W0018449

SAGE
50
YEARS

Environment and Fiscal Reforms in India

Thank you for choosing a SAGE product! If you have any comment, observation or feedback, I would like to personally hear from you. Please write to me at contactceo@sagepub.in

—Vivek Mehra, Managing Director and CEO,
SAGE Publications India Pvt Ltd, New Delhi

Bulk Sales

SAGE India offers special discounts for purchase of books in bulk. We also make available special imprints and excerpts from our books on demand.

For orders and enquiries, write to us at

Marketing Department
SAGE Publications India Pvt Ltd
B1/I-1, Mohan Cooperative Industrial Area
Mathura Road, Post Bag 7
New Delhi 110044, India
E-mail us at marketing@sagepub.in

Get to know more about SAGE, be invited to SAGE events, get on our mailing list. Write today to marketing@sagepub.in

This book is also available as an e-book.

Environment and Fiscal Reforms in India

Edited by
D.K. Srivastava
K.S. Kavi Kumar

SAGE www.sagepublications.com
Los Angeles • London • New Delhi • Singapore • Washington DC

First published in 2014 by

SAGE Publications India Pvt Ltd
B1/I-1 Mohan Cooperative Industrial Area
Mathura Road, New Delhi 110 044, India
www.sagepub.in

SAGE Publications Inc
2455 Teller Road
Thousand Oaks, California 91320, USA

SAGE Publications Ltd
1 Oliver's Yard, 55 City Road
London EC1Y 1SP, United Kingdom

SAGE Publications Asia-Pacific Pte Ltd
3 Church Street
#10-04 Samsung Hub
Singapore 049483

Published by Vivek Mehra for SAGE Publications India Pvt Ltd, typeset in 10/13pt Garamond by Diligent Typesetter, Delhi and printed at Saurabh Printers Pvt Ltd, New Delhi.

Library of Congress Cataloging-in-Publication Data

Environment and fiscal reforms in India / edited by D.K. Srivastava, K.S. Kavi Kumar.
pages cm
Includes bibliographical references and index.
1. Environmental impact charges—India. 2. Fiscal policy—India. 3. Environmental policy—Economic aspects—India. I. Srivastava, D. K., 1948– II. Kavi Kumar, K. S.
HJ5450.E58 363.7'060954—dc23 2014 2014027673

ISBN: 978-93-515-0041-4 (HB)

The SAGE Team: N. Unni Nair, Alekha Chandra Jena, Anju Saxena and Rajinder Kaur

Contents

List of Tables

List of Figures

List of Abbreviations

ANPR	Automatic Number Plate Recognition
APD	Air passenger duty
APM	Administered pricing mechanism
ASI	Annual Survey of Industries
BAU	Business-as-usual
BED	Basic excise duty
BHEL	Bharat Heavy Electricals Limited
BOD	Biochemical oxygen demand
CHP	Combined heat and power
CAC	Command-and-control
CCICED	China Council of International Cooperation on Environment and Development
CCL	Climate change levy
CFL	Compact fluorescent lamps
CGST	Central GST
CIS	Change in stock
CMAs	Catchment Management Agencies
CMCT	City maintenance and construction tax
CO_2e	Carbon dioxide equivalent
CPCB	Central Pollution Control Board
CSO	Central Statistical Organization
CT	Consumption tax
CVD	Countervailing duty
DALY	Disability adjusted life years
EC	Empowered Committee
ECB	Energy commodity balance
EEA	European Environment Agency
EEE	Energy–economy–environment

EI	Environment industries
EOF	Energy optimizing furnace
ET	Eco-taxes
ETR	Environmental tax reforms
FAIORT	Fixed assets investment orientation regulation tax
FOT	Farmland occupation tax
GAMS	General Algebraic Modelling System
GDP	Gross domestic product
GEF	Global environment facility
GFCE	Government final consumption expenditure
GFCF	Gross fixed capital formation
GGST	Green GST
GHG	Greenhouse gases
GRIHA	Green rating and integrated habitat assessment
GST	Goods and services tax
GVA	Gross value added
IAMs	Integrated Assessment Models
IARI	Indian Agricultural Research Institute
IGST	Integrated goods and services tax
IOT	Input–output table
IOTT	Input–output transactions table
IPPS	Industrial Pollution Projection System
ITC	Input tax credit
LTCS	Landfill Tax Credit Scheme
LRD	Longitudinal research database
MoEF	Ministry of Environment and Forests
NCV	Net calorific value
NDP	National domestic product
NEMA	National Environmental Management Act
NIA	National income accounts
NIC	National Industrial Classification
NICs	National Insurance Contributions
NIT	Net indirect taxes
PFCE	Private final consumption expenditure
PLS	Pollution levy system
PM	Particulate matter
PPP	Purchasing power parity
RNR	Revenue neutral rate

RRR	Revenue realization ratio
RSPM	Respirable suspended particulate matter
RT	Resources tax
SACAA	South Africa Civil Aviation Authority
SACU	South African Customs Union
SAD	Special additional duty of customs
SEEA	System of Environmental-Economic Accounting
SEZs	Special economic zones
SGST	State GST
SPM	Suspended particulate matter
SSIs	Small-scale industries
STPP	Sodium tri-poly phosphate
TERI	Tata Energy and Resources Institute
THFC	Thirteenth Finance Commission
TSP	Total suspended particulates
TSS	Total suspended solids
UTLUT	Urban and township land use tax
VAT	Value-added tax
VED	Vehicle excise duty
VRR	VAT revenue ratio
VVUT	Vehicle and vessel usage tax
WRI	World Resources Institute
YLL	Years of life lost

Preface

India is presently undertaking major tax reforms for the taxation of goods and services, which will integrate taxes such as State VAT, CENVAT, service tax, and a host of other small taxes on goods and services, and replace these by a comprehensive goods and services tax (GST). In a concurrent GST regime, at present as far as goods are concerned, two rates are being talked about: a core rate and a lower rate, apart from an exempted category of goods.

Pollution has serious implications for economic growth and welfare because of its impact on health, resource depletion and natural calamities linked to climate change. Though it is well established that market-based and fiscal instruments for pollution control (such as taxes, subsidies and trading instruments) have several desirable properties compared to the command-and-control mode of environmental regulation, many countries including India still use the latter. Carefully designed use of fiscal instruments such as eco-taxes (which tax the polluting inputs and outputs rather than pollution directly) provides a framework in which the central and the state governments can develop a coordinated intergovernmental approach to tackle issues of pollution in the light of India's growth requirements while keeping pollution within acceptable limits. Eco-taxes are not meant to be a revenue-augmenting device. Instead, the idea is to change the structure of taxation without putting additional burden on the tax payers. They reduce the use of resources and pollution by making them more expensive. At the same time, they facilitate reduction of distortionary taxes on labour and capital, making them cheaper, leading to increased output, employment and resource productivity. Many European countries have now extensively started using a number of eco-taxes for controlling pollution and meeting environmental targets including those relating to climate change.

Enthused by the pioneering work done by Professor Raja J. Chelliah, Madras School of Economics (MSE), Chennai, has been advocating the use of eco-taxes and eco-subsidies for effective environmental management in India. In continuation of research in this theme, MSE has recently explored the role of environmental tax reforms in the context of the emerging GST regime. The research was supported by the Ministry of Environment and Forests, Government of India and British Foreign and Commonwealth Office's Strategic Programme Fund. This book brings together the research carried out over the past two years in this regard.

We had the benefit of interacting with late Dr R. J. Chelliah in the initial stages of the study. Professor U. Sankar, Professor Emeritus at MSE, helped us immensely throughout the study and provided critical comments on all the technical papers. We would like to specially thank Professors Ramprasad Sengupta, JNU, Rita Pandey, NIPFP and Mahesh Purohit, FPEPR, for their valuable and detailed comments on the drafts of various Technical Papers that constituted the earlier versions of various chapters of this book. We are also grateful to Dr C. Bhujanga Rao, Dr Bodhisattva Sengupta, Dr Brijesh C. Purohit, Mr Subham Kailthya, Ms Ishwarya Balasubramaniam and Ms Asha Mariam Abraham for contributing generously to the chapters. We are also grateful to the members of the Advisory Committee with Dr C. Rangarajan as Chairman, for their valuable inputs.

We had occasion to discuss some of the international experience on the matter with Professor Paul Ekins, University College, London and Chairman, Green Fiscal Commission, UK and Professor Stephen Smith also of the University College, London. We also discussed these issues with Professor Anil Markandya of the University of Bath, and Dr Partho Shome, formerly Director and CEO, Indian Institute of Research on International Economic Relations, New Delhi. We had fruitful interactions with Dr Philip Summerton and Hector Politt of Cambridge Econometrics and Dr Karsten Neuhoff, Dr Mairead Curran and Dr Annela Anger of 4CMR, University of Cambridge. We also interacted with Dr Judith Rees, Dr Alex Bowen and Dr Ruth Kattumari of London School of Economics and Ms Helen Devenney, Chair of Environmental Taxes Working Group of the Chartered Institute of Taxation (CIOT), London, Mr Nick Goulding, Past President of CIOT, and Mr Maric Glaser, Technical Officer, CIOT.

We have greatly benefitted from interactions on the subject matter with Dr Kirit Parikh, former member of Planning Commission, Dr Vijay Kelkar,

Chairman, Thirteenth Finance Commission, Dr Atul Sarma and Dr Indira Rajaraman, Members, Thirteenth Finance Commission, Dr Pradipto Ghosh, former Secretary, Ministry of Environment and Forests, Shri Dhirendra Singh and Shri Vijay Shankar, Members of the Commission for Centre–State Relations, Shri Devendar Singh, Member-Secretary, Commission for Centre–State Relations, Professor Abhijit Sen, Member of Planning Commission, Shri R. C. Khwaja and Ms Meera Mehrishi, Secretaries in the Ministry of Environment and Forests and Shri R. S. Ahlawat, Economic Advisor, Ministry of Environment and Forests.

The views expressed in this book are those of the authors. Members of the Board of Governors of MSE are not in any way responsible for these views. Ms Sudha and Ms Jothi provided able secretarial assistance. Ms Geetha and Ms Getsie David helped with final revisions and formatting.

D.K. Srivastava
K.S. Kavi Kumar

1

Context and Overview

D.K. Srivastava and K.S. Kavi Kumar

1.1 INTRODUCTION

India is targeting the introduction of a comprehensive value-added tax (VAT) under the name of a goods and services tax (GST). By now, more than 140 countries have already adopted a VAT and as such India will be a latecomer into the VAT club although a kind of fragmented VAT system[1] is already in place with the reform of indirect taxes since the early 1990s. Many of the developed countries which had adopted VAT earlier are now introducing a conscious 'green shift' not only in their VAT but also in their entire tax structure so as to use economic instruments for achieving environmental objectives.

Since a major change in the system of taxation in India is being introduced, it is the appropriate time to also bring on board the environmental considerations. It is argued here that this will be welfare improving and facilitate the introduction of GST by allowing for a lowering of the overall GST rate, that is, the so-called revenue neutral rate (RNR), while taxing the environmental 'bads' at differentially higher rates. This will also give the Indian GST a forward-looking orientation where incentives will be in place to encourage growth of environmental-friendly industries rather than only correcting for past distortions.

Protection and improvement of environment is a constitutional responsibility cast on every citizen, the state governments and the central government. Under the Constitution, three important subjects concerning environment, namely, water, land, and gas and gas-works are placed in the State List of the Seventh Schedule of the Constitution as items 17, 18 and 25. Forests are in the Concurrent List. Under Article 48, protection and improvement of environment has been identified as state responsibility. This Article provides that 'the state shall endeavor to protect and improve the environment and to safeguard the forests and the wild life of the country.' The quality of environment has an important bearing on the right to life under Article 21 relating to the fundamental rights.[2]

Under Article 249, Parliament can legislate on matters of 'national interest'. Two major and vital Indian environmental laws, namely, The Air (Prevention and Control of Pollution) Act of 1981 and The Environmental (Protection) Act of 1986, have been enacted under these constitutional provisions. Article 51A(g) imposes a fundamental duty on the Indian citizen to protect and improve the natural environment, including forests, lakes, rivers and wildlife.

Given this background, the rest of the chapter provides an overview of the environmental concerns facing India and makes an argument in favour of integrating eco-taxes (ETs) and eco-subsidies in the emerging GST framework. The discussion also focuses on choice of polluting inputs and outputs that could be targeted for levying additional green taxes in India. The chapter ends with a brief description of the rest of the chapters.

1.2 POLLUTION IN INDIA: DIMENSIONS AND SEVERITY

The main forms of pollution are atmospheric pollution, land degradation and soil pollution, water pollution and noise pollution. The main sources of atmospheric pollution are (a) combustion of fuels to produce energy for heating and power generation in the household and industrial sectors; (b) exhaust emissions from the transport vehicles that use petrol, diesel oil, etc. and (c) waste gases, dust and heat from many industrial sites including chemical manufacturers and electrical power generating stations. Three main pollutants of ambient air quality are sulphur dioxide (SO_2), nitrogen dioxide (NO_2) and particulate matter, whereas carbon dioxide (CO_2) is the chief global pollutant. The main water pollutants are effluents and discharges from industries. The main land and soil pollutants are fertilizers and pesticides.

1.2.1 Air Pollution

In most of the Indian cities, the annual average concentrations of respirable suspended particulate matter (RSPM) and suspended particulate matter (SPM) reflecting presence of particulate matter exceed the National Ambient Air Quality Standards. The reasons for high particulate matter levels are vehicles, engine gensets, small-scale industries (SSIs), biomass incineration, boilers and emission from power plants, suspension of traffic dust, and commercial and domestic use of fuels.

Vehicles are a major source of atmospheric pollution. According to the relative share of major states in the India in terms of the total number of vehicles, Maharashtra had the highest share of 12.1 percent, followed by Tamil Nadu, with 11.9 percent. Gujarat was next with a share of 9.7 percent, followed by Uttar Pradesh with 8.8 percent. In terms of two wheelers, Tami Nadu had the highest share of 13.2 percent followed by Maharashtra with 11.8 percent. In terms of cars, Maharashtra had the largest share but in terms of goods vehicles, Tamil Nadu had the highest share.

There is a considerable inter-state variation in CO_2 emissions. State-level CO_2 emissions charts for 2000 indicate that Uttar Pradesh has the highest level of pollution followed by Madhya Pradesh, Maharashtra, Andhra Pradesh, West Bengal, Gujarat and Tamil Nadu (Table 1.1). Per capita CO_2 emissions as per these charts show that Madhya Pradesh has the highest emission at 660 metric tons followed by Delhi with 440 metric tons followed by Odisha and Goa. Punjab has a per capita CO_2 emission of 450 metric tons. High per capita emissions may be either due to the state undertaking production of polluting material as in the case of Madhya Pradesh, Chhattisgarh and Bihar or due to high per capita consumption as in Delhi, Goa, Gujarat and Maharashtra. States like Bihar, Odisha, Madhya Pradesh and Andhra Pradesh have India's major steel plants that consume a lot of coal. This makes their emission levels disproportionately high compared to their incomes. At the all-India level, nearly 77 percent of the CO_2 emissions are from coal and about 70 percent of the coal in India is consumed by the power sector.

1.2.2 Land and Soil Pollution

In India, about 130 million hectares of land (45 percent of total geographical area) is affected by serious soil erosion through ravine and gully, shifting cultivation, cultivated wastelands, sandy areas, deserts and water logging. The average degradation percentage is estimated at 18.8 considering all

Table 1.1
State-level CO_2 emissions: 2000

('000 metric tons of carbon)

Aggregate						
J&K	HP	Punjab	Haryana	UP	Rajasthan	Delhi
696.5	659.1	10845.7	5460.5	44268.3	8929.3	6033.8
Bihar	Odisha	WB	Assam	Gujarat	Maharashtra	Goa
9012	16172.3	23363.7	1097	18461.5	35595.4	652.2
MP	AP	Karnataka	Kerala	TN	Others	
39279.4	30126	9059.6	3034.2	17584.9	43712.6	
Per capita						
J&K	HP	Punjab	Haryana	UP	Rajasthan	Delhi
0.07	0.11	0.45	0.26	0.27	0.16	0.44
Bihar	Odisha	WB	Assam	Gujarat	Maharashtra	Goa
0.11	0.44	0.29	0.04	0.37	0.37	0.44
MP	AP	Karnataka	Kerala	TN	Others	
0.66	0.4	0.17	0.1	0.28	0.62	

Source: Ghoshal and Bhattacharya (2007).

the districts. Some districts of Mizoram, Maharashtra, Uttar Pradesh, West Bengal, Madhya Pradesh, Himachal Pradesh and Bihar have relatively higher percentage of soil erosion compared to the national average.

The activity of mining and quarrying covers underground and surface mines, quarries and wells, and includes extraction of minerals and activities such as dressing and beneficiation of ores, crushing, screening, washing, cleaning, grading, milling floatation, melting floatation and other preparations at the mine site. In India, coal is the most important energy source but Indian coal has a low calorific value with ash content ranging from 40 to 50 percent as well as high moisture content between 4 and 20 percent (Chikkatur and Sagar, 2007).

1.2.3 Water Pollution

Water is polluted by the effluents of industries. Some of the important industries in this context are ferrous and non-ferrous metallurgical industries, mining and ore processing, and industries relating to petroleum, petrochemicals, chemicals, ceramics, cement, textiles, paper, fertilizers, coal (including coke), power (thermal and diesel) generation, and industries processing animal or vegetable products. SSIs are also a major source of industrial water pollution.

Both land and water are polluted because of excessive use of pesticides. An inter-state comparison of consumption of pesticides shows that, according to the available data for 2004–05, the highest amount of pesticides was used in Punjab followed by Uttar Pradesh, Haryana, West Bengal, Maharashtra and Gujarat. These inter-state differences are the result of both the intensive use of pesticides and the area over which the pesticides are used.

The presence of iron in water has affected the largest number of habitations in India. These habitations are located largely in Odisha, Assam, Bihar and West Bengal. Next in terms of the pollutants affecting water for habitations was fluoride and the states most affected were Rajasthan, Karnataka, Madhya Pradesh, Gujarat and Uttar Pradesh. The arsenic contamination of water was limited to two states only namely, Bihar and Assam. The presence of nitrate was mostly in Rajasthan, Maharashtra, Karnataka and Bihar. Salinity was a problem in Rajasthan, Gujarat, Maharashtra and Punjab.

Apart from the national and state-wise picture, a number of 'environmental hotspots' in the country have also been identified calling for urgent policy intervention. The Blacksmith Institute of New York has been identifying the worst polluted places of the world on the basis of size of the affected population, severity of the toxin involved, impact on children's health and development, evidence of a clear pathway of contamination, and existing and reliable evidence of health impact. In the 2006 report, Ranipet in Tamil Nadu featured among the top 10 worst polluted places.[3] Within a distance of 5 kilometres around 68 tanneries operate in Dindigul leading to severe ground water pollution. Tannery effluents are reported to have left only 16 out of 56 wells in Kamatchipuram village uncontaminated, forcing people to walk long distances for water. The water and soil pollution from the tannery effluents has the potential to affect about 450000 people. In the 2007 report, Sukinda valley in Odisha featured among the top 10 worst polluted places. Sukinda valley contains about 97 percent of India's chromite ore deposits and is one of the world's largest open cast chromite ore mines. With over 12 mines still in operation, a large quantity of waste rock is spread over the surrounding areas and the Brahmani riverbank.[4] Besides these, the 2006 and 2007 reports also highlight other pollution hotspots of India including Kanpur (chemical pollutants from the tanneries), Ankleshwar (heavy metals and chemicals from the chemical units), Vapi (chemicals and heavy metals from the chemical units), Kolkata (lead pollution from lead factories producing lead ingots and lead alloys) and Mahad Industrial Estate in Karnataka (heavy metals and organic pollutants from the chemical units).

1.3 POLLUTION IN INDIA: IMPLICATIONS FOR GROWTH AND WELFARE

Pollution is an externality to economic activities associated with both production and consumption of goods and services. Pollution has serious implications for economic growth and welfare because of its impact on health, resource depletion and natural calamities linked to climate change.

Pollution has local, regional and global dimensions (as discussed in previous section). The local effects are largely on air, soil, water and plants from industrial emissions and discharges, noise and smell. The regional effects are due to eutrophication, contaminants in the soil and water and landscape changes due to mining or agriculture. The global effects relate to changes in the climate due to ozone depletion and the greenhouse effect. Accordingly, policies for controlling pollution and mitigating its impact need to have national, state-level and local dimensions.

With respect to the global dimension, climate change is linked to greenhouse gases (GHGs). India's contribution to carbon emissions in per capita terms[5] is still much less than many of the developed countries but its aggregate contribution is the fourth highest after China, the USA and Russia. In 1990, China and India combined to account for 13 percent of world emissions, but by 2004 that share had risen to 22 percent, largely because of a substantial increase in coal use in these two countries along with rapid economic growth. This trend is projected to continue; and by 2030, carbon dioxide emissions from China and India combined are projected to account for 31 percent of total world emissions, with China alone responsible for 26 percent of the world total.

In global terms, there is an asymmetry between who has relatively been more responsible for the adverse impact on climate and who will relatively face more adverse consequences. Effects on India will be disproportionately larger as compared to its contribution to global carbon emissions. According to the Geological Survey of India,[6] it is estimated that nearly

46000 glaciers (one-third of world's glaciers) in the Himalayas between 2000 and 5000 metres altitude have started receding by 10–15 metres every year causing concerns of rivers getting dry in summer. As a result, rice production in India may come down by 10 percent by 2030 and 25 percent by 2080. Wheat production would also be considerably reduced, as projected by the Indian Agricultural Research Institute (IARI). Many of the country's coastal areas are likely to get submerged.

Pollution, however, is a concern broader than the issue of climate change. The health hazards related to pollution affect quality of life, productivity of population, loss of work days and use of resources for treatment of chronic diseases. Data from the Central Pollution Control Board (CPCB) and other sources show that the environmental pollution—water, air as well as solid waste—have been in excess of the national ambient standards at several places across India. For instance, the water pollution levels measured in terms of biochemical oxygen demand (BOD) in several rivers is well above the water quality criteria. Similarly, the RSPM critically important from the viewpoint of health has been well above the national ambient air quality standard in several monitoring stations. The following charts give a snapshot picture of the status of the environmental pollution. Figure 1.1 shows the position of air pollution and Figure 1.2 that of water pollution compared to

Figure 1.1
Staus of air pollution across India—Mid-2000s

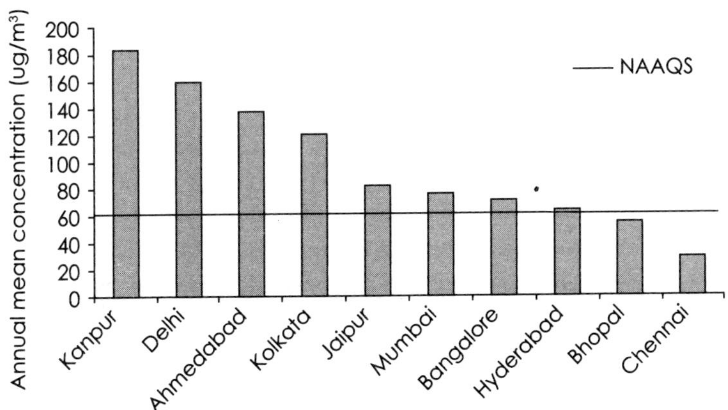

NAAQS: National Ambient Air Quality Standard.
Source: World Bank (2007).

Figure 1.2
Status of water pollution across India—Mid-2000s

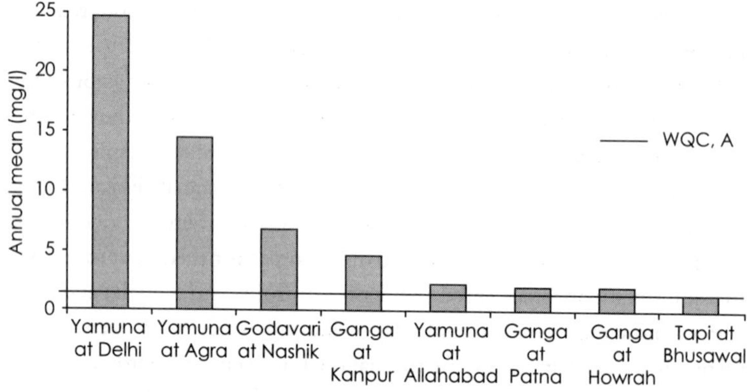

WQC, A: Water Quality Criteria for Class A Water Bodies.
Source: World Bank (2007).

the relevant benchmarks across various monitoring sites/stations in India in mid-2000s.

World Bank (2005) assessed that the annual economic cost of damage to public health from increased air pollution alone based on RSPM measurements for 50 cities with the total population of 110 million was close to US$ 3 billion in 2004. A significant health burden is also associated with the indoor air pollution resulting from the use of 'dirty' fuels such as firewood. Smith and Mehta (2002) have analysed the years of life lost (YLL) and disability adjusted life years (DALY) among the rural and urban children below the age of 5 years and estimated the YLL and DALY attributable to the use of solid fuels in the household in India to be about 20 million annually.

1.4 COPING WITH POLLUTION: ROLE OF ENVIRONMENTAL TAXES

There are two major groups of policy instruments for achieving the environmental objectives: regulatory and market-based economic instruments.[7] Regulatory instruments prescribe emission standards or effluent limits. These require considerable administrative costs for implementation and monitoring. Their effectiveness also depends on a number of conditions. Market-based instruments include taxes, subsidies and trading instruments. In comparison with the regulatory policies, market-based instruments may be able to reduce the costs of achieving a given level of environmental protection through incentives.

The OECD (2007) and the International Energy Agency and the European Commission (see Ekins, 2009) define environmental taxes as 'any compulsory, unrequited payment to general government levied on taxbases deemed to be of particular environmental relevance'. The taxbases include energy products, motor vehicles, water, measured or estimated emissions, natural resources, etc.

Environmental tax reforms (ETRs) constitute indirect, self-monitoring, incentive-based changes in the tax structure to achieve environmental objectives. These have the potential to induce appropriate environmental decisions through instituting an incentive structure by raising the relative costs of polluting inputs and outputs. ETR is not meant to be a revenue-augmenting device. Instead, the idea is to change the structure of taxation without putting additional burden on the tax payers. ETR reduces the use of resources and pollution by making them more expensive. At the same time, it reduces distortionary taxes on labour and capital, making them cheaper, leading to increased output, employment and resource productivity. Similarly, these can be used to reduce the overall GST tax rate (RNR) thereby reducing the deadweight losses associated with indirect taxes.

Environmental taxes have the attraction that they insulate polluters from the risk that regulatory requirements might involve in terms of excessive abatement costs. The tax rate per unit of emissions places an upper limit on the unit abatement cost to be incurred. If abatement turns out to be more costly per unit than the tax per unit, then firms will simply pollute and pay the tax, rather than paying for costly abatement. By contrast, regulatory policies which set a quantitative limit on emissions may risk requiring that abatement measures are undertaken which are far more costly than the resulting environmental benefits.

Environmental taxes can be advocated from the viewpoint of static and dynamic efficiency gains. Static gains arise through reallocation of abatement among various polluters. As the costs of pollution abatement vary across firms or individuals, environmental taxes have the potential to minimize costs, for two important reasons. First, taxes provide each polluter with incentive to abate in the least-expensive ways and thus achieve a given level of abatement at lower total abatement cost. Second, taxes can avoid the need for the regulatory authority to acquire detailed information on individual sources' abatement costs. This would lower the public sector's costs of regulation.

Dynamic gains arise through providing incentives for innovations. Regulatory policies, stipulating that polluters must use particular technologies, or maintain emissions below a specified limit, do not provide polluters with any encouragement to make reductions in pollution beyond what the regulations require. Environmental taxes provide a continuing incentive for polluters to seek ways to reduce emissions, even below the current cost-effective level. This incentive arises because the tax payment is made on each unit of residual emissions. New technologies may further reduce marginal cost below the tax rate and lead to further abatement. As the demand for green technologies is increasing globally, this can also lead to new comparative advantages, further stimulating employment and output. Figure 1.3 highlights three channels through which ETR can positively impact growth: (a) lower health management costs, (b) lower deadweight losses and (c) promotion of environmental industries through financing of eco-subsidies.

Studies suggest that energy use and corresponding emissions tend to rise with income, and that increases in energy prices will tend to reduce energy use. ETR tends to increase energy efficiency as well as reduce energy demand. The main challenge that India faces is as to how to reduce the energy intensity of growth so that potential growth can be achieved at lower levels of energy use and pollution.

1.5 INTERNATIONAL EXPERIENCE WITH ETRs

Internationally, ETR has become the norm for many countries and many beneficial effects are already visible. OECD (2007) observes that the number of environmentally related taxes in OECD countries has increased steadily over the years. The OECD and the European Environment Agency (EEA) mention about 375 environmentally related taxes in OECD countries (excluding measures of 250 environmentally related fees and charges). This includes the energy and transport sectors, and a number of taxes and charges linked to measured or estimated emissions. About 90 percent of the revenues from the environmental taxes stems from taxes on motor vehicle fuels and motor vehicles.

Figure 1.3
ETR and growth: Channels of interface

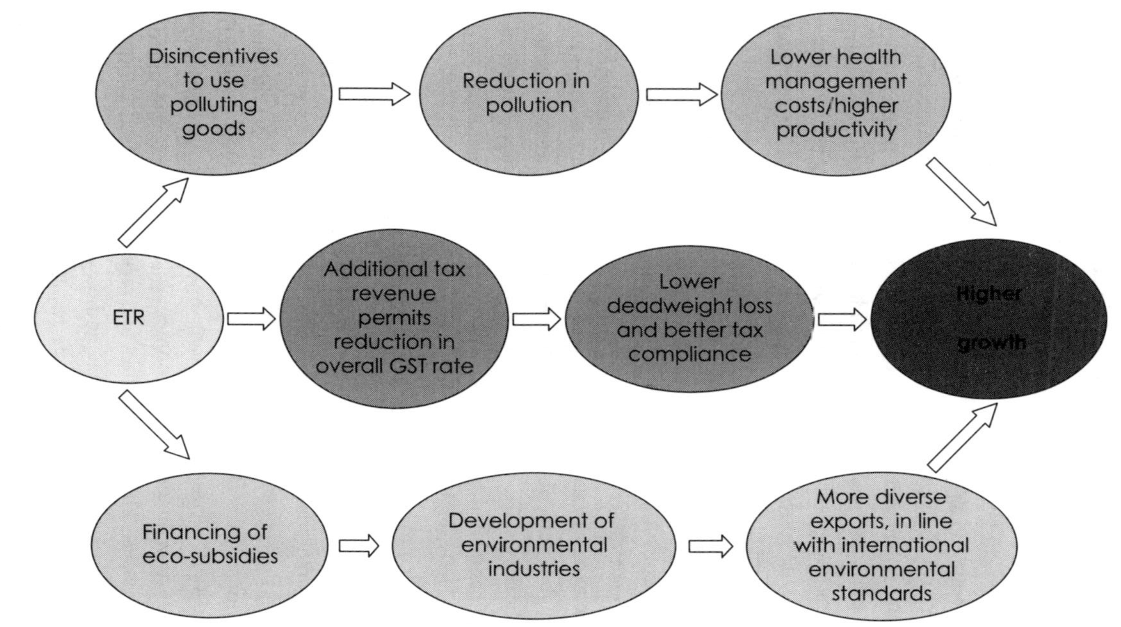

The implementation of ETR goes back to the early 1990s. Sweden, Denmark, Norway, Finland and the Netherlands were the early reformers. Sweden was the first European Union (EU) country to introduce ETR where specific charges for carbon dioxide, sulphur dioxide and nitrous oxide were introduced and later the ETR became more complex.

ETs can serve two purposes: one, stem the flow of additional pollution by discouraging the use of polluting inputs and outputs (disincentive effect), and two, generate additional revenue which can be used partly or fully for providing environmental public goods (revenue effect). An important issue is whether ET revenue should be fully earmarked for environmental public goods. Chapter 2 provides a detailed discussion on environmental public goods and ET revenue by introducing analytical framework involving the concept of *social marginal cost of public funds*. Given the practical difficulties involved in measuring social marginal cost of public funds, certain conventions or rules of thumb may have to be used while assessing the link between ET revenue and environmental public goods. It can be argued that such conventions need to be different between developed and developing countries. In developing countries, environmental taxes can be used to some extent in increasing the tax–gross domestic product (GDP) ratio and a higher percentage can be allocated for environmental public goods.

In the developed countries, given high tax–GDP ratio, the revenue from the environmental tax can be used to replace conventional distortionary taxes and to provide general public goods. In practice, this was what most developed countries followed. The revenue from the new tax regime was recycled into a reduced level of income tax and employers' contributions in order to benefit both households and industry.

Denmark initially targeted households, by increasing taxes on waste and recycling the revenue through reductions in income tax. Subsequently, in 1996, industry was targeted with energy taxes introduced alongside reductions in social security contributions. Since 1999, the tax burden has been shifted further, by raising environmental and corporate taxes and reducing personal taxes. The Netherlands has recycled increased energy tax revenue into both lower income tax and employers' contributions alongside a 3 percent reduction in corporate tax, greater tax credits for small business and increases in tax-free allowances. Reforms in Finland introduced a carbon dioxide tax in addition to other energy taxes, although electricity generation was exempted and gas subjected to a 50 percent reduction. Benefits were skewed towards households despite industry being equally affected by the new taxes. Finland's tax shift, estimated at 1.25 percent of GDP, was quite large.

Germany increased existing energy taxes and introduced a new electricity tax and recycled the revenue by reducing social security contributions. This amounted to a tax shift of almost 1 percent of GDP. The environmental taxes were complemented by special reductions and subsidies for renewable energy, bio-fuels and combined heat and power (CHP) facilities. Overall, the environmental taxes raised revenues in the order of 2–2.5 percent of GDP.

International experience has shown that environmental taxes can be quite effective in their environmental impact. It has been shown that the fuel taxes have had a significant environmental impact. In a recent study, Sterner (2007) reviews several studies for a number of countries and concludes: 'had Europe not followed a policy of high fuel taxation but had low US taxes, then fuel demand would have been twice as large.' Sterner observes that fuel taxes are the single most powerful climate policy instrument implemented to date. ETR can have a powerful effect on energy use. Ekins (2009) estimates the price elasticity of energy demand in the UK at about (–) 0.64, which implies that a 10 percent increase in the energy price will reduce energy consumption by 6.4 percent. He also finds that energy use tends to increase with value added with an elasticity of (+) 0.5 (meaning that a 10 percent increase in value added will tend to increase energy consumption by 5 percent). Other things being equal, this means that if a sector (or by implication the economy as a whole) is growing, its energy use will be growing too, unless it is restrained by a rising energy price. Table 1.2 provides a summary of the impact of the 'green shift' as evaluated by UK's Green Fiscal Commission. A more detailed analysis is given in Chapter 2.

With a reasonable change in the relative prices of labour and environmental resources, ETR may significantly change the incentives for innovation and technological development, inducing companies to devote more effort to increasing resource productivity, and less to increasing labour productivity. Industries that reduce pollution, increase resource productivity and encourage a switch to renewable resources. These industries are collectively being called the environment industries (EI) which have two distinct components: the supply of traditional *pollution control* technologies and services ('end-of-pipe treatment') and industries relating to *resource management* (management of materials and energy). Both components of the EI have contributed to environmental improvement in the EU. Some of the main environmental industries may be classified as given in Table 1.3.

Table 1.2
Impact of a green shift in taxation: Selected international evidence

Country and Tax	*Period Evaluated*	*Impact*	*Source*
Finland: energy and carbon tax	1990–2005	CO_2 emissions 7 percent lower than would have otherwise been; A shift from carbon tax to output tax on electricity in 1997 may have lessened impact	Nordic Council, 2006 Nordic Council, 1999
Norway: carbon and sulphur dioxide taxes	1991–2007	21 percent reduction in CO_2 from power plants by 1995; 14 percent national reduction in CO_2 in the 1990s; 2 percent attributed to carbon tax; 12 percent reduction in CO_2 emissions per unit of GDP	OECD, 2001 OECD, 2006a Nordic Council, 2006
Denmark: energy and carbon tax	1992	CO_2 emissions in affected sectors down by 6 percent and economic growth up by 20 percent between 1988 and 1997 and a 5 percent reduction in emission in one year in response to tax increase; In 1990s a 23 percent reduction in CO_2 from as usual trend and energy efficiency increased by 26 percent; Subsidy to renewables may have accounted for greater proportion of emissions reductions than tax	OECD, 2006a Nordic Council, 2006
Sweden: energy and carbon taxes	1990–2007	Emissions reductions of 0.5 million tons per annum; Emissions would have been 20 percent higher than 1990 levels without tax	Nordic council, 2006
The Netherlands: energy tax	1999–2007	Emissions 3.5 percent lower than would have otherwise been; Low tax rates may have limited impact	de Jaeger, 2007
Germany: environmental tax reform, taxes on transport, fuels and electricity	1999–2005	CO_2 reduced by 15 percent between 1990 and 1999 and 1 percent between 1999 and 2005; CO_2 emissions 2–3 percent lower by 2005 than they would have been without tax German re-unification an important factor in reductions	EEA, 2007 OECD, 2006a
UK: industrial energy tax	2001–2010	UK CO_2 emissions reduced by 2 percent in 2002 and 2.25 percent in 2003 and cumulative savings of 16.5 million tons of carbon up to 2005; Reduction in UK energy demand of 2.9 percent estimated by 2010	Cambridge Econometrics, 2005 HMT, 2006

Source: Green Fiscal Commission (2009).

Table 1.3
Upcoming environmental industries

Pollution Control	*Resource Management*	*Administration, Management and Research*
Waste water treatment	Solid waste management and recycling	General public administration
Air pollution control	Recycled materials	Private environmental management
Remediation/clean-up of soil/ground water	Renewable energy production	Environmental research and development
Noise and vibration control	Water supply	
Environmental monitoring	Eco-construction	
Nature protection		

Source: Based on Ekins (2009).

India needs to develop capacity in these industries where there is potential of considerable growth of demand rather than concentrating on polluting industries where already there is considerable excess capacity globally.

1.6 ETs AND GST IN INDIA

The system of taxation of goods and services in India has been subjected to extensive reforms since the 1990s. As a result, we have moved away from the earlier structure of cascading type of taxes like the central excise duty and the state sales taxes. Even after the levy of CENVAT and State VAT, the Indian tax system is replete with many distortions and inefficiencies. There is continuing cascading between CENVAT, State VAT and service tax. India is about to embark upon a major tax reform of its system of indirect taxes that will integrate central and state taxes on goods and services resulting into a comprehensive GST. The issue is as to how to handle ETR in the framework of GST. As already discussed, many countries that have VAT have also initiated ETR. We can opt for a suitable design learning from their experience so that we can have environmental taxes well integrated with GST from the very beginning.

At present, the Empowered Committee of State Finance Ministers has been working towards evolving a common structure of GST that will be acceptable to the Centre and the states. After extensive discussions, some features of the proposed GST appear to be taking a clear shape. Among various forms of GST, given our fiscal federal arrangements, India is headed towards a concurrent GST. The central and state governments will be entitled to tax the same tax base covering the value added up to retail for goods and services consumed in their jurisdictions. The GST will have two components: central GST (CGST) and state GST (SGST).

Once the reformed system is put in practice, it will subsume the service tax, the central excise duties, state sales taxes, additional excise duties in lieu of sales tax on textiles, tobacco and sugar and a number of other state taxes. The central sales tax (CST) on inter-state sale of goods will also go. The additional excise duties in lieu of sales tax for sugar, tobacco and textiles will also be integrated with GST.

In regard to the interface between GST and ETs, several features may be noted:

1. In a VAT regime, input taxes are fully rebated. As such, taxation of polluting inputs will be ineffective as the tax paid on the inputs will be fully rebated, unless a non-rebatable cess is levied on the inputs.
2. ETs call for differential rates of tax on polluting inputs and outputs but the accepted GST norm is to go for a uniform rate regime although some countries do have more than one rate.
3. In inter-state trade, the destination principle applies and the producing state where pollution may be localized does not get any part of tax revenue. It is only the consuming state that gets the tax revenue, whereas the pollution is suffered by the citizens of the producing state. A non-rebatable cess on the GST will provide some tax revenue for the producing state.
4. In GST, exports will be zero-rated. The importing country may tax the good but the country where production and pollution may take place does not get any tax revenue. The same argument at a more local level applies to special economic zones (SEZs).
5. ET provides additional tax revenue to enable reducing overall GST rate (RNR) than would otherwise be the case thereby reducing the deadweight costs.

6. Moving to GST with uniform rates may imply a lowering of the current tax load on polluting inputs and outputs where currently cascading may imply higher tax rates. As such without the incorporation of environmental cesses, the move to GST may be environmentally perverse. Appendix A1.1 provides information about the effective tax rates on polluting goods in India.
7. Introducing ETR into the GST framework requires coordination between the Centre and the states and among the states so that another kind of 'race-to-bottom' does not get initiated where industries start to relocate themselves in those states where environmental taxes or regulations are weak.
8. Many of the developed countries are imposing restrictions on their imports to ensure that goods imported by them meet environmental norms. The introduction of ETR in GST will incentivise Indian exporters to meet environmental norms and this will support the drive to increase India's exports.
9. In moving to a destination-based GST, many of the producing states will lose revenue because of the abolition of the central sales tax. Although some compensation is being estimated, this will only be for a few years. With the ETR in place, the producing states will have a longer-term mechanism in their hand to generate revenues that can support their activities for dealing with pollution in their jurisdictions.

A 'green shift' in taxation of goods and services implies that the overall tax burden does not increase on the system so that inefficiency costs of excess taxation such as deadweight losses, compliance costs and administrative costs do not increase. It will also improve inter-generational equity by spreading better among different generations the use of natural resources and fossil fuels as compared to their over-exploitation by the present generation. In any case, when the social welfare function is seen in the broader context where various positive externalities of green development and negative externalities of pollution are internalized, any 'green shift' in taxation is likely to be welfare improving without affecting the growth momentum adversely.

Global sources of pollution or pollution where state boundaries are generally crossed should be taxed at the national level, regional sources at the state level and pollution with strong local characteristics should be taxed at the local level. There should be inter-state coordination so that as a result of taxation of polluting inputs and outputs, industries do not attempt to relocate in other states where ETs are less stringent. This may happen if some states pursue more actively in pollution control while others are more relaxed and the CST also goes.

1.7 ECO-SUBSIDIES AND ETs

ETs should be complemented by eco-subsidies. Eco-subsidies can be given to provide incentives to producers and consumers for favouring goods and services that have environmentally favourable properties. Subsidies decrease the relative price of products and encourage their use. There could be direct subsidies financed by the general budget, as also subsidies linked to ETs where tax revenues are partially or fully earmarked for financing eco-subsidies. Eco-subsidies can also be administered through tax expenditures in the form of tax credits or allowances to encourage expenditure for usage of environmentally friendly inputs and outputs.

Internationally, there are several examples of eco-subsidies. In the Netherlands, a rebate is provided for replacement of old appliances; in Spain, Hungary and Denmark, a direct payment of subsidy is made for replacement of old appliances. In Italy, the consumers receive a tax rebate for the purchase of energy efficient refrigerators and freezers. In France, purchases of condensing boiler are promoted though a tax credit and in Australia there are region-specific subsidy schemes. In many EU and non-EU countries, purchases of compact fluorescent lamps (CFL) are encouraged through subsidies. In the USA, corporate tax credits are given to manufacturers of energy efficient appliances or to the owners of commercial buildings for the installation of energy efficient equipment. Many states in the USA provide subsidies and personal income tax credits for energy conservation. In India also, there are some subsidies to incentivise use of production of energy saving devices or alternative sources of energy.

There are several advantages in targeting environmental goals through subsidies. Subsidy schemes can be better targeted to specific consumer groups. In particular, some of the distributional concerns of energy taxation can be addressed through subsidies targeted to lower income groups. Also, direct subsidies can be more calibrated to the product characteristics. Some products need higher subsidies than others.

1.8 IDENTIFICATION OF POLLUTING INPUTS AND OUTPUTS

Pollution can be of different types: air, water, land, toxic and metal pollution. It is important to distinguish between pollution from production (industrial pollution) and that from consumption (pollution from residential and commercial sectors, transport and the use of harmful products like plastics, fertilizers, etc.). Further, industrial pollution can be traced to the use of polluting inputs and/or the manufacturing process. Process-related pollution can be reduced by using better processes. Thus, to reduce industrial pollution either inputs/outputs can be taxed, or facilitate adoption of environment friendly technologies through eco-subsidies, or both. In addition, bulk of the pollution can also be traced to the fuel used.

Since the design of GST should be such that only a limited number of polluting inputs and outputs should be selected for differential rates of taxation or levy of non-rebatable taxes on inputs, the selection of commodities has to be such as to maximize the environmental impact with a limited number of environmental taxes. It should also be dovetailed to regional environmental pollution characteristics.

It should be noted that environmental management needs multiple instruments including the ETs and other economic instruments, command and control (CAC) regulations, and information disclosure instruments. For effective environmental management, a combination of all these instruments is required. The discussion here with focus on ETs must not be construed upon as nullification of the need for other instruments.

1.8.1 Industry-wise Heavy Polluters

Appendix A1.1 identifies major polluting industries in India and their state-wise positions. It also describes the methodology used to derive the relative rankings and pollution loads. It is shown that at the all-India level, iron and steel industry is the highest polluting industry in terms of all four pollutants except air where it ranks second to cement. Iron and steel is the largest water polluting industry in India with 87.4 percent of the total pollution load. The pulp and paper and aluminium industries rank second and third, respectively, with their contribution to total water pollution load at 4.6 and 2.5 percent. Sugar and distillery industries rank fourth and fifth, respectively.

The cement industry is the biggest air polluter emitting nearly 34 percent of the total air pollution load. Iron and steel stands second, emitting 32 percent, while oil refinery ranks third contributing 7.4 percent to the total industrial air pollution load. The iron and steel industry is also the largest metal polluter accounting for more than 71 percent of the total metal pollution load. Aluminium industry is the second highest contributor (nearly 16 percent) to metal pollution. In the toxic pollution category also, iron and steel industry is the highest polluter contributing 39 percent of the total pollution load. The second most polluting industry in this category is leather with about 14 percent share in total toxic load. Iron and steel, leather, petrochemical and oil refinery industries together account for 70 percent of total toxic pollution load. The main implication of these results is that substantial reduction in total pollution loads can be achieved by focusing pollution control efforts in a limited number of industrial sectors.

1.8.2 State-wise Heavy Polluters

Since the sources, incidence and intensity of pollution are different across states, in determining state-level interventions these differences should be taken into account. As detailed in Appendix A1.1, the relevant ranking in each category of pollution are as follows:

1. Water: Bihar, Maharashtra, Madhya Pradesh, Odisha, West Bengal
2. Air: Maharashtra, Madhya Pradesh, Gujarat, Andhra Pradesh, Bihar
3. Toxic: Maharashtra, Gujarat, Tamil Nadu, Bihar, Uttar Pradesh
4. Metal: Bihar, Maharashtra, Odisha, West Bengal, Uttar Pradesh.

It may be noted that in determining the extent of intervention, population density of the states should be taken into consideration. A high density state (like West Bengal or Kerala) will face higher per capita burden of pollution and the policy needs to take this into account.

1.8.3 Petroleum and Energy

In designing ETs, considerable importance needs to be attached to taxation of fuel and energy. After a long period of administered prices for the petroleum sector, a dismantling of the administered pricing mechanism (APM) was announced and made effective from 01 April 2002. Subsidies for the public distribution system (PDS) kerosene and domestic LPG were continued on the ground that these were fuels of mass consumption. With a sharp and spiralling increase in international oil prices, particularly since late 2003, combined with sharp week-to-week and sometimes day-to-day volatility of petroleum prices, this arrangement has virtually collapsed. The explosive increase in the global crude prices increased the volume of subsidy on PDS kerosene and domestic LPG to unprecedented levels. The Centre has not been able to follow suitable principles of pricing reflecting the trade parity prices, as recommended by the Rangarajan Committee. Kirit Parikh Committee also made similar observations and suggested market determined pricing strategy for petrol and diesel.

The central excise levy on petrol and diesel has been a combination of ad-valorem and specific rates. The contribution of the petroleum sector to the total net excise revenues of the government was of the order of 40 percent. Moreover, taxes (including sales tax/VAT) and duties constitute a significant proportion of the retail prices.

State-level taxes are also high for petroleum products. Almost all state governments in India are also levying non-vatable sales tax on crude oil and petroleum products at special rates. Since states suffer different levels of pollution, related to vehicular and other uses of petroleum products, they are entitled to use different rates, reflecting their own environmental considerations. In particular, the higher income states, where per capita consumption of petroleum products may be higher, may levy a higher special rate of tax.

Fuel taxes are often criticized on distribution grounds. It is argued that fuel taxes may be regressive, that is, it burdens the poor proportionately more than the rich. Such a contention finds empirical evidence in developed countries. However, it is not the case for developing countries where fuel taxes are generally found to be progressive or neutral. This is attributed to the differences in income and expenditure pattern of households in developed and developing countries.

A study on fuel taxes in South Africa (Ziramba et al., 2009) finds that the distribution of fuel expenditure is progressive and hence suggests that fuel tax would not necessarily be regressive. When indirect use of fuel is included, the effect is still progressive. A similar result is found for China (Cao and Zeng, 2010). He uses micro-level household survey data and elasticity estimates to find out that the fuel tax reform is progressive at all levels, the progressivity being greater in the short run than in the long run. The case of carbon tax was studied for Indonesia using a general equilibrium model which indicates that a carbon tax is progressive in rural household, whereas it may be neutral or regressive in urban households depending on whether the revenues are recycled back or not (Yusuf, 2008).

Datta (2008) studies the distributional impact of fuels in the Indian context. His results indicate progressivity of transport fuel tax in both rural and urban sectors and a neutral effect of coal tax. However, tax on cooking fuels like kerosene imposes a greater burden on the poor and hence is regressive. For an environmental tax to be effective, the fuel should have both an elastic demand and a high emission potential. The emission potential of transport fuels is around 2.3 kilograms of carbon dioxide per litre of fuel. Different studies report different values for transport fuel elasticity which are price sensitive in the long run ranging from –0.84 to –0.42 (Datta, 2008). Hence, transport fuels are a good case for fuel tax as they are progressive and also effective in reducing emissions as they satisfy the above two conditions.

Kerosene is primarily used by poorer households as cooking and lighting fuel. Though kerosene has a highly elastic demand especially in the rural areas, it is not advisable to tax kerosene as it is found to be highly regressive. Besides being regressive, a tax on kerosene will also lead to switching to fuel wood which causes extensive indoor air pollution.

It should be noted that progressivity is not the same as equity. Progressivity implies that the rich pay proportionately more tax than the poor. This does not exclude the poor from paying the tax which can leave them with a lower budget to meet other expenditure. Thereby, the income distribution tends to become less equal. The effect of such equity patterns has not been studied widely. Such a negative impact of fuel taxes on equity could have serious implications for India especially since it is an energy poor country. This, however, can be addressed through a programme of targeted energy subsidies for the poor.

There is a case to tax electricity on account of the fact that the GHG emissions from thermal power plants are the highest. An electricity duty is currently being levied by the state governments. Under the GST regime, the effective rate of electricity duty could actually be higher than the current rate. This being the case, there is no need for an additional eco-cess to be levied on electricity. However, in states where the effective rate of electricity duty under the GST regime is lower than the current rate, and/or the national average, eco-cess could be levied.

1.8.4 Tax Treatment of Coal

Coal containing high ash content causes serious environmental pollution and health hazards in transportation and handling, industrial applications and generation of power. As discussed in Section 1.2, coal is the major source of CO_2 emission in India. Strong incentives are needed to promote coal cleaning and carbon capture technologies. Some initiatives have been taken in this regard. For promotion of clean coal technologies, action has been initiated with the cooperation of Indo-US Working Group, Indo-EU Working Group and Asia Pacific Partnership. The environmental management plans are now scrutinized by an Expert Committee setup by the Ministry of Environment and Forests. Under a jointly funded project by the Global Environment Facility, United Nations Development Programme and the Government of India, a 'coal bed methane recovery and commercial utilization project' has been approved with the objective of harnessing methane to minimize safety risks in mines and to utilize potential energy source and to mitigate damage to the atmosphere. It is also meant to bring to the country, a state-of-art methodology for source assessment and recovery techniques of coal bed methane recovery taking account of the Indian conditions.

As far as taxation of coal under customs duty and CENVAT is concerned, the following provisions apply. Under the Customs Duty Act, for all varieties of coal except bituminous coal, the tariff rate is 10 percent. For bituminous coal, the tariff rate is 55 percent. Under the Central Excise Act, the tariff rate is zero percent for all varieties of coal. Under a special notification, under the Coal Mines (conservation and development) Act 1974, a stowing excise duty has been levied at the rate of ₹10 per ton of coal irrespective of its grade with effect from 26 March 2003. This excise duty is collected by the Coal Controller on all raw coal produced and dispatched from all the collieries in India. It is realized from the consumers along with the coal sale bills raised by the coal companies. The net proceeds from the stowing excise duty during the preceding year or years is disbursed to the owners, agents or the managers for execution of stowing and other operations for the safety in coal mines or conservation of coal or any other purpose connected with development of coal mines or transportation, distribution or utilization of coal. The central government also levies a coal cess- -raised to ₹100 per tonne in 2014–15 budget from earlier value of ₹50 per tonne.

Based on the preceding discussion and the recommendations of the earlier ET studies (see Appendix A1.2 for details), the following could be taken for special consideration of ET and eco-subsidies under the GST regime. It should be noted here that the scope of the discussion here is to provide policy directions for the implementation of ETs, and not to give specific recommendations about the tax structure and tax rate.

1. *Coal:* In addition to the environmentally rational cess on coal (consistent with ash content), the producing states like Bihar, Assam, Odisha, Jharkhand, Madhya Pradesh and Chhattisgarh could be allowed to levy a higher cess than the floor rate to facilitate clean-up of production-related pollution.
2. *Petroleum products:* Even though the petroleum products are currently kept outside the GST, given the considerable revenue-importance of tax on these products, they should be eventually brought under GST and additional cess should be levied based on environmental considerations.
3. *Chemical fertilizers:* Given the adverse environmental effects caused by the non-point source pollution generated through the use of chemical fertilizers, the existing subsidy on these fertilizers should be eliminated in phases. Subsidy should instead be given to the bio-fertilizers.
4. *Chemical pesticides:* Similar to chemical fertilizers, indiscriminate use of pesticides, particularly in case of commercial crops like cotton, fruits and vegetables, results in significant environmental health damages. Combination of ETs and eco-subsidies should be used to disincentivize and incentivize the use of chemical and bio-pesticides,respectively.
5. *Plastics:* Local-level ETs (along with other incentive programmes) should be used for reducing demand for plastics by the consumers, promote biodegradable plastics and incentivize recycling.

1.9 OVERVIEW OF THE BOOK

Pollution in India is high relative to prescribed standards. It has serious implications for sustainability of growth due to depletion of natural resources, implications of climate change and health hazards. Of the two approaches to pollution control, namely regulatory approach and use of market-based instruments, the latter has certain advantages. The two approaches are not mutually exclusive and can be used to complement each other. The main fiscal instruments are ETs and eco-subsidies. Internationally, there has been a noticeable move towards ETR of the existing tax structures thereby giving rise to green shift in taxation.

India is likely to introduce a major change in its system of indirect taxation by bringing in a comprehensive GST. This paper has argued that this is the appropriate time to introduce a GST that is well integrated with ETR. This will facilitate the introduction of GST itself by reducing the overall GST rate while allowing for state-level variation in the ET component of GST in the form of non-rebatable cesses that allow for state-level flexibility. The ETs should bc accompanied by eco-subsidies so as to encourage the development of environmental induscries by providing incentives for non-polluting processes and goods.

Broadly, it is on these aspects this book focuses. The rest of the chapters in the book are organized as follows: As mentioned above, many developed countries have now started using ETs for controlling pollution and meeting environmental targets. The experience of developed and other developing countries with regard to what types of taxes are levied, how much revenue is generated from those taxes and how it is used and what have been the impacts of the taxes on the economy and the environment will guide us a long way while trying to design a tax system integrating ETs in India. The second chapter discusses the economic, environmental and social effectiveness of ETs practised by various countries.

Current debates on GST range from the uniform rate to be introduced, the list of goods to be exempted from the proposed GST as well as on the compensation schemes acceptable to states losing out on GST due to the consumption-based nature of GST itself. The third chapter highlights the key differences between various schools of thought with regard to implementation of GST in India and discusses the constitutional amendments being debated.

The primary objective of integrating environmental taxes into the framework of overall taxes is to provide adequate incentives to restrict environmental damage. This requires a detailed understanding of how taxes affect the consumption of goods, especially those that are polluting in nature, and subsequently its effect on pollution load and therefore on environmental quality at the national level. The fourth chapter describes the insights from a detailed modelling work that assessed the economic and environmental effectiveness of integrating environmental taxes in the GST framework in India.

Subsidy is an important fiscal instrument that the governments can use to induce greater consumption of environment friendly goods or promote innovations in efficiency enhancing technologies. The role of environmental subsidies in the GST regime in India is discussed in the fifth chapter.

Finally, the sixth chapter summarizes the main arguments of the book and provides policy recommendations. The chapter also discusses the prospects for a comprehensive integration of ETs in the GST regime in India.

NOTES

1. Currently, goods are taxed under CENVAT by the Central Government and State VAT by the state governments. Services are taxed separately. Taxation of petroleum products is subjected to sales tax as well as central excise duty. There is a central sales tax on inter-state trade of goods.
2. The Supreme Court in its verdict in the M.C. Mehta vs. Kamal Nath case has observed that any disturbance to the basic environment elements, namely, air, water and soil necessary for life, would be hazardous to life within the meaning of Article 21 of the Constitution.
3. While the state government had ordered closure of Tamil Nadu Chromates and Chemicals Limited a decade ago, the legacy of the same still continues with no solution still in sight for the safe disposal of 1500000 tons of solid waste generated by the factory over two decades before its closure. Blacksmith Institute and Asian Development Bank estimate that about 3.5 million people are potentially affected due to ground and surface water contamination.
4. As untreated water is discharged by the mines into the river and onto the soil, more than 60 percent of the drinking water is reported to contain hexavalent chromium at levels that are far above the national and international standards. Of the 2600000 potentially affected population in the area, a local NGO has estimated that about 25 percent are affected by various pollution-induced diseases.
5. A number of modelling exercises facilitated by the MOEF (2009) highlight that India's per capita GHG emissions in 2030–31 would be between 2.77 tons and 5.00 tons of CO_2e (carbon dioxide equivalent). Four of the five studies estimated that even in 2031, India's per capita GHG emissions would stay under 4 tons of CO_2e which is lower than the global per capita emissions of 4.22 tons of CO_2e in 2005. This would mean that even two decades from now, India's per capita GHG emissions would be well below the global average of 25 years earlier.
6. While it is acknowledged that the Himalayan glaciers are receding, a recent MOEF Discussion Paper (Raina, 2009) argues that this could be due to various factors and the link with climate change is not that clear-cut.
7. A third alternative is also emerging based on information disclosures. By disclosing the environmental performance of a firm, it is anticipated that the firm would adjust its environmental performance through the market feedback.

2

Environmental Tax Reforms: International Experience

D.K. Srivastava, K.S. Kavi Kumar and C. Bhujanga Rao

2.1 ENVIRONMENTAL MANAGEMENT: DIFFERENT APPROACHES

Various countries have adopted different approaches for managing environmental pollution and resource degradation. Considering that the environmental pollution is a classic externality problem, most countries have attempted to address it through regulatory 'command-and-control' (CAC) approach. Subsequently, market-based instruments have been adopted in several developed and few developing countries to provide requisite incentives for the polluters to comply with the pollution reduction. Recognizing that society at large is as much part of the pollution problem as the industry and government, recent advances in pollution management suggest information-based instruments that bring together all the relevant stakeholders. This chapter first provides a brief description of various approaches adopted worldwide for managing the environment and then discusses the evidence from the developed and developing countries on environmental tax reforms (ETR). The chapter also provides a brief discussion on the lessons for India based on the international experience.

2.1.1 Relative Merits of Regulatory and Market-based Instruments for Environmental Management

a. Regulatory Instruments

These involve state regulation of activities where the state prescribes emission or effluent standards, limits the production of certain goods beyond a prescribed limit, prohibits the use of polluting inputs and restricts location of polluting industries. Non-compliance to these standards results in punishment in the form of fine or other legal measures. Regulations could take the form of performance standards where the state dictates a certain level of performance or work practice standards where it imposes the use of a technique known to reduce pollution (Driesen, 2006).

The main criticism against the CAC instruments is the high cost of emission reduction and failure in government implementation. Given that all industries do not have the same abatement cost, it is cost efficient for some industries to abate more and others to abate lesser than required. However, regulations require all industries to adhere to similar standards irrespective of their cost of abatement which increases the overall cost of abatement. Regulation is also more difficult to implement as it requires considerable information and involves significant administrative costs for implementation and monitoring. Lastly, the penalty for non-compliance does not depend on the extent of non-compliance. In case of non-compliance, everyone pays the same fine irrespective of the difference in their level of compliance.

Regulatory instruments work best in cases of complete market failure and in cases where an activity or a pollutant could lead to excessive harm where the market forces are unable to react.

b. Market-based Instruments

Market-based economic instruments are intended to internalize environmental costs and externalities, and hence influence decisions of agents by sending signals through price and other variables. These provide financial incentives to make environment friendly decisions. It is in the economic interest of the polluter or the consumer to reduce pollution voluntarily by using better inputs and techniques or consume less polluting goods by conservation or substitution.

The main strength of economic instruments is the flexibility they allow leading to a reduction in the overall cost of abatement in comparison to other regulatory approaches. Economic instruments call for an overall level of environmental performance in the economy. The private players, depending on their relative costs, can decide their respective levels of abatement. This ensures that industries with lower abatement cost abate more than those with higher abatement costs.

Market-based instruments are of three broad types: price-based, quantity-based and informational-policy instruments.

(i) Price-based instruments: The price-based instruments can be further grouped into negative and positive instruments. A pigouvian tax is a typical negative price instrument used when the output produced of a 'bad' is at the point where the marginal cost of the firm meets the price. The socially optimum output would have been lesser if the social marginal cost (which is higher than the firm's private cost) had been considered. Since the firm ignores this externality, a tax is imposed on it to the extent that its private cost equals the social cost internalizing the externality and inducing the firm to produce at the socially optimal level. Thus, as resources and emissions become more expensive, consumers and producers have an incentive to consume lesser or pollute lesser. It works out to be more efficient than CAC regulations as firms which have a lower marginal abatement cost than the marginal tax rate will do so and those who do not will simply pay the tax.

Subsidies for environmental 'goods' which are generally under-produced or under-consumed, to encourage more production and consumption could fall into positive price instruments. The main drawback of price instruments is that the outcome level is allowed to vary and hence cannot be pre-determined.

(ii) Quantity-based instruments: As opposed to price instruments where price is fixed and output is allowed to vary as decided by firms' response, in the case of quantity-based instruments the government fixes the output and the private firms can choose prices to achieve the quantity limit. In a way, quantity instruments are similar to performance standards except that non-compliance to the limits is allowed if a firm could buy credits from another firm which has over-achieved the target, that is, reduced emissions beyond requirement. Such credits can be exchanged through instruments like tradable pollution permits. Such permits give an incentive for firms to pollute less as they could sell their permits if they achieve better performance. Such an instrument stems from the Coasean approach where it is argued that the socially optimal level of outcome will emerge if proper property rights are defined and it is the state's responsibility to define and enforce such rights. The ultimate outcome does not depend on who possesses the right as the polluter and the victim will bargain among themselves and reach the optimal outcome. The main advantage of quantity instruments is that they ensure the desired environmental outcome. However, the practical implementation of trade permits requires an effective legal and institutional structure, the lack of which acts as a major hurdle for its effectiveness especially in developing countries.

(iii) Informational-policy instruments: In addition to price and quantity instruments, informational instruments also provide incentives to pollute less. 'Right to Know' programmes require polluters to report the amount of pollution they generate. For example, in the USA, the Toxic Release Inventory forces firms to publicize their level of toxic chemical use and effluents (Driesen, 2006). Such programmes give incentives for the firm to reduce pollution to the extent it is conscious of its reputation and loss of market demand as a result of any adverse reputation. Voluntary environmental certification systems and eco-labelling reveal the environmental attributes of the company or the product to the consumer and hence the firm is tempted to improve its conduct to attract customers. Other instruments which provide information about the firm like awareness campaigns and information programmes on new deployable techniques could further help the firm to reduce pollution. However, information programmes may be used complementarily with other instruments and may not be effective if used alone.

In recent international experience, the reliance on using economic instruments has considerably increased. In this paper, we examine the reasons for this increased dependence on using economic instruments for environmental management internationally.

2.1.2 Eco-taxes: Taxing Pollution versus Taxing Polluting Inputs and Outputs

Eco-tax is a broad term used to denote a variety of negative price incentives including not only taxes that directly tax pollution but also other indirect taxes which discourage the consumption of polluting outputs and the use of polluting inputs in production. For example, a tax on automobiles would lead to a reduction in pollution indirectly through lesser usage of automobiles. A tax on coal, which is regarded to be highly polluting, will discourage its use as raw material in production process and encourage its substitution with other environment friendly materials.

Hence eco-taxes (the way they are referred here) can be levied directly on pollution or on pollution-causing inputs and outputs signalling the price for the unpaid factor of production, thereby internalizing the externality. However, taxing pollution directly is often difficult due to measurement problems. Further, in some countries like India pollution taxes necessitate significant legal and institutional reforms. In such circumstances, taxing polluting inputs and outputs is considered the second-best solution. Eco-taxes, levied on output, are aimed at raising the price of the output, inducing consumers to reduce consumption levels or shift to non-polluting substitutes. Reduction in consumption will subsequently lead to a reduction in production and hence in pollution load. Impact of eco-tax in this case depends on the price elasticity of the polluting good and the availability of close substitutes. If levied on inputs, the burden of the tax is borne partly by the producers and is partly passed on to the consumers in the form of increased prices. This will encourage producers to invest in technological innovations and to use non-polluting inputs if substitutes are available.

2.1.3 Revenue Neutral versus Revenue-augmenting ETR

ETR is a tax policy reform which seeks to apply revenue-raising economic instruments such as taxes or an emissions trading system to resource use and pollution. ETR generally involves three complementary activities. These are as follows:

1. Removal of existing taxes and subsidies that have negative environmental impacts (EEA, 1996).[1]
2. Restructuring existing taxes in an environmentally friendly manner.
3. Introducing new environmental taxes.

Considering the tax system as a whole, ETR could be revenue neutral or revenue augmenting. A revenue neutral ETR attempts to shift the burden of taxation from 'goods' such as labour and capital to 'bads' such as polluting inputs and outputs (Weizsacker, 1992). In this sense, it reduces the overall distortionary burden of the tax system. Additionally, it reduces resource use and pollution by implementing eco-taxes and increases output, employment and resource productivity by lowering taxes on capital and labour, thereby enhancing welfare.

On the other hand, environmental taxes can also be designed as fully or partially revenue augmenting. This may be relevant where environmental public goods are under-provided and environmental taxes add revenues to the overall revenue-pool so that the size of the public sector expands to provide environmental public goods.

An important issue in this context is whether eco-tax revenue should be fully earmarked for environmental public goods. Appendix A2.1 provides a detailed discussion on environmental public goods and eco-tax revenue by introducing analytical framework involving the concept of *social marginal cost of public funds (SMCPF)*. Given the practical difficulties involved in measuring SMCPF, certain conventions or rules of thumb may have to be used while assessing link between eco-tax revenue and environmental public goods. It can be argued that such conventions will need to be different between developed and developing countries. In developing countries, environmental taxes can be used to some extent in increasing the tax–GDP ratio and a higher percentage can be allocated for environmental public goods.

In the developed countries, given high tax–GDP ratio, the revenue from the environmental tax can be used to replace conventional distortionary taxes and to provide general public goods. In practice, this was what most developed countries followed. The revenue from the new tax regime was recycled into a reduced level of income tax and employers' contributions in order to benefit both households and industry.

2.1.4 Other Issues in Designing Eco-taxes

According to Chelliah et al. (2007), while designing a system of eco-taxes, several issues need to be carefully resolved. Some of those issues are outlined below:

1. Pollution can be from stationary/point sources or non-point sources. If pollution is from point sources such as emissions from factories, a CAC regime may also work. If pollution is from non-point sources, such as those that result from consumption, only

indirect instruments such as tax on inputs or outputs can be applied. When designing such indirect taxes, it is important to understand the extent to which the input/output is responsible for pollution as the effectiveness of the tax largely depends on this link.

2. In a federal structure of eco-taxes, it is important to allocate the responsibility of taxation between the Centre and the states. Preferably, the Centre can handle national level environmental problems and regional environmental management can be the responsibility of the states. Problems, such as air pollution and marine pollution, involving inter-state externalities should be the responsibility of the Centre, and local problems such as solid waste management and local water pollution can be entrusted to the states.
3. The choice of levying eco-taxes on inputs or outputs depends on whether the pollution occurs at the production stage or the consumption stage. If pollution occurs largely during production, especially when a particular input is used, it is desirable to tax the input which will push the producer to look for cleaner substitutes. If pollution occurs during consumption, for example, while driving a car, it is desirable to tax the output (gasoline or motor vehicles). Inadequate information in tracking the use of the output at the consumption stage makes output tax less feasible than input tax.

2.1.5 Managing Pollution and Climate Change through Environmental Taxes

The main forms of pollution are atmospheric pollution, land degradation, soil pollution, water pollution and noise pollution. Different environmental taxes may be suitable for different forms of pollution.

a. Air Pollution

The main sources of atmospheric pollution are: (a) combustion of fuels to produce energy for heating and power generation in the household and industrial sectors; (b) exhaust emissions from vehicles that use petrol, diesel, etc. and (c) waste gases, dust and heat from many industrial sites including chemical manufacturers and electrical power generating stations. Three main pollutants of ambient air quality are sulphur dioxide (SO_2), nitrogen dioxide (NO_2) and particulate matter (PM).

b. Water Pollution

Water is polluted by the effluents of industries. Some of the important industries in this context are ferrous and non-ferrous metallurgical industries, mining and ore processing, and industries relating to petroleum, petrochemicals, chemicals, ceramics, cement, textiles, paper, fertilizers, coal (including coke), power generation (thermal and diesel) and animal or vegetable product processing industry. Small-scale industries (SSIs) are also a major source of industrial water pollution.

c. Soil Pollution

Soil can be polluted through seepage of polluted water and use of chemicals and fertilizers. The main land and soil pollutants are fertilizers and pesticides.

d. Climate Change

Since the Industrial Revolution, anthropogenic activities such as energy generation from fossil fuels and deforestation have been increasing the atmospheric concentrations of greenhouse gases (GHGs) beyond their natural levels, resulting in an enhanced greenhouse effect. The main gases contributing to GHG concentration include carbon dioxide (CO_2), methane (CH_4), nitrous oxide (N_2O) and halocarbons. This increase in GHG concentration is believed to result in an increase in global temperatures. The temperature rise could be coupled with changes in rainfall pattern, sea level rise, and frequency and severity of extreme events such as cyclones, droughts, etc. The sum of all these potential changes is referred to as climate change.

So far, much of the global response to climate change problem has been on: (a) assessing the extent of mitigation of GHG emissions world over that could avoid 'dangerous' climate change; (b) distributing the mitigation burden across nations that fulfils the 'common but differentiated' principle of the Earth Summit in 1992 and (c) identifying cost-effective route for meeting mitigation targets and developing mechanisms and institutions that enable cost-effective mitigation. The role of environmental taxes in managing climate change has occupied considerable attention in the international arena.

Given these environmental concerns, a wide range of environmental taxes have been used. Some of these taxes are outlined here.

1. **Carbon tax:** A carbon tax on the use of fossil fuels is an eco-tax. It is a tax on energy sources which emit carbon dioxide. A carbon

tax aims at reducing emissions of carbon dioxide and thereby slow global warming. It can be implemented by taxing the burning of fossil fuels like coal, petroleum products such as gasoline and aviation fuel, and natural gas, in proportion to their carbon content. Unlike market-based approaches such as carbon cap-and-trade systems, it has the benefit of being easily understood and can be popular with the public if the revenue is earmarked to fund environmental projects. Other forms of carbon taxes are as follows:

- *CO_2 tax:* It is similar to carbon tax and it is levied on CO_2 instead of carbon content.
- *Energy tax:* It is a charge levied on quantity of energy consumed.
- *Implicit carbon tax:* It is a sum of all taxes on energy, including taxes on energy sales (excise duties). It may be noted that petrol and diesel are heavily taxed fuels due to their low demand elasticities; taxing them is an easy way to collect fiscal revenues.

2. **Effluent charges:** These are also a form of eco-tax, which is levied on effluents, pollution and other hazardous wastes. These are widely used in Western and Eastern European countries and are used to control a range of pollutants like carbon monoxide (CO), carbon dioxide (CO_2), sulphur dioxide (SO_2), biological oxygen demand (BOD), oxides of nitrogen (NO_x), total suspended solids (TSS), nitrogen (N), phosphate (P), landfill and hazardous waste.
3. **User charges:** These are the charges levied on those who directly benefit from a service, in order to finance its provisions. Examples are fuel taxes, congestion charges (used for traffic management), charges for disposing of landfill and hazardous wastes (used for solid waste management), product taxes on batteries, beverage containers, tyres (the revenue of which is used for its disposal).
4. **Insurance premium taxes:** These are used in the case of oil and chemical pollution and the amounts raised are used to clean up in cases where the liable party cannot be found or cannot pay the full cost. These are used in Belgium, Finland and the USA.
5. **Sales taxes:** Sales taxes are widely used all over the world.
6. **Deposit refund system:** These are used for environment regulation for disposal or recycling of hazardous waste.
7. **Severance taxes:** These are levied on the extraction of mineral, energy and forestry products.

8. **Licence fees:** These are used for enforcement of conservation in fishing and hunting.
9. **Specific taxes:** These are imposed on technologies and products, which are associated with substantial negative environmental externalities. Garbage disposal taxes and refundable fees are used for positive environmental results.

2.2 ENVIRONMENTAL TAXES: DEVELOPED COUNTRY EXPERIENCE

The application of eco-taxes as a tool for environmental management has been practiced in developed countries for a number of years now. Extensive tax reforms have been undertaken for a number of years now, particularly in the sub-continents and countries of Europe, Canada, Australia and New Zealand. Europe was among the pioneers to introduce eco-taxes with Sweden, Denmark, Norway, Finland and the Netherlands being some of the first countries to introduce environmental taxes. Presently, the UK and Germany are using eco-taxes in a significant way. This section focuses on the experiences with eco-taxes in the UK, Germany and Sweden among the European countries along with those of Canada and New Zealand.

2.2.1 Types of Taxes

For the discussion here, eco-taxes have been divided into three broad groups: energy taxes (including CO_2 taxes), transport taxes, and taxes on pollution, waste and natural resources (excluding taxes on oil and gas).

Energy taxes include taxes on all energy products irrespective of whether they are used for transport or other purposes (e.g. domestic fuels). Hence, taxes on petrol and diesel, though used for transport purposes, are included under energy taxes.

Pollution taxes (including taxes on waste) and natural resources taxes are levied to discourage the contamination and over-use of natural resources, respectively. Pollution taxes include taxes directly on pollution emitted into air, water, etc. CO_2 taxes, however, are included under energy taxes. Waste taxes are levied on the wastes dumped in landfills. Resource taxes are levied on water extraction, forestry and mining.

Transport taxes are levied on the ownership and use of motor vehicles. These taxes are applicable for any mode of transport—road, rail, air, etc. It can be levied at the time of purchase of a motor vehicle or when one uses a certain mode of transport (e.g. air travel).

a. Energy and Carbon Taxes

An energy tax provides incentives for energy efficiency, reduced consumption and switching to low emission fuels. Most energy taxes are levied on fuels according to their carbon or sulphur content. The most important energy tax is a fuel duty on petrol and diesel. A fuel duty on petrol and diesel used in vehicles adds to the marginal cost of driving. It is expected to reduce the number of trips made and/or distance travelled. In the long run, it also encourages people to buy more fuel efficient vehicles.

In the UK, two important energy taxes used are fuel duty and the climate change levy (CCL; Table 2.1). The rates for fuel duty were determined using a fuel duty escalator from 1993 to 1999 when it was abandoned. The CCL is designed to discourage excessive use of energy. Differential rates are charged for different fuels. Germany has an energy tax which is charged on different sources of energy. Sweden has a carbon tax and a separate sulphur tax aimed at reducing sulphur emissions. In Canada, fuel is subject to goods and services tax (GST)/HST. In addition, it is subjected to a non-rebatable federal excise tax and a provincial sales tax. In the Canadian province of British Columbia, a carbon tax is also levied. The Canadian example shows how fuel tax is subjected to both GST/HST and additional excise duties both at the federal and provincial levels.

b. Taxes on Waste, Pollution and Natural Resources

A tax on waste aims at reducing the externalities associated with waste disposal. These externalities include methane emissions, risk of contamination of water systems, disutility to local residents, health effects, etc. Examples of waste taxes are the Landfill tax of the UK and the Waste levy of New Zealand. Both these taxes are charged on landfill operators. However, the tax-incidence can be passed onto consumers through higher prices.

The main examples of taxes on natural resources are taxes on aggregates and taxes on water extraction. Aggregates refer to rock, gravel, sand and any materials naturally mixed with them. The tax is levied on quarry operators and other businesses that commercially exploit aggregates. This tax is charged to take account of the external costs of aggregates extraction which include emissions from transportation, noise, dust, pollution of groundwater, loss of habitat for wildlife, etc.

Table 2.1
Taxes on energy

Country	*Tax*	*Objective*	*Description*
UK	Climate change levy (CCL)	To encourage energy efficiency	Charged on business use of energy such as natural gas, electricity, LPG and solid fuels; different rates for different fuels
	Fuel duty	To reduce number of trips made by car	Tax levied on fuels based on emissions
Germany	Energy tax	To encourage energy efficiency	Tax charged on tax rate on mineral oil for fuel, gas and heating oil, coal and electricity
Sweden	Carbon tax	To reduce carbon emissions	Levied on oil, coal, natural gas, liquefied petroleum gas, petrol and aviation fuel in domestic traffic
	Sulphur tax	To reduce sulphur emissions	Levied on liquid fuels, coal and fuel oil according to the sulphur content
Canada	Fuel tax	To encourage use of efficient fuels	Fuel is subject to the GST/HST, the federal excise tax, provincial taxes and provincial sales taxes; hence, tax rates differ among provinces
	British Columbia's carbon tax	To reduce emissions of CO_2, methane and nitrous oxide	Levied on the purchase and use of fossil fuels such as gasoline, diesel, natural gas, heating fuel, propane, coal, etc based on emissions of CO_2 equivalent

Source: Leicester (2006), Kolhaas (2000), Branlund and Kristrm (1999), British Columbia Government (2008).

Taxes on water are seen in the UK and Mexico. In both countries, businesses are taxed for extracting water. Table 2.2 summarizes some notable examples of taxes on wastes and natural resources.

c. Transport Taxes

Transport taxes have been successfully implemented in several countries. Transport taxes seek to reduce pollution arising from transportation and fuel use by dis-incentivizing frequent or inefficient travel. These taxes are

Table 2.2
Taxes on waste and natural resources

Country	*Tax*	*Objective*	*Description*
UK	Landfill tax	To reduce externalities associated with waste disposal	Charge levied on landfill site owners and can be passed on to consumers via higher prices
	Aggregates levy	To reduce externalities associated with aggregates extraction	Tax levied on quarry operators and other organizations that commercially exploit aggregates; different rates for active and inactive wastes
	Water abstraction charge	Levied by the Environment Agency to cover the costs they incur in water resource management	Levied on businesses that extract and use over ground, underground or tidal water sources
New Zealand	Waste levy	To provide both an incentive to avoid waste, along with funding to help develop waste minimisation infrastructure	Charged on waste disposed at disposal facilities
Mexico	Water abstraction charge	To encourage efficient use of water	Different rates for specific types of uses of water; rate also determined by the relative scarcity or abundance of an area's water resources
	Pollution charges	To reduce discharge of polluting effluents	Different rates for different contaminants and different types of water bodies to which effluent is discharged

Source: Leicester (2006), OECD (2003) and Ministry of Environment, New Zealand.

levied on vehicles based on their emissions rating. A tax on vehicles represents a fixed cost of car ownership. As such, it does not give an incentive to drive less. Instead, it provides an incentive to buy more fuel efficient cars and encourages motorists to scrap older and more polluting cars. As shown in Table 2.3, this is the case with the vehicle excise duty (VED) in the UK,

Table 2.3
Transport taxes

Country	*Tax*	*Objective*	*Description*
UK	Vehicle excise duty (VED)	To encourage purchase of low emission cars	Annual tax on road vehicles based on the emissions rating of the vehicles
	Air passenger duty (APD)	To reduce the number of times a person flies	Levied on airlines based on the number of passengers flying domestically or internationally from the UK airports
	London congestion charge	To reduce level of congestion in Central London	Charged on any vehicle entering or parking in the charging zone between 7 a.m. and 6.30 p.m. on a weekday
	Taxation of company cars	To reduce emissions by company cars	Company cars are allocated a cash value on which company car drivers are liable to pay income tax and employers are liable to pay Class 1A National Insurance Contributions (NICs)
Germany	Vehicle tax	To reduce CO_2 emissions from road traffic	Tax based on cylinder capacity of vehicle, over which EURO 2 per gram of CO_2 emissions per kilometre (g/km) is charged if those exceed a threshold of 120 g/km
Sweden	Vehicle excise duty (VED)	To reduce CO_2 emissions from road traffic	Duty comprises of a base charge of 360 SKR plus a CO_2 charge of 15 SKR per gram of CO_2 exceeding 100 grams per kilometre (g/km)
Canada	Vehicle tax	To encourage purchase of low emission cars	Federal excise tax on automobiles based on the weighted average fuel consumption rating of the vehicle

Source: Leicester (2006), Kolhaas (2000), Borup (2007) and British Columbia Government (2008).

Germany, Sweden and Canada. Another form of transport tax is to levy a tax on the passenger depending on his use hence encouraging him to travel less. Such taxes are common in air transports like the air passenger duty (APD) of the UK. Use of a transport tax can also have a spatial dimension with a view to reduce congestion in areas with high vehicular density and heavy polluted air. An example of a local level tax is the London congestion charge.

2.2.2 Revenues from Eco-taxes

Figure 2.1 shows the revenue from environmental taxes in select European countries for the year 2004. It can be seen that the revenue is highest in Germany followed by the UK. France, Italy, the Netherlands and Spain also have significant revenues from environmental taxes. Figure 2.1 shows environmental tax revenues in absolute amounts, whereas Figures 2.2 and 2.3 show environmental tax revenues relative to GDP and total tax revenues, respectively.

The level of tax revenues is the product of tax rate and tax base. High tax rates reduce the tax base and this disincentive effect of the tax rate depends on the price elasticity of the use of polluting inputs and outputs. High revenues need not be interpreted as indicative of environmental

Figure 2.1
Revenues from environmental taxes (2004)

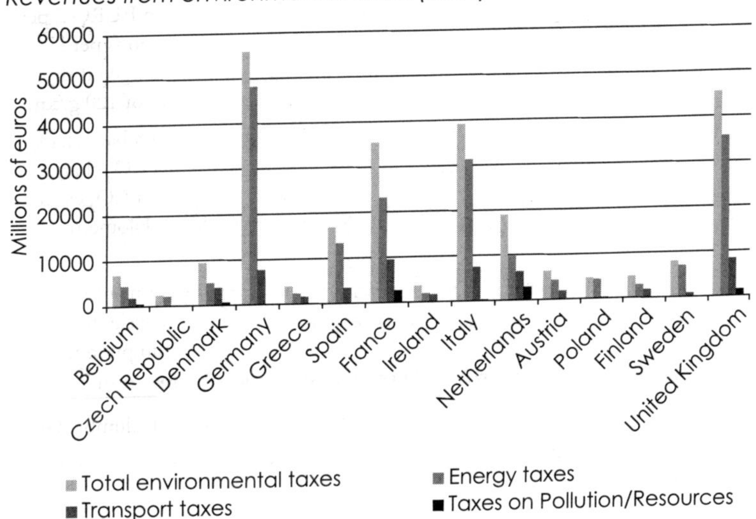

Source: http://www.swivel.com/workbooks/25744-Environmental-tax-revenue-in-Europe

Figure 2.2
Eco-tax revenues as percent of GDP

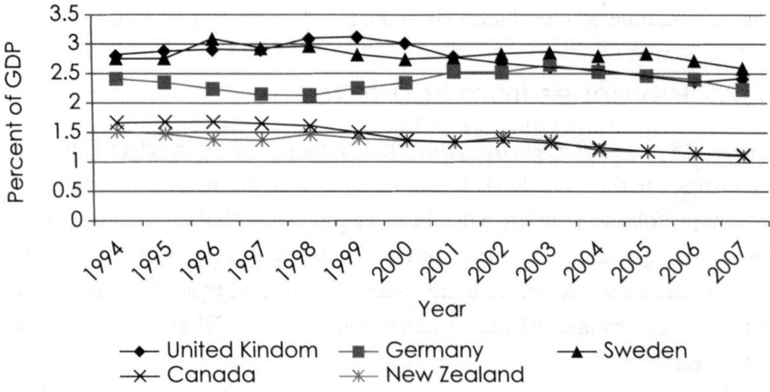

Source: http://www2.oecd.org/ecoinst/queries/TaxInfo.htm

Figure 2.3
Eco-tax revenues as percent of total tax revenues

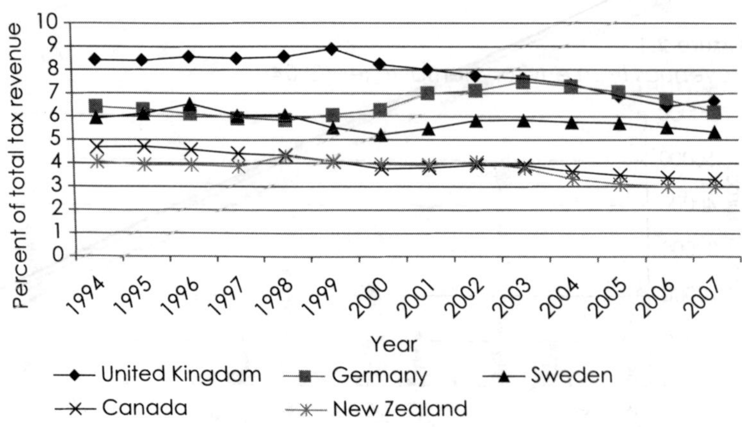

Source (Basic Data): http://www2.oecd.org/ecoinst/queries/TaxInfo.htm

effectiveness of the tax. The following considerations need to be borne in mind.

1. If a tax system is environmentally effective in inducing the desired outcome of reduced consumption of the 'bad', it leads to erosion of

the tax base itself. As a result, tax revenues fall. In this case, reduced revenues imply that the tax system is environmentally effective. On the other hand, reduced revenues could also occur because the system of eco-taxes is in its infancy and there are very few of such taxes to generate revenue from. In this case, lesser revenues correspond to lesser environmental effectiveness.

2. In some cases, if an environmental tax is levied on an inelastic good, consumption would change only to a limited extent irrespective of the tax rate. Such taxes are principally levied for revenue purposes. In this case, increased revenues do not necessarily mean high environmental effectiveness unless these revenues are used to promote environment friendly technological shifts. The link between high revenues and high environmental effectiveness could also be weak for other reasons: some environmental outcomes could be achieved at low rates and outcomes also depend on relative tax rates between related products (OECD, 2001). However, high revenues from environmental taxes could also imply the existence of a well-developed eco-tax system which may have positive impacts on the environment.

a. Country-wise Analysis

Overall, revenue potential from environmentally related taxes over the period 1996–2006 has shown a declining trend in most of the OECD countries. Figures 2.2 and 2.3 show revenue from eco-taxes for the countries under study as a percent of their GDP and as a percent of their total tax revenues, respectively.

Figure 2.2 shows that revenue from eco-taxes as a percent of GDP has been higher at about 2.5–3 percent in the UK, Germany and Sweden, whereas it has averaged at about 1–1.5 percent in Canada and New Zealand. It also shows that the revenue has been decreasing in all the countries especially after 2003. However, the declining trend of revenue from eco-taxes has to be interpreted bearing in mind that the decline could be either because (a) the number of such taxes and the tax rates are on the decline; or (b) as the tax rate increases, it induces change in behaviour leading to reduced consumption of the 'bad' and hence reducing the tax base and consequently the tax revenue. OECD observes that the reason for this decline in revenues from environmentally related taxes is due to the decline in the use of petrol per unit of GDP.[2]

Figure 2.3 highlights the trend in eco-tax revenues as a percent of total tax revenues. Eco-tax revenues constitute about 6–8 percent of total tax revenues in the UK, Germany and Sweden, whereas in Canada and New Zealand, eco-tax revenues constitute only about 4–5 percent.

b. Tax-wise Analysis

From Figure 2.3, it is seen that energy taxes contribute by far the most in terms of revenue for all the European countries and other OECD countries. Fuel taxes, especially taxes on transport fuels, contribute a major portion of energy tax revenues. Figure 2.4 shows the trends in eco-tax revenues from different sources as a percent of total tax revenues for the UK (top panel), Germany (middle panel) and Sweden (bottom panel). These also help explain the reasons for the declining trend observed in eco-tax revenues as a percent of total tax revenues shown in Figure 2.3.

Figure 2.4 indicates that the decline in eco-tax revenue in these countries is due to the declining trend observed in energy tax revenues, especially from petrol and diesel taxes. This pattern could be either due to a decrease in tax rates on these goods over the years or a decline in consumption in response to an increase in tax rates over time. Transport fuels are known to have an inelastic demand in the short run but are more elastic in the long run. In almost all countries, tax rates have increased, whereas consumption has shown a decline over the years leading to reduced revenues.

One notable feature of the international experience is the predominance of consumption-based taxes, especially of that on transport. This could be for various reasons, the major one being that it is easy to administer and has higher revenue potential. The system of eco-tax in its current state relies much less on direct taxation of pollution.

c. Utilization of Revenue

Environmental taxes can either be revenue augmenting or revenue neutral. Revenue neutral eco-taxes are advocated by many economists for economies characterized by high levels of distortionary taxes. In this case, apart from achieving environmental objective, environmental taxes could reduce overall distortionary impact of the tax system, thereby making it more efficient. For countries where the tax–GDP ratio is low relative to international norms, environmental taxes could be used to raise

Figure 2.4
Revenue from transport, energy and pollution taxes as a percent of total tax revenues—the UK, Germany, Sweden

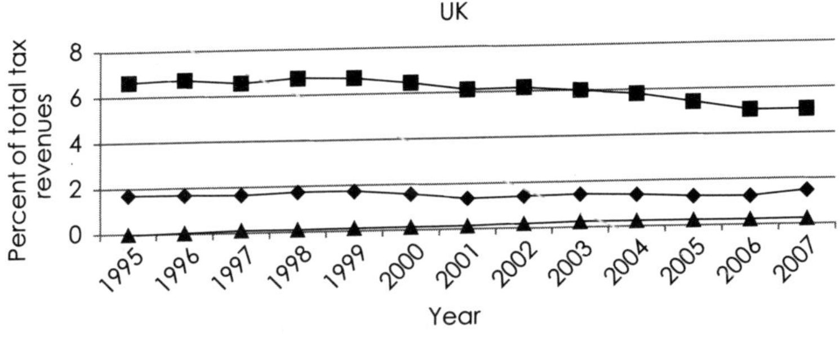

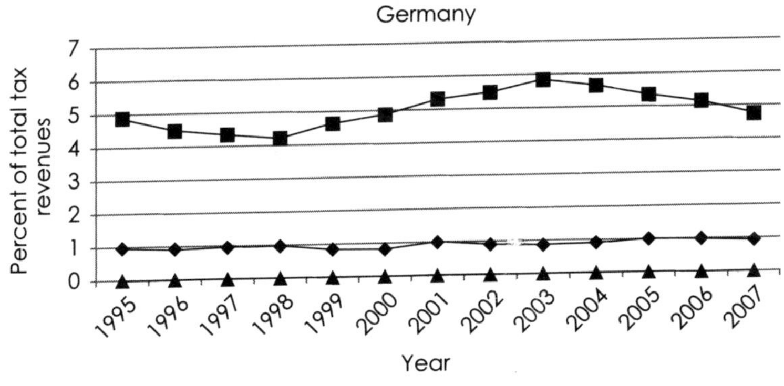

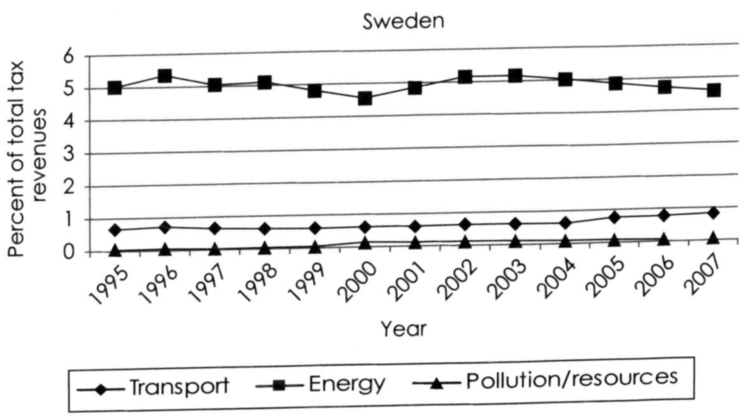

Source (Basic Data): http://ec.europa.eu/environment/enveco/mbi.htm

additional revenues while partially reducing the distortion. Revenues from environmental taxes can be utilized in several ways as discussed below.

1. *Revenue generated from environmental 'bads' can be re-invested in the environment:* Apart from regulating the misuse of the environment through economic or non-economic instruments, considerable investment needs to go into the protection of the environment in the form of research and development of new technologies. Revenue generated from environmental taxes can be used to facilitate this and for strengthening the institutional structures for more effective implementation as also for investing in the development and maintenance of natural resources.

   An example of environmental taxes being used for environmental purposes is the landfill tax of the UK. The revenue from landfill tax is not directly spent on the environment. However, a rebate on the landfill tax was given in proportion to the money spent on the environment. The Landfill Tax Credit Scheme (LTCS) was introduced by which landfill site owners can donate to designated bodies undertaking approved local community environment projects and in return receive a credit of 90 percent of the value of their donation from their landfill tax bill, up to a fixed limit. This limit, which was initially 20 percent of total liability, was reduced to 6 percent in 2003. From 2003, two-thirds of the funds raised was diverted away from local community environment projects and allotted to public spending to encourage sustainable waste management (Leicester, 2006).

   Similarly, water abstraction charges of Mexico, as discussed later in the next chapter, are levied by the Environment Agency to cover the costs they incur in water resource management.

   New Zealand's waste levy aims to provide both an incentive to avoid waste along with funding to help develop waste minimization infrastructure, such as reprocessing facilities and collection systems. It could also help to develop markets for compost and recyclables. The Waste Minimization Act in New Zealand provides for a waste levy of $10 per ton of waste disposed of at disposal facilities. Half of the levy funds are distributed to territorial authorities, on a population basis, to help implement their waste minimization and management plans. The other half of the levy, less administration costs, is available for funding waste minimization projects.[3]

2. *Environmental tax revenues can also be used to reduce the overall tax rate or reduce other distortionary taxes such as those on labour and capital:* In Germany, the ecological tax revenue was primarily used to reduce non-wage labour costs and contribute towards public pension scheme. In 2003, the revenue generated by the eco-tax amounted to approximately 18.7 billion euros, of which about 90 percent, that is, 16.1 billion euros, went into the public pension scheme. Employers and employees could thus benefit from a reduced contribution rate, from 20.3 percent in 1998 to 19.5 percent in 2005 (Kolhaas, 2000). The relief offered by the ecological tax reform is however larger: without the ecological tax reform, contributions to the public pension scheme would have further increased in the same time period as a result of demographic and economic pressures. Without the ecological tax reform, contributions in 2005 would thus have been at least 1.7 percent points higher at 21.2 percent.

   Another example of environmental taxes used to reduce the rates of other distortionary taxes is the carbon tax of Canada. The carbon tax is forecasted to generate an estimated $2.27 billion over the next three years.[4] The carbon tax revenues for the year 2008–09 are estimated at $300 million. Since the carbon tax is designed to be revenue neutral, this revenue will be returned to the public through reductions in other taxes. This is achieved through the following:[5]

   a. A cut in the two lowest provincial personal income tax rate by 5 percent.
   b. A reduction in the general corporate income tax rate from 12 to 11 percent.
   c. A reduction in the small business corporate income tax rate from 4.5 to 3.5 percent.
   d. Provision of a Northern and Rural Homeowner benefit of up to $200 beginning in 2011.
   e. A reduction in school property taxes for farm land by 50 percent beginning in 2011.

3. *Sometimes, the revenue generated from environmental taxes could be earmarked for certain specific purposes:* Earmarking of revenues could increase the environmental effectiveness if environmentally motivated but could also be detrimental if it drives inefficient spending that need not or would not have happened if these taxes were not levied. Hence, the

possible economic and environmental consequences of earmarking revenues should be carefully explored (OECD, 2001). The experiences of countries that are currently implementing eco-taxes reveal that large amounts of revenues from fuel taxes are allocated to road infrastructure and related activities.

In New Zealand, for example, revenue from fuel excise duty and road user charges is meant to provide an estimated extra $35 million above what would have been provided under the current funding commitments. This additional funding is projected to rise to about $600 million by the year 2016. The funds will be used for improving road and public transport. Road user charge in New Zealand is set at a rate which recovers the cost that heavy vehicles impose on the public road system. The money collected is used for maintenance and construction of the road system, traffic enforcement and safety programmes. Similarly, all the revenue collected from motor vehicle license fee goes to the public road system to pay for road construction and maintenance, traffic enforcement and road safety programmes.

However, earmarking revenues in this manner should be done with caution.

2.2.3 Impact of Eco-taxes

ETR impacts both the environment and the economy through the following ways:

1. By making the polluting inputs and outputs more expensive, ETR *reduces pollution and resource use.*
2. By shifting the burden of taxation away from labour and capital, ETR makes these cheaper, which in turn leads to an *increase in output, employment and resource productivity.*
3. By encouraging green industries, ETR *leads to green innovation and development of green technology.*

The theoretical discussion on the impacts of ETR focuses on the double dividend hypothesis (Patuelli et al., 2002). The double dividend hypothesis states that environmental taxes will not only lead to a cleaner environment (first dividend) but also boost employment, resource productivity and GDP (second dividend). ETR involves taxing environmental 'bads' and recycling the revenues to reduce distortionary taxes on other 'goods'. As pointed out by Heady et al. (2000), there is a distortionary effect associated with taxation in the form of reduced employment that results from taxes that are related to employment (income tax, social security tax) and taxes that affect the real value of worker's wages [value-added tax (VAT) and excise duties]. The source of double dividend therefore is increased employment resulting from a reduction of these taxes. There will be a strong employment dividend, however, only when there is involuntary unemployment in the system. Reduced taxes on 'goods' (such as labour and capital) also improve their productivity and enhance GDP. The occurrence of a double dividend will depend on the balance between the economic losses caused by the environmental tax and the benefits from revenue recycling.

There is a distinction between a strong dividend and weak dividend in the literature as introduced by Goulder (1995).The strong dividend hypothesis relates to gains in productivity and employment as a result of replacing some existing taxes with environmental taxes that will reduce the distortionary cost of raising the current level of government revenue. The weak dividend hypothesis is only concerned with the use of the revenues from the environmental taxes suggesting that it is better to use it to reduce distortionary taxes. There is surprisingly little evidence of the existence of a strong double dividend. The existence of a strong dividend assumes that the existing tax structure is not revenue optimal, and the environmental tax takes the tax structure in the direction of revenue optimality. Hence, strong dividend cannot be empirically shown if it is assumed that the tax structure is already optimum. However, there is substantial empirical evidence to show the existence of a weak double dividend. This section discusses the available empirical evidence from the literature on these aspects.

Literature on ETR, particularly in the European Union (EU), shows a positive impact on the environment and a neutral or positive impact on the economy. Ekins (2009) has estimated the potential impact of a green tax shift in the EU on GHG emissions, GDP, employment and environmental industries (EIs). Some of his findings are as follows:

a. ETR in EU: Potential Impact on Economy and Environment

So far, ETR in Europe has been small. Ekins (2009) studied the potential impact of a much more substantial tax shift in EU. Six scenarios were devised to investigate the implications of using ETR to achieve large-scale reductions in CO_2 emissions to meet EU targets for 2020 (20 percent GHG reductions from 1990s level by 2020, or 30 percent in a context of global cooperation). There were two baseline scenarios, one with a high energy price (BH) and one with a low energy price (BL); one scenario based on BL to achieve the 20 percent target with all revenues from the environmental taxes recycled back through reductions in income tax and employers' social security contributions (S1L); and three scenarios based on BH, one the same as S1L, except for the energy price (S1H), one with 10 percent of the environmental tax revenues recycled instead to stimulate green technologies (S2H) and one to achieve the 30 percent EU target (S3H). All the scenarios were modelled using two large macro-econometric models (E3ME, GINFORS) with detailed representation of EU countries and, in GINFORS, other world regions as well.

The results of the models for achieving the 20 percent target (S1L, S1H, S2H) are as follows:

1. ETR reduces CO_2 emission and resource consumption.
2. The effect on GDP is small. It is slightly positive in E3ME and slightly negative in GINFORS.
3. ETR increases employment in both models.
4. The carbon prices that are needed to reach the GHG targets are of the same order of magnitude in both models (€53–68 in S1H and S2H) and lower in S2H when some of the revenues from the taxes are invested in low-carbon technologies.
5. Results from S2H show that investment in green technologies could significantly reduce both the carbon price and GDP loss in reaching the 20 percent target.

Overall, the results suggest that an ETR will meet the 20 percent GHG emissions reduction target and will raise employment, lower resource consumption and have negligible effects on GDP. Achieving the 30 percent target (S3H) requires a much higher carbon price (€180–200/tCO_2). In GINFORS, it also requires a correspondingly higher negative impact on EU GDP (–1.9 percent). However, the global impacts, which are insignificant in the unilateral scenario (S1H), are substantial in the scenario of global climate cooperation (S3H). Global CO_2 emissions are effectively stabilized by 2020, and are 15.6 percent below the baseline, and global resource consumption has also dropped by more than 5 percent. Global GDP is about 1.4 percent below the baseline in S3H.

Overall, it has been shown that ETR can increase well-being through its environmental and economic effects. ETR in Europe could play an important and cost-effective role in meeting the EU's emission reduction targets for 2020.

b. ETR and EI: Potential Impact

An EI is one which reduces pollution, increases resource productivity or switches from non-renewable to renewable resources. EIs are essential for sustainable development. Not only are they an important source of employment and exports but they also control negative environmental factors which would otherwise place constraints on growth and welfare.

ETR promotes the formation of EIs by making pollution and resource use more expensive. In order to increase resource and environmental productivity, companies will invest more in green innovation and technology development.

EIs have significant revenue and employment potential. According to Ekins (2009), EI in the EU-25 countries generated a turnover of around €270 billion and also created 3.4 million full-time job equivalents in 2004.

Figure 2.5 shows different countries' market share of the global EI. Germany's share has been increasing over the years and it is now the highest, surpassing even the USA.

Figure 2.5

Environmental industry: World market share of OECD countries

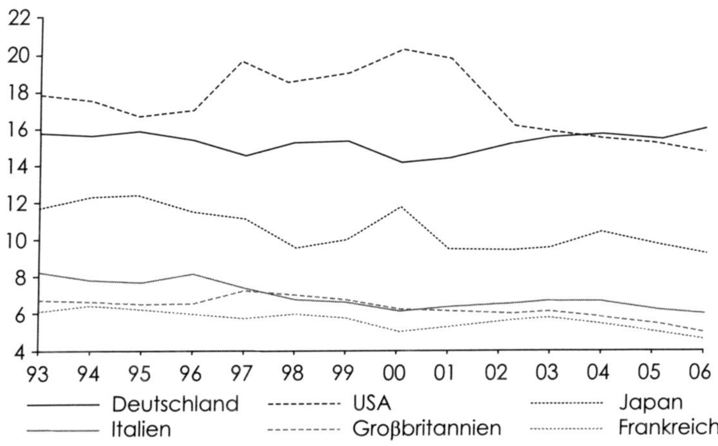

Source: Ekins (2009).

The EI has two distinct components: the supply of traditional pollution control technologies and services ('end-of-pipe treatment'); and those industries concerned with resource management (management of materials and energy). While pollution control technologies are important in reducing the environmental impact, it may increase costs and material use, and therefore reduce resource productivity. Thus, it may lead to a trade-off between environmental improvement and GDP growth. There is no such trade-off in the case of resource management. More efficient resource use increases resources productivity and reduces costs.

Table 2.4 gives a breakdown of the EI for EU-25, Germany and the UK, measured by turnover. Resource management is the largest and the fastest growing component of EI. It accounts for 62 percent of EI turnover. The

Table 2.4
Environmental industries for EU-25, Germany and the UK: Turnover 2004 (bn €)

	EU25	*Germany*	*UK*
A. Pollution Control	**82.0**	**26.5**	**4.7**
Waste water treatment	52.2	19.3	1.6
Air pollution control	15.9	4.5	1.7
Remediation/clean up of soil/groundwater	5.2	1.1	0.3
Noise and vibration control	2.0	0.4	0.1
Environmental monitoring/instrumentation	1		
Nature protection	5.7	1.2	1.0
B. Resource Management	**168.5**	**75.3**	**14.8**
Solid waste management and recycling	52.4	14.9	6.4
Recycled materials	24.3	6.8	3.5
Renewable energy production	6.1	2.2	0.4
Water supply	45.7	11.4	4.5
Eco-construction (estimated)	>40	40 (2005)	
C. Administration, Management, Research	**19.8**	**4.4**	**2.0**
General public administration	11.5	4.4	1.6
Private environmental management	5.8		0.4
Environmental research and development	2.5		
TOTAL	**>270.3**	**>106.2**	**>21.5**

Source: Ekins (2009).

demand for pollution control technologies has largely stagnated in advanced European economies like Germany.

Ekins (2009) studied four areas of German EIs—low energy houses, fuel consumption of cars, industrial recycling and green electricity. He finds that in all four cases, government intervention (through a mix of policy instruments) was essential in achieving environmental and economic benefits. The economic benefits included innovation, growth, exports and employment. German 'green power', in 2007, avoided 115 Mt CO_2 emissions, up from 85 Mt in 2005. The improvements in waste management have also reduced greenhouse gas emissions, with savings since 1990 of around 40 Mt CO_2e, mainly by closing own landfill sites. The German eco-tax of 1999 seems to have played an important role in the reduction of traffic-related CO_2 emissions and the reduction of the use of heat energy by households. The change in relative prices—whether through taxes, subsidies or market price movements—was found to have been the dominant influence across the case studies.

c. *Impact of ETR: Examples from International Experience*

The previous section gave the potential impacts of ETR in the EU. This section gives the impact on the environment and the economy of some of the important taxes introduced earlier in Europe and other developed countries.

(i) Energy taxes: Distributional effects: Energy taxes consist of taxes on transport fuels and taxes on other energy sources. Fuel taxes reduce fuel use by increasing the marginal cost of driving. It is difficult to exactly estimate the impact of fuel duty on fuel use because it depends on the own price elasticity of demand for petrol which in turn is affected by the availability and price of substitutes such as public transport and alternative fuels.

The price elasticity for the consumption of petrol is estimated to be about –0.65 to –0.1, whereas that for the consumption of diesel is lower at –0.6 (EEA, 2000). Studies also estimate the long-term price elasticity for the number of kilometres driven at about –0.1 to –0.4. The four panels in Figure 2.6 show the consumption of motor fuels along with their tax rates for the UK, Canada, Germany and Sweden. The long-term effect of a tax rate in decreasing the consumption of motor fuels (though not to a large extent as shown by the magnitude of price elasticity) is evident from Figure 2.6.

In order to reduce demand for transport fuels in the UK, the fuel duty was introduced. The fuel price escalator was introduced in 1993 which

Figure 2.6

Consumption of motor fuels along with their tax rates for the UK, Canada, Germany and Sweden

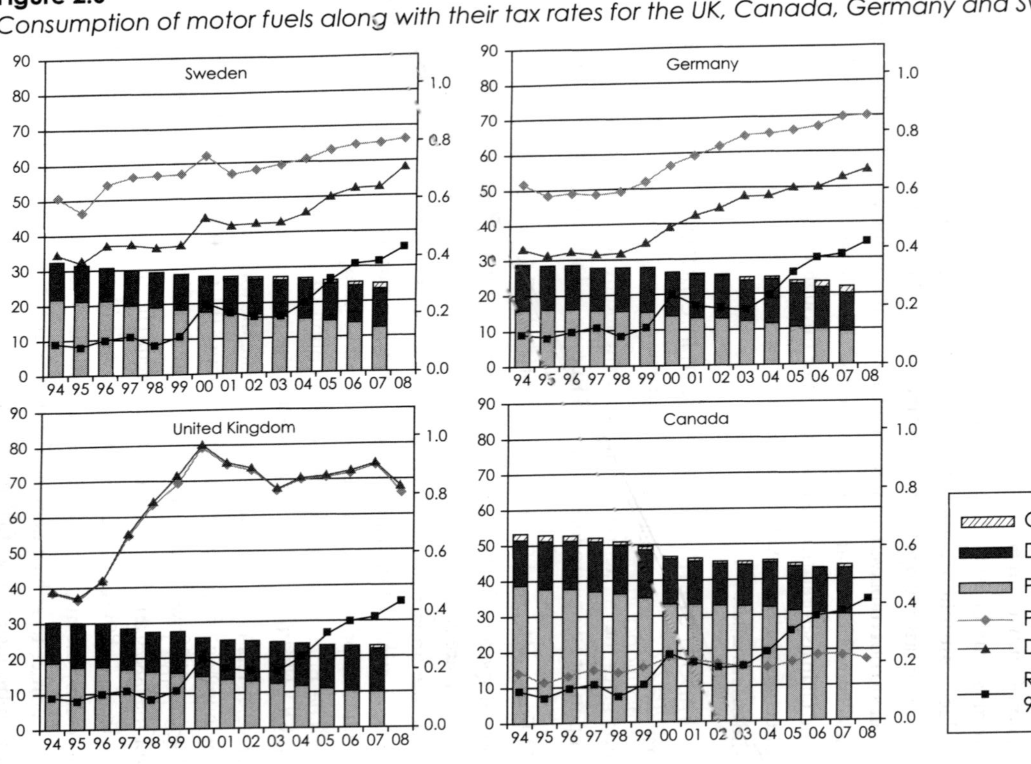

Source: http://www2.oecd.org/ecoinst/queries/TaxInfo.htm

meant that the fuel duty would be increased by at least 3 percent above the normal rate of inflation. The escalator was increased to 5 percent in 1995 and then to 6 percent in 1997 before being abandoned in 1999. Real fuel duty has decreased since then. Evidence shows that in the period 1993–98 when the fuel duty escalator was in place, average fuel efficiency of articulated lorries over 33 tons increased by 13 percent. Leicester (2006) estimates the price elasticity of fuel in the UK to be around –0.25. Owing to the fuel duty escalator, the fuel consumption from the transport also went down as can be seen in Figure 2.6.

The distributional impact of a fuel tax has often been considered a constraining factor if the tax is regressive. However, it may be progressive if the poor do not own cars or if the rich own inefficient cars that use a lot of fuel. Leicester (2006) looks at the distributional impact of a 5 percent rise in fuel price. He uses data from 2003–04 and compares it with data from 1999. He looks at its effect across all households and across car-owning households only. This is shown in Figure 2.7.

Figure 2.7
Distributional impact of a 5 percent fuel price rise

(a) All households

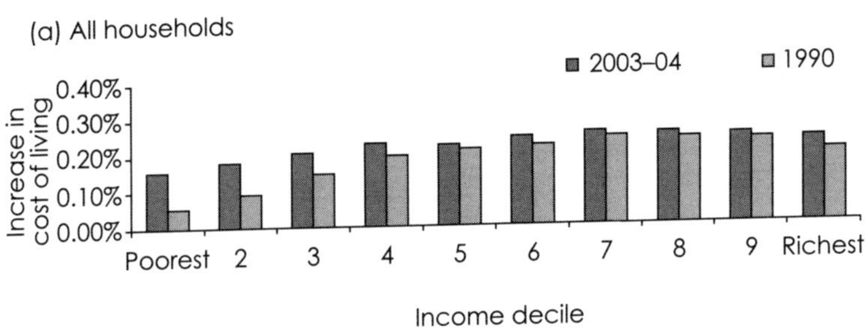

(b) Car-owning households only

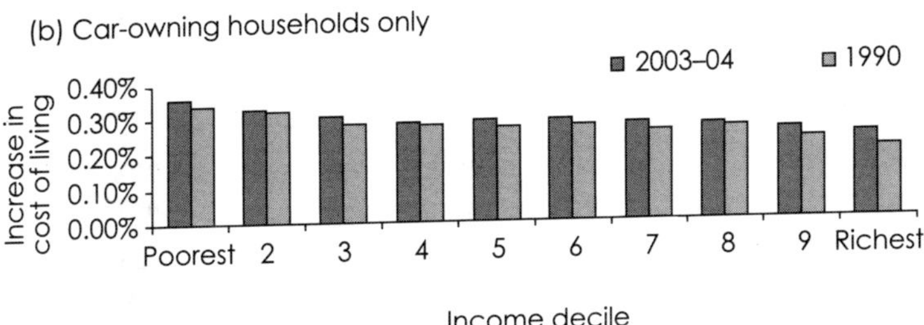

Source: Leicester (2006).

It shows the effect of the fuel price rise on all households. This is clearly not regressive with the 7th and the 8th deciles bearing most of the impact. However, in 2000, the impact has increased more strongly for the bottom deciles. This is due to an increase in car ownership. Looking at only car-owning households (Figure 2.7), the impact is certainly regressive.

Evidence from Canada tells a different story. Table 2.5 shows the impact of a $30 per ton carbon tax on different income groups.

It is observed that though the absolute cost is lesser for lower quintiles, the impact of the carbon tax as a percentage of income is higher for the lower income groups. To reduce the impact of the carbon tax on the poor, a Climate Action Tax Credit of $115.50 per adult and $34.50 per child was introduced. In all, it is estimated that individuals and businesses will receive tax reductions of $494 million which is $194 million more than the carbon tax revenue.

The CCL of the UK is a tax on the business use of energy. This tax is estimated to lead to a reduction in both business uses of energy and carbon emissions. Part of CCL revenues has been recycled back into the business sector by a reduction in employer's NICs by 3 percentage points. This along with the reduction in energy demand is estimated to lead to

Table 2.5
Impact of carbon tax on household income groups in Canada

	Income Groups					
	Average All Groups	*Lowest Quintile*	*Second Quintile*	*Third Quintile*	*Fourth Quintile*	*Top Quintile*
Average household income (2005) $	68102	16686	34599	55302	81349	152572
Average household size	2.51	1.45	2.11	2.56	2.99	3.41
Carbon tax ($30/ton) impact:						
Direct cost per family	266	96	184	259	341	450
Indirect cost	513	185	355	499	658	868
Total cost	779	281	539	758	1000	1318
Percent of average Income (percent)	1.14	1.68	1.56	1.37	1.23	0.86
Per person	310	194	255	296	334	386

Source: CUPE (2008).

a reduction in business costs. The CCL has also proved to be effective in reducing emissions while also supporting competitiveness of energy intensive businesses.

Energy taxes in Sweden, Denmark and Germany have led to a significant reduction in carbon emissions (Table 2.6). In Sweden, the most obvious effect of the carbon tax has been the expansion of biomass use in the system. The tax has led to the development of methods of biomass extraction and a biomass market and increase in biomass demand.

The sulphur tax of Sweden has led to a reduction in sulphur emission and has also encouraged the use of low sulphur content fuels and adoption of improved engine technology.

(ii) Taxes on waste and natural resources: Taxes on waste have been found to have a significant impact on the environment by reducing the generation of waste and the waste dumped into landfills. In this section, the impact of the waste taxes in the UK, Sweden and Denmark and the aggregates levy of the UK are discussed (Table 2.7). In Sweden, it was found that waste generation reduced in spite of an increase in production and consumption. In the UK, the dumping of both active and inactive waste has reduced.

The landfill tax of the UK also had a positive impact on waste management. A part of the revenue from the landfill tax is used for investment in sustainable waste management. As a result of this, in England, approved planning decisions (i.e. where planning permission has been granted) for landfill sites fell by 14 percent between 2002–03 and 2003–04, while approved decisions for waste treatment sites rose by 52 percent and composting facilities increased by 55 percent (Seely, 2009).

With regard to natural resources, there has been a reduction in the aggregates extracted in the UK. This can be attributed both to the aggregates levy and the landfill tax. While the former raised extraction costs, the latter increased waste disposal costs and therefore encouraged the reuse of hard core and other inert wastes instead of virgin aggregates in road building, etc.

Another positive indicator in the UK is that the sales of aggregates fell by 8 percent between 2001 and 2003 in spite of increasing construction activity. However, this could have been due to factors other than the aggregates levy and the landfill tax. During the same period estimated production of recycled aggregates in England increased by 3.1 million tons.

Table 2.6

Impact of fuel duty, industrial energy tax and sulphur tax in the UK, Sweden, Denmark and Germany

Country	*Tax*	*Impact*
UK	Fuel duty	Studies suggest that a 10 percent rise in the price of fuel reduces fuel consumption by around 2.5 percent and traffic volume by 1 percent after a year, all other things remaining constant (Leicester, 2006). Increases in fuel duty are estimated to have produced annual carbon savings of between 1 and 2.5 MtC by 2010. Average fuel efficiency of lorries over 33 tons increased 13 percent between 1993 and 1998 (GFC, 2009).
	Climate change levy (CCL)	CCL reduces overall energy demand in the economy by 0.2 percent in 2000, 1 percent in 2001, 1.8 percent in 2002 and 2.9 percent by 2010 compared with a situation where the CCL package had not been announced or implemented. Carbon emissions are reduced by an estimated 0.2 percent in 2000, 1 percent in 2001, 2 percent in 2002 and 2.3 percent in 2010. CCL is estimated to lead to a 0.13 percent reduction in overall unit cost for businesses by 2010. Due to its exemption from CCL, good quality CHP (combined heat and power stations) will increase by 1.2 gigawatts of electricity (GWe) by 2010. (HMRC website, http://www.hmrc.gov.uk/)
	Industrial energy tax	UK CO_2 emissions reduced by 2 percent in 2002 and 2.25 percent in 2003 and cumulative savings of 16.5 million tons of carbon up to 2005. Reduction in UK energy demand of 2.9 percent estimated by 2010 (GFC, 2009).
Sweden	Energy and carbon taxes	Emissions reductions of 0.5 million tons per annum. Emissions would have been 20 percent higher than 1990 levels without tax. The Use of Biomass has been increased in industry since 1990 from 45 TWh/yr to 54 TWh/yr (Branlund and Kristrm, 1999).

	Sulphur tax	The annual sulphur emissions from 1989 to 1995 have been reduced by 19000 tons due to the tax. This represents 30 percent of the total emissions reduction in that period for which the tax is responsible. Sulphur content of fuels fell 80 percent between 1980 and 1998 (Branlund and Kristrm, 1999).
Denmark	Energy and carbon tax	CO_2 emissions in affected sectors down by 6 percent and economic growth up by 20 percent between 1988 and 1997 and a 5 percent reduction in emission in one year in response to tax increase. In the 1990s, a 23 percent reduction in CO_2 from usual trend and energy efficiency increased by 26 percent. Subsidy to renewables may have accounted for greater proportion of emissions reductions than tax (GFC, 2009).
Germany	Environmental tax reform, taxes on transport , fuels and electricity	CO_2 reduced by 15 percent between 1990 and 1999 and 1 percent between 1999 and 2005. CO_2 emissions 2–3 percent lower by 2005 than they would have been without tax. German re-unification an important factor in reductions (GFC, 2009).

Source: Author's compilation.

Table 2.7
Impact of taxes on waste and natural resources in the UK, Sweden and Denmark

Country	*Tax*	*Impact*
UK	Landfill tax	Waste disposed into landfill sites has reduced from 86.9 million tons in 1998–99 to 52.5 million tons in 2008–09, a reduction of around 39 percent.
		The amount of active waste disposed reduced by 32 percent while inactive waste reduced by 74 percent (HMRC website http://www.hmrc.gov.uk/).
		Land filled waste has decreased in spite of increasing total waste over the years (Leicester, 2006).
	Aggregates levy	The total amount of aggregates extracted fell from 266.5 million tons in 2003–04 to 224.4 million tons in 2008–09, a fall of around 15 percent (HMRC website http://www.hmrc.gov.uk/).
Sweden	Waste taxes	In spite of a 7 percent increase in production and consumption, waste generation has declined by 0.5 percent.
		Total waste to landfill has fallen (GFC, 2009).
Denmark	Household waste tax	26 percent reduction in waste delivered to municipal sites between 1990 and 1996 (GFC, 2009).

Source: Author's compilation.

(iii) Impact of transport taxes: Transport taxes that include taxes on vehicles are found to have a positive impact on the environment by reducing pollution, emissions and fuel use. Vehicle taxes, such as the VED in the UK and Sweden, have led to a shift in consumer preferences to fuel efficient cars. Changing consumer preferences have further encouraged the vehicle manufacturers to produce cars with lower emissions rating. However, in studying the impacts of vehicle taxes on the environment, it is hard to disentangle the contribution made by the VED and changes made to the manufacturing process or changing preferences (Leicester, 2006).

The VED is expected not to affect the poor adversely as it is less likely that the poor own cars. However, there is no evidence to prove or contradict this.

APD tries to reduce GHG emissions by increasing the marginal cost of air travel. The effectiveness of an Air duty depends on the price elasticity of air travel which has been estimated by studies to be quite low. It has been estimated that a 10 percent increase in price would reduce demand for long haul business flights by 2.5 percent and short haul business flights by 7 percent (Leicester, 2006).

Leicester suggests various measures to improve the impact of the APD on emissions. These include taxing the flight instead of individual passengers, taxing according to the distance and taxing according to the type of aircraft and its fuel efficiency. There is not much information on the distributional impact of an air duty. This would depend on the number of flights taken across income classes.

Another interesting example of a transport tax is the London congestion charge which is a local tax. This tax has led to a reduction in carbon emissions within the charging zone by allowing traffic to flow more freely and reducing time spent idling in traffic queues. It is also likely to increase demand for public transport by around 1–2 percent (Blow et al., 2003). Revenue from this tax has been used to improve London's transport system (Table 2.8).

2.2.4 Summary

The following are the basic messages that emerge out of the experience of developed countries:

1. The centrepiece of environmental taxes is taxes on energy which may take the form of fuel taxes or carbon taxes.
2. In addition to fuel taxes, a number of other taxes have also been levied primarily aimed at reducing use of inefficient vehicles. Further, there are a number of taxes on waste and natural resources.
3. Revenue raised from environmental taxes has ranged from 4 to 14 percent of total tax revenues in different countries.
4. The revenues from environmental taxes have generally been used to reduce other distortionary taxes. Partially, these are also used to encourage environment friendly technologies.
5. The overall impact of environmental taxes has been shown to have negligible adverse impact on growth and positive effect on employment due to promotion of EIs.
6. There may be some adverse distribution impact of environmental taxes which needs to be neutralized through carefully designed subsidies.
7. Most studies found that the eco-taxes have significant environmental impact.

Table 2.8

Impact of transport taxes imposed in the UK and Sweden

Country	*Tax*	*Impact*
UK	Vehicle excise duty (VED)	The average emissions rating of new cars purchased has reduced from 190 g/km in 1997 to 165 g/km in 2007, a drop of 13 percent (Butcher, 2009). This is still far above the EU target of 140 g/km by 2008–09. Since 1997, there has been a changing of consumer preferences away from cars that come under higher bands. However, these trends existed even before the reforms in 2001 (Leicester, 2006).
	Air passenger duty (APD)	Studies estimate that demand for long-haul leisure flights are reduced by 10 percent and short-haul leisure flights by 15 percent (Leicester, 2006).
	London congestion charge	The monitoring report of Traffic for London (2006) suggests that congestion has fallen by around 25–30 percent relative to pre-charging baselines. Carbon emissions have been reduced by around 16 percent within the charging zone (Blow et al., 2003).
	Taxation of company cars	The number of company cars has reduced from 1.6 million in 2001 to 2.1 million in 2005. CO_2 emissions from cars have reduced by around 0.2–0.3 MtC for 2005 and are estimated to reduce by 0.35–0.65 MtC by 2010. Also, average CO_2 emissions were around 15 g/km lower in 2004 than would have been without the reforms. Percentage of company cars running on diesel increased from 33 percent in 2002 to 50–60 percent in 2004. The number of company car drivers receiving free fuel has reduced by around 600000 since 1997. The proportion of company car drivers receiving free employer provided fuel for private use has also decreased significantly from around 57 percent in 1997 to around 30 percent in 2006 (HMRC website, http://www.hmrc.gov.uk/).
Sweden	Vehicle excise duty (VED)	The use of eco-friendly car increased from 52 percent in 2003 to 66 percent in 2006. From 2005 to 2007, the total share of more efficient cars increased from 2.9 to 14.3 percent with the amount of new cars with emissions less than 120 gCO_2/km increasing by a factor 3 from 2006. As a result, average CO_2 emissions for new cars decreased from 198 gCO_2/km in 2003 to 191 gCO_2/km in 2006 (Borup, 2007).

Source: Author's compilation.

2.3 ETR: EVIDENCE FROM SELECTED DEVELOPING COUNTRIES

This section discusses the experience of developing countries in environmental fiscal reform. Most developing countries have largely used regulations and CAC instruments for environmental management. More recently, apart from fuel taxes, environmental taxes are being used in developing countries. Compared to quantity-based instruments, price-based market instruments are quite feasible in developing countries as the institutional framework is not a barrier.

The concept of an ETR is similar in developed and developing countries in that it is used as a tool to achieve environmental goals while simultaneously generating revenues. However, one key difference in the design and rationale of implementation of ETR is that in the developed countries, ETR generally aims at reducing other distortionary taxes. In developing countries that have low tax–GDP ratios, environmental taxes are used for raising additional revenues and for achieving other developmental and environmental goals (Speck, 2008). Implementation of ETR in developing countries should not only satisfy the environmental objectives but also ensure that ETR does not conflict with growth and poverty reduction objectives.

According to an OECD (2005) study, ETR could have fiscal as well as environmental benefits in developing countries. In addition, it may also facilitate poverty reduction by lowering health cost and pollution hazards for the poor. Some of these are discussed below.

1. Fiscal benefits
   - ETR can be used as one of the ways to mobilize revenues to finance basic public services when raising revenue through other sources proves to be difficult or burdensome.
   - Environmental taxes such as those on natural resources extraction, transport fuel and other energy consumption also have a high potential to generate revenues.
   - ETR revenue can be used to reduce other distorting taxes so that gains in economic efficiency and employment could be realized along with gains in environmental quality. This leads to 'fiscal dividend'.

2. Environmental benefits
   - ETR helps to internalize the externalities associated with pollution by sending appropriate price signals. By revealing the true cost of pollution or scarce resources, environmental taxes create direct incentives for polluting less and using fewer resources.
   - Environmental management requires a lot of investment in order to finance research and development of new technologies, and implementing, monitoring and enforcing them. ETR can provide additional funds to cover these expenses.
   - ETR also requires that the polluter pays for the clean-up costs which would otherwise have to be paid by the government. In this way, ETR frees up funds.
3. Poverty reduction benefits
   - The impact of environmental degradation is largely felt by the poor. ETR addresses the environmental concerns of the poor and directly helps in poverty reduction by providing improved access to water, sanitation and other resources and also by reducing the adverse health impacts. Additional employment opportunities can also be created in new environmental goods and services sector.
   - The revenue from eco-taxes can also be used to invest in many poverty alleviation and other pro-poor investments.

Given the heavy reliance on regulatory instruments, developing countries may need to design the environmental taxes as complementary instruments. Also, given high levels of poverty, the distributional implications of the environmental taxes need to be in specific context. Any trade-off between growth and improved environment needs to be carefully examined. Similarly, any major regressive effect of removal of certain subsidies from an environmental viewpoint and introduction of eco-taxes needs to be estimated.

Taxation of natural resource extraction may suit resource abundant developing countries from the viewpoint of sustainability. Developing countries are often resource rich and also resource dependent, which leads to over extraction and depletion of natural resources. Taxes on extraction of resources can address the issue of over-exploitation of natural resources. At the same time, such taxes yield large amounts of revenue. Against this background, this section discusses the experience of three developing countries—China, South Africa and Mexico, in the way they have evolved from a purely CAC regime to adoption of selected eco-taxes.

2.3.1 South Africa

South African environmental legislation like many other developing countries is largely based on the traditional 'CAC' model where regulations are set and non-adherence to these regulations are punished by way of fines. Though the environmental legislations have been introduced as early as the 1930s, environment protection has gained attention only in the last decade with the introduction of National Environmental Management Act (NEMA) in several spheres including bio-diversity, air quality, coastal management, protected areas and waste. Some of the important Acts enacted from time to time are given below.[6]

1. Atmospheric Pollution Prevention Act, 1965
2. Environmental Conservation Act, 1989
3. National Forests Act, 1998
4. National Water Act, 1998
5. National Environmental Management: Protected Areas Act, 2003
6. National Environmental Management: Biodiversity Act, 2004
7. National Environmental Management: Air Quality Act, 2004
8. National Environmental Management: Integrated Coastal Management Act, 2008
9. National Environmental Management: Waste Act, 2008

The importance of regulations in environmental management is particularly evident from the recent National Environmental Management Amendment Bill whereby the fines and penalties associated with contraventions of environmental laws have been greatly increased.

An alternative way of environmental management is to incentivize environmental compliance through fiscal instruments. Some environmental taxes do exist in South Africa though many of them are still in their infancy. In South Africa, revenues from environmentally related taxes are comparable to other countries accounting for about 2 percent of GDP and 10 percent of total tax revenues. Consistent with the international pattern, taxes on transport fuels, especially the general fuel levy on petrol, diesel and bio-diesel constitute a majority of the revenue accounting for about 65–74 percent of the revenue from environmental taxes. Table 2.9 provides details about the eco-taxes in South Africa.

Table 2.9
South Africa: Eco-taxes

Sector	*Tax*	*Objective/Description*	
Transport fuels	General fuel levy	To finance general government expenditure programmes	Levied on petrol, diesel and bio-diesel but are zero rated for VAT purposes. Diesel taxed at lower rate than petrol.
	Road accident fuel levy	To compensate victims of motor vehicle accidents	
	Equalization fund levy	Used to smooth retail fuel prices in times of significant price shocks	
	Customs and excise levy	Source of funding for the member countries of South African Customs Union (SACU)	
Vehicle taxation	Ad-valorem customs and excise duty	VAT on all motor vehicle sales. Ad-Valorem duty based on price of vehicle is imposed on passenger and light commercial vehicle (LCV) purchases.	
	Road licensing fees	Imposed by the Provincial Government (including motor vehicle licenses, operator licenses and motor vehicle registration). For provincial road management and traffic control.	
Aviation taxes	Aviation fuel levy	Payable by wholesale distributors on the sale of aviation fuel.	
	Airport charges	Payable by the operators of aircraft in South Africa and consists of a landing charge, parking charge, and passenger service charge. To fund the operation of the South Africa Civil Aviation Authority (SACAA).	
	Air passenger departure tax	Departure tax on international air travel from South Africa, revenues of which goes to the national revenue account. Additional revenues for tourism promotion.	
Product taxes	Plastic shopping bag levy	National levy of 3 cents per plastic bag to discourage use of plastic bags.	
Electricity	NER electricity levy	A national levy per kWh is implemented on all electricity generated to fund the National Electricity Regulator.	
	Local government electricity surplus	Some municipalities are generating surplus from electricity sales. Hidden surplus could be viewed as implicit tax.	

Table 2.9 continued

Table 2.9 continued

Sector	*Tax*	*Objective/Description*
Water supply	Water resource management charge	To cover the costs associated with planning and implementing catchment management strategies, management of water quality and use, water resource protection, and water demand management. Eventually, this charge will be used to fund the operations of the Catchment Management Agencies (CMAs).
	Water resource development and use of water works charge	Seeks to cover the construction, operation and maintenance costs of different water schemes.
	Water research fund levy	To fund the operations of the Water Research Commission.
Wastewater	Waste water discharge charge system (proposed)	To recover the costs associated with different water treatment and water quality management programmes, and to provide incentives for water users returning water back to the water resource to reduce their pollution loads.

Source: Compiled based on information from Policy paper, National Treasury of South Africa (2006).

As indicated in Table 2.9, environment-related taxes have often been levied for revenue objectives or other sector-specific objectives. The general fuel levy is the largest source of revenue and is used to finance general government expenditures, whereas other levies or charges are used to fund the operations of the respective authorities.

These taxes can be further reformed to strengthen their environmental impact. For example, the *general fuel levy* generates significant revenues. It also provides incentives to reduce consumer demand for transport fuels, increase demand for public transport and more fuel efficient technologies. The environmental impact could be more pronounced if differential tax rates are introduced whereby the use of dirtier fuels is discouraged by taxing them at a higher rate.

Another reform in the transport sector could be changing the *ad-valorem customs and excise duty on motor vehicles.* Currently, VAT is based on the price of the vehicle and hence more expensive the vehicle, more is the tax. This could be due to revenue objectives. It could however be better aligned with environmental objectives as well if the tax is based on the environmental costs imposed by different vehicles (e.g. the emissions rating of vehicles). In doing so, care should be taken that all vehicles come into the tax net and revenues are not compromised.

The South African environmental taxes are in its infancy. Hence, there is scope to introduce new taxes besides reforming the existing taxes to address the environmental concerns in South Africa.

2.3.2 China

Chinese environmental policy consists mainly of regulatory instruments and legislations although China is now considering implementation of a carbon tax. Environmental legislation in China started with the adoption of the Environmental Protection Law in 1989. This law lays down provisions for pollution control and environmental impact assessments. It also makes the state responsible for environmental management. Other important laws passed since then are the Water Pollution Prevention and Control Law (1984), the Air Pollution Prevention and Control Law (2000) and the Environment Impact Assessment Law (2002).

This section looks at the various environmental policy instruments in use in China. Fiscal instruments such as environmental public expenditure and environmental pricing have started gaining prominence of late. There are also several taxes which could have potential positive impacts on the environment. These, along with regulatory instruments, are explained below:

a. Pollution Levy System

The Pollution Levy System (PLS) in China, introduced in 1982, is one of the most comprehensive environment regulatory systems in the world. Under this system, a standard for pollution discharge is set and all discharges exceeding this standard are charged a fee. Discharges into air and water, solid waste and noise pollution are included in this system. Presently, around 200 polluting substances and about 25 percent of Chinese industries are covered under the PLS. In 2006, the PLS yielded a revenue of around 14.4 billion RMB. This revenue is mostly used for pollution abatement and environmental clean-up activities.

b. Fiscal Instruments

The environmental fiscal instruments used in China are environmental fiscal expenditures, environmental taxation, and fees and environmental pricing. These are explained below:

Environmental fiscal expenditures: A major step in environmental policy of the Chinese government has been the setting up of the Environmental Fiscal Expenditure Account in 2007 in order to budget for spending in environmental protection activities. In order to cover environmental damage expenses, the Forest Ecological Benefit Compensation Fund was set up in 2004.

Environmental taxation and fees: In addition to these fiscal instruments, there are several taxes which have indirect environmental implications. A list of these taxes are given in Table 2.10. This also includes environmental fees in China, that is, the water fees.

The VAT, consumption tax and the VVUT are taxes on transport, fuels and other energy sources. Vehicles are charged a consumption tax at the time of purchase according to engine type and cylinder capacity. Vehicle owners also have to pay the VVUT every quarter. The consumption tax provides a differential tax on gasoline and diesel, while other energy sources are taxed under VAT.

Of all the taxes, the RT has the most direct environmental benefit. Although introduced to adjust the incomes of companies and promote market competition, this tax can potentially reduce exploitation of resources such as crude oil, natural gas, coal, etc. The water fee is used to regulate the use of urban water resources.

The other taxes on the list are charged on ownership of land, incomes of businesses and on investment in fixed assets. The government of China is planning to introduce more eco-taxes in future including a carbon tax. The China Council of International Cooperation on Environment and Development (CCICED) and the Environmental Economics Working Group have suggested introducing various taxes such as a SO_2 tax on coal, a tax on gasoline and diesel, water pollution taxes, taxes on agricultural inputs, etc.

Environmental pricing: Environmental pricing has been implemented in the electricity sector. The preferential grid price of desulphurized electricity has been made higher than non-desulphurized electricity. This has

Table 2.10
Environment-related taxes in China

Tax	*Description*
VAT	Coal gas, liquefied petroleum gas, natural gas, methane gas, and coal/charcoal products for household use charged at 13 percent; crude oil charged at 17 percent.
Vehicle and vessel usage tax (VVUT)	Quarterly tax payable by vehicle owners.
Urban and township land use tax (UTLUT)	Tax payable by businesses and individuals for land owned in urban areas.
Consumption tax (CT)	Tax on consumption of goods including gasoline (leaded charged at 0.28 Yuan per litre and unleaded at 0.2 Yuan per litre), diesel (0.1 Yuan per litre), motor vehicle tyres (10 percent), motor cycles (10 percent) and motor cars (charges according to type and cylinder capacity of car).
Resources tax (RT)	Tax on exploitation of mineral resources such as crude oil, natural gas, coal, other non-metal ores, ferrous metal ores and non-ferrous metal ores.
City maintenance and construction tax (CMCT)	Tax on businesses and individuals who pay VAT, consumption tax and/or business tax. Tax rate based on the amount paid under above mentioned taxes.
Farmland occupation tax (FOT)	Tax on businesses and individuals who use farm land for non-farm purposes.
Fixed assets investment orientation regulation tax (FAIORT)	Tax on businesses and individuals who invest in fixed assets within the territory of the People's Republic of China.
Water fees	Fee on the use of urban water .

Source: Eschborn/Bonn (2004), Beijing Local Taxation Bureau.

also been used to fund the installation of desulphurization technology. This promotion of desulphurization has led to a reduction in SO_2 emissions by 1.8 million tons per year (GTZ, 2007).

2.3.3 Mexico

Mexico has several legislations in place for environmental management. Environmental management has been done for air, water and waste through various measures, predominantly regulations. For air, quality targets have been established for major metropolitan areas using the Air Quality Metropolitan Index. The 2001–06 National Programme on Environment and Natural Resources stresses the need for local governments to monitor air quality and air pollutant emissions periodically. The official Mexican standard NOM-001-ECOL-1996 sets limits on concentrations of contaminants in waste water effluent discharged into various types of water bodies. Mexico has formulated a practical water quality index to describe the quality of its surface waters. The General Law on Ecological Balance and Environmental Protection (LGEEPA, 1988; updated 1996) is the current legal basis for waste management. It includes the Hazardous Waste Regulation and provides the basis for issuing Official Mexican Standards, for example, on hazardous waste classification and operation of landfills.

Apart from the regulations, Mexico has only a few environmental taxes as given in Table 2.11. Unlike the other developing countries considered here, Mexico's taxes are environmentally motivated and intend to reduce incidence of environmentally harmful behaviour. For example, charges such as water abstraction charge and water effluent charge are purely levied to achieve environmental goals by providing incentive to use water efficiently and to reduce discharge of polluting effluents.

Table 2.11
Eco-taxes in Mexico

Tax	*Description*	*Revenue Utilization*
Surcharge on petrol sold in Mexico city (1995–97)	Levied on leaded and unleaded petrol only in the metropolitan region of Mexico city.	The revenue was earmarked for financing the introduction of new technology in gas stations that would allow the recovery of organic fumes.
Water abstraction charge	To encourage efficient use of water. Different rates for specific types of uses of water. Rates also determined by the relative scarcity or abundance of an area's water resources.	The revenues are earmarked to the building and maintenance of hydraulical infrastructure.

Table 2.11 continued

Table 2.11 continued

Tax	*Description*	*Revenue Utilization*
Entrance fees to natural protected areas	Differentiated fees according to ecosystem charge capacity. Higher fee to enter areas with low carrying capacity.	For conservation of the natural protected areas.
Excise on new automobiles	Levied on cars and trucks applied on the sales price.	–
Special excise on products and services	Levied on diesel, petrol and natural gas used for transport purposes.	–
Tax on vehicle ownership	Levied during registration or use of motor vehicles. Different rates for different vehicles.	–
Water effluent charges	Levied on quantity of wastewater in excess of permissible contents of chemical oxygen demand (COD) and TSS, depending on carrying capacity of recipient body.	–

Source: Compiled based on information from OECD website.

In terms of contribution of eco-taxes to the overall tax revenues, the trend shows a fall in recent years. As percentage of GDP, eco-taxes accounted for close to 2.5 percent share in the late 1990s, which has since fallen to about 0.5 percent. A similar pattern is observed for their contribution relative to overall tax revenues.

Figures 2.8 and 2.9 show that tax revenues follow a fluctuating pattern and have been steeply declining since 2002. To trace the source of decline, Figure 2.10 plots the time trend of revenues from the different eco-taxes in Mexico (in US dollars). It can be seen that the revenue from transport fuel taxes (special excise on products and services) contributes to the majority of revenues from eco-taxes.

A similar pattern was observed with respect to the developed countries where a fall in energy tax revenues led to a fall in overall revenues. As discussed earlier, this pattern could be either due to a decrease in tax rates

Figure 2.8
Eco-tax revenue as percent of GDP

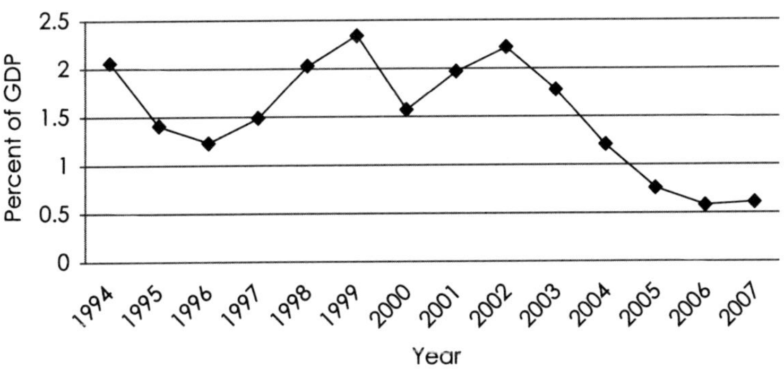

Source (Basic Data): http://www2.oecd.org/ecoinst/queries/TaxInfo.htm

Figure 2.9
Eco-tax revenue as total tax Revenues

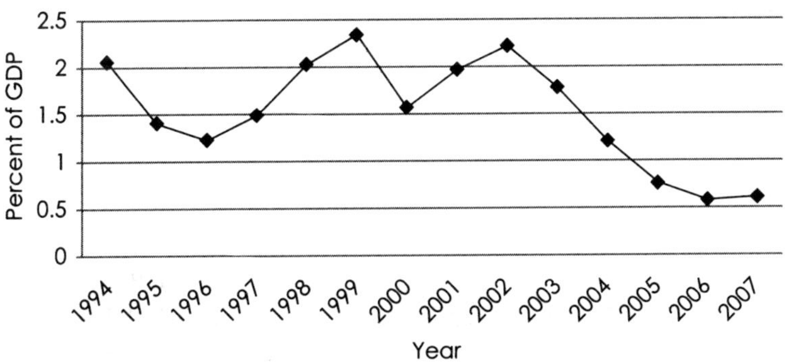

Source (Basic Data): http://www2.oecd.org/ecoinst/queries/TaxInfo.htm

on these goods over the years or a decline in consumption in response to an increase in tax rates over time. In the developed countries, it was observed that the tax rates have increased and revenues had fallen owing to the decrease in consumption. However, in Mexico, a contrasting pattern seems to appear, which can be seen from Figure 2.11.

Figure 2.11 shows that the tax rate on petrol and diesel have fallen quite steeply since 2002 and in response consumption of both petrol and

Figure 2.10
Revenues from different eco-taxes in Mexico

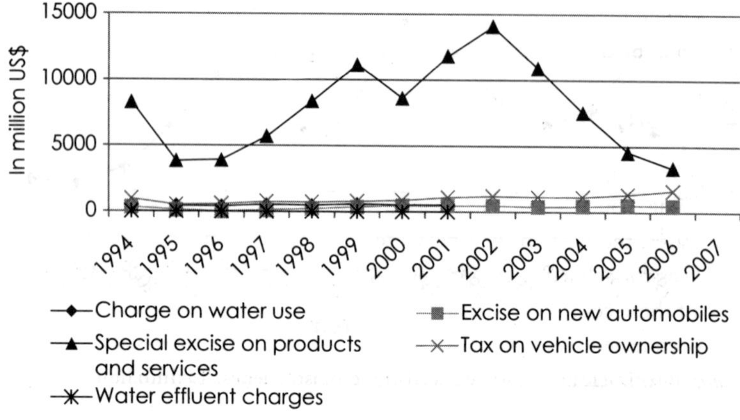

Source (Basic Data): http://www2.oecd.org/ecoinst/queries/TaxInfo.htm

Figure 2.11
Tax rates on petrol, diesel and other products in Mexico

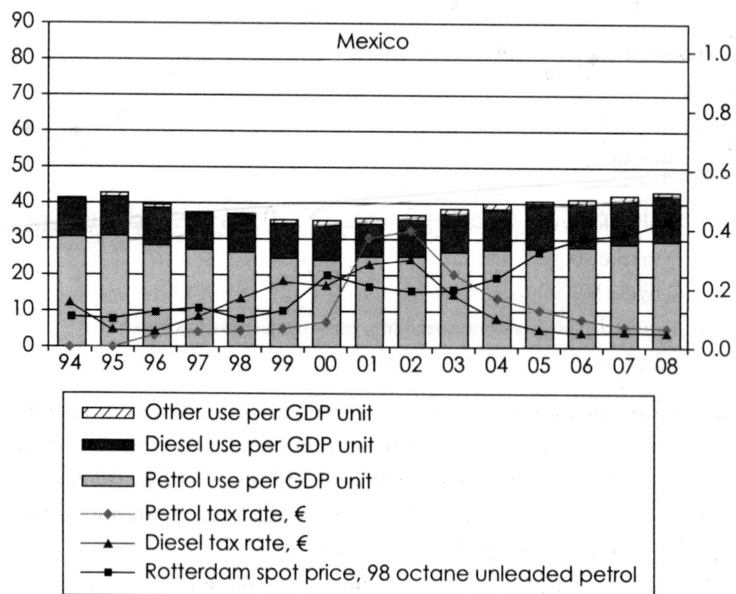

Source: http://www2.oecd.org/ecoinst/queries/

diesel has increased. Hence, the fall in revenues is clearly due to the fall in fuel prices which indicates that fuel taxes in Mexico have not succeeded in achieving the desired environmental goal of reduced fuel consumption. This could be due partially to political reasons.

2.3.4 Summary

In this section, we have looked at the experience with eco-taxes in select developing countries, namely, South Africa, China and Mexico. In all these cases, there has been a heavy reliance on regulations and CAC type of polices for achieving environmental objectives. However, progressively more of these countries are using environmental taxes. Many of these taxes have been levied for revenue purposes and can be reformed to strengthen their environmental impact. Taxes on fuels are the most common taxes but in addition taxes on ownership and taxes on water effluents and resource taxes are also being used.

2.4 LESSONS FOR INDIA

International experience has shown that eco-taxes have been successfully implemented in other countries. The purpose of this section is to derive lessons for India from international experience. The following issues are worth examining in this context:

Issue 1: Should India complement the present CAC approach with market-based instruments for achieving environmental objectives? What are the relative merits of price-based instruments over quantity-based instruments?

Issue 2: In India, should tax be charged on pollution directly or on polluting inputs and outputs?

Issue 3: Should ETR be designed as revenue neutral or a revenue-augmenting tool? In the latter case, it is implied that the size of the public sector will increase.

Issue 4: In the environmental tax regime, what would be the relative roles of central, state and local governments?

Issue 5: How should environmental taxes and the GST together be part of an overall regime of taxation of goods and services in India?

Issue 6: What would be a suitable strategy to utilize additional tax revenues from environmental taxes?

2.4.1 Complementing CAC with Eco-taxes

International experience in developing instruments for environmental management indicates that countries start with CAC instruments, and then move to user charges and finally complement these with environmental taxes. India already has an extensive regulatory regime in place. Many states have user charges, fines and penalties. This might be the appropriate time to use environmental taxes extensively.

In moving to a GST, there are certain initial revenue risks that depend on what the core GST rate will be. Even if the rate is revenue neutral for the Centre and the states as a group, it will entail revenue losses for a select set of states. These states are likely to be the so-called 'producing' states which presently earn relatively larger revenues from the central sales tax. These states are generally mineral-rich and/or manufacturing states that suffer considerable pollution damage. The revenue potential of environmental taxes can be used to partly or fully offset the revenue loss on account of the elimination of CST. This will require permitting a levy of non-rebatable excise duties and/or cesses on polluting inputs and outputs to complement the GST.

2.4.2 Direct versus Indirect Taxation of Pollution

Internationally, there are very few examples of attempts to directly tax pollution. Instead, taxes are usually charged on polluting inputs and outputs. The main examples are the five Scandinavian countries and the UK. The direct taxation of pollution is analytically more efficient but extremely difficult to administer because of measurement and implementation difficulties.

Some recent works argue that implementing a tax on inputs (upstream taxation) such as fuels and other sources of carbon emissions can be considered equivalent to taxing the pollution itself (in this case, carbon emission) with certain qualifications. For example, considering the US case in the context of climate externalities, Metcalf and Weibasch (2009) argue that

> there are two principles, one physical and one economic, which allow us to substantially reduce the collection and enforcement costs for a tax on emissions from fossil fuels. The first is that a unit of fossil fuel will emit the same amount of carbon regardless of when or where it is burned. For

> carbon emissions from fossil fuel combustion, there is a perfect correspondence between input and output. Therefore, we can tax the input—the fossil fuel—rather than the output—the emission.

They recognize that exceptions to this rule will have to be provided as is the case when the fossil fuel is permanently sequestered such as fuel used for tar or carbon that is captured and stored. They argue that as far as the economic principle relating to the incidence of a tax and its efficiency effects are concerned, these are unrelated to the statutory obligation to remit the tax. Thus, the point of the levy of the tax can be determined so as to minimize collection and monitoring costs and to ensure maximum coverage. They observe that,

> in general, imposing the tax upstream (i.e. at the earliest point in the produc tion process) will achieve these goals as (a) there are far fewer upstream producers than there are downstream consumers; and (b) because of economies of scale in tax administration, the cost will be lower per unit of tax. (Metcalf and Weibasch, 2009)

These observations are well worth considering in the Indian case also. Implementation of this strategy requires identifying those taxes and industries which maximize positive environmental impact and compliance while minimizing administrative costs. Some of these aspects are discussed below.

a. Fuel and Energy Taxes

Fuel and energy taxes in other countries have been the centrepiece of environmental taxes. They have been successful in the long run in reducing the consumption of fuel and encouraging consumers to switch to cleaner fuels. These also contribute significant revenues which have been used to reduce other distortionary taxes.

The main criticism against fuel taxes is on distributional grounds. The popular perception is that fuel taxes are regressive. However, academic evidence does not favour this view. It was in the early 1990s that the question of regressivity in fuel taxation was raised for the first time. It was argued that fuel taxation imposes a larger burden on poor people.

Experiences of the UK and Canada give mixed results in this regard. While Leicester (2006) shows that fuel tax in the UK is not regressive, other studies have shown British Columbia's carbon tax on fuel to be regressive in nature. In order to counteract this effect, a tax credit was given to the poor.

Datta (2008) studies the distributional impact of fuels in the Indian context. His results indicate progressivity of transport fuel tax in both rural and urban sectors and a neutral effect of coal tax.

For an environmental tax to be effective, the fuel should have both an elastic demand and a high emission potential. Transport fuels are a good case for fuel tax as they are progressive and satisfy the above two conditions. Their emission potential is around 2.3 kilograms of carbon dioxide per litre of fuel. Different studies report different values for transport fuel elasticity which are price sensitive in the long run (Datta, 2008).

There is also a strong case for the taxation of coal. Figure 2.12 shows India's GHG emissions from fuel combustion for the period 1971–2000. It can be seen that coal is the major contributor to GHG emissions. Emissions from coal have been dramatically increasing over the years. Also, as already mentioned, Datta's study shows that the distributional impact of coal is almost neutral.

The next step is to look at the level of tax already levied on fuel and coal in India. Figures 2.13 and 2.14 show the gasoline and diesel prices in different countries including India for the year 2008.

As can be seen from Figure 2.13, petrol price in India is high but not as high as many of the European countries. However, the USA, Canada and China have lower gasoline prices than in India. Diesel price in India

Figure 2.12

CO_2 emissions from fuel combustion in India

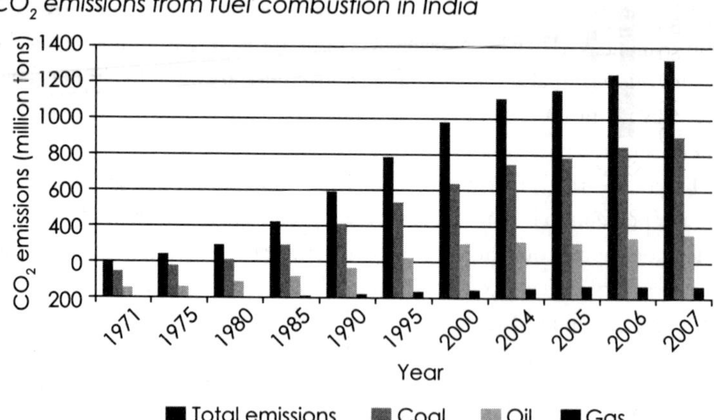

Source: IEA (2009a).

Figure 2.13
Gasoline prices (2008)

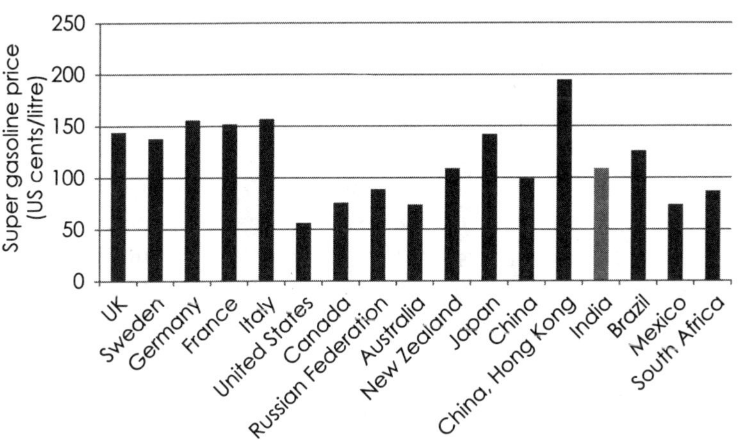

Source: GTZ International Fuel Prices (2009).

Figure 2.14
Diesel prices (2008)

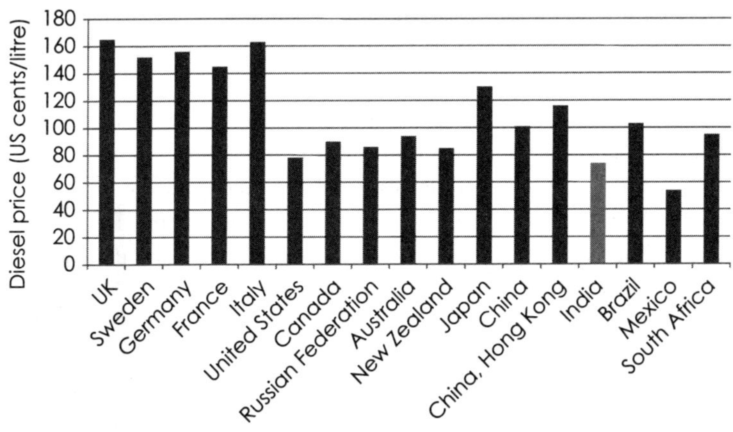

Source: GTZ International Fuel Prices (2009).

(as shown in Figure 2.14) is also comparable on an average with other countries. Whether there is scope for further increase in petroleum and diesel prices is linked with the impact that these prices will have on growth

Figure 2.15

Steam coal prices for electricity generation (2008)

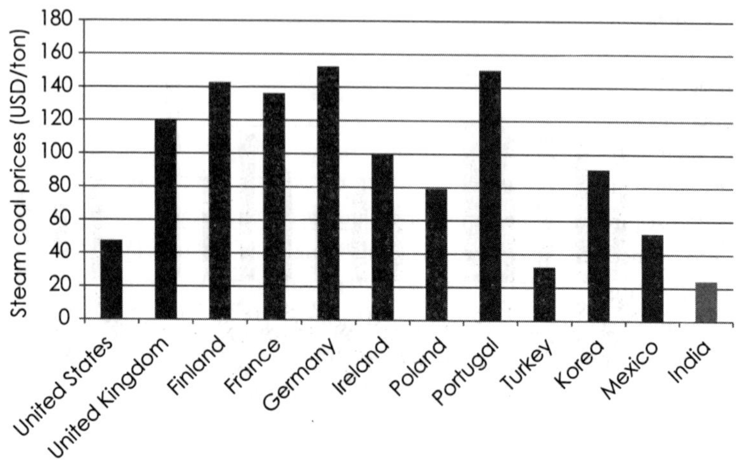

Source: IEA (2009b).

and distribution. From the input–output tables (IOTs) for India published by the Centre for Statistical organization (CSO), the effective tax rate on the petroleum products industry was found to be 31.86 percent for the year 2006–07.

The steam coal prices for electricity generation in different countries including India is given in Figure 2.15 for the year 2008.

The steam coal prices are lowest for India among the countries considered. Again, from the IOTs, the effective tax rate for the coal industry was found to be 2.46 percent for the year 2006–07, which is very low. This further strengthens the case for a coal tax and demonstrates the need to increase tax on coal in India.

b. Taxes on Polluting Industries

Taxes on polluting industries are levied to decrease the discharge of pollutants into air, water or any other media. A review of the international experience with respect to eco-taxes reveals that taxes on the industries that cause pollution or on direct pollution are almost completely ignored. The reasons for the predominance of consumption taxes vis-à-vis taxes on direct pollution have already been discussed. However, taxes on polluting industries are extremely important to shift production to cleaner methods. In a GST regime, only a limited number of polluting inputs and outputs can be charged at a higher rate or exempted from rebatable taxes on inputs. Thus, only a few industries can be chosen for taxation. These industries must be selected so as to maximize the environmental impact with a limited number of environmental taxes.

In their papers, Gupta (2002) and Pandey (2005) have identified the most polluting industries in India. Pollution loads for these industries were estimated according to the nature of pollutants (water, air, toxic and metal) and also by medium (air, water and land) for the toxic and metal pollutants.

The five largest polluting industries along with the states in which they are located are given in Table 2.12.

The relative contribution of each industry to total pollution load at the all-India level shows that the iron and steel industry is the highest polluting industry in terms of all four pollutants except air where it ranks second to cement. Iron and steel is the largest water polluting industry in India with 87.4 percent of the total pollution load. The pulp and paper and aluminium industries rank second and third, respectively, with their contribution to total water pollution load at 4.6 and 2.5 percent. Sugar and distillery industries rank fourth and fifth, respectively (Table 2.12).

The cement industry is the biggest air polluter emitting nearly 34 percent of the total air pollution load. Iron and steel stands second, emitting 32 percent, while oil refinery ranks third contributing 7.4 percent to the total industrial air pollution load.

The iron and steel industry is also the largest metal polluter accounting for more than 71 percent of the total metal pollution load. Aluminium

Table 2.12
Five largest polluting industries

Industry	*States*
Iron and steel	Bihar and Madhya Pradesh
Oil refinery	Maharashtra and Tamil Nadu
Fertilizer	Gujarat, Maharashtra and Uttar Pradesh
Sugar	Uttar Pradesh and Maharashtra
Cement industry	Madhya Pradesh and Andhra Pradesh

Source: Pandey (2005), Gupta (2002).

industry is the second highest contributor (nearly 16 percent) to metal pollution. In the toxic pollution category also, iron and steel industry is the highest polluter contributing 39 percent of the total pollution load. The second most polluting industry in this category is leather with about 14 percent share in total toxic load. Iron and steel, leather, petrochemical and oil refinery industries together account for 70 percent of total toxic pollution load.

The current level of taxes for these industries is given in Table 2.13.

As can be seen from the table, most polluting industries have a high effective tax rate. Under the GST, this rate will be reduced to the common GST rate. This necessitates a system of eco-tax integrated in the GST regime.

Table 2.13
Effective tax rate as percent of value added

	2003–04		*2006–07*	
Industries	*Effective Tax Rate (percent)*	*Rank out of 107 Industries*	*Effective Tax Tate (percent)*	*Rank out of 103 Industries*
Cement	9.89	61	12.54	50
Drugs and medicines	24.97	30	23.30	32
Fertilizers	28.08	26	24.67	28
Iron and steel casting and forging	34.95	13	35.48	14
Iron and steel foundries	56.68	6	52.04	7
Iron, steel and ferro alloys	17.09	42	9.11	55
Leather and leather products	17.05	43	8.21	59
Motor vehicles	34.07	17	36.98	11
Non-ferrous basic metals	24.08	31	31.97	16
Paper, paper products and newsprint	31.45	22	35.30	15
Pesticides	23.35	34	20.15	38
Petroleum products	56.94	5	31.86	17
Sugar	6.69	68	24.07	31
Coal and lignite	2.46	79	2.46	79
Average of all industries	17.41		18.15	

Source (Basic Data): CSO, 2003–04 and 2006–07 IOTs. Authors' calculation.

c. Transport Taxes

The contribution of vehicles towards air pollution is significant in most metro cities in India. This is seen by the high level of respirable suspended particulate matter (RSPM) and suspended particulate matter (SPM) in major cities of India, the main source of which is vehicles. There is a strong case for taxing vehicles on account of its contribution to the pollution load, which is as high as 76–92 percent for CO and 32–74 percent for NO_x. Currently, encouraging new vehicular technology that is more efficient in fuel use and upgrading older technology is implemented through a series of norms and regulations in India. Several committees such as the Expert Committee on Auto Fuel Policy (2006) have recommended the use of economic instruments to control vehicular pollution.

From the IOTs, we see that in India, the effective tax rate (as percent of GDP) is quite high for motor vehicles at about 36.98 percent for 2006–07. So, the impacts of raising motor vehicles taxes beyond this should be evaluated. However, in designing a motor vehicle tax, the most important point is to provide an incentive for fuel efficient cars in the form of a tax differentiation.

2.4.3 Eco-taxes: Revenue Neutrality versus Revenue Augmentation

The international experience shows that eco-taxes were often planned as revenue neutral interventions accompanied by reduction in the tax rates of the more distortionary taxes. In most developed countries, the aggregate tax–GDP ratio is already quite high and additional tax burden on account of eco-taxes would face considerable resistance. In India, the tax–GDP ratio at about 17–18 percent is relatively low and there is a need to increase the size of government particularly if the additional revenue can be used for promoting environmental management.

In the context of GST, it may be argued that the revenue potential of the eco-taxes can be used partly to cover the revenue risk associated with GST and partly to safeguard the revenues for environment-specific uses. The revenue risk arises because of the uncertainty regarding the revenue-neutral rate. The Task Force of the Thirteenth Finance Commission (THFC) has estimated it as 12 percent, whereas many analysts find it to be an underestimate of the revenue neutral rate. A second use of the revenue potential of the eco-taxes is that it can provide cover to the so-called producing states in respect of the additional revenue shock on account of the elimination of the central sales tax.

Under the GST, a common tax rate for all goods and services will be implemented. As the international experience shows, many countries where VAT is in place, this has been supplemented by eco-taxes. This takes the form of non-rebatable excise taxes on selected polluting inputs in addition to GST and earmarked cesses on top of the GST rate on outputs that pollute or intensively use polluting inputs.

2.4.4 Eco-taxes: Central, State and Local Dimensions

Another aspect to be considered is that unlike most countries considered in Chapter 2, India has a federal setup. This means that tax responsibilities must be differentiated between the Centre and the states. Centre should be given the responsibility to tax those pollutants whose externality is felt at the national or global level. Local pollutants should be the responsibility of the state. Also, different states have different polluting industries, and the nature of pollution is not the same across states. This means that taxation of polluting goods across states cannot be uniform as will be the case under GST. Local level taxes, such as a congestion tax, can be made the responsibility of the local authorities.

The last two issues of how the environmental considerations could be integrated in the emerging GST regime and what strategy should be adopted for utilizing the environmental tax revenue are discussed while describing the current debate on GST in India in the next chapter.

NOTES

1. For example, subsidies on intensive agriculture, fossil fuels or road and air transport will counteract the effect of an environmental tax. http://www2.oecd.org/ecoinst/queries/TaxInfo.htm
2. Ministry of Environment, New Zealand.
3. British Columbia Government (2009).
4. Ministry of Small Business and Revenue, British Columbia (2008).

5. Some of the other related legislations are given below:
   Sea-Shore Act, 1935; Prince Edwards Islands Act, 1948; Sea Birds and Seals Protection Act, 1973; National Parks Act, 1976; Dumping at Sea Control Act, 1980; Sea Fisheries Act, 1988; Antarctic Treaties Act, 1996; Wreck and Salvage Act, 1996; Environment Conservation Act Extension Act, 1996; Environmental Laws Rationalization Act, 1997; Marine Living Resources Act, 1998; National Veld and Forest Fire Act, 1998; National Environmental Management Act, 1998; World Heritage Convention Act, 1999; Western Cape Planning and Development Act, 1999; National Heritage Resources Act, 1999; Municipal Systems Act, 2000; South African Weather Service Act, 2001; Western Cape Environmental Implementation Plan, 2002.

3

Goods and Services Tax in India: The Current Debate

D.K. Srivastava

After the central government adopted CENVAT and the state governments adopted State VAT, the idea of a comprehensive goods and services tax (GST) has been pursued as the logical next step in reforming India's indirect taxes. The issue has been examined so far by (a) the Empowered Committee (EC) of State Finance Ministers, (b) the Thirteenth Finance Commission (THFC) and (c) the model implicit in central government's proposed constitutional amendment. Some important suggestions were also made by the Centre-State Financial Relations Commission headed by Justice Poonchi. There have been many hurdles in implementing the GST. The matter now has also been referred to the Fourteenth Finance Commission. States have a number of concerns with the design of GST.

3.1 EC GST MODEL

The EC of State Finance Ministers has been deliberating on the design of a suitable GST for some time now. The EC has favoured a concurrent GST with central and state GST components. The EC had put forward a 'First

Discussion Paper' outlining the key features of its suggested GST design. Its main features are summarized below:

1. The GST will have two components: one levied by the central GST (CGST) and the other to be levied by the State GST (SGST). The basic features of law such as chargeability, definition of taxable event and taxable person, measure of levy including valuation provisions, basis of classification, etc. should be uniform across these statutes as far as practicable.
2. The CGST and SGST would be applicable to all transactions of goods and services made for a consideration except for the exempted goods and services, goods which are outside the purview of GST and the transactions which are below the prescribed threshold limits.
3. The CGST and SGST are to be paid to the accounts of the Centre and the states separately. Taxes paid against the CGST and SGST will get input tax credit (ITC) within the CGST and SGST chains, respectively, but cross-utilization of ITC between CGST and SGST would not be allowed.
4. The administration of the CGST will be with the Centre and that of SGST with the states.
5. A uniform SGST threshold across states is desirable.
6. The following central taxes should be, to begin with, subsumed under the GST: (a) central excise duty, (b) additional excise duties, (c) excise duty levied under the Medicinal and Toiletries Preparation Act, (d) service tax, (e) additional customs duty, commonly known as countervailing duty (CVD), (f) special additional duty of customs (SAD), (g) surcharges and (h) cesses.
7. The following state taxes and levies should be, to begin with, subsumed under GST: (a) value-added tax (VAT)/sales tax, (b) entertainment tax (unless it is levied by the local bodies), (c) luxury tax, (d) taxes on lottery, betting and gambling, (e) state cesses and surcharges in so far as they relate to supply of goods and services and (f) entry tax not in lieu of Octroi.

Alcoholic beverages would be kept out of the purview of GST as part of demerit goods. Sales tax/VAT can be continued to be levied on alcoholic beverages as per the existing practice. Tobacco products would be subjected to GST with ITC. Centre may be allowed to levy excise duty on tobacco products over and above GST without ITC. As far as petroleum products are concerned, that is, crude, motor spirit (MS) [including aviation turbine fuel (ATF)] and high-speed diesel (HSD) would be kept outside GST as is the prevailing practice in India. Sales tax could continue to be levied by the states on these products with prevailing floor rate. Similarly, Centre could also continue its levies. On natural gas, whether it should be kept outside the GST, a final view has not been taken yet.

In this model, the Centre would levy integrated goods and services tax (IGST) which would be CGST plus SGST on all inter-state transactions of taxable goods and services with appropriate provision for consignment or stock transfer of goods and services. The inter-state seller will pay IGST on value addition after adjusting available credit of IGST, CGST and SGST on purchases. The exporting state will transfer to the Centre the credit of SGST used in payment of IGST. The importing dealer will claim credit of IGST while discharging his output tax liability in his own state. The Centre will transfer to the importing state the credit of IGST used in payment of SGST. The relevant information will also be submitted to the central agency which will act as a clearing house mechanism, verify the claims and inform the respective governments in respect of transfer of funds.

3.2 THFC: GST MODEL

The THFC proposed what they called the 'model GST' in which petroleum products are also covered under GST except that there will be an additional non-rebatable levy on the petroleum products. The THFC model is also a concurrent GST model with CGST and SGST as its two components. The THFC did not take a view on IGST vis-à-vis the modified bank model in regard to taxation of inter-state sales.

The THFC provides that no exemptions should be allowed other than a common list applicable to all states as well as the Centre, which should only comprise: (a) unprocessed food items; (b) public services provided by all governments 'excluding railways', communications and public sector enterprises; (c) service transactions between an employer and employee and (d) health and education services. It also says that the present area-based exemption schemes should be terminated. The existing schemes should not be grandfathered. Alternative options like refunding taxes paid by industries in these locations could be considered.

The THFC has suggested that the taxation of petroleum products and natural gas should be rationalized by including them in the tax base. HSD, MS and ATF could be charged GST and an additional levy by both the central and state governments. No input credit would be available against either CGST or SGST on the additional levy. A similar treatment would be provided to alcohol and tobacco. Such an arrangement would ensure protection of existing revenues while taking care of environmental concerns. In the EC Model, taxation of petroleum products would remain outside GST subject to non-rebatable sales tax by the states and excise duty by the Centre.

3.3 GST MODEL IMPLICIT IN THE PROPOSED CONSTITUTIONAL AMENDMENT

The central government has not directly spelt out the GST model that it advocates. However, the model implicit in the proposed constitutional amendment bill of 2011, and later of 2013, may be taken as indicative of the features of GST desired by the central government. This amendment bill seeks to confer simultaneous power on Parliament as well as the state legislatures including every union territory with legislature to make laws for levying GST on every transaction of supply of goods or services or both. The proposed central and state GST would be levied on all transactions involving supply of goods and services except those that are exempt or kept out of the purview of the GST.

Some of the key changes in the proposed GST-related constitutional amendments in the 2011 bill relate to Articles 246, 249, 268 and 270 and the Seventh Schedule. A summary of the key constitutional articles where amendments have been proposed is given in Table 3.1.

The constitution amendment bill proposes, under Article 279 A, the constitution of a 'GST Council'. The GST Council shall consist of the following members: (a) The Union Finance Minister: Chairperson; (b) The Union Minister of State in charge of Revenue: Member; (c) The Minister in charge of Finance or Taxation or any other Minister nominated by each state government: Members.

Table 3.1
Key proposed constitutional amendments and related articles

Article No.	*Subject*	*Nature of Amendment*
246A	Power to levy GST	Power extended to Parliament; Exclusive power to Parliament for GST in the course of inter-state trade and commerce
249(1)	Council of States	Parliament to have overriding power in GST matters through the instrumentality of the Council of States
268	Service tax; existing provision for services tax to be dropped.	States also have power to levy service tax
269	GST on inter-state trade	Parliament also to levy; apportionment to be determined
270	Sharing of GST	Sharing of GST on the basis of recommendations of the Finance Commission
271	Surcharges	Centre to have power to levy surcharge except on GST
279A	GST Council	Composition of the GST Council and the responsibilities of the GST Council
279B	GST Dispute Settlement Authority	Constitution of the GST Dispute Settlement Authority and responsibilities
286	Imports and sale outside the state	Parliament to have exclusive jurisdiction of GST matters in respect of imports and sale outside the state
287	Consumption of electricity by central government institutional authorities in states	Earlier exemption to be withdrawn
366 and 29A	Definition of goods and definition of sale of goods and services	Definition of goods to exclude: (i) Petroleum crude; (ii) High-speed diesel; (iii) Motor spirit (commonly known as petrol); (iv) Natural gas; (v) Aviation turbine fuel and (vi) Alcoholic liquor for human consumption Supply to cover lease-based supply of goods and services and works contracts

Table 3.1 continued

Table 3.1 continued

Article No.	*Subject*	*Nature of Amendment*
Seventh Schedule	Entries 84 and 92C	Services to be added to the State List Excise Tax in the State List on (a) Tobacco and tobacco products; (b) Petroleum crude; (c) High-speed diesel; (d) Motor spirit (commonly known as petrol); (e) Natural gas and (f) Aviation turbine fuel

Source: GoI (2011).

The members of the GST Council referred to in sub-clause (1) of clause (2) shall, as soon as maybe, choose one amongst themselves to be the Vice-Chairperson of the Council for such period as they may decide. The GST Council shall make recommendations to the union and the states on the following:

1. The taxes, cesses and surcharges levied by the Centre, the states and the local bodies which may be subsumed in the GST.
2. The goods and services that may be subjected to or exempted from the GST.
3. The threshold limit of turnover below which GST may be exempted.
4. The rates of GST.
5. Any other matter relating to the GST, as the Council may decide.

While discharging the functions conferred by this article, the GST Council shall be guided by the need for a harmonized structure of GST and for the development of a harmonized national market for goods and services.

One-third of the total number of members of the GST Council shall constitute the quorum at its meetings. The GST Council shall determine the procedure in the performance of its functions. Every decision of the GST Council taken at a meeting shall be with the consensus of all the members present at the meeting. No act or proceedings of the GST Council shall be invalid merely by reason of (a) any vacancy in, or any defect in, the constitution of the Council; (b) any defect in the appointment of a person as a Member of the Council and (c) any irregularity in the procedure of the Council not affecting the merits of the case.

Under Article 279B, parliament provides scope for the establishment of a 'GST Dispute Settlement Authority' to adjudicate any dispute or complaint referred to it by a state government or the Government of India arising out of a deviation from any of the recommendations of the GST Council constituted under Article 279A that results in a loss of revenue to a state government or the Government of India or affects the harmonized structure of the GST. The GST Dispute Settlement Authority would be required to look into principles and amounts of compensation to states. Most states resisted the idea for a dispute settlement authority and current indications are that this may be dropped. The idea of achieving a 'consensus' as the deciding rule for the GST Council is also being viewed as unworkable. The revision in 2013 has dropped the idea of a dispute resolution authority and provided for a rule for majority decision instead of consensus.

The proposed amendment seeks to cover all goods and services under the ambit of GST except petroleum products and alcoholic liquor for human consumption. The amendments relate to Article 366 of the Constitution, which after amendment would provide for the following changes:

- Unless the context otherwise requires, the following expressions have the meanings hereby, respectively, assigned to them, that is to say—(12) 'goods' includes all materials, commodities and articles; (12A) 'GST' means any tax on supply of goods or services or both except taxes on the supply of the following goods, namely: petroleum crude, high-speed diesel, motor spirit (commonly known as petrol), natural gas; aviation turbine fuel; and alcoholic liquor for human consumption.

The coverage of goods and services under CGST and SGST is determined by amendments to the Seventh Schedule. The following amendments are proposed:

- For the Union List, for entry 84, the modified entry will be: duties of excise on the following goods manufactured or produced in India namely: petroleum crude, high-speed diesel, motor spirit (commonly known as petrol), natural gas, aviation turbine fuel and tobacco and tobacco products; Entry 92 and 92C, which mentions 'Taxes on Services' are to be omitted.

- For the State List, the proposed changes are: (a) entry 52—taxes on the entry of goods into a local area for consumption, use or sale therein to the extent levied and collected by a Panchayat or a Municipality; (b) entry 54—taxes on the sale, other than sale in the course of inter-state trade or commerce or sale in the course of international trade and commerce of, petroleum crude, high-speed diesel, natural gas, motor spirit (commonly known as petrol), aviation turbine fuel and alcoholic liquor for human consumption; (c) entry 55 shall be omitted; (d) entry 62—taxes on entertainments and amusements to the extent levied and collected by a Panchayat or a Municipality or a Regional Council or a District Council.

One related matter is about states being given power to levy SGST on imports. In the note prepared and circulated by the Joint Working Group on GST on the Constitutional amendments, it is mentioned that assigning the power to levy SGST on imports to the states would entail extra-territorial jurisdiction particularly in the case of land-locked states and that it would be impractical for them to collect the tax for the simple reason that SGST being destination based, the revenue would accrue to the consumption state, while the collection would essentially have to be at the port of importation. These problems would be overcome if necessary constitutional amendment is made to empower the states to collect taxes levied by the Centre and to assign them to the same central agency as created for IGST for subsequent transfer of revenue to the respective consumption states.

The Ministry of Finance, Government of India has introduced a negative list of services in the implementation of service tax. A negative list approach is by far a more comprehensive approach. It allows the tax chain to be extended automatically to a wide range of economic activities where sometimes the distinction between goods and services become blurred. It allows input tax rebates for many services that may otherwise be left out in a positive list of services. For the overall logic of GST to go through both goods and services should be approached through a negative list.

In the discussions that preceded the implementation of the negative list, an apprehension was expressed that by a negative list concept, the central government may bring unto its own jurisdiction services for taxation that may have been taxed by the state governments unless these services are included in the negative list. Now that the negative list concept has been invoked, the ambit of the service tax has been increased resulting in higher revenues. The state governments would eventually be in a better position to assess the value of the additionality of service tax as part of the proposed grand bargain.

3.4 BRINGING ENVIRONMENTAL CONSIDERATIONS IN THE CONSTITUTIONAL AMENDMENT

In order to bring environmental considerations in the proposed constitutional amendment and to make taxation of polluting goods and services at par with other demerit/s in goods and services, we suggest that a clause pertaining to notified polluting goods and service be added in clause 12 of Article 366, entry 84 of the Union List and entry 54 of the State List under the Seventh Schedule of the Constitution. As per the proposed amendment, Article 366 is to be amended with respect to the following:

- Unless the context otherwise requires, the following expressions have the meanings hereby, respectively, assigned to them, that is to say—(12) 'goods' includes all materials, commodities and articles; (12A) 'goods and service tax' means any tax on supply of goods or services or both except taxes on the supply of the following goods, namely: petroleum crude, high-speed diesel, motor spirit (commonly known as petrol), natural gas, aviation turbine fuel, alcoholic liquor for human consumption and other goods and services notified by the union government, any state government, or government of a union territory as 'polluting goods and services'.

For the Union List, for entry 84, the following is proposed as the modified entry:

- Duties of excise on the following goods manufactured or produced in India namely: petroleum crude, high-speed diesel, motor spirit

> (commonly known as petrol), natural gas, aviation turbine fuel, tobacco and tobacco products, and other goods and services notified by the union government or government of a union territory as *polluting goods and services*; Entry 92 and 92C, which mentions 'Taxes on Services' are to be omitted.

To enable the states to tax petroleum products under a non-rebatable sales tax along with other polluting goods and services, entry 54 of the State List of the Seventh Schedule should be modified. It should include the following items: petroleum crude; high speed diesel; motor spirit (commonly known as petrol); natural gas; aviation turbine fuel; tobacco and tobacco products and other goods and services notified by the state government as *polluting goods and services.*

4

Integrating Environmental Considerations in GST Regime

D.K. Srivastava and K.S. Kavi Kumar

4.1 CONTEXT AND ISSUES

The planned nationwide indirect tax reform in India discussed in the previous chapter will eliminate the multiplicity of indirect taxes present in the current system, simplify the tax structure and broaden the tax base. Under the goods and services tax (GST) regime, tax will be levied on goods and services at each point of sale or provision of service, with the seller or service provider claiming credit for input tax which he has paid while purchasing the goods or procuring the service.

At present, there are parallel systems of indirect taxation at the central and state levels with overlapping tax bases with respect to value added up to the stage of manufacturing. This leads to cascading of indirect taxes. Apart from variations in tax rates, the levy of inter-state sales tax also fragments the all-India market. The tax system in India remains a mix of destination- and origin-based levies. The proposed reforms aim to bring about a comprehensive GST that eliminates cascading, removes tax barriers in the inter-state movement of goods and services, and ushers in a system where taxation will be destination-based, goods and services will be taxed at the same rates, rates will be common across states, inter-state sales tax will be eliminated and the country as a whole will become a genuine integrated common market.

However, GST in this form may have perverse environmental consequences unless suitable provisions are built into the system. For instance, if a polluting good is taxed at a lower rate under the GST regime than the present tax structure (after taking account central and state taxes), the resulting consumption of the polluting good is expected to be higher. Further, in a destination-based system, the tax revenue will accrue to the consuming states rather than the producing states. This will not only increase emissions in the producing states but will also leave them with lesser revenues to cope with the negative externalities of production. India, with a third of the world's poor and with 80 percent of its billion plus population living on less than $2 a day, economic growth remains at the top of its development agenda. However, development can occur only when growth is sustainable. This means that India must follow a resource use pattern that explicitly accommodates environmental concerns.

This chapter focuses on integrating environmental considerations in the GST regime. After reviewing the literature on energy–economy–environment (EEE) models that have been extensively used in various country-level/region-level analyses, the chapter proposes a detailed modelling framework for assessing the implications of introducing eco-taxes in the GST regime. The implications on economic growth, tax revenue and environmental pollution are estimated using a macro-economic model coupled with input–output modelling framework for sectoral disaggregation.

4.1.1 EEE Linkages in India

Energy use and the economy have been observed to be growing together in most countries and India is no exception. Energy as an input in several critical sectors like petroleum, steel, cement, aluminium, etc. is one of the most important catalysts for the development process. Rapid expansion of the energy sector is thus a necessary condition for sustaining the growth of the economy. At the same time, energy intensive sectors are major contributors of India's growth and hence targeted higher growth rates imply that energy requirements are poised to increase steeply in the near future. Figure 4.1 shows how energy and the economy have grown together in India.

Figure 4.1
Growth of energy, electricity and the Indian economy

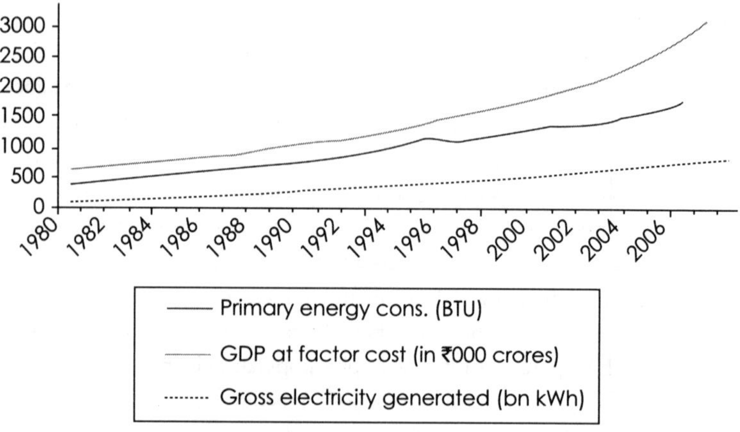

Source: Compiled by the authors using data from International Energy Agency (www.iea.org).

The energy use of the economy has been rapidly increasing with coal being the predominant source of primary energy supply. Coal still contributes about 63 percent of India's energy requirements followed by petroleum products and natural gas (Figure 4.2).

As a consequence of the energy–economy interactions and the high predominance of fossil fuels in the total energy mix, the environment has been severely affected. Energy-related activities are the prime cause of accumulation of greenhouse gases (GHGs), especially CO_2, which results in several global environmental issues such as ozone depletion and climate change. Figure 4.3 shows the emissions profile of India. Energy-related emissions constitute about 67 percent of total GHG emissions and 94 percent of CO_2 emissions.

Energy-intensive growth of the Indian economy has led to a steep rise in emissions over time. Though India does not rank very high on global emissions currently, future emissions are poised to grow at a staggering rate. Also, India will be among the countries which will be highly vulnerable to adverse effects of changing climate. This necessitates integration of energy, environment and economic policies to simultaneously achieve high growth with low pollution and energy security.

Figure 4.2
Primary energy supply by energy source

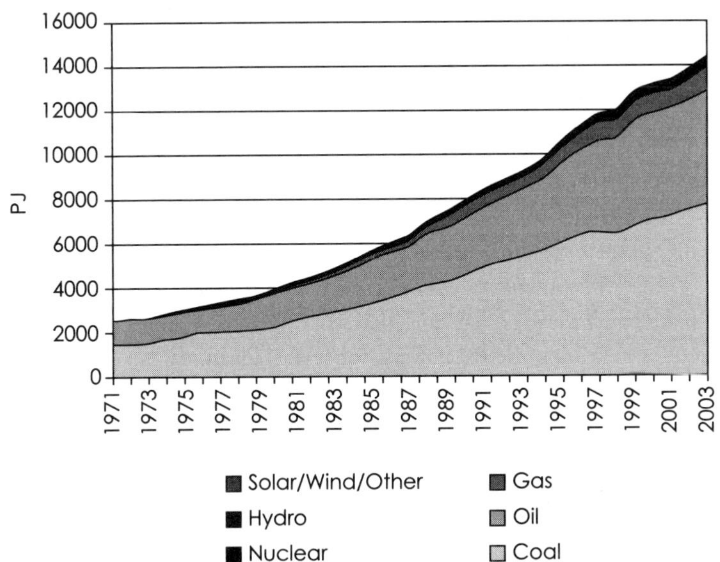

Source: Compiled by the authors using data from International Energy Agency (www.iea.org).

Figure 4.3
GHG emission in India by source

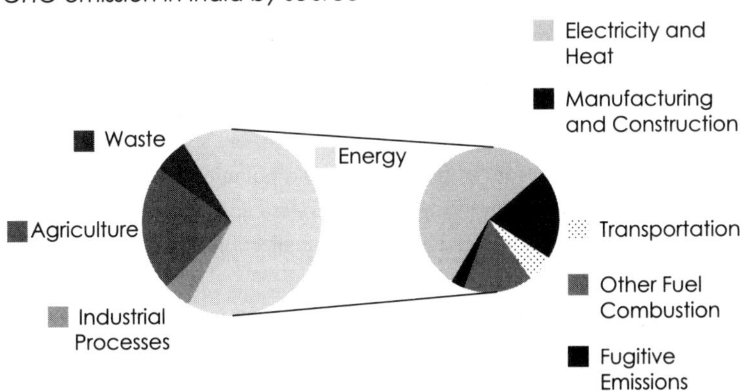

Source: Compiled by the authors using data from World Resources Institute (http://cait.wri.org).

4.1.2 Objectives of the Study

In the context of a planned GST regime and the possible detrimental effects it could have on the environment, the present study has the following objectives:

1. Project the output till 2029–30 under the business-as-usual (BAU) GST scenario. Calculate the corresponding pollution under the GST scenario.
2. Simulate different scenarios of eco-tax and observe its impact on macro-economic outcomes (output and revenue) and pollution.
3. Identify the set of tax rates that will help achieve long-term objective of increasing the fiscal space for taking advantage the demographic dividend and produce high-growth low-pollution scenarios.

4.2 EEE MODELS: REVIEW

The interaction between energy, environment and economy is complex and non-deterministic. The impact of policy measures such as levying an eco-tax or allowing trade in emission permits (i.e. a cap-and-trade system) on energy use, environment and economy is arguably a long-term issue requiring a detailed understanding of how these systems interact with each other. The objective of EEE modelling is to study the interactions among the inter-dependent systems. Moreover, modern computing prowess has made it possible to develop models that simulate the complex EEE interactions to generate detailed future scenarios. For instance, using EEE models it is possible to study the effect of a policy measure, say levying a carbon tax, on future gross domestic product (GDP) and pollution levels. Depending on how the different components of the system and their interactions are represented, these models lead to different projections.

4.2.1 Evolution of EEE Models

The links between energy and the economy were established several decades ago. Energy use and the economy have been observed to be growing together. Energy consumption rises as the economy expands and an increase in energy supply has been regarded as a critical spur to economic growth. As the dependence of world economies on energy increased, the oil crisis of the early 1970s brought about fears about depleting fossil fuel reserves and its possible impact on the economy. This led to the development of energy–economy modelling in the early 1970s, also known as decision-aid models, aimed at facilitating decision-making. The objective of these energy–economy models was often energy forecasting for governments and international institutions. Some of the important issues that energy–economy models tried to address are the following:

1. What would be the projected energy demand growth?
2. Can energy supply keep pace with the energy demand growth without affecting prices?
3. How would energy use constraints affect fuel prices?
4. How would end-use constraints affect the demand for energy-using services?
5. To what extent will the shortfall of energy supply affect the growth of the economy?
6. By how much will future international energy demand growth lag economic growth?
7. Which factors contribute most to the decoupling of energy demand and economic growth in various regions?
8. How will improvements in energy-supply technology affect the energy balance of the economy?

Over the years, beyond energy problems, governments became increasingly sensitive to environmental issues which started gaining prominence. The energy–economy interactions lead to adverse consequences on the environment. Energy-related activities are the prime cause of accumulation of GHGs, especially CO_2, leading to climate change. Similarly, release of CFCs by the industrial activities has led to depletion of ozone layer. Fears relating to energy–economy interactions affecting the environment, translated into demands for technical and economic evaluation of the risks involved and designing appropriate responses. Since the 1980s, energy–economy models initially developed for energy planning were altered to incorporate the environment and were replaced by EEE models. Apart from the issues that energy–economy models address, EEE models try to address the following issues:

1. What will be the BAU trajectory of GHG emissions?
2. How will changes in technology affect the overall energy system cost, energy use and emissions?
3. What is the least cost response to environmental constraints like emission reduction targets?
4. What is the impact of regulations and market-based instruments like taxes and subsidies on emissions?
5. How to develop mitigation strategies?

Although EEE models capture the EEE linkages, these models do not consider the secondary feedback effects of the environment on energy use and economy. A recent development since the 1990s popularly known as Integrated Assessment Models (IAMs) seeks to evaluate the impact of human activities on *bio-physical systems* including atmospheric composition, climate and sea level change, and ecosystems. It also tries to capture the feedback effects of these changes in bio-physical systems on energy use and economy. IAMs use inter-disciplinary knowledge and evaluate the cause and effect chain of climate change. IAMs hence explore how economic–environment interactions lead to GHG emissions, how emissions lead to concentrations, how these concentrations affect the bio-physical systems (temperature, sea level change) and how these changes have a feedback effect on the economy and the eco-system. The typical issues that IAMs can address beyond those that can by tackled by EEE models are the following:

1. What are the potential bio-physical consequences of GHG emissions?
2. How and to what extent do bio-physical changes affect the economy and the eco-system?
3. What are the macro-economic and sectoral impacts of pollution reduction policies?
4. Comparison and evaluation of different scenarios of mitigation and adaptation.

Figure 4.4 illustrates the evolution of EEE models. Models that were developed for energy planning in the wake of the energy crisis have evolved

Figure 4.4
Evolution of EEE models

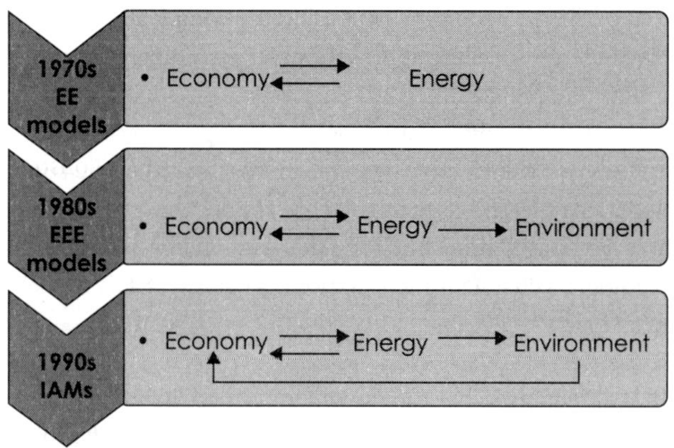

Source: Compiled by the authors.

into complex models combining inter-disciplinary knowledge that model the interactions and feedback effects between the economy, energy and the environment.

4.2.2 Typology of EEE Models

Over the last four decades, several EEE models have been developed ranging from simple models developed for energy forecasting to recently developed IAMs which model the bio-physical changes and their feedback on the economy.

The energy models developed in the 1970s had simple structures. Energy demand was a function of the output which was represented by a Leontief production function. Energy demand was governed by the parameters of the production function and the coefficient relating energy to output. The supply of energy was modelled according to the supply of individual fuels (which were considered to be perfect substitutes) depending on their respective production. Prices were generally irrelevant in the determination of energy demand and supply.

From this simple representation of the energy economy relationships, energy models evolved in trying to represent the complex interactions more precisely by introducing several methodological advances. The emergence of new technologies and strategies in the production process and improved distribution of skills among the modelling institutions have forced better representation of the system by increasing the complexity. This has led to a huge diversity of modelling approaches and accordingly different typologies of models can be identified.

Models can be classified based on their scope in terms of their economic and environmental coverage, the approach used in the construction of the model, the method used to solve the model, the level of aggregation, geographic coverage, time horizon, the way energy is treated and the way technological change is incorporated. Typically, EEE models can be classified as follows:

1. Based on approach—top down, bottom up, hybrid;
2. Based on method—macro-economic, general equilibrium, input–output, simulation, optimization, accounting framework;
3. Based on time—static/dynamic, short/medium/long/very long term;
4. Based on level of aggregation—aggregated/disaggregated and
5. Based on geographical coverage—global/regional/national/local.

EEE models can be broadly classified as top-down models and bottom-up models based on the approach used to construct the models. Top-down models are those in which macro-economic features predominate, whereas bottom-up models use technical and engineering information about the production process. Models which assume that the strategies of the agents in the economy are essentially influenced by decisions at the 'top' adopted a top-down approach. Whereas, those that believe that the strategies of agents are constrained by specific local concerns and with different objectives adopted a bottom-up approach. In the recent years, hybrid models have been developed which include both top-down and bottom-up features that take interest in decisions taking place at the top and the bottom.

Once the model has been constructed as a top-down or bottom-up model, the method to solve the model has to be chosen (Table 4.1). Typically, top-down models can be solved using macro-economic (or Keynesian) framework, general equilibrium framework or an input–output framework. Bottom-up models can be solved using optimization, iterative equilibrium/simulation or accounting frameworks. Individual models may use multiple methods and tools to solve the model.

Table 4.1
Comparison of top-down and bottom-up approaches

Features	*Top-down Approach*	*Bottom-up Approach*
Data	Use aggregated economic data	Use detailed data on fuels, technologies and policies
Cost/benefit	Assess costs/benefits through impact on output, income, GDP	Assess costs/benefits of individual technologies and policies
Capturing costs	Implicitly capture administrative, implementation and other costs	Can explicitly include administration and programme costs
Perception of market	Typically assume efficient markets, and no 'efficiency gap'	Do not assume efficient markets, overcoming market barriers can offer cost-effective energy savings
Capturing interactions	Capture inter-sectoral feedbacks and interactions	Capture interactions among projects and policies
Usage	Commonly used to assess impact of carbon taxes and fiscal policies	Commonly used to assess costs and benefits of projects and programmes
Less suitable for	Examining technology-specific policies	Predicting the macro-economic impact on the economy as a whole
Treatment of capital	Precise description of capital equipment	Homogeneous and abstract concept
Treatment of technology	Menu of technological options introduced	Trend rates (endogenous or exogenous)
Potential efficiency improvements	Usually high, costless improvements	Usually low constraint on economy

Source: Compiled by the authors.

Models can also be classified based on whether they are static or dynamic. In static models, a comparative static analysis is done where two equilibria are compared. In dynamic models, the time factor is explicitly introduced by considering dependencies between stock and flow variables. Models can also be classified by the time horizon of their projections. Typically, bottom-up models are suitable for short-term forecasts, whereas top-down models are suitable for medium- to long-term forecasts.

A classification of EEE models can also be made based on the level of aggregation which may be assessed by the number of equations, exogenous variables, economic sectors, energy products and pollutants. The aggregation level determines the precision with which the interactions between the energy system, economy and environment are captured.

Models can also be classified as global, regional, national or local models based on the geographical cover for which the model gives projections.

4.2.3 Select EEE Models for India

This section discusses some models specific to India which were developed with assistance from the Ministry of Environment and Forests (MoEF) to project the trajectory of GHG emissions in India (MoEF, 2009). These include the NCAER-CGE model, IRADe-Activity Analysis model, TERI-MoEF and TERI-Poznan MARKAL models. The discussion there focuses on one bottom-up model (MARKAL), two top-down models (GEM-E3 and GEMINI-E3) and a hybrid model (E3ME) aiming to understand how the components of economy, energy and environment are represented in these models. MARKAL model uses a bottom-up optimization framework; GEM-E3 and GEMINI-E3 use a CGE framework while the E3ME model uses a macro-econometric framework. All of them are dynamic models and are wide in scope of the geographical and sectoral coverage.

a. TERI-MoEF (MARKAL) Model

Basic features

1. Bottom-up representation of energy producing, transforming and consuming technologies;
2. Cost minimization model based on linear programming version of MARKAL model;
3. Prescriptive model that predicts the future evolution of energy sector and GHG emissions only under the validity of cost minimization objective and all the assumptions;
4. Technological change is incorporated through TFPG (assumed to be 3 percent) and AEEI and is assumed to be limited;
5. Finds a least cost set of technologies that satisfies exogenously specified end-use demands. The resulting energy-technology combinations are shown as outputs;

6. Scope: 35 energy consuming sectors + energy supply options (coal, oil, gas, hydro, nuclear, renewables, biomass);
7. GHGs covered: only CO_2 (from energy and industry);
8. Timeframe: 2001–31.

Model outputs: The environmental trajectory in 2030–31 as predicted by the MARKAL model is as follows:

1. CO_2 emissions (aggregate): 4.9 billion tons;
2. CO_2 emissions (per capita): 3.4 tons;
3. Commercial energy use: 1567 mtoe;
4. Fall in energy intensity: 0.11 (2001–02) to 0.06 (2031–32) kgoe per $GDP at PPP;
5. Fall in carbon intensity: 0.37 (2001–02) to 0.18 (2031–32) kg CO_2 per $GDP at PPP.

b. TERI-Poznan Model

The TERI-Poznan study uses the same linear programming cost minimization MARKAL framework as is used by the TERI-MoEF model except that it differs in some key assumptions. The main differences in assumptions between the two models are with respect to the following:

1. *GDP growth:* 8.2 percent per annum during 2001–31 (MoEF model: 8.84 percent CAGR of GDP during 2003–30 from NCAER-CGE projections).
2. *Energy prices:* Considered to evolve based on expert judgement (MoEF model: international energy prices form IEA and domestic energy prices from CGE projections).
3. *Factor productivity:* No improvements assumed (MoEF model: TFPG = 3 percent per annum).
4. *Energy efficiency:* Limited improvements based on past trends and expert judgement (MoEF model: AEEI = 1.5 percent per annum subject to technical feasibility limits).

The difference in assumptions leads to different results even though the basic model framework is the same. The prediction by the TERI-Poznan model with respect to key environmental variables is more unfavourable to the environment compared to the TERI-MoEF model. The results are as follows:

1. CO_2 emissions (aggregate): 7.3 billion tons;
2. CO_2 emissions (per capita): 5.0 tons;
3. Commercial energy use: 2149 mtoe;
4. Fall in energy intensity: 0.11 (2001–02) to 0.08 (2031–32) kgoe per $GDP at PPP;
5. Fall in carbon intensity: 0.37 (2001–02) to 0.28 (2031–32) kg CO_2 per $GDP at PPP.

c. Activity-analysis Model

The activity-analysis model is a 'stand-alone' top-down model that uses the activity analysis framework to model the linkages between economy and environment.

Basic features

1. Uses a linear programming framework that maximizes welfare (the discounted sum of total construction streams) given the constraints imposed by resource availability and various technological possibilities for using them.
2. Scope: multi-sectoral—includes 34 producing sectors producing 25 commodities + government, intertemporal—planning horizon is from 2003 to 2033.
3. GHGs covered: CO_2 (from energy, industry, households and government consumption only).
4. The sectoral output as given by the input–output matrix is based on the updated social accounting matrix of 2003–04 prices.
5. This model is also prescriptive and works given the validity of the assumptions and consumption maximizing objective.

Model outputs: The results of the activity-analysis model with respect to key parameters are as follows:

1. CO_2 emissions (aggregate): 4.23 billion tons;
2. CO_2 emissions (per capita): 2.9 tons;
3. CAGR of GDP (2010–11 to 2030–31): 7.66 percent;

4. Commercial energy use: 1042 mtoe;
5. Fall in energy intensity: 0.1 (2003–04) to 0.04 (2030–31) kgoe per $GDP at PPP;
6. Fall in carbon intensity: 0.37 (2003–04) to 0.18 (2030–31) kg CO_2 per $GDP at PPP.

d. NCAER-CGE Model

Basic features: The top-down macro-economic CGE model developed by NCAER in collaboration with Jadavpur University is based on the neo-classical CGE framework and incorporates specific institutional factors of the Indian economy. It covers more than 37 sectors and is recursively dynamic.

A system of non-linear equations simultaneously determines the endogenous variables in the model. The 37 sector CGE model is calibrated to the benchmark equilibrium data set for the Indian economy for 2003–04 by constructing a SAM for that particular year. A sequence of equilibria, from 2003–04 to 2030–31, is generated by using a time-series data of exogenous variables which is solved on General Algebraic Modelling System (GAMS).

Model outputs: The model projects GHG emissions in 2030–31 to be 4 billion tons of CO_2e with per capita GHG emissions at 2.77 tons CO_2e. The growth in GDP is projected to be 8.84 percent. Total commercial primary energy in 2030–31 is estimated to be 1087 mtoe. Energy intensity is estimated to decline at an annual compound rate of 3.85 percent. CO_2 intensity is also projected to decline from 0.37 kg CO_2e in 2003–04 to 0.15 CO_2e kg CO_2e in 2030–31 per $GDP at PPP.

In addition to the above-mentioned models, a number of other regional global models connect energy, economy and environment. Table 4.2 provides an overview of some of the widely used models.

4.3 MODEL-BASED PROJECTIONS OF MACRO-AGGREGATES

In this section, we discuss the overall methodological framework adopted by the study and also the specific modelling approach used to project macro-economic aggregates.

Table 4.2
Overview of widely used EEE models

Model	*Time-Horizon*	*Spatial Coverage*	*Theme of Application*	*Approach*	*Aggregation Level*	*Reference*
AIM	Dynamic/long-run projections	Regional (Asia-pacific)	IAM: energy–environment–climate–economy	Hybrid (simulation, optimization)	Disaggregated	Kainuma et al. (2003)
ASF	Long run (1985–2100)	Global (9 regions)	IAM: energy–economy–climate	Top-down (optimization)	Disaggregated (4 modules: energy, agriculture, industry, land use)	EPA (1990), CIESIN (1995)
LEAP	Medium to long-term modelling tool	Can be applied at a local, national or regional scale	Energy–economy–environment tool	Bottom-up (accounting framework)	Depends on data availability. Can be aggregated or disaggregated	LEAP (2005)
MESSAGE	Dynamic (medium to long term)	Global (11 macro-regions)	IAM: energy supply–economy–climate	Hybrid (optimization)	Disaggregated	IIASA (2005), Nakicenovic and Riahi (2003)
E3MG	Dynamic/long run	Global (20 regions)	Energy–economy–environment	Hybrid (macro-econometric framework)	Highly disaggregated (42 sectors, 28 consumer spending categories, 14 atmospheric emissions, 12 fuel types)	Cambridge econometrics (http://www.camecon.com/EnergyEnvironment/EnergyEnvironment Global/Modelling Capability/E3MG.aspx)

SGM	Dynamic: recursive/long run (1990–2050)	Global (13 regions)	IAM: energy–economy–climate	Top-down (general equilibrium framework)	Disaggregated (14 multi-sector regional models)	Edmonds et al. (2004)
NEMESIS	Recursive dynamic/short or medium run	Regional (EU-27, USA, Japan)	Energy–economy–environment	Top-down (macro-econometric framework)	Disaggregated (32 production sectors, 160 eqns)	Brécard et al. (2006)
PRIMES	Dynamic/ medium term (1990–2030)	Regional (15 European Union countries)	Energy–economy–environment	Bottom-up (optimization) + top-down (general equilibrium)	Disaggregated (24 energy forms, demand sector and supply sector disaggregation)	European Commission (1995)

Source: Compiled by the authors from various sources listed.

Notes: AIM: Asia-pacific Integrated Model; ASF: Atmospheric Stabilization Framework model; E3MG: EEE Model for the Globe; SGM: Second Generation Model; LEAP: Long-Range Energy Alternatives Planning System; MESSAGE: Model for Energy Supply Strategy Alternatives and their General Environmental impact; NEMESIS: New Econometric Model of Evaluation by Sectoral Interdependency and Supply; PRIMES: Price-Induced Model of the Energy System.

4.3.1 Overall Methodological Framework

Here, we provide a brief discussion on the methodological framework adopted at different stages in the estimation process. Broadly the discussion covers, projecting under a set of assumptions how the economy as measured by its gross value added (GVA) is likely to perform in the next two decades, its effect on local and global pollution and the effectiveness of GST and environmentally motivated taxes in shifting the trajectory of output and pollution in the long term.

Figure 4.5 illustrates the four important components of the modelling exercise. The first component involves forecasting the performance of the

Figure 4.5
Overall modelling framework

I. Macro-economic Projections	II. Sectoral Disaggregation
• Projection of GVA at eight-sector level till 2029–30 using macro-econometric model • GVA at eight-sector level decomposed to 14-sector level to facilitate realistic estimates of the effect of GST on the economy	• Estimation of output from GVA using Leontief inverse matrix derived from Input-Output tables for 2006–07 • Values of output divided into 51 sectors based on GVA ratios corresponding to 2006–07 to bring it in line with available pollution coefficients
III. Estimation of Environmental Pollution	**IV. Response to Fiscal Measures**
Local emissions: • Product of output vector and pollution coefficient vector from IPPS database yield estimates of local pollution such as SO_2 and TSP *Global emissions:* • Product of output vector with carbon intensity estimates from MoEF report yield estimates of CO_2 emissions	• Assessment of the effect of GST and eco-tax on: ▪ output; and, ▪ environment

Source: Prepared by the authors.

macro-economy till 2029–30. This is done at an eight-sector level to minimize the complexity of the model while capturing the structural changes in the economy. The next component disaggregates the economic performance into 51 sectors to bring it in line with available pollution coefficients. The product of output and pollution coefficient vectors yields a vector of pollution load corresponding to each of the 51 sectors. This constitutes the third component. The fourth and the final component assesses the effect of GST and eco-tax on output and the environment. The eight-sector output is further disaggregated into 14 sectors and the 51 sectors of the input–output matrix are compressed into the same 14 sectors for aligning the projections of sectoral outputs estimation of pollution load.

The discussion in this section mainly focuses on the first component of the overall modelling framework, namely macro-economic projections. Brief description of two other key components, namely sectoral disaggregation and estimation of environmental pollution is provided in the next two sections before describing assumptions underlying the macro-economic projections for India over the period 2010–11 to 2029–30.

4.3.2 Sectoral Disaggregation

The macro-model projects GDP (at factor cost and constant 1999–2000 prices) at an eight-sector disaggregation for the years 2006–07 to 2029–30. This feeds as an input in the input–output module from which the output vector is calculated for the year 2006–07 to 2029–30 as explained below.

The Centre for Statistical Organization (CSO) publishes the input–output transactions table (IOTT) once in every five years. The CSO provides the input flow (absorption) matrix and the output (make) matrix. The input flow matrix is a (commodity × industry) matrix which gives the value of each commodity *j* that flows as input into each industry *i*. The make matrix is a (industry × commodity) matrix which gives the value of each commodity *j* that is produced as output by each industry *i*. Using these matrices, we obtain the (commodity × commodity) I-O coefficient matrix (*A*) that gives the number of units of each commodity *j* that flows as input to produce one unit of output of each commodity.[1] Similarly, we also obtain the (industry × industry) I-O coefficient matrix which gives the number of units of output of each industry *i* that flows as input to produce one unit of output of each industry. We assume industry technology for constructing these matrices.[2]

Hence, in the input–output tables (IOTs), each industry/commodity is listed as a consuming sector across the columns and as a supplying sector across the rows. It is assumed that the inputs used in producing an output are related to that output by a linear and fixed coefficient production function. Hence, each column is a technique of production by which only one product is produced. The output vector of each commodity/industry is denoted by X. The output of each commodity/industry is the sum of its use as inputs for other commodities/industries plus the final demand for that commodity/industry.

Mathematically, the input–output model can be expressed as

$$X = AX + F, \tag{3.1}$$

where A = coefficient matrix, X = output vector and F = final demand vector.

The solution for this is

$$X = (I - A)^{-1} F,$$

where $(I - A)^{-1}$ is the Leontief matrix.

Using the (commodity × commodity) matrix (A), we calculate the Leontief matrix. The IOT for 2006–07 as provided by CSO is at a 130 × 130 level of sectoral disaggregation. For convenience, we first collapse the original IOT to 51 × 51 matrix. The eight sectors for which GDP is projected (from the macro-model) are then matched to these 51 sectors so that we have a (51 × 1) matrix of final demand for a given year. Subsequently, further aggregation into 14 sectors was done. This aggregation was undertaken after taking into account both contribution of sectors to indirect tax revenues and to pollution.

4.3.3 Estimation of Environmental Pollution

The strong inter-linkages between the economy and the environment have already been discussed in Chapter 2. What is clear from the discussion is the need to find cost-effective pathways that balance the benefits of growth with its associated environmental cost at the margin. Industrial emissions contribute significantly to environmental pollution. This takes the form of emissions into the air or water or through waste disposals in landfills or incineration.

However, as already pointed out earlier, pollutants can be divided into flow pollutants and stock pollutants on the basis of their lifetime. Stock pollutants such as CO_2 have a lifetime of more than 100 years while flow pollutants have much shorter durations. Therefore, the true cost (or benefit) of additional emissions (or reduction in emissions) is the present value of the stream of future costs (or benefits). It is in this context that the effectiveness of any policy measures needs to be evaluated. It is because of this reason that we have presented emissions from flow and stock pollutants separately.

In estimating emission of flow pollutants, we use sectorally disaggregated information on economic output from the most recently available IOTs and pollution coefficients from the Industrial Pollution Projection System (IPPS) to generate the associated pollution load corresponding to each of the sectors. For measuring the level of a stock pollutant (CO_2), we use information on consumption, net calorific value (NCF) and emission factor (EF) of different fuels. Further, the macro-econometric model provides projections of output till 2029–30. This allows us to estimate future pollution levels under a set of assumptions.

It needs to be stated up-front that although it is the ambient concentrations of pollutants that impact health and the environment, modelling concentrations are far more complex and involve using detailed transportation models that translate emissions from a source to ambient concentrations at a receptor. The Central Pollution Control Board (CPCB) has recently drafted common guidelines for air quality monitoring and source apportionment studies for Indian cities and detailed studies have been carried out in select cities—e.g. Mumbai (NEERI, 2010). However, the purpose of this study is to provide broad aggregates of pollution levels and present the likely future trend till 2029–30.

4.3.4 Macro-economic Projections

The emphasis is on highlighting the underlying trends in components of aggregate demand and output. For this purpose, we utilize a macro-econometric model, which provides a disaggregated treatment of the supply side and emphasizes structural changes in the economy. Long-term modelling of the macro-economy for two or more decades into the future needs to be different from short-term modelling in several crucial respects. In particular, long-term models need to emphasize the supply side of the economy far more than the demand side. In short- to medium-term modelling, the focus is on the management of cyclical movements, where the demand side is important. On the other hand, the supply side gains central importance in long-term models which need to focus on growth, productivity and technological change. However, models of the Indian economy with a long-term perspective emphasizing supply side factors are not available especially within the context of questions that are examined in this study.

Long-term growth is conditioned by a suitable policy environment. Management of policies, both monetary policy and fiscal policy, requires to be aimed at providing a stable economic environment and addressing issues of sustainability rather than short-term policy calibration.

In the Indian context, the impact of the demographic changes such as the slowing down of the population growth, changes in the age structure, and consequently on the availability of the work force and the dependency ratio, needs to be endogenized. Similarly, the long-term model should provide for structural changes in the economy like the growing share of the service sector and the falling share of the agricultural sector. Furthermore, as capital stock increases, the ratio of older capital stock to total capital stock also increases. This implies that consumption of fixed capital will increase at an accelerated rate over time. With technological progress, productivity of factors of production may increase but there will also be diminishing returns to capital. Technological change can also be a reason for accelerated rate of obsolescence of capital stock.

In this model, four sectors are considered: real, monetary, fiscal and trade. The real sector is specified in a disaggregated way both on the demand side and the output side. These are the focus areas of the study. Specific policy rules are followed with reference to fiscal, monetary and trade policies.

A major structural change that will progressively affect the economy is the demographic shift in India where the dependency ratio (defined as the ratio of population below 14 years and above 60 years) will reach a peak and then decline. Correspondingly, the share of working age population to total population will increase.

Figure 4.6 shows the projected share of working age population (in the age group of 15–60 years) to total population in India based on UN country-wise population projections. The minimum of this ratio at about 54 percent was in 1970 and the highest of the ratio at about 64 percent is

Figure 4.6
Share of working population in total population

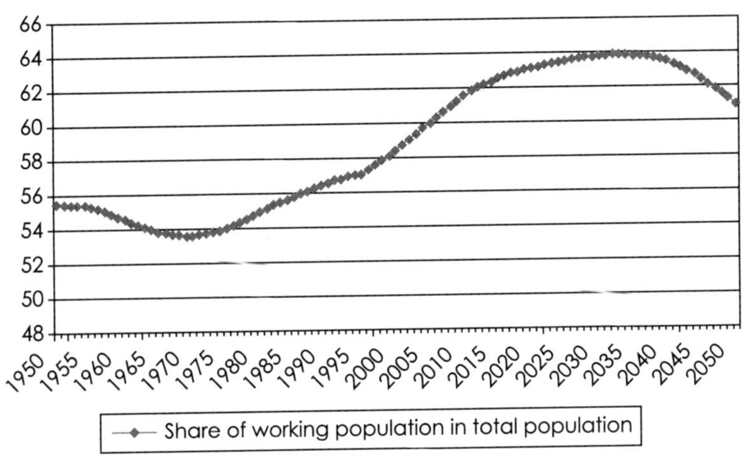

Source: Based on UN population projections.

projected to occur around 2033. There is noticeable acceleration of this ratio soon after 2000. Although it continues to rise, there is a deceleration after 2007. The window from now up to 2035 is the critical growth window for India with the growing availability of labour force and a falling dependency ratio. It benefits growth from the output side by making available the human resources needed for sustaining a high rate of growth. It also augments the saving rate and therefore the supply of investible resources. However, adequate provision is required for government expenditure on education and health to improve the capabilities of these human resources who require education, skills and training for productive absorption in the growing service sectors of the economy.

Policy Environment

The policy environment focuses on sustainability and support for a long-term high growth profile of the Indian economy. In the fiscal sector, consistent with the central and state fiscal responsibility legislations, policy is geared towards achieving balance on the revenue account and reducing government debt to sustainable levels. As government debt falls, interest payments relative to GDP also fall, creating space for additional primary expenditure geared towards supporting the education and health sectors.

For this purpose, fiscal deficit broadly follows a rule consistent with the fiscal responsibility legislations of the central and state governments and the recommendations of the Twelfth and Thirteenth Finance Commissions. Fiscal deficit is determined as 6.9 percent of the previous year's GDP at market prices.[3] This, assuming a 15 percent growth of nominal income on average, keeps the combined fiscal deficit at about 6 percent of current years' nominal GDP at current market prices. After achieving the desired margin of reduction in government debt, an asymmetric path for fiscal deficit can be followed by allowing it to increase to levels higher than 6 percent of GDP, if higher growth would still provide a stable debt–GDP ratio. The suggested target for the combined debt of the central and state governments by the Twelfth Finance Commission was 56 percent of GDP. On the revenue account, the target of the FRBMAs of the central and state government endorsed by both the Twelfth and Thirteenth Finance Commissions is to achieve balance or surplus on the revenue account.

Monetary policy is geared towards long-term target of reducing the inflation rate to about 4 percent per annum. We generate broad money (M3) by a rule such that the annual growth rate of M3 is kept at 17 percent per annum. It is shown that this progressively reduces the inflation rate to reach a 4 percent level on a sustained basis.

With respect to the external sector, the long-term target is to bring the current account in balance. This is kept as a target but introduced in incremental steps. Current account deficit to GDP ratio is taken as exogenous and its time path provides for a gradual reduction in the current account deficit to GDP ratio.

Model Specification

In specifying the model, the following notations are used. The natural log of a variable is denoted by prefixing a variable by *l*. The deviation of the actual value of a variable from its long-term equilibrium value is denoted by prefixing a variable name by *Z*. The long-term equilibrium value of a variable is indicated by suffixing a variable name by *F*. The first difference of variable is denoted by prefixing a variable name by *D*. Structural breaks are captured by intercept and slope (intercept dummy * time trend) dummies that are indicated by *D* and *S*. Thus, *D*71 means that intercept dummy has a value 0 from 1950–51 to 1969–70, and a value 1 from 1970–71 onwards. The time trend is indicated by TT which ranges from 1 to 80 covering the 80 years from 1950–51 to 2029–30. Thus, *S*70 will have value (*D*70 * TT) equal to zero up to 1969–70, and 31, 32, …, 80 from 1970–71 to 2029–30. The model is specified as follows. Please refer to Appendix A4.1 for a description of various variables used in the model specification.

A1. Aggregate supply: Aggregate output is divided into eight sectors. The production functions depend on the capital stock of each of these sectors. In addition, they use as inputs, outputs of the other sectors. This provides for the interdependence of inter-sectoral growth. Given the increasing size of the work force, labour is not considered a constraint, either of skilled or unskilled variety. However, the study acknowledges that availability of skilled manpower may become a constraint for certain sectors. Keeping these considerations in mind, output is divided into the following eight categories: (a) agriculture and allied services; (b) industry, consisting of sub-sectors of (i) manufacturing, (ii) mining and quarrying, and (iii) electricity, gas and water supply; and (c) services, consisting of sub-sectors of (i) construction, (ii) trade, hotels, transport and communications, (iii) finance, insurance, real estate and business services and (iv) community, social and personal services.

For each aggregate output category, a production function is specified. For each sector, capital stock and outputs of other sectors are seen to have a significant influence.

Output in agriculture and allied services (GDP at factor cost at 1999–2000 prices)

1. *LYAR* = *F*[*DRAIN*10, *LKAR*, *LYAR*(–1), *D*88, *S*88]

The *DRAIN*10 is (0, 1) variable taking a value 1 for years when the rainfall is less than average rainfall by a margin of more than 10 percent of the average.

Output in manufacturing (GDP at factor cost at 1999–2000 prices)

2. *LYMANR* = *F*[*LKMANR*, *LYFIEBR*, *LYMANR*(–1)]

Output in mining and quarrying (GDP at factor cost at 1999–2000 prices)

3. *LYMQR* = *F*[*D*71, *D*72, *LCBPRE*, *LYMQR*(–1)]

Output in construction (GDP at factor cost at 1999–2000 prices)

4. *LYCRR* = *F*[*LKAR*, *LKCRR*, *LYTHTCR*, *LYCRR*(–1)]

Output in trade, hotels and restaurants (GDP at factor cost at 1999–2000 prices)

5. *LYTHTCR* = *F*[*LKCRR*, *LYCRR*, *LYCSPR*, *LYFIEBR*, *LYTHTCR*(–1)]

Output in electricity, gas and water supply (GDP at factor cost at 1999–2000 prices)

6. *LYEGWSR* = *F*[*LCBPRE*, *LKCRR*, *LKFIEBR*, *LYMQR* *LYEGWSR*(–1)]

Output in financial investment, business and related services (GDP at factor cost at 1999–2000 prices)

7. *LYFIEBR* = *F*[*LKCSPR*, *LYAR*, *LYMQR*, *LYTHTCR*, *LYFIEBR*(–1)]

Output in community, social and public services (GDP at factor cost at 1999–2000 prices)

8. *LYCSPR* = *F*[*D*101, *D*90, *D*91, *D*99, *LCBPRE*, *LYTHTCR*, *LYCSPR*(–1)]

GDP at factor cost at 1999–2000 prices

9. *YR* = *YAR* + *YIR* + *YSER*

GDP at factor cost in industries

10. *YIR* = *YEGWSR* + *YMANR* + *YMQR*

GDP at factor cost in services

11. *YSER* = *YCRR* + *YCSPR* + *YFIEBR* + *YTHTCR*

Sectoral Capital Stocks

For each sector, capital stock is generated. The overall gross investment is generated by the sum of private and government investments. From this, the increase in net fixed capital stock is generated after deducting consumption of fixed capital, investment in inventories, investment in valuables and an errors and omissions term. Different sectors claim a share in the increase in net fixed capital stock. Seven of these shares can be independently determined. One of the shares can then be residually determined.

12. Capital stock in agriculture: *KAR* = *KAR*(–1) + *IAR*

13. Capital stock in construction: *KCRR* = *KCRR*(–1) + *ICRR*

14. Capital stock in community, social and personal services: *KCSPR* = *KCSPR* + *ICSPR*(–1)

15. Capital stock in finance, insurance, real estate and business services: *KFIEBR* = *KFIEBR*(–1) + *IFIEBR*

16. Capital stock in manufacturing: *KMANR* = *KMANR*(–1) + *IMANR*

17. Capital stock in trade, hotels and restaurants: *KMQR* = *KMQR*(–1) + *IMQR*

18. Capital stock in mining and quarrying: *KTHTCR*=*KTHTCR*(–1) + *ITHTCR*

19. Capital stock in electricity, gas and water supply: *KEGWSR* = *KEGWSR*(–1) + *IEGWSR*

Sectoral Investment Shares in Total Investment

Sectoral investments are generated by applying sector-specific ratios to net addition of fixed capital stock. Net addition to fixed capital stock is derived from gross investment after deducting consumption of fixed capital, inventories, investment in valuables, errors and omissions, and statistical discrepancies.

Share of investment in community, social and public services in aggregate investment

20. *LSICSPR* = *F* (*D*85, *LSICSPR*)

Share of investment in manufacturing in aggregate investment

21. *LSIMANR* = *F*(*D*102, *D*103, *LSIMANR*)

Share of investment in trade, hotels and restaurants

22. *LSITHTCR* = *F*(*D*83, *D*84, *LSITHTCR*)

Four of these shares are taken as policy driven and taken as exogenous. These are *SIAR*, *SEGWSR*, and *SICRR*, *SIMQR*. *SFIEBR* is determined residually. The share of the agricultural sector in the total increment to net fixed stock has been falling over time. From a value of about 55 percent in the early 1950s, its value has fallen to about 5.5 percent. From the viewpoint over all food security and for its strategic position, the share of agricultural investment in total fixed capital stock is kept at 6 percent throughout the forecast period up to 2030. Since the sum of the eight sectoral investment shares should add to 1, one of these is residually determined. The remaining four sectoral investment ratios are determined by a VAR model, which is embedded into the overall model as a recursive block.

Aggregate Capital Stock

23. *KR* = *KR*(–1) + *GIR*

A2. Aggregate demand: Private consumption expenditure at 1999–2000 prices

1. *LCPR* = *F*(*D*58, *D*59, *D*79, *D*81, *D*95, *LCPR*(–1), *LDRATIO*, *LPVDYR*, *S*95)

Since the dependency ratio is an important influence, this equation is estimated in two steps. First, the equation is estimated without the lagged variable, i.e. only with the private disposable income (*PVDYR*) and the dependency ratio. A structural break is identified in 1981 and introduced in the parameter with respect to the income variable. The coefficient of the dependency ratio is then fixed. Using that as a restriction on the coefficient of the *DRATIO* variable, the equation is re-estimated using the lagged-dependent variable.

Government consumption expenditure at 1999–2000 prices

2. *LCG* = *F*(*LCBPRE*, *LCG*)

Government consumption is directly related to government's primary revenue expenditure. This equation merely translates the budgetary primary revenue expenditure into the government consumption constraint in the National Income accounts. Government includes not only administrative departments but also the public sector enterprises.

Private investment expenditure at 1999–2000 prices

3. *LIPR* = *F*(*LDRATIO*, *LIPR*, *LPVDYR*, *LRLN*)

Government investment expenditure at 1999–2000 prices

4. *LIGR* = *F*(*LCBFDD*, *LIGR*)

Exports (in rupees at 1999–2000 prices)

5. $LEXPR = F(LEXPR, LWEXP)$

Exports depend on growth of world exports which in turn depend on growth of world income. Unit value of exports by itself or relative to unit value of imports was not found to be significant. Since the current account deficit is being generated through a rule, imports get determined through an identity described later.

Indirect taxes net of subsidies

6. $LIDLS = F(D90, LCBITR, LIDLS)$

Indirect taxes net of subsidies are at current prices. This term is used for taking the GDP at factor cost to GDP at market prices. It is linked to the combined indirect taxes and this equation links the budgetary aggregate to the income accounting aggregate after deflating it by the implicit price deflator of GDP at market prices, defined below.

GDP at market prices (at constant 1999–2000 prices)

7. $YMR = YR + IDLS/PYN$

Change in stock (CIS; real sector closure)

8. $QYMR = YMR - (CPR + CG/PYR + IPR + IGR + EXPR - IMPR)$

GDP at current market prices

9. $YN = YMR * PYN$

Gross fixed investment

10. $GGIR = IPR + IGR - CFCR - WGIR$

Private disposable income

11. $PVDYR = YR - WPVDYR$

B. Fiscal sector: Since both direct and indirect taxes are undergoing extensive reforms, we expect them not to follow a historical path. In both cases, these are generated by buoyancy parameters that are subject to exogenous control.

Combined direct taxes

1. $CBDTR = (1 + BCBDTR * GYN) * CBDTR(-1)$

Combined indirect taxes

2. $CBITR = (1 + BCBITR * GYN) * CBITR(-1)$

Since a revenue deficit rule is followed, if interest payments are determined within the model, then primary revenue expenditure will get determined through an identity. The revenue receipts on the combined account of central and state governments are given by the following identity where non-tax revenues are exogenous.

Primary revenue expenditure

3. $CBPRE = CBRD + CBRR - CBIP$

Combined fiscal deficit (rule)

4. $CBFDD = YN(-1) * FDRATIOLAG$

Combined debt

5. $CBDEBT = CBDEBT(-1) + CBFDD$

Effective interest rate on government debt

6. $LCBEIR = F(D64, D66, LCBEIR, LRLN)$

Interest payment (on combined account of central and state governments)

7. $CBIP = CBEIR * CBDEBT(-1)$

C. Monetary sector: Money supply rule

1. $M3 = M3(-1) * [1 + GYR(-1)]$

Nominal long-term interest rate

2. $LRLN = F(LRLN, LRSN)$

Nominal short-term interest rate

3. $LRSN = F[DLM3, IPR(-1), RSN(-1)]$

The monetary sector closure requires that demand for money should be set equal to supply of money. Since demand for money is a function of the interest rate, the monetary sector closure is used to determine the short-term interest rate, which is linked to the long-term rate through a term structure.

Change in money supply

4. $DLM3 = LM3 - LM3(-1)$

D. External sector: External investment

1. $LFINV = F(LFINV, LYR)$

Current account surplus

2. $CAS = CASRATIO * YN$

The current account surplus is determined by an exogenous rule that gradually reduces its level relative to GDP. From this, the trade balance can be determined. Given other current transfers, either exports or imports will be determined by the balance of payments identity. We select imports to be determined by this rule since exports are less under the control of an economy.

Trade balance

3. $TBL = CAS - NIB$

Imports at constant prices

4. $IMPR = ((EXPR * PEXP/100) - TBL) * (100/PIMP)$

E. Prices: Implicit price deflator of GDP at factor cost

1. $LPYR = F(LM3, LPYR, LYR)$

This is the basic price equation in which both output and money supply are used. All the remaining price equations are linking equations that are linked to the implicit price deflator of GDP at factor cost.

Implicit price deflator of GDP at market prices

2. $LPYN = F(D62, D69, D80, LPYR, S69, S80)$

Implicit price deflator of investment goods

3. $LPI = F(D72, D98, LPI, LPYR, S72, S98, TT)$

Unit value of imports (index, 1999–2000 = 100)

4. $LPIMP = F(D75, LPIMP, LPYR)$

Unit value index of exports ((index, 1999–2000 = 100)

5. $LPEXP = F(D64, D74, D91, LPEXP, LPYR, S64, S74)$

Thus, the model has 54 equations with the following sector-wise equations:

Real sector: aggregate supply side: 23

Real sector: aggregate demand side: 11

Fiscal, monetary and external sectors: 20

Exogenous Variables

Exogenous variables: There are 16 exogenous variables (excluding structural break dummies) of which six are policy variables.

Policy variables: *BCBDTR*, *BCBITR*, *CASRATIO*, *CBRDRATIO*, *FDRATIOLAG*, *GM3*

Investment shares: *SIAR*, *SICRR*, *SIFIEBR*

Others: *DRAIN10*, *DRATIO*, *CBNTR*, *NIB*, *WEXP*, *WGIR*, *WPVDYR*

The structural break dummies are given in Table 4.3.

Estimation Methodology

Equations are estimated by two-stage least squares with a set of instruments for the first stage. The sample period is from 1950–51 to 2008–09. In the case of levels of variables, the following predetermined variables are used commonly as instruments. In addition, there are equation-specific variables that incorporate all other predetermined variables appearing in the equation.

Table 4.3
Structural break dummies

1950s	*1960s*		*1970s*		*1980s*		*1990s*	*Current Decade*
D55	*D62*	*S64*	*D71*	*S72*	*D80*	*S80*	*D90*	*D101*
D58	*D64*	*S65*	*D72*	*S74*	*D81*	*S88*	*D91*	*D102*
D59	*D65*	*S67*	*D73*		*D83*	*S91*	*D92*	*D103*
	D66	*S69*	*D74*		*D84*	*S93*	*D93*	*D104*
	D67		*D75*		*D85*	*S95*	*D94*	
	D68		*D78*		*D88*	*S98*	*D95*	
	D69		*D79*				*D96*	
							D98	
							D99	

Source: Prepared by the authors.

*C, TT, DRAIN*10, *LWEXP, LCBPRE, LYAR*(–1), *LYMANR*(–1), *LYCSPR*(–1), *LYFIEBR*(–1), *LYTHTCR*(–1), *LYCRR*(–1), *LKAR*(–1), *LKMANR*(–1), *LCBITR*(–1), *LCPR*(–1), *LIPR*(–1)

All variables are tested for stationarity. It has been shown that most aggregate variables in the Indian economy can be seen (a) either as trend-stationary with structural breaks or (b) first-order integrated series with or without structural breaks (Srivastava et al., 2010). For details of estimated equations and other model details, see Srivastava (2011). This raises the problem whether structural relations should be estimated using co-integration and error correction or by using structural breaks along with co-breaking. In this model, we have used error correction wherever the error correction term is significant. In other words, all equations are estimated first in levels to estimate the long-run equilibrium relation. Then, the first difference of the levels provides the dynamics around the long-run equilibrium relation. In case of structural breaks, we use the equation in levels along with the error, which is taken as an exogenous variable.

Forecasts

For generating the forecasts, projections for exogenous variables are provided by the following procedures:

*DRAIN*10*:* This is dummy variable reflecting drought years where average annual rainfall is less by a margin of 10 percent or more from the long-run average. This has a value of 1 every four years from the last observed shortfall year, reflecting roughly the four-year cycle of rainfall. Other years are kept at zero.

DRATIO: Dependency ratio. The forecasts are taken from the UN projections.

FDRATIOLAG: This reflects the target ratio of fiscal deficit to GDP at market prices. As the target is taken as 6 percent of current year GDP, it is kept at 6.15 percent of previous year's GDP at market prices after an adjustment period that extends up to 2014–15 so that it is brought down from its present level in incremental steps.

SIAR: This is the share of investment in agriculture in total increase in net fixed capital stock. This ratio is exogenously determined to ensure that at least 6 percent of increase in net fixed capital stock is invested in agriculture. Historically, this ratio has been coming down and during 2005–06 to 2008–09 it had fallen below 6 percent. The agriculture sector does not attract much investment from private sector since its growth rate is low and subject to high volatility, implying that risk adjusted return to agriculture is low. From a strategic viewpoint, the government must ensure that the share of investment in agriculture does not fall below the current levels.

The estimated equations are described in detail in Srivastava (2011). The error correction mechanism is used in the case of the following demand side equations:

1. Private consumption expenditure (LCPRE)
2. Private investment expenditure (LIPE)
3. Exports (LEXPR)

On the production side, it is used in one case, agriculture, where the long-term relation itself has a cyclical pattern. In other cases, short-term dynamics is not emphasized.

SICRR: This is the share of investment in construction in total increase in net fixed capital stock. This ratio is exogenously determined to ensure that at least 4 percent of increase in net fixed capital stock is invested in this sector. Historically, this ratio has been low although it has been rising marginally. It is a low capital high growth sector. Its minimum investment is kept at 4 percent of increase in net fixed capital stock.

SIFIEBR: This is the share of investment in financial services, real estate and insurance. This ratio is exogenously determined to ensure that at least 11 percent of increase in net fixed capital stock is invested in agriculture. Historically, this ratio has been low although it has been rising marginally. It is also a low capital high growth sector. Its minimum investment is kept at 4 percent of increase in net fixed capital stock.

WEXP: Index of world exports. This is assumed to grown at 10 percent per annum in the forecast period.

WGIR: This indicates investment in valuables, inventories, errors and omissions, and statistical discrepancies taken into account in the National Income Accounts in arriving at gross investments.

Table 4.4
Aggregate demand variables: Growth rates (in percent per annum)

Year	*Private Consumption Expenditure*	*Private Investment Expenditure*	*Government Investment Expenditure*	*Exports*	*Imports*
2011–12	7.088	8.557	1.455	24.931	21.804
2012–13	6.624	9.162	1.638	1.997	3.488
2013–14	6.753	10.515	1.949	–4.390	–2.391
2014–15	6.536	11.033	2.251	7.487	8.148
2015–16	6.015	10.782	2.487	21.005	19.582
2016–17	6.995	11.652	2.665	20.131	18.810
2017–18	6.251	11.393	2.871	11.957	11.332
2018–19	6.823	11.980	3.017	6.014	5.917
2019–20	6.582	12.003	3.175	7.767	7.618
2020–21	6.426	11.944	3.302	12.949	12.526
2021–22	7.262	12.451	3.406	14.151	13.752
2022–23	6.862	12.680	3.539	12.442	12.165
2023–24	7.422	13.390	3.629	9.463	9.344
2024–25	6.985	13.297	3.727	9.550	9.399
2025–26	8.169	14.664	3.785	9.629	9.463
2026–27	7.753	14.648	3.886	10.881	10.633
2027–28	8.514	15.707	3.943	10.266	10.008
2028–29	8.205	15.832	4.017	9.995	9.688
2029–30	9.458	17.435	4.055	8.252	7.926

Source: Based on model projections.

WPVDYR: This term reflects net transfer of payments to private sector. It is assumed to grow at 15 percent per annum in the forecast period (Table 4.4).

An increasing trend is observed for both private consumption and investment expenditure growth rates, with the rates being nearly 10 and 17 percent, respectively, by 2029–30. Rate of growth of exports and imports fluctuates a lot owing to changing external demand conditions, but finally settles at around 10 percent for both by 2023–24 (Table 4.5).

Table 4.5
Implicit price deflators: Inflation rates (in percent per annum)

Year	*Implicit Price Deflator of Exports*	*Implicit Price Deflator of Investment Goods*	*Implicit Price Deflator of Imports*	*Implicit Price Deflator of GDP at Market Prices*	*Implicit Price Deflator of GDP at Factor Cost*
2011–12	8.935	6.916	8.089	8.092	8.135
2012–13	7.566	6.462	6.268	6.899	6.934
2013–14	6.111	6.065	4.940	6.022	6.052
2014–15	5.172	5.810	4.438	5.562	5.588
2015–16	4.898	5.733	4.585	5.552	5.579
2016–17	4.925	5.693	4.832	5.497	5.524
2017–18	5.097	5.720	5.021	5.624	5.651
2018–19	5.241	5.742	5.083	5.670	5.698
2019–20	5.330	5.765	5.090	5.727	5.754
2020–21	5.415	5.802	5.133	5.826	5.854
2021–22	5.369	5.773	5.077	5.694	5.722
2022–23	5.247	5.732	4.958	5.588	5.614
2023–24	5.048	5.659	4.774	5.386	5.411
2024–25	4.890	5.613	4.645	5.304	5.329
2025–26	4.645	5.508	4.439	5.001	5.024
2026–27	4.370	5.407	4.204	4.768	4.790
2027–28	4.043	5.279	3.924	4.446	4.465
2028–29	3.760	5.179	3.698	4.242	4.260
2029–30	3.399	5.027	3.399	3.839	3.854

Source: Based on model projections.

The inflation rate (implicit price deflator of GDP at market prices) falls to just above 5.5 percent per annum by 2014–15, and thereafter steadily falls to about 4 percent by 2029–30. Inflation rates with respect to other implicit price deflators also show a similar time path. Only the empirical price deflator with respect to the investment goods remains higher than 5 percent per annum (Tables 4.6a and b).

Industrial output and manufacturing show a fairly steady rate of growth. Mining and quarrying rate remains stable at around 6 percent per annum. The case of interest is the agriculture sector, which shows considerable

Table 4.6a
Sectoral outputs: Growth rates (in percent per annum)

Year	*Agriculture and Allied Services*	*Industrial Output*	*Manufacturing*	*Mining and Quarrying*	*Electricity, Gas and Water Supply*
2011–12	7.730	6.476	6.380	6.322	7.306
2012–13	3.950	6.352	6.353	5.848	6.820
2013–14	5.696	6.361	6.470	5.504	6.382
2014–15	3.925	6.153	6.313	5.180	5.923
2015–16	–1.094	6.056	6.297	4.862	5.439
2016–17	11.039	5.984	6.170	5.135	5.430
2017–18	1.465	5.710	5.814	5.284	5.349
2018–19	7.706	6.096	6.282	5.474	5.317
2019–20	3.107	5.989	6.138	5.609	5.252
2020–21	0.295	6.141	6.422	5.307	4.828
2021–22	11.128	6.166	6.419	5.560	4.829
2022–23	2.758	6.060	6.274	5.710	4.763
2023–24	8.375	6.533	6.847	5.879	4.717
2024–25	–1.577	6.545	6.864	5.954	4.591
2025–26	14.521	6.857	7.231	6.134	4.545
2026–27	2.292	6.716	7.056	6.211	4.404
2027–28	10.647	7.396	7.888	6.333	4.284
2028–29	–1.180	7.417	7.918	6.372	4.077
2029–30	16.530	7.878	8.466	6.519	3.940

Source: Based on model projections.

fluctuations and variations in the rates. This is occurring on account of the built-in cyclical trend in the model to take note of the climate cycles. Since agrarian sector is highly weather-dependent in India, the trends reflect the impact of droughts (or any similar calamity, with an occurrence rate of every four years on average) on agricultural growth performance.

In the disaggregated analysis of service sector, it is found that the sub-sector of trade, hotels, transport and communications services have highest growth rates. After a falling trend till 2018–19, the sector shows a sustained increase in rate of growth (14 percent in 2029–30). Construction sector reveals growth, albeit at a falling rate. From 9 percent in 2010–11, it falls to

Table 4.6b
Sectoral outputs: Growth rates (in percent per annum)

Year	*Construction*	*Community, Social and Public Services*	*Financial, Real Estate, and Business Services*	*Trade, Hotels, Transport and Communications*	*GDP at Factor Cost*
2010–11	9.404	10.196	9.248	10.544	8.660
2011–12	8.962	9.539	9.799	10.251	8.930
2012–13	8.542	8.987	10.519	9.638	8.182
2013–14	8.024	8.503	10.174	9.558	8.289
2014–15	7.654	8.124	10.098	9.632	7.965
2015–16	7.419	7.844	9.675	9.576	7.182
2016–17	7.210	7.879	8.463	9.679	8.591
2017–18	7.069	7.887	9.610	9.717	7.564
2018–19	6.942	7.930	8.923	9.693	8.305
2019–20	6.793	7.946	9.452	10.093	7.984
2020–21	6.787	7.842	9.171	10.173	7.708
2021–22	6.695	8.011	8.429	10.512	8.936
2022–23	6.693	8.167	9.706	10.716	8.374
2023–24	6.686	8.336	9.319	10.903	9.095
2024–25	6.661	8.461	9.965	11.431	8.455
2025–26	6.753	8.701	8.891	11.796	10.085
2026–27	6.827	8.906	10.714	12.310	9.517
2027–28	6.948	9.172	10.132	12.631	10.504
2028–29	7.007	9.393	11.058	13.448	10.034
2029–30	7.211	9.751	9.895	13.998	11.744

Source: Based on model projections.

approximately 7 percent. But this may be due to saturation in this particular field. All other sectors show robust growth, with an initial declining trend which transforms into an increasing trend from around 2020. It may be noted that the forecasts aim to capture the potential growth rather than actual growth (Table 4.7).

The share of combined direct and indirect taxes shows a steady increase. They account for one-fourth share relative to GDP from around 2025–26. The fiscal trend is encouraging, with government debt following a declining

Table 4.7
Fiscal variables: Relative to GDP at market prices (percent)

Year	*Combined Direct Taxes*	*Combined Indirect Taxes*	*Combined Interest Payments*	*Combined Fiscal Deficit*	*Government Primary Revenue Expenditure*	*Government Debt*
2010–11	7.373	9.743	4.941	6.752	21.24	65.726
2011–12	7.593	9.743	4.861	6.380	19.94	62.292
2012–13	7.593	9.808	4.831	6.058	18.87	59.965
2013–14	7.789	9.935	4.790	6.011	18.09	58.251
2014–15	7.980	10.118	4.776	6.052	17.37	57.147
2015–16	8.167	10.354	4.807	6.095	16.67	56.572
2016–17	8.375	10.619	4.791	6.018	17.04	55.357
2017–18	8.577	10.875	4.824	6.068	17.38	54.751
2018–19	8.795	11.151	4.836	6.024	17.75	53.820
2019–20	9.015	11.430	4.867	6.038	18.12	53.136
2020–21	9.238	11.712	4.918	6.048	17.48	52.623
2021–22	9.482	12.022	4.928	5.987	17.91	51.644
2022–23	9.723	12.327	4.976	6.024	18.32	51.111
2023–24	9.978	12.651	5.015	5.995	18.76	50.405
2024–25	10.228	12.967	5.096	6.036	19.16	50.127
2025–26	10.506	13.320	5.127	5.963	19.66	49.280
2026–27	10.778	13.664	5.201	6.007	20.12	48.912
2027–28	11.068	14.032	5.258	5.972	20.63	48.302
2028–29	11.353	14.394	5.356	6.009	21.11	48.074
2029–30	11.669	14.795	5.403	5.939	21.68	47.321

Source: Based on model projections.

trend. In addition, the fiscal deficit is stable at around 6 percent of GDP, and combined interest payments show only a marginal increase in the period under study. A notable thing is the rise in government primary revenue expenditure. The additional fiscal space for higher primary revenue expenditure comes mainly by an increase in the tax–GDP ratio, both from the side of direct taxes and indirect taxes (Table 4.8).

Private consumption expenditure registers a decline, but is matched with a corresponding rise in private investment spending. The domestic

Table 4.8
Aggregate demand variables: Relative to GDP at market prices (percent)

Year	*Private Consumption Expenditure*	*Private Investment Expenditure*	*Government Investment Expenditure*	*Exports*	*Imports*
2010–11	59.212	25.840	7.357	30.133	34.878
2011–12	58.211	25.751	6.852	34.559	38.999
2012–13	57.372	25.985	6.437	32.583	37.307
2013–14	56.558	26.519	6.060	28.768	33.628
2014–15	55.809	27.272	5.740	28.641	33.685
2015–16	55.202	28.188	5.488	32.334	37.582
2016–17	54.391	28.983	5.189	35.771	41.118
2017–18	53.727	30.014	4.962	37.231	42.559
2018–19	52.992	31.033	4.720	36.444	41.620
2019–20	52.304	32.188	4.510	36.371	41.480
2020–21	51.682	33.454	4.325	38.140	43.335
2021–22	50.888	34.534	4.106	39.966	45.251
2022–23	50.178	35.906	3.923	41.467	46.834
2023–24	49.408	37.319	3.726	41.606	46.941
2024–25	48.739	38.986	3.564	42.027	47.349
2025–26	47.890	40.607	3.360	41.852	47.082
2026–27	47.119	42.509	3.187	42.374	47.561
2027–28	46.270	44.510	2.998	42.282	47.348
2028–29	45.501	46.856	2.834	42.267	47.199
2029–30	44.570	49.242	2.639	40.946	45.587

Source: Based on model projections.

economy, therefore, does not face any deficiency in aggregate demand. A feature that stands out is the increasing role of private sector investment in driving demand. Share of government investment expenditure falls steadily, while that of private sector increases. Further, projections reveal that India will get increasingly integrated with the world economy, as the market share of exports and imports as a percentage of GDP increase to almost 40 percent by 2029–30.

4.3.5 Concluding Observations

In this section, besides providing an overview of the overall methodological framework adopted in this study, we have described the macro-econometric framework developed for projecting aggregate demand based on a disaggregated growth profile of the Indian economy. The final demand vector consisting of consumption, investment and net exports can then be used in conjunction with the input–output model to generate the pollution loads up to 2029–30. Economic growth is projected in a policy framework that supports growth and takes into account anticipated structural changes.

The main features of the macro projections may be summarized as follows:

1. The share of the agriculture sector falls to about 7 percent of GDP and that of the service sector increases to about 80 percent.
2. The tax–GDP ratio increases to about 25 percent of GDP by 2029–30.
3. The Indian economy becomes more globalized: market share of exports as percentage of GDP increases to more than 40 percent of GDP by 2029–30.
4. The domestic consumption demand falls but it is compensated largely, by an increase in domestic investment demand.
5. The key feature of the Indian economy in the next two decades will be the increasing role of private investment.
6. The results depend on adequate progress in infrastructure projects which will also contribute to improving the human capital. The model provides for additional fiscal capacity for the needed expenditure on infrastructure and human development sectors. If this additional fiscal capacity is not created, then realized growth will be less than the projected growth.

4.4 SECTORAL DISAGGREGATION IN AN INPUT–OUTPUT FRAMEWORK

4.4.1 Description of IOTs

The CSO publishes IOTs every five years. These tables provide the sale and purchase relationships between producers and consumers in an economy. For the purpose of our analysis, we have used the latest IOTs corresponding to the year 2006–07. Two crucial matrices that help us understand the flow of goods and services (final and intermediate) in an economy are the input flow and output flow matrices. While the input flow matrix tabulates the value of each commodity that flows as an input into each industry, the output flow matrix tabulates the value of output of each commodity produced by each industry. Both these matrices—the input flow matrix and the output flow matrix—are presented at a 130-sector disaggregation level.

In the input flow matrix, different commodities form the rows and different industries form the columns. The sum across columns for each row gives the total use of that particular commodity as input (in ₹ lakhs) for industrial use which is given as IIUSE in a separate column. In addition to this, private final consumption expenditure (PFCE), government final consumption expenditure (GFCE), gross fixed capital formation (GFCF), CIS and net imports for each commodity are given as separate columns. The sum of PFCE, GFCE, GFCF, CIS (EXP – IMP) gives total final use (TFUSE) for each commodity which is the final demand vector. Summing TFUSE across commodities gives the overall GDP of the economy. Output of a commodity is given as the sum of its use as input in all the industries plus the final demand and hence is the sum of IIUSE and TFUSE.

The sum across rows for each column gives the total inputs (in ₹ lakhs) of all commodities that are used by a particular industry. In addition to this, net indirect taxes (NIT) and the GVA for each industry are given as separate rows. The sum of NIT and GVA across industries gives the overall GDP of the economy and matches with the sum of TFUSE across commodities. Output of an industry is given as the sum of total inputs that the industry uses along with NIT and GVA. In order to maintain consistency, the value of output across industries equals the value of output across commodities.

In the make matrix, the sum across columns gives the total output of that industry, whereas the sum across rows gives the total output of commodities. Again, to be consistent, the total output of industry equals the total output of commodities.

4.4.2 Estimation of Leontief Matrix

The Leontief matrix for 2006–07 is not explicitly provided by CSO at the time of this analysis. However, it is possible to estimate the Leontief matrix from the absorption and make matrices which are available for 2006–07.

The CSO manual states the method and the assumptions followed by the statistical agency in deriving other related matrices from the absorption and make matrices. Two assumptions can be made for analysing outputs of secondary products, namely (a) *industry technology assumption* where input structure of a secondary product is considered to be similar to that of the industry where it has been produced and (b) *commodity technology assumption* where the input structure of the secondary product of an industry is assumed to be similar to that of the industry where it is primarily produced. Besides these two main assumptions, the mixed technology assumption which includes the characteristics of both industry and commodity technology is followed. In the present analysis, industry technology has been assumed uniformly for all sectors.

Using the methodology described in CSO, the (commodity × industry) coefficient matrix (B), the product mix matrix (C) and market share matrix (D) are calculated. Further, assuming industry technology, the (commodity × commodity) coefficient matrix (A) and the (industry × industry) coefficient matrix (E) is derived using the following relationship:

$$A = BD; E = DB.$$

The Leontief inverse is then computed for both the matrices as $(I - A)^{-1}$ and $(I - E)^{-1}$ where I is an identity matrix of the same dimension as A or E.

4.4.3 Reducing Matrix Dimensions

As mentioned earlier, the input–output matrices are available at a 130-industry disaggregation level. However, the pollution coefficients from IPPS database used to calculate pollution load are available only for 51 industries. Therefore, in order to facilitate the calculation of pollution load, the 130 industries are aggregated into 51 industries. Three important considerations are made while aggregating the 130 industries into 51 industries: (a) the polluting nature of the industry; (b) industries which contribute more than 5 percent of the total GVA in 2006–07 are treated as separate industries and (c) industries where cascading will continue in the existing GST framework such as beverages (alcohol) and petroleum are not merged with other industries (Table 4.9).

Table 4.9
Mapping of input–output sectors with IOTT sectors

Industry	*Group-code*	*IOTT Sectors*
Animal husbandry	1	21–24
Banking and insurance	2	118, 199
Beverages	3	44
Cash crop	4	8–13, 17
Cement	5	75
Ceramic	6	74
Coal and lignite	7	27
Coal tar products	8	64
Communication	9	115
Construction	10	106
Crude oil	11	29
Drugs and medicines	12	70
Edible oil	13	40, 41
Electrical machinery and equipment	14	88–91, 93
Electricity	15	107
Electronic and non-electrical machinery	16	87, 92, 94
Fertilizers and pesticides	17	67, 68
Fishing	18	26
Food crops	19	1–7
Forestry and logging	20	25
Fruits and vegetables	21	18, 19
Gas and water supply	22	108
Industrial chemical except fertilizer and other chemicals	23	65, 66, 69, 71
Integrated iron and steel	24	77–79
Leather and leather products	25	59, 60
Machinery, tools and implements	26	83–86
Mineral products	27	30–37
Miscellaneous food products	28	43
Miscellaneous manufacturing	29	101–105

Table 4.9 continued

Table 4.9 continued

Industry	*Group-code*	*IOTT Sectors*
Miscellaneous metal products	30	81, 82
Natural gas	31	28
Non-ferrous basic metals	32	80
Other chemicals	33	73
Other crops	34	20
Other non-metallic mineral prods.	35	76
Otherservices1	36	114, 117, 120–128
Otherservices2	37	129, 130
Paper, paper prods. and newsprint	38	57, 58
Petroleum products	39	63
Plantation crop	40	14–16
Plastic products	41	62
Rail and other transport equipment	42	95–100
Railway and other transport service	43	109–113
Rubber products	44	61
Sugar	45	38, 39
Synthetic fibres, resin	46	72
Tea and coffee processing	47	42
Textiles and apparel	48	46–54
Tobacco products	49	45
Trade	50	116
Wood and wood products	51	55, 56

Source: Prepared by the authors.

4.4.4 Mapping Scheme for Industries

Having collapsed the original 130 × 130 input–output matrices into 51 × 51 matrices, we obtain Leontief inverse of the (industry × industry) coefficient matrix (E) with a 51 × 51 dimension which is in line with the vector of pollution coefficients. However, the macro-model provides final demand only at an eight-sector disaggregation which is divided into 14 sectors using the ratio of GVA of that sector to total GVA in 2006–07. Hence, it is required

Table 4.10
Mapping 130 industries to 14 sectors

Sector/industry	*Sec code*	*IOT Code*
Agriculture and allied	1	1–26
Mining and quarrying		
Coal and lignite	2	27
Crude petrol	3	29
Other mining, N.E.C.	4	28,30–37
Manufacturing		
Petroleum products including LPG	5	63
Other polluting goods	6	38–39, 46–51, 56–60, 64–75, 77–80
Beverages including alcoholic beverages	7	44
Remaining manufacturing goods N.E.C.	8	40–43, 52–55, 61–62, 76, 81–105
Construction	9	106
Electricity, gas and water supply	10	107, 108
Transport, storage and communication	11	109–115
Trade, hotels and restaurants	12	116–117
Financial services, real estate and other services	13	118–120
Community, social and personal services	14	121–130

Source: Prepared by the authors.
N.E.C.: not elsewhere classified.

to map these 14 sectors into 51 industries so as to get a more disaggregated final demand (net of taxes). To this end, we first map the 14 sectors to the 130 industries (as the mapping is clearly defined, see Table 4.10) and then aggregate the final demand (net of taxes) of 130 industries into 51 industries as described earlier.

After mapping the 14 sectors to the 130 industries, the final demand (net of taxes) of each of the 14 sectors is divided amongst the corresponding industries (from the 130 industries). This division is based on the proportion of GVA contributed by a particular industry in relation to the sum of GVA contributed by all the industries constituting a particular group in 2006–07. Once the final demand of eight sectors is mapped to

130 industries, it is then collapsed to 51 industries based on the mapping as given in Table 4.9.

4.5 ECO-TAXES IN GST FRAMEWORK: REVENUE POTENTIAL

4.5.1 Introduction

The macro-model discussed in Section 4.3 produces a set of sectoral outputs comprising eight sectors. These outputs are used to meet the final demand in these sectors. However, in generating these outputs, considerable intermediate outputs are also required. These intermediate outputs are important both for the determination of the pollution impact of meeting the sectoral final demands as also for generating indirect tax revenue in a system in which cascading to a partial extent continues. To take these considerations into account, we combine the macro-model, which is more aggregated but provides a longer-term dynamic perspective with an IOT which is more disaggregated but gives a static perspective as the input–output coefficients are with reference to a specific year. In the present analysis, we use the 2006–07 IOT for the Indian economy.

The projected outputs can be used to generate the pollution load by multiplying the vector of outputs at constant 1999–2000 prices with the pollution load coefficient vector. The matrix of intermediate output and the vector of final demand/outputs can also be used to generate tax revenue from taxation of goods and services. Since tax revenue is in nominal terms, the tax base would need to be defined at current prices by multiplying the constant price matrices by a vector of implicit price deflators.

Given the current debate on GST, it is likely that some taxation of intermediate outputs will continue and some cascading may also continue. Tax revenue from intermediate outputs will relate to the exempt sectors and the goods that are subject to excises like tobacco and alcoholic beverages. Similarly, as per the present discussion, petroleum products will be out of GST and in their respect cascading type of taxation will continue. In our scheme, the polluting inputs or inputs that are used intensively in producing polluting outputs should also be subjected to a non-rebatable excise or cess and in their case also cascading will continue. Exports will be zero-rated and in their respect any taxation of inputs under GST will be rebated.

Many exercises that have recently been undertaken with a view to calculating the revenue neutral rate (RNR) like Poddar and Bagchi (2007), Task Force on GST (2009), NCAER (2009), Kavita Rao (2010) and Empowered Committee (EC) of State Finance Ministers have all focused on working out an RNR limited to taxes on goods and services to be merged in the GST. In this study, we consider options for the taxation of goods and services in a broader framework covering all taxation of goods and services in a longer-term perspective. This covers imports duties as well as domestic taxation including the taxation of petroleum products, taxation of vehicles, stamp duty and registration fees, taxation of alcoholic beverages, and excises and cesses on polluting inputs and outputs. In this framework, the GST rates and revenue potential options are considered.

Over the longer run, as the Indian economy is progressively more globalized, the external sector, and consequently the import duties will continue to play an important role. Import duties are meant first to neutralize any cost disadvantages that domestic producers may be facing. Thus, inclusive of import duties, the prices of the imported goods may be such that domestically produced goods remain competitive. Over and above this 'protection' role, there may be countervailing duty on imports that are equal to the tax rate for the domestically produced goods both under GST and for the cascading type of taxes. Under the GST, imports that are used as intermediate goods, the countervailing duty equivalent to the GST rate will be rebated at later stages of the value-added chain. Only the cascading type of levies will not be rebated.

The IOT reports indirect taxes net of subsidies. The indirect taxes here include central and state taxes on goods and services. In addition to this, the local taxes on goods are also included. The present analysis focuses only on the central and state taxes. Since net indirect taxes, that is indirect taxes net of subsidies, are given sector-wise, it would be useful to separate the indirect taxes and subsidies for the desired level of disaggregation. Cascading type of taxes that may continue are state excise duties, electricity duty, purchase tax if it is allowed to continue under GST, entry tax/octroi, tax on petroleum products, non-rebatable component of tax on polluting goods and services, mandi tax, and municipal taxes and cesses. Compared to 2006–07, when CST was at 4 percent, in the GST regime the CST would go away.

4.5.2 Macro-model and IOT

As described earlier, the macro-model and the IOT are used together for the generation of pollution and indirect taxes. For this purpose, the following steps are utilized:

1. *Disaggregation of output into 14 sectors:* In the macro-model, output at factor cost is generated for eight sectors. These are further disaggregated into 14 sectors. These sectors are chosen at the appropriate level of aggregation keeping in mind implications both of taxation and pollution.
2. *Generation of intermediate output:* Intermediate output is generated linked to the projected domestic output.
3. *Definition of tax bases:* The relevant tax bases are defined by using both intermediate demand for cascading type of taxes and domestic output that is domestically used, i.e. netting out exports and adding that part of import that goes for final consumption. Tax bases are distinguished according to the possibility of application of differential rates in the GST framework.
4. *Generation of tax revenue:* Tax revenues are generated by application of sectoral tax rates, sectoral subsidies, cascading taxes and non-cascading taxes.

These steps are described in detail below.

a. Disaggregation of Output and Imports

In the model described in Section 4.3, output was disaggregated into the following eight sectors defined at 1999–2000 prices:

1. Agriculture and allied sectors (*YAR*)
2. Mining and quarrying (*YMQR*)
3. Manufacturing (*YMANR*)
4. Construction (*YCRR*)
5. Electricity, gas and water supply (*YEGWSR*)
6. Financial, real estate and business services (*YFIEBR*)
7. Trade, hotels, transport and storage services (*YTHTCR*)
8. Community, social and personal services (*YCSPR*)

Given the relative importance of sub-sectors from the viewpoint both of pollution and GST, the following sectors are further divided.

Mining and quarrying output: The mining and quarrying sector output (YMQR) is further divided into three sectors using sub-sectoral shares as defined below:

Output of coal and lignite: $YCLR = AYCLR * YMQR$, where $AYCLR$ is the share of output of coal and lignite within the mining and quarrying sector.

Crude petroleum: $YCPETR = AYCPETR * YMQR$, where $AYCPETR$ is the share of output of coal and lignite within the mining and quarrying sector.

Correspondingly, other mining output may be determined as:

$$YOMQR = (1 - AYCLR - AYCPETR) * YMQR$$

Manufacturing sector: The manufacturing sector output is divided into four sub-sectors.

Petroleum products including liquefied petroleum and gas

$$YPETROLR = AYPETROL * YMANR,$$

where $AYPETROL$ is the share of output of petroleum products within the manufacturing sector.

Beverages group:

$$YBEVR = AYBEV * YMANR,$$

where $AYBEV$ is the share of output of beverages in the manufacturing sector.

Other polluting goods (mainly metals, plastics and leather)

$$YOPOLLR = AYPOLL * YMANR,$$

where $AYPOLL$ is the share of output of other polluting goods in the manufacturing sector.

Correspondingly, other manufacturing can be derived as follows:

$$YOMANR = (1 - AYPETROL - AYPOLL - AYBEV) * YMANR$$

Trade, hotels, transport, storage and communications: In the service sector, trade, hotels, transport and storage are divided into two sectors.

Transport, storage and communications,

$$YTCR = AYTHC * YTHTCR,$$

where *AYTHC* is the share of output of communications in the overall transport, storage and communications group of the service sector.

Correspondingly, output in trade, hotels and restaurants in this group is given by

$$YTHR = (1 - YTHC) * YTHTCR.$$

In all, there are six parameters used for this disaggregation. These are: *AYCLR*, *YCPETR*, *AYPETROL*, *AYBEVR*, *AYPOLL* and *AYTHC*. The others are residually determined. The parameter values, based on the 2006–07 IOT, are given in Table 4.11. The intra-sectoral shares are taken as fixed for the forecast period in the base run. However, sectoral outputs in terms of the eight-sector division changes in the forecast period as emerging from the macro-model.

A similar decomposition is needed for the corresponding groups with respect to imports. Imports are used as intermediate inputs or for final

Table 4.11
Intra-sectoral shares (2006–07)

	Variable Name	*Intra-sectoral Shares*
Mining and quarrying		
Coal and lignite	AYCLR	0.010
Crude petroleum	AYCPETR	0.022
Other M & Q	AYOMQR	0.968
Manufacturing		
Beverages	ABEVR	0.024
Petroleum products	AYPETROL	0.053
Other polluting goods	AYPOLL	0.192
Other manufactured goods	AYOMANR	0.732
Trade, hotels, transport, storage and communications		
Trade hotels and transport	AYTHT	0.587
Storage and communications	AYTHC	0.413

Source: Based on IOT 2006–07, CSO.

consumption. That part which is used for final consumption will add to the tax base of GST. The part used as inputs will be part of the tax base for cascading taxes. We need 14 coefficients to divide the overall imports into 14 sectors. In addition, one parameter is needed to divide imports into two components, namely that used for final demand and that used as inputs. Table 4.12 gives the relevant export and import shares. For the base solution, these intra-sectoral as well as export and import shares are taken as fixed. In effect, these shares are changing in line with the projected change in the concerned sectoral aggregate (mining and quarrying, manufacturing, trade, hotels, transport, storage and communication, aggregate exports and aggregate imports). These can be further changed in simulations keeping in mind the projections of the relevant sectoral aggregates.

b. Generation of Intermediate Demand

GDP at factor cost is divided into 14 sectors. That part of GDP which is exported will be zero-rated and will not constitute the tax base and needs to be deducted except for cascading taxes like petroleum products, alcoholic

Table 4.12
Sectoral shares of imports and exports

	Exports	*Imports*
Agriculture and allied sectors	0.034	0.017
Coal and lignite	0.000	0.010
Crude petroleum	0.001	0.139
Other mining, N.E.C.	0.054	0.082
Petroleum products including LPG	0.030	0.025
Other polluting goods	0.133	0.221
Beverages including alcoholic beverages	0.000	0.000
Remaining manufacturing goods N.E.C.	0.400	0.427
Construction	0.000	0.000
Electricity, gas and water supply	0.000	0.000
Transport, storage and communication	0.059	0.007
Trade, hotels and restaurants	0.099	0.017
Financial services, real estate and other services	0.010	0.016
Community, social and personal services	0.180	0.038

Source: Based on IOT 2006–07, CSO.

beverages and tobacco products. Imports can be subjected to the customs duty and the equivalent of countervailing GST. The countervailing duty will be rebated at different stages of value added and finally GST revenue will be collected only on that component of imports that is used directly for final consumption.

In the case of the exempt sectors and purchases by dealers below the threshold limits, where if the purchases are made from registered dealers, tax paid on intermediate uses will not be rebated at later stages. For petroleum, beverages and polluting goods also cascading may continue requiring estimation of intermediate use.

For this purposes, we have used the coefficients from the IOT:

1. $\Sigma a_{ij} = I_j/Z'_j$ (sum over i) indicates intermediate uses of the jth output for all i commodities, where Z'_j is the gross output of the jth sector inclusive of intermediate output, GVA and NIT_j.
2. The model projects values of GDP at factor cost, without indirect taxes net of subsidies, which is the GVA for the jth sector (say, X_j).
3. Intermediate use ratio with respect to gross output is recalculated as $i_j = I_j/Z_j$, where $Z_j = (Z'_j - NIT_j)$.
4. Since $Z_j = I_j + X_j$, we calculate I_j/X_j as follows:
   $X_j = Z_j - I_j = Z_j - i_j.Z_j = Z_j(1 - i_j)$
   or $Z_j = X_j/(1 - i_j)$
   or $I_j/X_j = i_j/(1 - i_j)$, where $i_j = \Sigma ea_{ij}$.

It is also useful to distinguish between intermediate use of the jth good/service within its own sector ($i = j$) and all other sectors.

Intermediate demand per unit of final value added (GDP at factor cost net of indirect taxes less subsidies) is generated by using the 2006–07 commodity by commodity (industry technology) matrix A. Table 4.13 gives the estimated sectoral input-use coefficients describing the proportion of output of any sector j used as inputs in the production of all goods and services (other than that used in own sectors).

In the case of petroleum products, we calculate intermediate use of petroleum products used in sectors other than petroleum products and crude petroleum as given vertical integration cascading may not be there in the intermediate use of petroleum products/crude petroleum within the sector. Similarly, in the case of beverages, intra-sector use of the product is taken out for calculating cascading.

Table 4.13
Intermediate use coefficients (wrt X_j) other than use in own sector

Agriculture and Allied	*Coal and Lignite*	*Crude Petroleum*	*Other Mining, N.E.C.*	*Petroleum Products Including LPG*	*Other Polluting Goods*	*Beverages Including Alcoholic Beverages*
0.32	0.27	0.27	0.20	0.82	0.74	0.70

Remaining Manufacturing Foods N.E.C.	*Construction*	*Electricity, Gas and Water Supply*	*Transport, Storage and Communication*	*Trade, Hotels and Restaurants*	*Financial Services, Real Estate and Other Services*	*Community, Social and Personal Services*
0.79	0.64	0.69	0.56	0.26	0.16	0.19

Source: Based on IOT 2006–07, CSO.

c. Adjustment for Prices

The output vector is projected in real terms at 1999–2000 prices and then converted into nominal terms. For this purpose, we require projection of sectoral prices for the forecast period. Additional equations for the implicit price deflators for the eight sectors of output are developed for this purpose, where each of these are linked to the deflator for the deflator of GDP at factor cost and other determinants. For the sub-sectors within the mining and quarrying, manufacturing, and transport, storage and communications and trade and hotels sector, the overall sectoral prices are used. Only in the case of petroleum products, an additional equation is developed. Each sectoral price is related to the overall price index (*PYR*) in the model and its own lagged terms and other determinants.

For the petroleum products, a price index is developed with reference to wholesale price index for the fuel group. The petroleum prices respond to the international crude oil prices and domestic tax rate on petroleum products. The prices for the polluting goods and beverages group are scaled up by a mark-up factor to reflect the influence of the higher rate of taxation compared to the core GST rate. The mark-up is a function of the elasticity of demand and the excess of the tax rate compared to core GST rate.

4.5.3 Estimation of GST Tax Base

Every sector will have a combination of cascading tax and non-cascading GST. For the cascading taxes, both intermediate and final outputs provide the tax base. For the GST, the final outputs provide the tax base.

Adjustments need to be made for exemptions and exports that will bear no tax. For estimating the tax base, we use the following steps:

1. GST base is taken as final demand proxied by domestic output net of exports plus imports meant for final consumption.
2. We estimate the base for taxation of un-rebated intermediate using the input–output coefficients and along with projection of sectoral outputs along with adjustments. This is needed for capturing (a) the tax base relating to exempt sectors where intermediate purchases are made from registered dealers and (b) for polluting goods, petroleum products, alcoholic beverages and tobacco where the whole or part of tax would be allowed to cascade.
3. Import duties and countervailing duty: projection of imports along with sectoral decomposition.
4. We also estimate the rebate that exporters would get on the GST paid on their intermediate purchases.

For a comparison, we look at the approaches followed by the Task Force on GST (2009) and the NCAER (2009) study on GST.

GST Base: Task Force of Thirteenth Finance Commission and NCAER Studies

For the estimation of the GST base, we make reference to one of the five approaches followed by the Task Force of the Thirteenth Finance Commission on GST (hereinafter the *Task Force*), namely, the approach that was based on the IOT. The *Task Force* took note of the fact that, in 2007–08, the combined statutory incidence of CENVAT, CST and State-level VAT on goods was in the range of 27–30 percent. The high rate also necessitated the need for multiple rates and multiple exemptions. The central taxes that are to be subsumed in the GST are CENVAT, service tax and countervailing duty on imports along with various cesses and surcharges. The central government will levy excise duties on petroleum products and tobacco products. The year of reference used by the Task Force is 2007–08.

We briefly discuss the various adjustments undertaken by the Task Force for calculating the RNR. The total collection from these central taxes in 2007–08 was ₹233435 crore (including collection from petroleum and tobacco products referred to as SIN-goods) of which collection from non-SIN goods and services was ₹157733 crore only. The breakup of the

Table 4.14
Revenues from the central taxes

Tax	*Non-sin Goods*	*POL*	*Tobacco*	*Total*
CVD	53510	5199	0	58709
Union excise duties	52922	60231	10272	123425
Service tax	51301	0	0	51301
Total	157733	65430	10272	233435

Source: Task Force on GST (2009)—Table 1.
Note: Union excise duties include additional excise duties and various cesses that will be subsumed in the CGST.

collections is given in Table 4.14 (Table 1 of the Task Force Report). Since the SIN-goods will continue to be subject to excises as at present, the RNR for the CGST is sought to be calculated only in respect of ₹157733 crore, being the collections from non-SIN goods and services.

In the case of state taxes, sales and excise taxes on petroleum and alcohol products would be outside of GST while taxation of tobacco products will be part of GST. The *Task Force* estimated that the total collection from 'EC-taxes' in 2007–08 was ₹118356 crore (excluding collection from petroleum, alcohol and tobacco products). The *Task Force* itself suggested a bigger list which included land and property transactions and stamp duty also. These were referred to by them as the TF-taxes. The total collection from 'TF-taxes' (excluding collection from petroleum, alcohol and tobacco products) was estimated by them at ₹188285 crore in 2007–08 as per details presented in Table 4.15. Since we are of the view that all the 'TF-taxes' should be subsumed in the SGST, our RNR for the SGST is sought to be calculated in respect of an amount of ₹188285 crore.

The Task Force has used the share of the unorganized sector in GDP at factor cost as representing the dealers below the threshold level. They observe that, in general, the unorganized sector in terms of the National Accounts Statistics is a good proxy for the unregistered dealers under the GST. The share of the unorganized sector in the non-agriculture net domestic product in 2007–08 is 48.69 percent and 90.27 percent in the agricultural sector.

The Task Force used the final demand vector (consumption expenditure, investment expenditure, etc.) in order to estimate the tax base. For

Table 4.15
State taxes to be merged in the goods and services tax

S. No.	Taxes	Non-sin Taxes	POL	Tobacco	Alcohol	Total
1	Stamp duty	38473				38473
2	Taxes on vehicles	15549				15549
3	Taxes on goods and passengers	6719				6719
4	Taxes and duty on electricity	9188				9188
5	Sales tax/VAT inc. CST and purchase tax	110826	56442	3000	11450	181718
6	Entertainment tax	1062				1062
7	Entry tax not in lieu of octroi	3914				3914
8	Other taxes and duties*	2554				2554
9	Total	188285	56442	3000	11450	259177
10	TF taxes sum 1–8	188285				
11	EC-taxes: sum 5–8	118356				

Source: Report Task Force on GST (2009)—Table 2.
Note: *Includes taxes on (a) lottery, betting and gambling (b) luxury tax and (c) cesses and surcharges by states.

estimating the value of purchases forming part of the PFCE that will form part of GST base, the Task Force used the share of purchases from the unregistered dealers in the same ratio as the share of the unorganized sector in the total national domestic product (NDP). This ratio in 2006–07 was 59 percent.

In the case of GFCE, it comprises of two elements, namely compensation to employees and net purchase of goods and services. Since compensation to employees will be outside the scope of the GST base, we exclude public administration in the input flow matrix from the GFCE to arrive at the net purchases of goods and services by government.

GFCF comprises two broad components, that is, construction and machinery equipment. The machinery equipment component is in the nature of capital goods which, under the GST, are proposed to be treated as intermediate inputs. Therefore, this element is not included as part of the GST base. Similarly, expenditure on construction by the public sector and the private corporate sector is also proposed as intermediate input by allowing full and immediate input credit on capital goods. Therefore, for the purposes of this exercise what is relevant is the estimate of the GFCF in the household sector.

The expenditure on construction as reported in Statement 19 of National Accounts Statistics, 2009 is ₹500036 crore comprising of ₹366855 crore towards construction and ₹133181 crore towards plant and machinery. The household sector in general would be in the un-organized sector (unregistered dealers or final consumers) and therefore, the expenditure on plant and machinery and construction by the household sector would be in the nature of final consumption. The expenditure on construction in the household sector would comprise of two components, namely, material and labour. In general, tax would be payable on the material component only since the labour component being from the un-organized or own labour will not be captured under the GST. Accordingly, we estimate the labour component as one-third of ₹366855 crore, that is, ₹122285 crore. Hence, the final consumption component in the GFCF in the household sector in 2006–07 is estimated at ₹377751 crore.

Some elements of the food sector, and education and health services are proposed to be exempt from the GST. Similarly, services categorized under the labels 'other commercial, social, personal services', 'others services' and 'public administration' are also proposed to be excluded since these would essentially be rendered by entities with turnover below the threshold limit or by government or by the non-profit sector.

The estimate of the non-land GST base for 2006–07 was obtained by aggregating the PFCE on goods and services from registered dealers (organized sector), the net purchases of goods and services by the government and the component relating to final consumption in the GFCF in the household sector. In Table 4.16, the size of the non-land GST base for 2006–07 is estimated at ₹2898520 crore, which accounts for 76.69 percent of the GDP at factor cost at current prices (₹3779385 crore). Applying the same ratio, the size of the non-land GST base in 2007–08 is estimated to be ₹3313817 crore. The GST base relating to land for 2007–08 is estimated to be ₹429260 crore as computed under the SI method. Therefore, the aggregate GST base in 2007–08 is estimated at ₹3743077 crore. This estimate is significantly higher than the size of the GST base estimated under the SI method (Table 4.17).

Table 4.16
Estimation of GST base—Task Force of the Thirteenth Finance Commission

S. No.	*Description*	*Units*	*Amount*
1	Aggregate PFCE	₹ in crs	2260042
2	PFCE relating to purchases from unregistered dealers (unorganized sector)	₹ in crs	1247433
3	PFCE (organized sector) (Row 1 – Row 2)	₹ in crs	1012609
4	GFCE on goods and services	₹ in crs	421059
5	GFCF in household sector (excluding labour)	₹ in crs	377751
6	Intermediate inputs from unregistered dealers	₹ in crs	1713887
7	Gross total (Row 3 + Row 4 + Row 5 + Row 6)	₹ in crs	3525306
8	Exemption for food, health, education and some services	₹ in crs	626786
9	Estimated non-land GST base in 2006–07 (Row 7 – Row 8)	₹ in crs	2898520
10	GDP at factor cost in 2006–07	₹ in crs	3779385
11	Non-land GST base as a proportion of GDP (Row 9 divided by Row 10)	in percent	76.69
12	GDP at factor cost in 2007–08	₹ in crs	4320892
13	Estimated non-land GST base in 2007–08 (Row 11* Row 12)	₹ in crs	3313817
14	GST base relating to land for 2007–08[1]	₹ in crs	429260
15	Estimated GST base in 2007–08 (Row 13 + Row 14)	₹ in crs	3743077

Source: Task Force on GST (2009)—Table 6.
Note: [1]The GST base relating to land in 2006–07 is estimated at ₹366855 crore.

Revenue Realization Ratio

In this analysis, for each tax, revenue is generated by estimation of the tax base multiplied by a core tax rate, and a revenue realization ratio (RRR). Thus,

$$\text{Tax revenue} = \text{tax base} * \text{tax rate} * RRR.$$

In the case of VAT, the concept of 'VAT revenue ratio (VRR)' has been used extensively. In case, there is single tax rate, and it is applied on

Table 4.17
Estimation of GST base—NCAER

S. No.	*Description*	*Units*	*Amount*
1	Estimated GST base (excluding land and the threshold exemption) in 2003–04	₹ in crs	2450042
2	Impact of the threshold exemption (purchases from the unorganized sector)	₹ in crs	894152
3	Non-land GST base in 2003–04 adjusted for threshold exemption (Row 1 – Row 2)	₹ in crs	1555890
4	GDP at factor cost in 2003–04	₹ in crs	2538170
5	Estimated non-land GST base in 2003–04 (Row 3 divided by Row 4)	in percent	61.30
6	GDP at factor cost in 2007–08	₹ in crs	4320892
7	Estimated non-land GST base in 2007–08 (Row 5* Row 6)	₹ in crs	2648692
8	GST base relating to land for 2007–08[1]	₹ in crs	429260
9	Estimated GST base in 2007–08 (Row 7 + Row 8)	₹ in crs	3077952

Source: Task Force on GST (2009)—Table 7.
Note: [1]The GST base relating to land in 2003–04 is estimated at ₹197305 crore.

the full tax base without any leakages or exemptions capturing the entire tax base, the RRR should be equal to 1. In practice however, the full tax base is not captured and the leakages can be for a variety of reasons. First, part of the tax base may not be captured due to policy decisions. Some part of the base may be exempt and some may be taxed at one or more levels of concessional rates. Secondly, there may be leakages in view collection inefficiencies.

In the case of VAT, the Task Force makes reference to VRR. They observe that a VAT system is, in absolute terms, 'efficient' when it covers the whole of the potential tax base (consumption by end users) at a single rate and where all the tax due is collected by the tax administration. Therefore, the ratio of the revenues actually collected and the revenues that would arise from a theoretically 'pure' VAT system with a single rate applied to all final consumption and 100 percent compliance would be a good measure to evaluate the performance of VAT. Such a VRR gives an indication of the efficiency of the VAT regime in a country compared to a standard norm. In theory, the closer the VAT system of a country is to the 'pure' VAT regime, the more its VRR is close to 1. This value can be taken as an indicator of a VAT bearing uniformly on a broad base with effective tax collection. On the other hand, a low VRR may indicate an erosion of the tax base at the standard rate. This can result from exemptions, reduced rates, registration thresholds for small traders, poor compliance or poor tax administration or a combination of these.

Estimation of RRR is not straightforward. The estimation of the potential VAT tax base (i.e. consumption by end users or national consumption) is difficult to assess with precision. In general, the charts of national consumption used to calculate the VRR are taken from the national accounts, but 'consumption' within the meaning of national accounts does not exactly match the potential VAT tax base. The Task Force estimated for India a VRR of what they call the 'flawless' GST as 0.79. They saw it as the product of a 'policy efficiency ratio' (comparing the theoretical revenue from actual VAT law and revenue from a pure VAT system) and a 'compliance efficiency ratio' (comparing actual VAT revenues with theoretical revenue from actual tax law). The 'flawless' GST recommended by the Task Force envisages very limited number of exemptions. These are essentially restricted to food, education and health services, the threshold exemption for registration of small dealers and public administration.

As regards the Report of the Task Force on GST, the recommended threshold exemption for registration of small dealers has both a positive and a negative impact on revenues. To the extent sales by unregistered dealers is exempt, there is a revenue loss. However, part of the revenue loss is recouped since purchases from unregistered dealers are not eligible for input tax credit. Similarly, a large part of the food items is distributed by small dealers and therefore there is significant overlap in the revenue effect of the threshold exemption and the food sector. The same also holds well in the health and education sector. The Task Force estimated the net impact of the exemptions under the 'flawless' GST on the tax base is estimated to be ₹206830 crore only. This accounts for 6.2 percent in the potential tax base. The 'policy efficiency ratio' was estimated by the Task Force to be 0.938.

The compliance level, although difficult to measure directly, can be seen as the ratio of the VRR to the 'policy efficiency ratio'. The Task Force estimates the implicit compliance level to be 0.84. It has been pointed out by some that given the cross-country estimates of the VRR, their estimate of VRR is extremely high. It is argued that if the VRR is aligned to the international norm, the RNR would be substantially higher than the 11 percent estimated by the Task Force. Therefore, it is best to use VRR as a tool to measure a single country's performance over a number of years rather than as a tool for comparison across countries. Nevertheless, five countries (i.e. Korea, Japan, Switzerland, Luxemburg and New Zealand) from amongst 29 OECD countries indeed have a VRR exceeding 0.7; another 17 countries have a VRR ranging between 0.5 and 0.7 and the balance seven countries have a VRR of less than 0.5.

The existing VRR in the case of central government levy on goods and services is extremely low. The current base is estimated to be as low as 0.3649. Further, the factor representing standard rate as the weighted sum of statutory rates was estimated to be 0.7550. Therefore, the 'policy efficiency ratio' is estimated to be a low of 0.2751. The Task Force observes that while no estimate of the compliance level is available, based on anecdotal information, they assumed compliance ratio to be 0.84, giving the VRR for central taxes on goods and services at a low level of 0.2352.

The value of exemptions (excluding threshold exemption) was estimated by the Task Force to be ₹1889096 crore (₹1358344 crore plus ₹530752 crore) and the estimated potential base is ₹2949748 crore. Therefore, the share of exemptions in the potential base is estimated to be 0.64. Hence, the share of the actual base is 0.36. The standard rate is 16.48 percent and the weighted average of statutory rates is estimated to be 12.28 percent. Therefore, the ratio of weighted average of statutory rates to standard rate is 0.75. This is the product of 0.36 and 0.75. This is the product of the 'policy efficiency ratio' (0.27) and the 'compliance efficiency ratio' (0.84).

de Mello (2008) empirically analyses 38 OECD and non-OECD countries and concludes that VAT efficiency is inversely related to the statutory rate and the share of tax administration costs in tax revenue (proxying for tax administration efficiency). The VAT efficiency is affected adversely by the level of the statutory rate. The coefficient in the tax is small in magnitude, although it is highly significant so that the loss in efficiency due to an increase in the VAT rate is relatively modest. The elasticity of VAT revenues to VAT rate is (–) 0.3 approximately. Silvani and Wakefield (2002) analyse a sample of 22 countries in the 1990s and show that, if the

VAT tax rate is raised by one percentage point, then the productivity falls by 3.6 percent.

The Task Force observes that the existing tax structure is riddled with a plethora of incentives and multiple rates. Therefore, the 'policy efficiency ratio' is extremely low. Once these policy deficiencies are removed, the VRR would automatically increase to a substantially higher level of 0.76. The purpose of introducing the flawless GST is precisely to achieve this policy objective.

4.5.4 Determination of Tax Base and Revenues: GST and Non-GST Taxes

As discussed earlier, we determined the total tax revenues raised from taxation of goods and services consisting of both GST and non-GST taxes. The GST will involve subsuming of CENVAT and service taxes and countervailing duties on imports and various cesses and surcharges as far as the central government is concerned and State VAT, purchase tax, central sales tax, entertainment tax, entry tax unless levied by the local bodies as far as the states are concerned. The taxation of petroleum products will continue outside GST both by the central government in the form of excise duties and by the state governments in the form of sales tax. State excises will continue on alcoholic beverages outside of GST. Taxation of tobacco will be part of GST but in addition there will be a non-rebatable component of central excise/sales tax. These arrangements are consistent with the constitutional amendment that has been introduced in Parliament by the central government. In addition, we are suggesting that provision can be made of a non-rebatable excise/cess on selected polluting goods and services. Further, indirect taxes other than GST would consist of import duties, stamp duties and registration fees and taxation of vehicles. The tax base for GST consists of two parts: (a) domestic output pertaining to non-exempt sectors and (b) intermediate output that continues to be taxed under GST. In addition, there will be stamp duties and registration fees and local taxes that are not getting merged with the GST (Table 4.18).

In order to determine the GST base, we may use the projections of outputs as divided into 14 sectors adjusted for exports and imports as discussed in the following paragraphs. The projected outputs are at factor cost and do not contain existing indirect taxes and subsidies.

Table 4.18
Composition of indirect taxes: 2006–07

Tax	*Revenue*	*Share in Total Tax Revenue*
Customs	86353	17.00
Excise	147353	29.00
Sales tax	162382	31.96
Service tax	37602	7.40
Stamps	32892	6.47
Other taxes and duties	41508	8.17
Total	508090	100.00

Source: Based on GoI (2009), Statement 43.

a. Adjustment for Threshold Level

Like the Task Force estimates, we can use the share of the unorganized sector as representing the share of dealers below the threshold level. To the extent goods and services are purchased from them, these will not be part of the GST base. If their own purchases of inputs are from the unorganized sector, that will also not be subjected to GST. It is only to the extent that their purchases of inputs are from the organized sector, that there will be taxation, which will be on intermediate use of goods and services. The share of the unorganized sector in NDP as given in the National Income Accounts differs from sector to sector (Table 4.19). However, for our purposes, the important ratios are those that pertain to the exempt sectors like food and education services or those sectors where higher or cascading taxation is relevant like petroleum products, tobacco, electricity and gas, and goods classified as polluting goods. Table 4.20 gives the relevant ratio for 2006–07 for this purpose.

b. Adjustment for Exempt Sectors

In the food sector, certain items particularly the cereals are likely to be exempted. Similarly, medical and health services and education services are likely to be exempted. Table 4.20 gives the relevant shares.

c. Adjustment for Sin-goods and Polluting Goods

The composition of final consumption also indicates those sectors that are to be subjected to excises or higher cesses like tobacco, petroleum products and beverages. We also have a list of polluting inputs and goods, which can be subjected to a non-rebatable component of tax.

Table 4.19
Share of unorganized sector in NDP at current prices for 2006–07

Sector	*Amount of Organized*	*Sectoral Total*	*Sector-wise Share of Organized Sector*	*Share of Unorganized Sector*
Agriculture, forestry and allied	62500	642349	0.10	0.90
Mining and quarrying	77618	90455	0.86	0.14
Manufacturing	319397	470803	0.68	0.32
Electricity	27901	29453	0.95	0.05
Construction	132810	310503	0.43	0.57
Trade, hotels, and restaurants	138981	611540	0.23	0.77
Transport, storage and communications	83753	258480	0.32	0.68
Financing, insurance and real estate	273855	462444	0.59	0.41
Community, social and personal services	331062	466320	0.71	0.29
All sectors	1447877	3342437	0.43	0.57

Source: Based on GoI (2009), Statement 76.

Table 4.20
Purchases for intermediate use by unregistered dealers from registered dealers

Sector	*Sector-wise Share of Organized Sector*	*Share of Unorganized Sector*	*Proportion of Purchases by Unorganized Sector from Organized Sectors*
Agriculture, forestry and allied	0.10	0.90	0.09
Mining and quarrying	0.86	0.14	0.12
Manufacturing	0.68	0.32	0.22
Electricity	0.95	0.05	0.05
Construction	0.43	0.57	0.24
Trade, hotels, and restaurants	0.23	0.77	0.18
Transport, storage and communications	0.32	0.68	0.22
Financing, insurance and real estate	0.59	0.41	0.24
Community, social and personal services	0.71	0.29	0.21
All sectors	0.43	0.57	0.25

Source: Based on GoI (2009), Statement 76.

d. Derivation of Customs Duty Revenue

Customs duty revenues are generated by application of a core rate and a customs revenue ratio that reflect the current structure of exemptions and rate differentials.

e. Derivation of Other Taxes

The main taxes left out are stamp duties and registration fees and taxation of vehicles that are both state taxes. To complete the revenue profile, we provide a growth path for these by using a growth rate on a base chart.

Following this route, we define the tax base in the following parts:

BASE GST: This consists of the sum of sectoral outputs other than those relating to cascading or exempt sectors and corresponding exports. In the model, this consists of the following:[4]

$$BASE1 = 0.10 * YARN + 0.86 * YCLRN + 0.86 * YCPETRN + 0.86 * YOMQRN + 0.68 * YOMANRN + 0.43 * YCRRN + 0.95 * YEGWSRN + 0.59 * YFIEBRN + 0.32 * YTHCRN + 0.23 * YTHTRN - CSHAREEXPORTS * EXPR * (PEXP/100) + BASEIMPORTS * IMPR * (PIMP/100)$$

The coefficient attached to nominal value of output indicates the share of registered dealers, i.e. after deducting from 1 the share of below threshold dealers. These coefficients represent the share of the organized sectors (Table 4.19). Exports undertaken by the unorganized sector is already taken out since the outputs represent output by the organized sector meant for domestic use as well as exports. We further need to zero-rate the share of exports by the organized sector. '*CSHAREEXPORTS*' is the coefficient indicating the share of the organized sector considering all sectors together and kept at 61 percent. This is derived as the weighted sum of the share of organized sector where the weights are given by the share of exports of each sector in the 2006–07 IOT. '*BASEIMPORTS*' represents that part of imports which may be used for final consumption and is kept at 10 percent.

Further to this GST base, an additional tax base would be provided by (a) purchases by dealers in the exempt sectors from registered dealers of non-exempt sectors on which tax will be paid on the intermediate purchases, which will not be rebated at later stages and (b) purchases for intermediate use by below threshold dealers from above threshold dealers in the non-exempt sectors.

$$RCASCADE1 = TCORE * (0.09 * 0.32 * YARN + 0.12 * 0.27 * YCLRN + 0.12 * 0.27 * YCPETRN + 0.12 * 0.20 * YOMQRN + 0.22 * 0.79 * YOMANRN + 0.24 * 0.64 * YCRRN + 0.05 * 0.69 * YEGWSRN + 0.24 * 0.16 * YFIEBRN + 0.22 * 0.56 * YTHCRN + 0.18 * 0.26 * YTHTRN + 0.21 * 0.19 * YCSPRN)$$

In the equation for *RCASCADE*1, within the parenthesis, the first coefficient attached to the output variables represents purchases by the unorganized sector from the organized sector (Column 3 of Table 4.20), the second coefficient indicates the extent of use of intermediate inputs in any sector from other sectors (Table 4.13).

BASEPETROL: Base 2 consists of the tax base for the petroleum products:

$$BASE2 = YPETROLRN + RCASCADE2 + MYPETROLR * (AWPIFUEL/100)$$

Here the cascading part is calculated as follows:

$$RCASCADE2 = (TCORE + TPETROL) * YPETROLRN * IUSEPETROL$$

where *TPETROL* and *IUSEPETROL* represent the additional tax and the intermediate use coefficient of petroleum products, respectively.

BASEPOLL: Base 3 consists of the polluting goods (mainly metals, plastics and leather; refer Table 4.10).

$$BASE3 = YPOLLRN + RCASCADE3$$

Here, the cascading part is calculated as follows:

$$RCASCADE3 = (TCORE + TPOLLN) * YPOLLRN * IUSEPOLL$$

where *TPOLLN* and *IUSEPOLL* represent the additional tax and the intermediate use coefficient of polluting goods, respectively.

BASEBEVR: This tax base relates to the excise duties on alcoholic beverages.

$$BASEBEVR = YBEVRN + RCASCADE4$$

The cascading part is calculated as follows:

$$RCASCADE4 = (TCORE + TBEVR) * YBEVRN * IUSEBEVR$$

where *TBEVR* and *IUSEBEVR* represent the additional tax and the intermediate use coefficient of alcoholic beverages, respectively.

BASETOBACCO is defined as consumption of tobacco products (*CTOBACCO*)

To cover the imports duties also, base 6 is defined as follows:

$$BASECUTOMS = IMPR * (PIMP/100)$$

In this system of indirect taxes on goods and services, the following are main sources of revenue:

GST: Revenue consists of taxation on the final value of all goods and services except the exempted sectors and exports + taxation of intermediate output of the exempted sectors + equivalent of countervailing GST on imports used directly for consumption.

Petroleum products: This is subject to a levy of excise by the central government and sales tax by the state governments.

Alcoholic beverages: This is subject to a levy of excise duty by the state governments.

Tobacco products: This is subject to an excise duty by the central government and GST by both the central and state governments.

Polluting goods and services: These may be subject to GST by both the central and state governments and an additional excise/cess that is not rebatable; if this is not permitted, then the polluting goods may be subjected to an entry tax by the local bodies.

Other than import duties, other taxes that may continue are stamp duties and registration fees and motor vehicle tax are grown by a growth rate on a base chart.

4.5.5 Projection of Tax Revenues

Tax revenues for different categories are projected by applying a core or modal tax rate on the tax base, modified by a 'tax revenue' ratio (similar to the VRR), which reflects a combination of factors including compliance, lower rate categories, exempted categories not taken into account and tax collection efficiency. Summarily, this ratio has been called as the compliance rate. For any benchmark year, the compliance rate can be determined by taking the actual revenue and comparing it with the product of the modal tax rate, tax base and compliance rate.

Thus, compliance rate (*COMPRATE*) = core rate * tax base/actual tax revenue for each relevant category.

Total tax revenue under indirect taxes will then be the sum of the following:

$$TRGST = COMPRATE * TCORE * BASE1 + RCASCADE1$$

$$TRPETROL = COMPRATE * (TCORE + TPETROL) * BASE2$$

$$TRPOLL = COMPRATE * (TCORE + TPOLLN) * BASE3$$

This can be seen as consisting of two parts: tax revenue from polluting goods at the core GST rate, and tax revenue from the additional non-rebatable component in the form of an excise or cess.

For purposes of distinguishing the revenue that is generated by the core GST rate and that raised by the additional excise/cess on the polluting goods, we divide this tax revenue into two parts:

$$TR3A = COMPRATE * TCORE * BASE3, \text{ and}$$

$$TR3B = COMPRATE * TPOLLN * BASE3 \text{ (this should have a cascading part)}$$

$$TRBEVR = COMPRATE * (TCORE + TBEVR) * BASE4$$

$$TRTOBACCO = (TCORE + TTOBRATE) * CTOBACCO$$

$$TRCUSTOMS = IMPDUTYRATE * BASE5$$

$$TROTHERS = TROTHERS(-1) * (1 + GROTHERS)$$

where *GROTHERS* is the growth rate applied for the residual category.

Given these, the total tax revenue from taxes on goods and services, taking into account both domestic and international taxes, is given by

$$TRINDIRECT = TRGST + TRPOLL + TRPETROL + TRBEVR + TROBACCO + TRCUSTOMS + TROTHERS$$

Alternative GST models: Three versions of GST, given the current debate in India, may be distinguished: version recommended by the Task Force of the Thirteenth Finance Commission (GST0), a modified version being suggested here, and the version implied by the proposed constitutional amendment (GST1), which partially reflects the views of the EC of State Finance Ministers, with elements that the central government has introduced (GST2). These are briefly discussed below.

GST0: Model recommended by the Task Force of Thirteenth Finance Commission includes all goods and services under GST including petroleum products, tobacco products, alcoholic beverages and polluting goods; some local taxes are also included including property tax, no entry tax, etc.; provision for non-rebatable excises/cess on the 'sin/demerit' goods that include petroleum products, tobacco products, alcoholic beverages and polluting goods.

GST1: All goods and services under GST including petroleum products, tobacco products, alcoholic beverages and polluting goods; local taxes are not included but provision for non-rebatable excises/cess on the 'sin/demerit' goods that include petroleum products, tobacco products, alcoholic beverages and polluting goods.

GST2: This is the model implied in the proposed constitutional amendment introduced to parliament by the central government. In this model, petroleum products are outside GST and will continue to cascade; state excise on alcoholic beverages is outside GST and will continue to cascade; tobacco is part of GST but the central government retains powers to levy and excise duty in addition to GST; there is no provision for an excise/cess on polluting goods and services.

Our empirical exercises start with the GST model (GST1) and examine the possibilities of revenue neutrality arguing that the core GST rate can start with 16 percent divided into two parts for the centre and states. It argues that if provision is made for a non-rebatable excise/cess on polluting goods, then it is possible to reduce the core GST rate within a few years, if revenue neutrality is considered in a broader context where the overall contribution of taxation of goods and services (excluding local taxes) is taken into consideration. Three important features are: with the international crude oil prices continuing to rise in the future, the tax on petroleum products will continue to contribute progressively higher amounts; with the

Indian economy progressively opening out, import duties will continue to have significant revenue importance; and with provision of non-rebatable excise on polluting goods, these will lead to additional tax revenues permitting reduction in the core GST rate and more environment friendly output structure.

From the GST2 model, moving to GST1 model will only mean somewhat higher excise tax rates for the sin/demerit goods and services but it will provide producers of these goods also rebate on non-sin/demerit goods when used as inputs.

Relative share of different components: In the projected revenues shown in Figure 4.7, the relative shares of different components are given in Table 4.22. The following are some of the noticeable features:

1. The core GST rate is kept at 14 percent.
2. Without changing the core rate, and compliance rate, the desired buoyancy comes from the petroleum taxes.
3. The core rate can be further reduced if higher rate is charged on polluting goods/petroleum products or if the compliance rate improves.
4. Over time the GST share in total tax revenues goes down as the share of exports in GDP increases, but this is compensated by the higher share of import duties (Table 4.21).

Figure 4.7
Target and projected tax revenue under GST framework

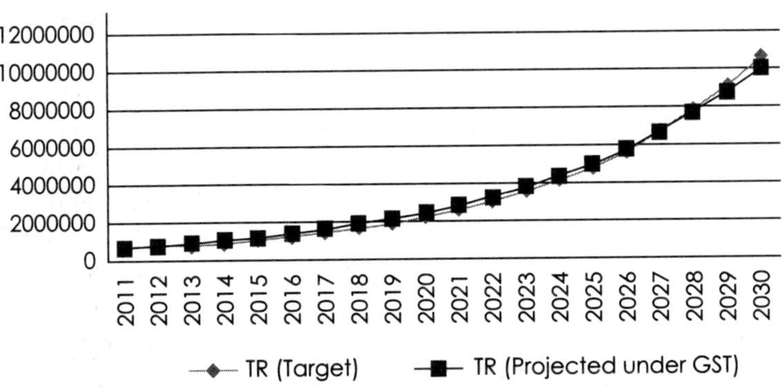

Source: Based on model projections.

Table 4.21
Relative shares in total tax revenue from goods and services

Year	*TRGST*	*TRPOLL*	*TRPET-ROL*	*TRBEVR*	*TRTO-BACCO*	*TRCUS-TOMS*	*TROTH-ERS*
2011	33.44	9.39	15.35	4.64	0.30	18.27	18.60
2012	31.39	9.54	16.14	4.49	0.28	20.24	17.93
2013	32.31	9.47	16.08	4.45	0.26	19.45	17.97
2014	34.27	9.32	15.68	4.44	0.26	17.68	18.35
2015	34.50	9.25	15.68	4.36	0.25	17.49	18.47
2016	32.88	9.31	16.13	4.22	0.24	18.91	18.31
2017	31.28	9.36	16.60	4.07	0.22	20.34	18.12
2018	30.69	9.34	16.79	3.98	0.21	20.81	18.16
2019	31.06	9.27	16.75	3.94	0.21	20.41	18.35
2020	31.16	9.20	16.79	3.89	0.20	20.28	18.48
2021	30.38	9.21	17.07	3.82	0.19	20.89	18.43
2022	29.46	9.22	17.41	3.73	0.18	21.68	18.31
2023	28.77	9.21	17.69	3.65	0.17	22.24	18.26
2024	28.66	9.17	17.81	3.60	0.16	22.31	18.28
2025	28.49	9.13	17.93	3.55	0.16	22.40	18.34
2026	28.45	9.07	18.03	3.50	0.15	22.43	18.36
2027	28.20	9.03	18.19	3.43	0.14	22.65	18.36
2028	28.17	8.98	18.28	3.38	0.14	22.68	18.36
2029	28.17	8.92	18.36	3.34	0.13	22.67	18.40
2030	28.67	8.82	18.29	3.31	0.13	22.29	18.49

Source: Based on model projections.

4.5.6 Concluding Observations

This section uses the macro-model with information from the IOT to determine tax bases for different goods and services including petroleum products, demerit goods like tobacco and alcoholic beverages and other polluting goods. We take note of the importance of the external sector when exports are zero-rated and the Indian economy becomes more globalized, part of the domestic production will go out of the tax base and import duties become more important. Revenue is generated by application of core rates to tax base along with a RRR. Results show that taxation of polluting goods and service by means of non-rebatable excise and/or cess can facilitate fixing the GST rate at about 14 percent and generate an increase in the tax–GDP ratio providing additional fiscal capacity for realizing potential growth as discussed in Section 4.3.

4.6 GROWTH, TAXES AND ENVIRONMENTAL POLLUTION: SOME ESTIMATES

4.6.1 Introduction

Growth of economic activities produces output as well as pollution. If the Indian economy grows at its potential rate as discussed in Section 4.3, then it will carry a certain pollution load. In this section, we estimate this pollution load. These estimates are made on the basis of estimated pollution load coefficients defined per unit of gross output. Given the present pattern of growth, a change in the structure of output favouring the less polluting service sector is already visible as discussed in Section 4.3. For further reducing pollution, the two broad considerations are (a) accepting growth at levels lower than the potential rate; (b) accelerating structural change in favour of less polluting output by means of fiscal interventions including eco-taxes within the GST framework and eco-subsidies. We examine some of these possibilities in this section.

4.6.2 Estimation of Local Pollution

a. Industry-specific Pollution Coefficients and the IPPS Database

The IPPS is a database on industrial pollution intensity developed by the World Bank. It is a modelling system that combines the US Environmental Protection Agency (EPA) data for pollution emissions and the Longitudinal Research Database (LRD) on industrial activity at the plant level to calculate pollution intensity of industrial sectors. Pollution intensity as provided by IPPS is defined as the ratio of pollutant output to manufacturing activity. Three measures of manufacturing activity are provided—value of output, value added and employment. For our purpose, value of output is the most suitable as it is being projected through the model at a suitable level of disaggregation. Therefore, data on pollution intensity given in terms of pounds (of a pollutant) per million US$ (of economic activity) measured at 1987 prices has been used, with necessary adjustments to express the coefficients in kilograms per ₹ crore of output at constant 1999–2000 prices.

The IPPS provides pollution coefficients for major air and water pollutants. The major air pollutants covered by IPPS are SO_2^-, NO_x, CO, fine particulates (FP), volatile organic compounds (VOC), total suspended particulates (TSP). Major water pollutants include biological oxygen demand (BOD) and total suspended solids (TSS).

One of the major limitations of using the IPPS data set is that it represents pollution intensity estimates for the USA. Applying the same factors to estimate pollution levels for a different country would neglect country-specific factors that might affect the accuracy of the results. This limitation needs to be recognized in interpreting the results from this study. Assuming that India uses inferior technology compared to the USA, actual pollution in India would be higher than that estimated using the IPPS coefficients. Hence, the estimated pollution using IPPS coefficients should be considered a lower bound for pollution estimates.

b. Estimating Local Pollution from Industrial Sources in India

Flow pollution from a particular industry is measured as the product of its pollution intensity (given by the IPPS database) and its corresponding value of output.

i. Mapping the industries of the 51 × 51 matrix to the ISIC codes: The IPPS database follows the ISIC classification in presenting industry-wise estimates of pollution intensity. Information on output is available from the IOT for 2006 which is disaggregated into 130 industries. We aggregated IOT into a 51 × 51 matrix to match-up with the ISIC classification. However, out of the 51 industry groups, only 33 industries could be mapped with ISIC codes. The mapping scheme used to match industries to its nearest ISIC codes is given in Appendix A4.2. These 33 industries include the 16 CPCB industries (excluding electricity) in 13 industry groups. Of these 16 CPCB industries, aluminium, zinc and copper have been classified into one industry group—'non-ferrous basic metals'—and mapped to a single four-digit ISIC code (3720). Similarly, fertilizers and pesticides appear as two different industries in the CPCB list, but is treated as a single industry group—'fertilizers and pesticides'—and mapped to ISIC code 3512. Apart from these 13 industry groups, these 33 industries which have been mapped to ISIC codes include two other sectors known for their high pollution intensities—coal and lignite and coal tar products. Both of them have been mapped into a single ISIC code (3540).

The remaining 18 industry groups could not be mapped to ISIC codes for which IPPS coefficients were available. These industry groups are mainly service-related sectors except electricity which is a highly polluting sector. Hence, we attribute the highest coefficient of all the 33 industries with available pollution coefficients to electricity. For the remaining 17 industry groups which are predominantly service sectors, the smallest of all the coefficients is used.

ii. Expressing the pollution intensities in appropriate units: The pollution intensities given by IPPS are in terms of pounds per 1987 million US dollar of output value. To calculate the pollution load for a particular industry, we need to multiply the industries' pollution intensity with a corresponding value of output. This requires both of them to be expressed in the same currency. In our report, we convert pollution intensity from pounds per million US dollar of output (at 1987 prices) to kilograms per 1000 rupee value of output (at 1987 prices). To convert US dollars into rupees, we use the purchasing power parity (PPP) exchange rate of 1987. This allows us to express intensity in terms of kilograms per 1987 value of output in 1987 prices. On the other hand, the output of 2006 as given by IOT is in 2006 prices. In order to be consistent with macro-economic projections, we convert both the pollution intensity coefficients and output to 1999–2000 prices by using the appropriate price deflators. The next step is to estimate the industry-wise pollution load by multiplying the industry-specific pollution intensity with its value of output. This gives the industry-wise pollution load of 2006 expressed in 1999–2000 prices.

iii. Pollution Load from Select Flow Pollutants: In order to devise effective strategies to promote cleaner growth, it is important to understand the contribution of different industries to the pollution process. We highlight here industries that have been major polluters of air and water in 2006.

a. Air Pollutants

Sulphur dioxide: Sulphur dioxide is one of the major air pollutants. Major sources of sulphur emissions include burning of coal, high-sulphur oil and diesel fuel. Electricity sector contributes 51 percent of sulphur emissions

Figure 4.8
Largest emitters of sulphur dioxides from industrial processes

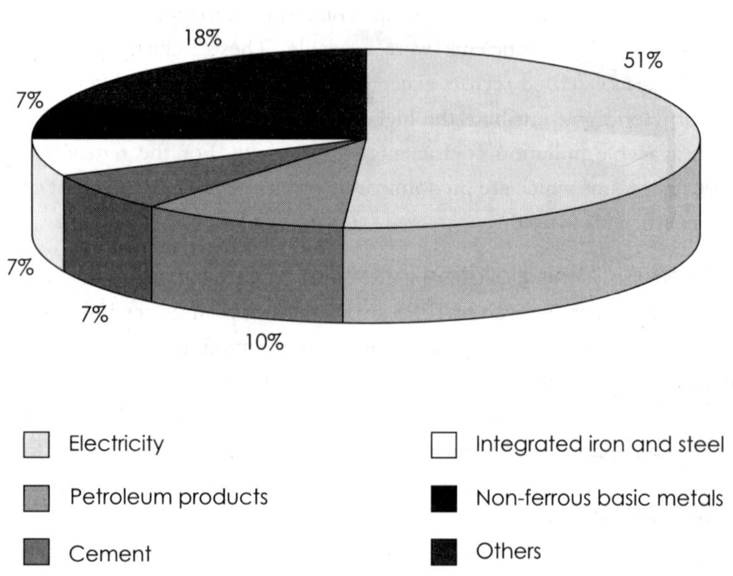

Source: Estimated based on IPPS data and IOTs 2006–07.

in India, followed by petroleum products (10 percent), cement, integrated iron and steel and non-ferrous basic metals (all at 7 percent; Figure 4.8). High concentration of sulphur dioxide adversely affects vegetation as well as human health. In fact, exposure to sulphur dioxide in the ambient air has been associated with reduced lung functions, increased incidence of respiratory symptoms and diseases, irritation of the eyes nose and throat, and premature mortality.

Nitrous dioxides: Nitrogen dioxides (NO_2) along with nitric oxide (NO) contribute to acid rain, depletion of ozone layer and adversely affect human health. Major emitters of nitrogen dioxides include fuel combustion, biomass burning and certain production processes. As expected, majority of NO_2 emissions come from the electricity sector (47 percent). Petroleum products (12 percent), cement (7 percent), integrated iron and steel (6 percent) and crude oil (5 percent) (Figure 4.9).

Figure 4.9

Largest emitters of nitrogen dioxides from industrial processes

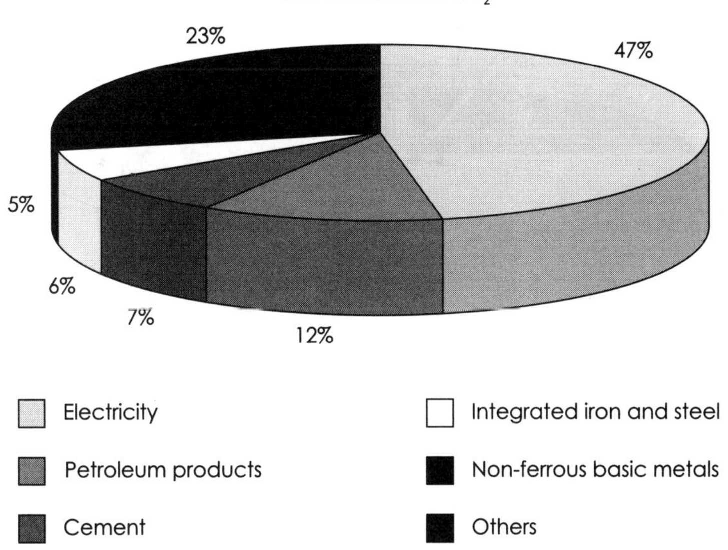

Source: Estimated based on IPPS data and IOTs 2006–07.

Fine particles: Fine particles constitute the tiny sub-divisions of solid matter suspended in air. For instance, soot expelled from a coal plant's smokestack find its way into the atmosphere as fine particles. Figure 4.10 shows that 81 percent of fine particles in the atmosphere is emitted by the electricity sector, followed by cement (12 percent), integrated iron and steel (4 percent), edible oil (1 percent) and petroleum products (1 percent).

b. Water Pollutants

Biological oxygen demand (BOD): BOD refers to the biochemical oxygen demand of water. It is an indirect measure of the concentration of biologically degradable material present in organic wastes. The paper and pulp industry contributes 43 percent of BOD emissions. Industrial chemicals (except fertilizers and other chemicals) contribute another 22 percent. Non-ferrous basic metals industry such as aluminium and copper smelters emit 14 percent of BOD, followed by other chemicals (12 percent) and sugar (2 percent) (Figure 4.11).

Figure 4.10
Largest emitters of fine particles from industrial processes

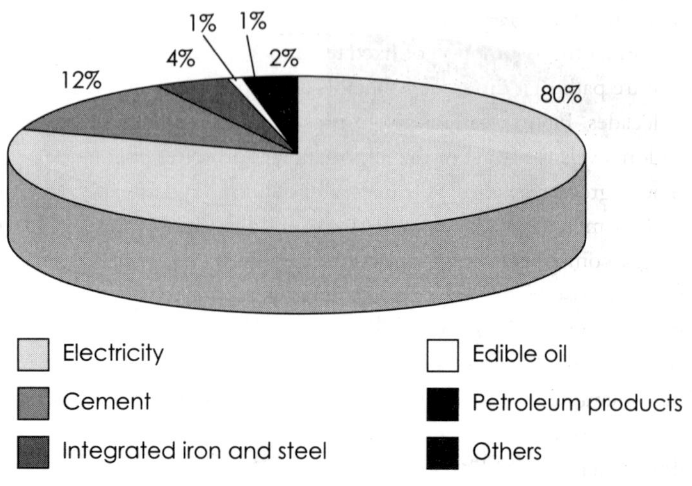

Source: Estimated based on IPPS data and IOTs 2006–07.

Figure 4.11
Largest emitters of BOD from industrial processes

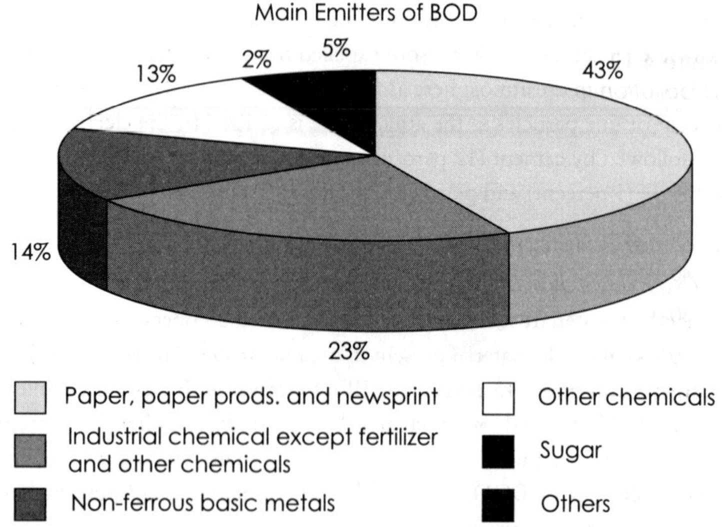

Source: Estimated based on IPPS data and IOTs 2006–07.

iv. Estimating future pollution load: Pollution levels in future will depend on a host of factors including technological innovations, regulations that mandate the use of more energy-efficient processes and the changes in demand for different goods. In this report, future output is estimated under the assumption of fixed technology. This allows us to estimate the future path that different pollutants are expected to follow in the next two decades. Figures 4.12 and 4.13 present future estimates of aggregate pollution levels for some of the important air and water pollutants.

The aggregate level of SO_2 from all pollution level is expected to rise from 10.1 million tons in 2006–07 to 54.4 million tons in 2029–30 representing a compound annual growth rate of 7.61 percent. NO_2 levels are expected to rise from 5.07 million tons to 27.67 million tons by 2029–30 growing at a rate of 7.66 percent. The level of FP emitted annually will grow from 5.23 million tons to 24.88 million tons at a CAGR of 7.02 percent. Water pollution, captured by BOD, is also expected to increase from 0.36 million tons of emissions per annum to 2.33 million tons per annum which represents a growth rate of 8.45 percent.

4.6.2 Estimation of Global Pollution

The IPPS database does not provide pollution intensities for global pollutants or GHGs that lead to global warming such as methane and carbon

Figure 4.12
Air pollution from specific pollutants till 2029–30

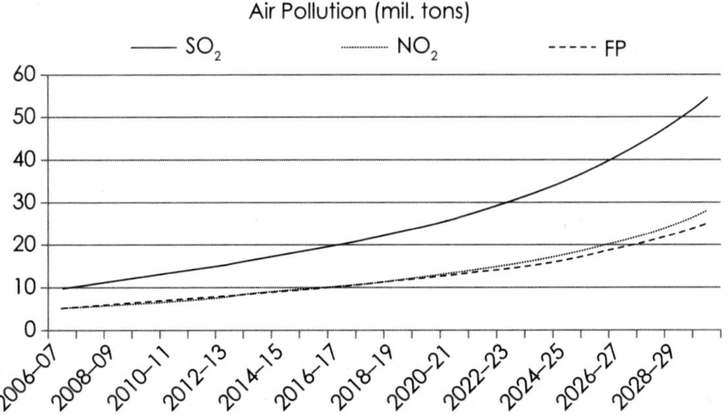

Source: Based on IPPS data and model projections.

Figure 4.13
Water pollution from specific pollutants till 2029–30

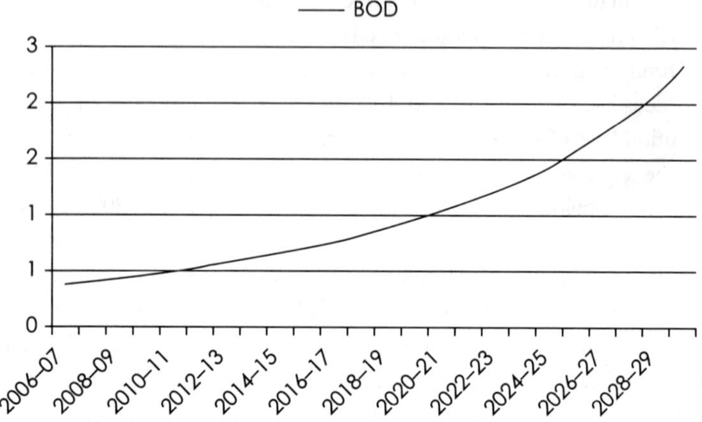

Source: Based on IPPS data and model projections.

dioxide. The emissions of these gases from different sources are therefore calculated using a different methodology.

The World Resources Institute (WRI) estimated that in 2005 CO_2 emissions accounted for 66 percent of the total emissions of GHGs in India (see Figure 4.14). CH_4 accounted for another 29.5 percent and N_2O constituted 3.8 percent of the total GHGs. Since CO_2 accounts for a major proportion of the total GHGs emitted in India, we restrict our analysis to estimating only emissions of CO_2 from fossil fuel combustion.

Although carbon dioxide is emitted from different sources, the primary source of CO_2 emissions is combustion of fossil fuels namely coal, oil and gas. Fossil fuels contain carbon which when combusted, oxidizes and is emitted as CO_2 into the atmosphere. Additionally, some carbon is also emitted in the form of CO, CH_4 and other hydrocarbons. Other gases like N_2O, SO_2 and black carbon are also emitted during the combustion of fossil fuels. Fossil fuel combustion mainly takes place in sectors like electricity, other energy industries (petroleum refining and solid fuel manufacturing), transport, residential, commercial and institutional sector, agriculture, fisheries and certain energy intensive industries (see Figure 4.15). Apart from fossil fuel combustion, CO_2 emissions may also result from industrial

Figure 4.14
GHG emissions in India (2005)

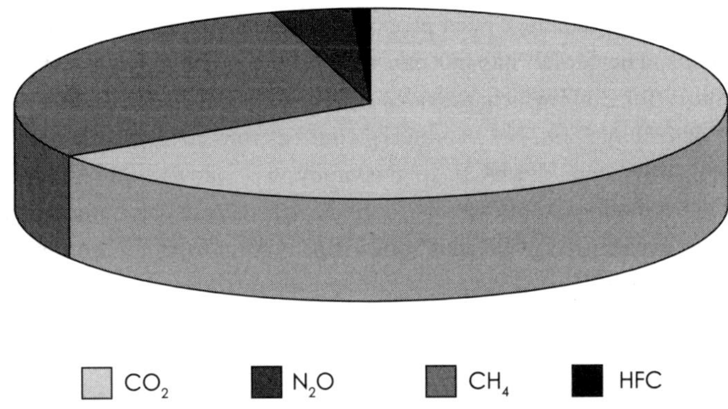

Source: Prepared by the Authors using data from http://cait.wri.org

Figure 4.15
CO_2 emissions by source

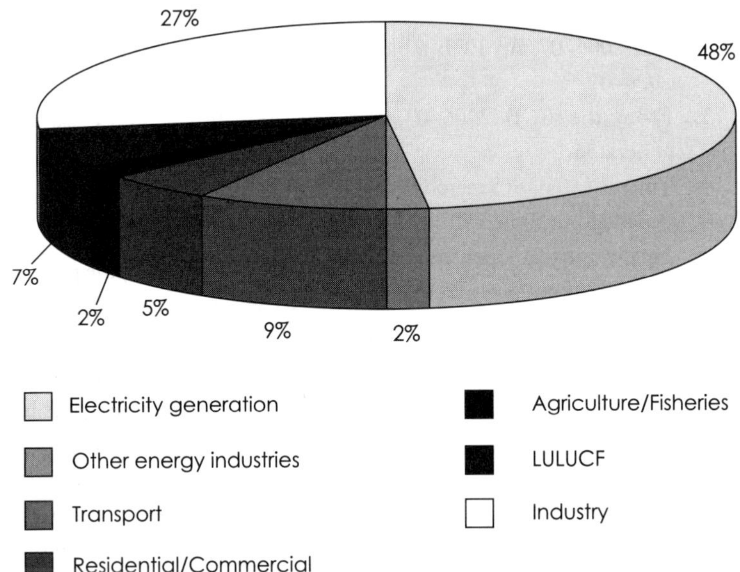

Source: Prepared by the authors using data from MoEF (2010).

processes, non-energy product use and from land use, land-use change and forestry (LULUCF).

Several methods have been proposed in the literature to calculate CO_2 emissions. The MoEF has recently released a report on GHG Emission Inventory for 2007 which provides official information on India's emissions of GHGs (CO_2, N_2O and CH_4) emitted from energy, industry, agriculture, waste and LULUCF. In this study, we follow the methodology used in estimating CO_2 inventory in the MoEF report. The different steps involved in calculating CO_2 emissions intensity from fossil fuel combustion are given below:

1. The energy commodity balance (ECB) for 2007–08 is available from CSO. Using the ECB 2007–08 and data from other sources (CMIE, Indiastat) to check for consistency, emissions for 2007–08 are generated at a sectoral level. These emissions are checked with the official emissions published by the MoEF. This validates the sectoral mapping of fossil fuel consumption.
2. If the emissions generated for 2007–08 are comparable with those of the official estimates, then the same method of allocation of fossil fuel consumption to different sectors may be adopted for the year 2006–07. An ECB table needs to be constructed for the year 2006–07.
3. From the ECB 2006–07, the emissions for 2006–07 can be generated.
4. The next step is to match the sectors for which emissions have been generated to those of the 51 sectors of the collapsed IOT.
5. Finally, the CO_2 intensity is calculated from the calculated emissions and the output given in the IOT.

Validation of Emissions for 2007–08

The CO_2 emissions for 2007–08 are calculated on the basis of the IPCC revised guidelines of 1996. As a first check, we need to see if our overall estimate of emissions is comparable with those of the MoEF. The data for apparent consumption[5] (in kilo tons) of all primary fossil fuels and secondary fuels are taken from the CSO. The NCV and the CO_2 EFs are borrowed from the MoEF report (Table 4.22).

The NCV of a fuel is a measure of its value for heating purposes, that is, it denotes the amount of energy that is released during the combustion of

Table 4.22
Parameters used in the calculation of CO_2 emissions

Fuels	*NCV (in tj/kt)*	*EF (in t/tj)*
Coal	21.905	94.71
Lignite	9.69	106.15
LPG	47.3	63.1
Petrol	44.3	69.3
Naphtha	43.0	74.1
Kerosene	43.8	71.9
ATF	44.1	71.5
Diesel oil	43.0	74.1
Fuel oil	40.4	77.4
Lubricants	40.2	73.3

Source: Based on MoEF (2010), Table 5.2.

a fuel. EF gives the amount of carbon-di-oxide released per unit of energy released.[6] Apparent consumption of each fuel multiplied by the corresponding NCV and EF gives the amount of CO_2 emissions generated from each fuel. Adding CO_2 emissions across each fuel, we obtain the total CO_2 emissions from fossil fuel combustion which comes to 1433207 thousand tons. This compares reasonable well with the MoEF estimate of CO_2 emissions of 1497029 thousand tons. It should be noted, however, that the MoEF estimate includes CO_2 emissions not only from fossil fuel combustion but also those from industrial processes, non-energy product use and LULUCF (Table 4.23).

The next step is to calculate sector-wise emissions and validate it with the sector-wise emissions of the MoEF. ECB for the year 2007–08 is available from the CSO. Additionally, other data sources[7] which give the sectoral consumption of coal, lignite and petroleum products have also been used. Using these data sources, we compile the sector-wise consumption of the fuels. Using the NCV and EF values used to calculate the overall emissions, we calculate the sector-wise emissions. The calculated sector-wise emissions and the MoEF emissions are compared in Table 4.24. It can be seen that the sector-wise emissions also compare well with the MoEF emissions.

Table 4.23
Comparison of MoEF emissions and calculated emissions (in '000 tons)

MoEF		*Calculated*	
Electricity generation	715830	Electricity	789957
Other energy industries	33788	Other energy industries	5985
Transport	138858	Transport	124056
Residential/commercial	71084	Residential/commercial	65617
Agriculture/fisheries	33277	Agriculture/fisheries	28721
Cement production	129920	Cement	45890
Glass and ceramic production	278	Glass and ceramic	57
Chemicals(including fertilizers)	27889	Chemicals	36508
		Fertilizers	14171
Iron and steel production	116958	Iron and steel	128229
Other non-ferrous metals	5413	Other non-ferrous metals	1502
Pulp and paper	5223	Pulp and paper	5837
Food processing	27626	Food processing	28801
Textile and leather	1861	Textile and leather	1746
Mining and quarrying	1460	Mining and quarrying	1188
		Engineering	344
Non-specific industries	87800	Non-specific industries	147827
Non-energy product use	849	Non-energy product use	6748
Grand total	1497029	Grand total	1433186

Source: Based on MoEF (2010), Table 10.3 and own estimates.

Construction of ECB Table for 2006–07

Having validated the emissions for 2007–08, the same sectoral allocation of fuel consumption is adopted for 2006–07 and an ECB table is constructed for the year 2006–07. Using the calorific value and EFs, CO_2 emissions from fuel combustion is calculated for the year 2006–07. CO_2 emissions have been calculated for 16 industry groups.

Mapping the Sectors Generating CO_2 Emissions with the IO Sectors

The 16 industry groups for which CO_2 emissions have been generated and three additional industry groups for which energy-related emissions are non-existent have been mapped to the 51 industries of the IOT. After mapping

Table 4.24
Estimation for CO_2 emissions: 2006–07 (in '000 tons)

Industry	*CO_2 Emissions*
Electricity	726349
Other energy industries	5597
Transport	123104
Residential/commercial	61532
Agriculture/fisheries	11467
Cement	41973
Glass and ceramic	67
Chemicals	12665
Fertilizers	28889
Iron and steel	112693
Other non-ferrous metals	232
Pulp and paper	5656
Food processing	26653
Textile and leather	2546
Non-specific industries	155006
Mining and quarrying	2423
Total	1316851

Source: Prepared by authors using ECB data from www.mospi.gov.in

the 19 industries with the 51 industries of the input–output matrix, we derive CO_2 intensities for the 16 industry groups for which emissions are calculated. The calculated emissions are divided by the corresponding output (at constant 1999–2000 prices) to arrive at intensity estimates. The CO_2 emission intensity for the remaining industry groups has been assumed to be zero as we have considered only energy-related emissions which can be safely assumed to be absent or negligible for these industries.

4.6.3 Estimating Future Pollution Load

We generate future pollution load by estimating (a) growth of output (GDP at factor cost) up to 2029–30 under specified assumption divided into 14 sectors, (b) using technology assumptions from the 2006–07 IOT to convert output in to gross output (sum of GDP at factor cost/GVA, net indirect taxes and input requirements), (c) pollution load matrix giving pollution per unit of gross output. Pollution levels into the future can then be analysed and modified either by changing the growth and/or structure of output, or by changing the input-use coefficients (substitution of inputs/changed technology) or by changing the pollution load coefficients (more environment friendly technology). The pollution load coefficients for different types of pollution are summarized in Table 4.25.

The policy options used in the scenario simulations are summarized below:

1. Allow growth at less than potential rate as deliberate policy;
2. Modify the input-use coefficients of major sources of pollution and
3. Restructure output in favour of less polluting sectors while maintaining growth at about potential rate.

a. Estimates of Pollution: Base Growth Scenario

In the base growth scenario, sectoral growth is projected as per potential growth using the model discussed in Section 4.3. These growth rates can be considered potential growth since they assume a supporting policy scenario and are based on supply side considerations. Pollution load, both of local and global pollutants are generated using the projected output at 1999–2000 prices, generating gross output from these, and then applying the pollution coefficients given in Table 4.26.

In the base scenario, the structure of output keeps changing in favour of the services sector. As a result, even while the input-coefficients and the pollution load coefficients are held constant, the CO_2 intensity of output falls as shown in Figure 4.16.

b. Simulation 1

As a benchmark, we examine the impact of reduction of achieving less than potential growth on the pollution load. In this scenario, we reduce each sectoral growth by one percentage point except agriculture and allied services, which are allowed to growth at the estimated potential rate. The effect on the pollution load is summarized in Figures 4.17 and 4.18.

c. Simulation 2

In simulation 2, we change the pollution load of selected sectors by 5 percent and in the case of 'other polluting goods' and 'electricity, gas, and water

Table 4.25

Sector-wise pollution load matrix

Sectors	*In kg per ₹ Crore of Output (GDPfc at 1999–2000 Prices)*						*In Tons Per ₹ Crore of Output*
	SO_2	NO_2	*CO*	*VOC*	*FP*	*TSP*	CO_2
Agriculture and allied	19.15	169.854	42.170	1.137	0.532	5.701	21.583
Coal and lignite	9609.29	5978.520	4526.028	1500.847	295.196	3686.032	38.655
Crude petroleum	5851.68	3366.194	3039.971	3098.192	59.145	516.134	38.785
Other mining, N.E.C.	0.39	1.946	0.389	0.389	0.000	0.778	117.305
Petroleum products including LPG	33646.64	20933.610	15847.752	5255.171	1033.619	12906.533	604.954
Other polluting goods	18180.98	9512.785	13496.490	3823.649	5879.727	5588.306	1180.950
Beverages including alcoholic beverages	438.74	66.475	5.698	0.950	0.000	45.583	392.589
Remaining manufacturing goods N.E.C.	2615.13	1233.597	343.397	932.645	422.400	1106.878	439.789
Construction	0.85	4.271	0.854	0.854	0.000	1.709	320.494
Electricity, gas and water supply	73295.45	34031.897	16632.867	7606.496	60944.523	35448.284	11997.042
Transport, storage and communication	0.55	2.755	0.551	0.551	0.000	1.102	483.951
Trade, hotels and restaurants	0.31	1.550	0.310	0.310	0.000	0.620	22.867
Financial services, real estate and other services	0.21	1.073	0.215	0.215	0.000	0.429	28.358
Community, social and personal services	0.41	2.055	0.411	0.411	0.000	0.822	97.776

Source: Constructed by the authors based on various sources indicated in the text.

Table 4.26
Pollution load: Base scenario

	In Kilotons						*In Million Tons*
Year	SO_2	NO_2	*CO*	*VOC*	*FP*	*TSP*	CO_2
2006–07	9801.83	5062.65	4252.88	1633.79	4896.29	3942.28	1330.53
2007–08	10460.48	5405.60	4564.28	1750.00	5189.08	4198.47	1424.53
2008–09	11039.55	5698.85	4796.26	1832.85	5531.70	4441.31	1528.42
2009–10	11846.37	6105.60	5138.06	1964.76	5947.83	4768.86	1650.03
2010–11	12710.88	6547.58	5507.86	2106.59	6390.15	5118.97	1781.21
2011–12	13555.35	6982.01	5866.31	2244.08	6827.52	5462.30	1913.66
2012–13	14412.00	7420.45	6235.53	2385.24	7262.19	5808.37	2047.11
2013–14	15296.90	7876.61	6624.78	2533.07	7699.94	6163.11	2184.48
2014–15	16183.32	8332.96	7019.80	2682.66	8130.39	6516.49	2323.58
2015–16	17075.63	8788.30	7424.97	2835.74	8550.83	6869.07	2463.51
2016–17	18007.12	9277.66	7849.97	2995.25	8989.81	7237.17	2613.14
2017–18	18947.98	9760.49	8273.60	3155.76	9438.31	7610.21	2767.74
2018–19	19983.15	10301.26	8749.65	3334.60	9918.57	8017.41	2935.41
2019–20	21054.44	10854.98	9240.76	3519.83	10415.87	8438.88	3112.85
2020–21	22168.20	11429.51	9766.13	3716.74	10909.62	8871.37	3296.29
2021–22	23345.98	12053.04	10326.10	3925.26	11428.59	9327.97	3495.48
2022–23	24562.21	12684.99	10902.04	4141.01	11964.16	9799.39	3706.00
2023–24	25916.56	13399.97	11557.95	4384.69	12540.75	10319.50	3937.58
2024–25	27335.40	14132.97	12247.11	4641.92	13136.72	10862.39	4185.25
2025–26	28889.84	14966.48	13018.05	4926.19	13772.79	11453.07	4460.55
2026–27	30489.68	15803.71	13810.55	5220.31	14422.36	12059.79	4755.17
2027–28	32313.20	16778.71	14740.02	5561.53	15127.86	12742.79	5085.81
2028–29	34229.52	17780.30	15723.13	5923.90	15852.30	13456.43	5446.39
2029–30	36364.83	18939.71	16846.00	6332.49	16628.44	14244.06	5855.26

Source: Based on model projections.

supply' by 10 percent and combine it with reduction in growth of 1 percentage point in coal and lignite, crude petroleum and petroleum products, polluting goods, alcoholic beverages, and electricity, gas, and water supply. In this scenario, growth across the board is not reduced. It is reduced only

Figure 4.16
CO_2 intensity of output: Base scenario

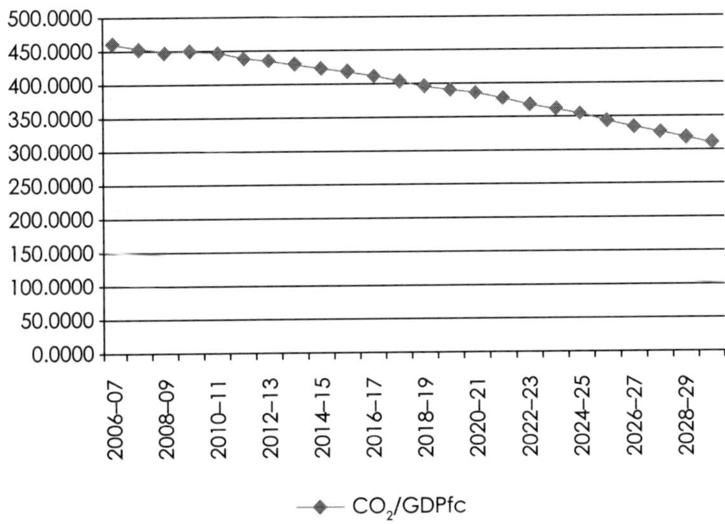

Source: Based on model projections.

Figure 4.17
Pollution load (SO_2): Base and simulation 1

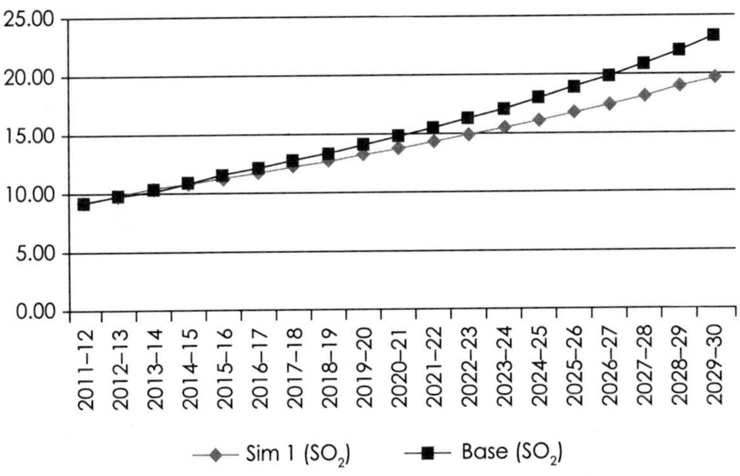

Source: Based on model projections.

Figure 4.18
Pollution load (CO_2): Base and simulation 1

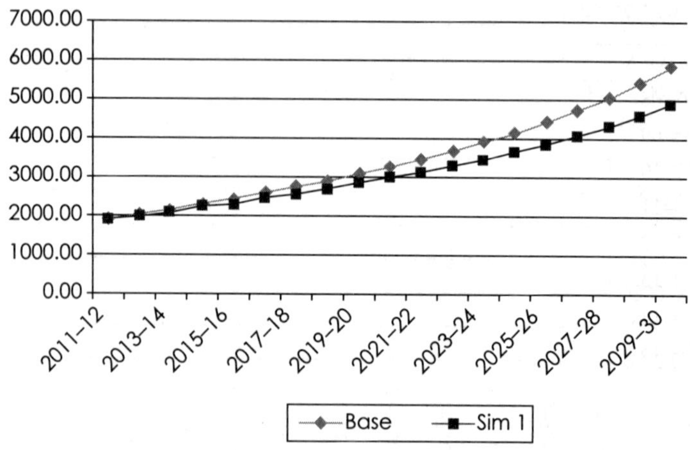

Source: Based on model projections.

Figure 4.19
Pollution load (CO_2): Base and simulation 2

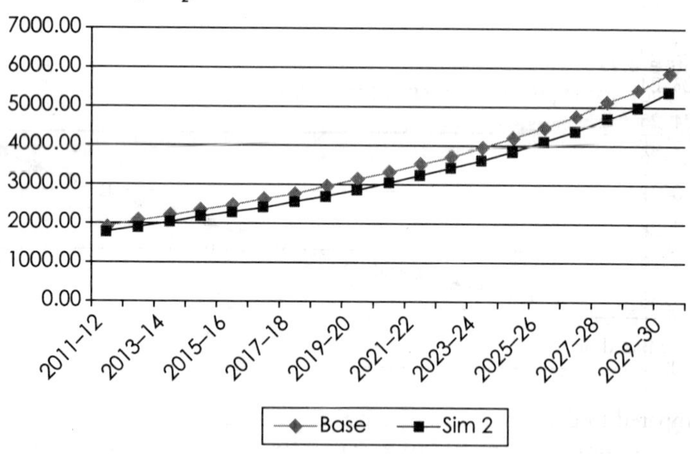

Source: Based on model projections.

in sectors more directly responsible for pollution combined with improvement in technology that causes less pollution.[8] Figure 4.19 shows the CO_2 pollution under the base scenario and simulation 2. Tables 4.27 and 4.28 summarize the reduction over time in carbon intensity across simulations

Table 4.27
Progressive reduction in carbon intensity (progressive percent reduction relative to 2006–07 level)

Year	*Base*	*Sim1*	*Sim2*
2007–08	1.78	1.78	1.70
2008–09	3.16	3.16	3.04
2009–10	2.87	2.87	2.72
2010–11	3.47	3.47	3.29
2011–12	4.74	4.88	5.04
2012–13	5.73	6.00	6.50
2013–14	7.02	7.40	8.23
2014–15	8.29	8.78	9.91
2015–16	9.15	9.72	11.16
2016–17	11.12	11.80	13.48
2017–18	12.32	13.08	15.02
2018–19	13.97	14.82	16.97
2019–20	15.33	16.24	18.62
2020–21	16.55	17.50	20.10
2021–22	18.57	19.60	22.31
2022–23	20.11	21.18	24.03
2023–24	21.96	23.09	26.03
2024–25	23.25	24.36	27.46
2025–26	25.45	26.64	29.71
2026–27	27.14	28.32	31.44
2027–28	29.19	30.42	33.49
2028–29	30.75	31.92	35.03
2029–30	33.05	34.30	37.23

Source: Based on model projections.

compared to the base scenario, and the CO_2 emission levels under all the scenarios, respectively.

The policy options available can be summarized as follows:

1. Allow growth at less than potential rate as deliberate policy;
2. Modify the input-use coefficients of major sources of pollution and
3. Restructure output in favour of less polluting sectors while maintaining growth at about potential rate.

Table 4.28
CO_2 emission levels over years (in million tons)

Year	*Base*	*Sim1*	*Sim2*
2007–08	1330.5	1330.5	1235.1
2008–09	1424.5	1424.5	1323.4
2009–10	1528.4	1528.4	1420.5
2010–11	1650.0	1650.0	1534.0
2011–12	1781.2	1781.2	1656.5
2012–13	1913.7	1896.0	1769.1
2013–14	2047.1	2009.4	1881.2
2014–15	2184.5	2124.3	1995.9
2015–16	2323.6	2238.4	2111.1
2016–17	2463.5	2351.0	2226.1
2017–18	2613.1	2470.5	2349.1
2018–19	2767.7	2592.1	2475.3
2019–20	2935.4	2723.4	2612.4
2020–21	3112.8	2861.0	2757.3
2021–22	3296.3	3001.2	2906.8
2022–23	3495.5	3152.9	3069.8
2023–24	3706.0	3311.5	3242.0
2024–25	3937.6	3485.8	3432.3
2025–26	4185.3	3670.4	3636.2
2026–27	4460.5	3875.8	3864.4
2027–28	4755.2	4093.4	4109.6
2028–29	5085.8	4337.9	4386.7
2029–30	5446.4	4602.4	4690.8

Source: Based on model projections.

4.6.4 Summary

In this chapter, we looked at the link between growth in the Indian economy with the pollution load that it carries. Both local and global pollutants are considered. The estimates are based on the IPPS coefficients for local pollution and the MoEF energy balance matrix for the CO_2 emissions. The policy options that reduce pollution are achieving growth rates less than potential as a conscious policy option and/or reducing pollution load by reducing the input use of polluting goods and services and reducing growth rates specifically of polluting goods and services without sacrificing overall growth. The latter can be facilitated by eco-taxes and eco-subsidies.

4.7 FINDINGS AND CONCLUSIONS

This study addresses two major considerations in planning for India's future growth. First, there is a need to recognize what the pollution load that is growing at potential rates implies. Secondly, while the proposed transition to GST might imply efficiency effects and therefore facilitate growth, left to itself it might also encourage pollution. We examine the case for integrating eco-taxes in the GST regime, which can then provide a modern green version of GST, which can facilitate environment friendly growth.

4.7.1 Methodology and Analytical Framework

While a number of alternative methodologies have been developed in the literature to examine energy–growth–pollution linkages, none of these provide a suitable framework to discuss fiscal policies and their impact on the choices regarding growth and pollution. Our methodology consists of using a macro-econometric model to generate future demand and output profiles and an input–output model to examine inter-sectoral choices.

We have developed a macro-econometric model to estimate potential growth as well as potential tax revenues under suitable policy configurations for fiscal, trade and monetary policies. It takes a long-term view and projects growth based on supply side considerations. Such growth can be considered potential growth achievable for the Indian economy. The model projects such growth up to 2029–30. It is shown that the structure of output changes by the implicit inter-sectoral drivers particularly the allocation of investment in these sectors. The model is used to generate both tax revenues and pollution.

The emphasis is on highlighting the underlying trends in components of aggregate demand and output. For this purpose, we utilize a macro-econometric model, which provides a disaggregated treatment of the supply side and emphasizes structural changes in the economy. Long-term modelling of the macro-economy for two or more decades into the future needs to be different from short-term modelling in several crucial respects. In particular, long-term models need to emphasize the supply side of the economy far more than the demand side. In short- to medium-term modelling, the focus is on the management of cyclical movements, where the demand side is important. On the other hand, the supply side gains central importance in long-term models which need to focus on growth, productivity and technological change.

Long-term growth is conditioned by a suitable policy environment. Management of policies, both monetary policy and fiscal policy, requires to be aimed at providing a stable economic environment and addressing issues of sustainability rather than short-term policy calibration.

In the Indian context, the impact of the demographic changes such as the slowing down of the population growth, changes in the age structure, and consequently on the availability of the work force and the dependency ratio, needs to be endogenized. Similarly, the long-term model should provide for structural changes in the economy like the growing share of the service sector and the falling share of the agricultural sector. Furthermore, as capital stock increases, the ratio of older capital stock to total capital stock also increases. This implies that consumption of fixed capital will increase at an accelerated rate over time. With technological progress, productivity of factors of production may increase but there will also be diminishing returns to capital. Technological change can also be a reason for accelerated rate of obsolescence of capital stock.

In this model, four sectors are considered: real, monetary, fiscal and trade. The real sector is specified in a disaggregated way both on the demand side and the output side. These are the focus areas of the study. Specific policy rules are followed with reference to fiscal, monetary and trade policies.

A major structural change that will progressively affect the economy is the demographic shift in India where the dependency ratio (defined as the ratio of population below 14 years and above 60 years) will reach a peak and then decline. Correspondingly, the share of working age population to total population will increase.

4.7.2 GST: Integrating Eco-taxes

At present, there are parallel systems of indirect taxation at the central and state levels with overlapping tax bases with respect to value added up to the stage of manufacturing. This leads to cascading of indirect taxes. Apart from variations in tax rates, the levy of inter-state sales tax also fragments the all-India market. The tax system remains a mix of destination- and origin-based levies. The proposed reforms aim to bring about a comprehensive GST that eliminates cascading, removes tax barriers in the inter-state movement of goods and services, and ushers in a system where taxation will be destination-based, goods and services will be taxed at the same rates, rates will be common across states, inter-state sales tax will be eliminated and the country as a whole will become a genuine integrated common market.

However, GST in this form may have perverse environmental consequences unless suitable provisions are built into the system. For instance, if a polluting good is taxed at a lower rate under the GST regime than the present tax structure (after taking account central and state taxes), the resulting consumption of the polluting good is expected to be higher. Further, in a destination-based system, the tax revenue will accrue to the consuming states rather than the producing states. This will not only increase emissions in the producing states but will also leave them with lesser revenues to cope with the negative externalities of production.

We note that there are clear elements and proposals for integrating eco-taxes in the GST framework in the Report of the Thirteenth Finance Commission and even in the proposals of the EC. These can be accommodated even within the proposed amendment to the constitution by the central government. The role of the GST Council will be of considerable importance in this context.

In the Green GST proposed in this study, the main features of GST may be summarized as follows:

1. GST will consist of CGST, SGST and IGST.
2. There will be single and uniform rate for both CGST and SGST with IGST rate being equal to CGST rate plus SGST rate.
3. Both centre and states will have the power to levy non-rebatable excise/sales tax or cess over and above the CGST and SGST rates on petroleum products, demerit goods and polluting goods and services. The list of goods selected for such non-rebatable excise/cess may be determined by the GST Council.

4.7.3 Pollution–Growth Trade-off

We demonstrate that using eco-taxes in the GST framework works better for the sustained environment friendly growth for India. It enables fixation of the core GST rate at relatively lower levels (initially at 14 percent) thereby generating efficiency effects and better compliance. With low overall GST rate resource allocation and compliance would be better, unleashing the productive forces of the economy taking the economy towards achievable potential growth.

The reduction in output of polluting goods and services is to be brought about by an increase in the non-rebatable component of the tax. Any increase in the tax needs to be translated into an increase in prices, which will reduce the demand for and output of the polluting goods. This will depend in a partial equilibrium setting on tax-elasticity of price and price-elasticity of output. If both are set at a unity, a desired 10 percent reduction in the quantity of use of the polluting goods will require a 10 percent increase in the tax rate. It may, however, be noted that for petroleum products and many of the other polluting goods as well as beverages, prices are administered and even if upward revision of tax is translated fully or partially into a change in price, there may be a time lag. In case of a unit tax-elasticity of output, the additional tax revenue due to the higher rate will be balanced out by the fall in the quantity used of the polluting goods and services. Additional tax revenues will only result if the tax-elasticity of output is less than one and under the assumption that the tax-increase is passed through to the prices. In the model, the additional tax revenues on polluting goods and services are generated by the higher non-rebatable component of the tax applied to the lower outputs of polluting goods and services. The policy experiments need to take into account the desired reduction in the output of the polluting goods and services, the impact of these changes on other outputs while maintaining the production relations, the required increase in the non-rebatable component of the tax rates over and above the core GST rates given tax-elasticities of prices and price-elasticities of output, and the impact on tax revenues.

The eco-taxes in the form of non-rebatable excises and cesses may be further supplemented by local level eco-taxes to regionally disperse growth so that local pollution can be dispersed and kept within acceptable limits. For global pollution such as that of CO_2, focus has to be on limited number of industries or sectors.

The policy options available may be summarized as follows:

1. Allow growth at less than potential rate as deliberate policy;
2. Modify the input-use coefficients of major sources of pollution and
3. Restructure output in favour of less polluting sectors while maintaining growth at about potential rate.

4.7.4 Fiscal Instruments and Pollution

Eco-taxes and eco-subsidies provide a set of instruments that can enable reaching desired environment objectives with minimum compromise on growth. In a complementary paper on eco-subsidies, we have argued that eco-taxes and eco-subsidies should be jointly used to bring about necessary changes in incentives change both input choices and technology choices so that these can be made more environment friendly. Since GST is on the anvil and a constitutional amendment bill has already been introduced in parliament, it is the appropriate time to make the case for integrating eco-taxes in the GST framework.

4.7.5 Scope for Future Research

While the work reported here on the integration of environmental taxes in India's indirect tax system in the context of a planned shift towards GST regime provides crucial policy insights, like every field of research there is scope for future work in several important directions. Some of these are outlined here:

1. A bottom-up approach to energy modelling focusing on a gradual shift to low-carbon growth via regulatory- and incentive-based mechanisms can be undertaken which would facilitate desired reduction in GHG emission intensity. The results from such an exercise can be further used to understand the macro-economic implications.
2. The feasibility of endogenizing energy prices or the energy input coefficients as function of the relative prices can be explored and the scope for promotion of energy efficiency and reduction of carbon intensity through public policies can be assessed.
3. Multiple uses of eco-tax revenue—say, to reduce industry pollution abatement burden, development of a few major clean technologies—can be demonstrated through large-scale macro-modelling aimed at achieving high and sustainable economic growth.
4. Sectoral studies can be undertaken to supplement the work reported here for identifying the list of polluting goods and services that need different treatment under the GST regime. Further, the distributional effects of the sectoral interventions may also merit detailed and careful examination.

NOTES

1. The methodology to calculate commodity × commodity table and industry × industry table from the input flow matrix and output flow matrix is as given in Appendix 2 of CSO's manual for input–output tables.
2. The commodity × commodity and industry × industry matrices can be constructed either with commodity technology or industry technology.
3. Benchmarking with previous year's GDP is useful since governments can overstate current GDP to validate higher borrowing in the current year even with fixed fiscal deficit GDP ratio. If the target with respect to current year GDP is 6 percent and the economy grows at 15 percent in nominal terms, we have '*A*'.
   '*A*': the fiscal deficit to previous year GDP (say, *FDRATIOLAG*), given by
   Fiscal deficit = $(.06)Y = (.06) * (Y_{-1} * 1.15)$; or
   $FDRATIOLAG = \text{fiscal deficit}/Y_{-1} = (.06) * (1.15) = .069$
4. The suffix '*N*' in the output of each sector indicates output in current prices.
5. Apparent consumption = production + imports – exports – international bunkers stock changes.
6. CO_2 emissions factor = carbon emission factor * 44/12.
7. CMIE, www.indiastat.com
8. It may be noted that the reduction in output of polluting goods and services is brought about by an increase in the non-rebatable component of the tax. However, there is no one-to-one relationship between tax rate and output reduction. The policy experiment needs to take into account the desired reduction in the output of the polluting goods and services, the impact of such changes on other outputs, the required increase in the non-rebatable component of the tax rates over and above the core GST rates given tax elasticities of prices and price elasticities of output, and the impact on tax revenue.

5

Role of Environmental Subsidies in India

D.K. Srivastava, Rita Pandey and C. Bhujanga Rao

5.1 SUBSIDIES: MEANING AND MEASUREMENT

Subsidies and indirect taxes are both indirect fiscal instruments aimed at modifying market-determined outcomes. In both cases, relative prices of the subsidized/taxed goods are affected relative to others. In the case of subsidized goods, the relative price is lowered, while for the taxed good, it is raised. Taxes reduce disposable income while subsidies inject money into circulation. Subsidies cater to positive externalities while taxes take care of negative externalities. Subsidies can promote environment-promoting technologies and use of environment friendly inputs. Subsidies can be targeted to specific sectors more easily than taxes, where adopting a sector-specific approach is not preferred.

5.1.1 Defining a Subsidy

Defining subsidy has not been an easy task and more so defining environmental subsidies, which can both be environment-promoting or environmentally harmful. As OECD (2006b) notes, there is no universally accepted definition of a subsidy. The literature on subsidy has recognized that the definition of a subsidy is a useful part of the framework for a policy discussion and that the term subsidy should be differently defined for different contexts.[1] Barg (1996) proposed three different definitions of subsidies for economic, fiscal and environmental issues as follows:

Economic definition: A government-directed, market-distorting intervention, which decreases the cost of producing a specific good or service, or increases the price charged for it.

Fiscal definition: Government expenditure, provision for exemption from general taxation or assumption of liability which decreases the cost of producing a specific good or service or increases the price charged for it.

Environmental definition: An environmental subsidy consists of the value of uncompensated environmental damage arising from any flow of goods or services.

Environmental subsidies have been defined in the broadest way, incorporating any flow of benefits that arise from reduction of environmental degradation, even if they are not government-directed, and do not pass through a market mechanism, and reflect indirect costs. For example, harvesting a forest without reforesting, or without recognizing non-timber values, involves an unpaid cost. This amounts to subsidization of these harvesters, to the extent of the unpaid cost, by the user of the environment, that is, the society. However, even this definition does not fully address the potential irreversible harm to an ecological system for which there may be no substitute.

In studies dealing with budgetary subsidies, subsidies have often been defined as unrecovered costs of public provision of private goods (Mundle and Rao, 1991; Srivastava et al., 1997). In the environmental definition of subsidies given by Barg (1996) also subsidies are taken as unrecovered costs. The concept of cost, however, is broader than the one usually applied in the budgetary studies. In environmental context, the cost to the society arises from uncompensated damage to the environment commonly shared by all members of the society by activities producing private goods (even if sometimes provided by the public authorities). These uncompensated losses may arise both when the concerned private goods are subsidized and when they are not subsidized. When a budgetary subsidy is used to encourage the production/use of such a good (e.g. fertilizer), there are two types of unrecovered costs: those that constitute the difference between the cost of provision of the good and the receipts from the users, and those that amount to the value of the damage to the environment because of the use of the good, which needs to be paid by its users to the society for the damage to the environment. The two unrecovered costs are both subsidies, and can be added up. However, the latter involves crucial issues of identification and quantification of such costs.

5.1.2 Measuring Subsidies: Alternative Approaches

a. Explicit Budgetary Subsidies

It is commonly recognized that entries in the budget under the head 'subsidies' would give a very incomplete picture of subsidies. An alternative approach is used in the national income accounting framework. Another possibility is to define subsidies as unrecovered budgetary costs.

b. National Income Accounting Approach

In national income accounts (NIA), indirect taxes net of subsidies constitute the difference between gross domestic product (GDP) at factor cost and GDP at market prices. Indirect taxes that are part of the sale price of commodities do not create incomes for factors of production. These are, therefore, deducted from GDP at market prices to get GDP at factor cost. On the other hand, subsidies have the reverse effect. A subsidy received by a firm will be paid out as wages, rents or profits, and would therefore, become incomes of the factors of production. However, this component of their income is not generated by the sale of output. Hence, subsidies must be added to expenditure, that is, GDP at market prices.

In India, in the Central Statistical Organization's NIA methodology, subsidies include grants on current account which private industries, public corporations and government enterprises receive from the government. These may be in the form of direct payments or those estimated on the basis of differentials between buying and selling prices of government trading organizations. The NIA approach focuses only on firms/producers or government departments. It does not fully cover all the budgetary costs in the public provision of non-public goods.

c. Budgetary Subsidies: Subsidies as Unrecovered Costs

Under this approach, subsidies are measured as 'unrecovered' costs of governmental provision of goods/services that are not classified as public goods. The unrecovered costs are measured as the excess of aggregate costs over receipts from the concerned budgetary head. The aggregate costs comprise two elements: (a) current costs and (b) annualized capital costs. Current costs consist of revenue (current) expenditures directly related to the provision of services classified under different heads. Transfers to funds are not included, as these do not contribute to the provision of service in the current cost. Transfers from funds are included. Transfers to individuals are also separated out, as these add to incomes of individuals and do not constitute provision of goods/services. For capital costs, a distinction is made between three forms of government investment resulting in accumulated capital stock. If services are departmentally provided, there is investment in physical capital. In addition, there is investment in the form of equity and loans including those given to public enterprises. The annualized cost of capital is obtained by applying the interest rate at which funds have been borrowed by the government to capital stock. This represents the opportunity cost of capital. In the case of physical capital, a depreciation cost is calculated, in addition. The receipts come in three forms: revenue receipts from the user charges, interest receipts on loans and dividends on equity investment.

In terms of symbols, these costs may be written as:

$$C = \mathrm{RX} + (i + d^*)\, K_o + iZ_o,$$

where RX = revenue expenditure on the service head net of adjustments; i = effective interest rate; d^* = depreciation rate; K_o = aggregate capital expenditure at the beginning of the period and Z_o = sum of loans and equity investment at the beginning of the period. Adjustments in deriving RX relate to transfer to funds which are deducted and transfer from funds which are added. Transfers to individuals are also not counted, although these are separately compiled. Expenditure on running secretariat social and economic services are also not counted as these relate to general administration, and are also not decomposable among different heads of services.

Receipts are:

$$\mathrm{R} = \mathrm{RR} + (I + D),$$

where RR = revenue receipts; I = interest receipts; D= dividends.

Subsidy is defined as: $S = C - R$.

Other parameters are effective interest rate and depreciation rate. The depreciation rate is to be calculated with reference to the stock of capital at the beginning of the year. This stock of capital is the sum of nominal investments in previous years.

5.1.3 Environmentally Harmful and Environment-promoting Subsidies

In the context of environment, subsidies are often interpreted as opportunity costs which arise due to negative environmental externalities. For example, car drivers pollute the atmosphere for all citizens and gain a benefit at everyone's expense implying that common citizens subsidize the car owners. Similarly, when farmers spray pesticides, they introduce toxic effluents into the commonly shared ecosystems. Industrialists often introduce pollutants into commonly shared water bodies. Although this kind of subsidization is widespread, it almost goes unnoticed. The conventional gross national product (GNP) accounting generally presents such activities as economic pluses, whereas there is a case to consider these as making a negative contribution to output. When soil erosion causes farmers to apply extra fertilizer to compensate for loss of plant nutrients, this is viewed as an economic activity to be recorded as an additional item for GNP—while the costs to society are not taken into account. Barg (1996) gives these examples to illustrate the point. The Exxon oil spill caused clean-up efforts costing $3 billion; the GNP arithmetic counted them as an advance for GNP.

Environmental degradation may result from both market failures and policy failures. Policy instruments for containing environmental degradation within acceptable thresholds have mainly focused on market failures. However, when economic policy leads to the use of such fiscal instruments as subsidies which themselves become a cause of environmental degradation, these may be cited as instances of policy failures. Several examples of the environmentally harmful subsidies which are introduced as part of a conscious economic policy may be cited. For example, subsidization of agriculture through subsidization of water or fertilizer or support prices can foster over-loading of croplands, leading to erosion and compaction of top soil, pollution from synthetic fertilizers and pesticides, and de-nitrification of soils. Subsidies for road transportation can engender atmospheric pollution. Subsidies for water encourage misuse and overuse of this scarce resource. Some examples of environmentally beneficial subsidies are afforestation programmes, subsidies to promote renewable energy, cleaner fuels, energy efficiency, wasteland development, and soil and water conservation.

Subsidies that encourage human action causing damage to the environment are harmful because they create incentives to behave in ways which decrease social welfare. In order to analyse such situations, one must first examine the environmental problems that arise from the human activity that is encouraged by these subsidies. Thus, one must come at the problem from both directions: define the subsidy and how it affects the human behaviour, and define the environmental situation and how it is affected by the subsidy-induced behaviour. Panayotou's list of economic manifestations of environmental degradation is a useful starting point for analysing such situations. This is presented in Box 1.

As long as subsidies nurture hidden costs in the form of environmental damage, they may be considered harmful/perverse subsidies. Figure 5.1 illustrates broadly the ways in which ill-targeted subsidies in agriculture could be harmful.

Box 1: Representative List of Economic Manifestations of Environmental Degradation

- Overuse, waste and inefficiency co-exist with growing resource scarcity (shortages).
- An increasingly scarce resource is put to inferior, low-return and unsustainable uses, even though superior, high-return and sustainable uses exist.
- A renewable resource, capable of sustainable management is exploited as an extractive resource (i.e. it is mined).
- A resource is put to a single use, when multiple uses would generate larger net benefits.
- Investments in the protection and enhancement of the resource base are not undertaken, even though they would generate a positive net present value by increasing productivity and enhancing sustainability.
- A larger amount of effort and cost is incurred, when a smaller amount of effort and cost would have generated a higher level of output, more profit and less damage to the resource.
- Local communities and tribal and other groups, such as women, are displaced and deprived of their customary rights of access to resources, regardless of the fact that, because of their specialized knowledge, tradition and self-interest, they may be the most cost-effective managers of those resources.
- Public projects are undertaken that do not make adequate provision for, or generate sufficient benefits to, compensate all those affected (including the environment) to a level where they are decidedly better off 'with' than 'without' the project.
- Failure to recycle resources and by-products, when recycling would generate both economic and environmental benefits.
- Unique sites and habitats are lost and animal and plant species go extinct without compelling economic reasons which counter the value of uniqueness and diversity and the cost of irreversible loss.

Source: Panayotou (1992).

Figure 5.1
Effects of ill-targeted subsidies in agriculture

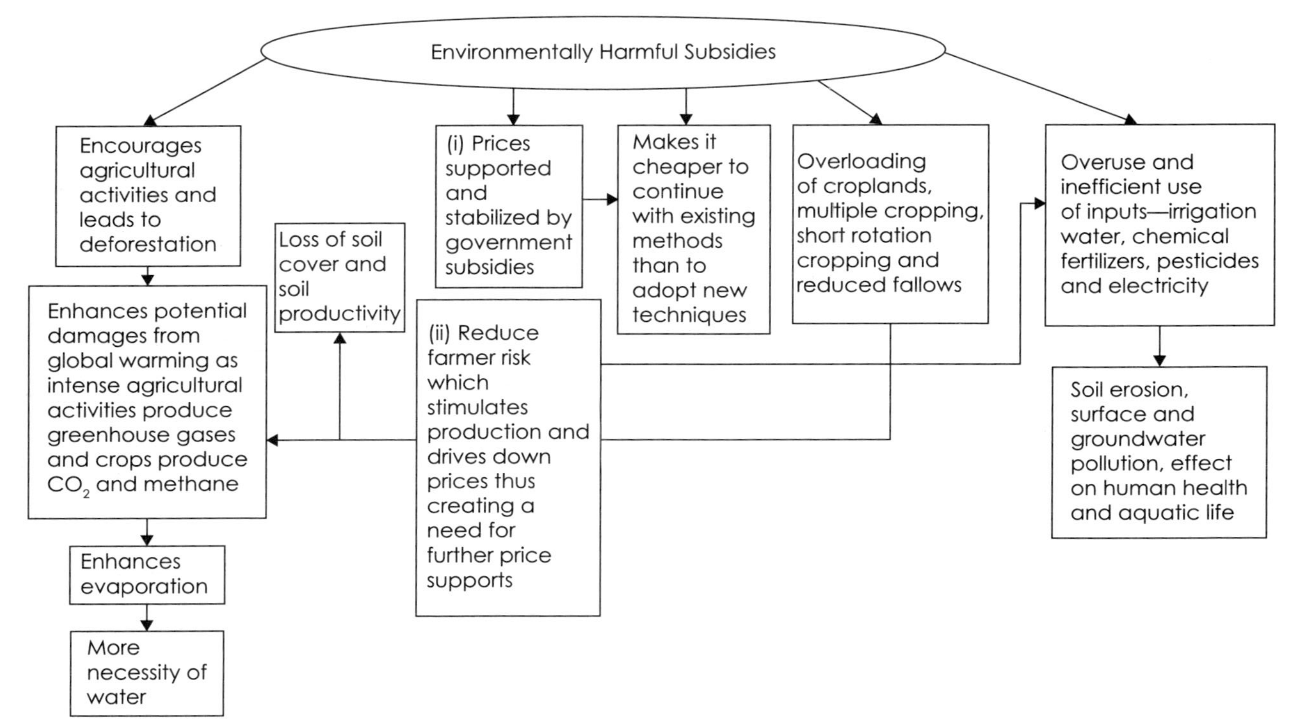

Environmentally harmful subsidies: Growing international concern: In recent years, the phenomenon of environmentally harmful subsidies has been recognized in the literature, and there is also a widespread international concern about environmentally harmful subsidies. This is both because of their huge monetary costs and the cross-country effects. For instance, subsidies for fossil fuels contribute to pollution effects such as acid rain, urban smog and global warming. These also have cross-border effects.

It has been estimated (Myers and Kent, 2001) that perverse subsidies in the world may amount to as much as $1.5 trillion, which is larger than the economies of all but five countries in the world (using purchasing power parity (PPP) for the GNPs of China and India). Ironically, the total of almost $1.5 trillion is two and a half times larger than the Rio Earth Summit's budget for sustainable development—a sum that governments dismissed as unthinkable. The main findings of Myers and Kent indicate that: (i) total subsidies in the world may be around $1900 billion per year, and perverse subsidies may be as large as $1450 billion; (ii) perverse subsidies have the capacity to (a) exert a highly distortive impact on the global economy of $28 trillion and (b) inflict grand scale injuries on our environment. It is also noted that the OECD countries account for two-thirds of all subsidies and an even larger share of perverse subsidies; that the USA accounts for 21 percent of perverse subsidies; and that the single sector of road transportation accounts for 48 percent of all subsidies and 44 percent of perverse subsidies.

While the two totals—overall subsidies of almost $1.9 trillion per year, and perverse subsidies, approaching $1.5 trillion per year—may appear to be large, these might still be underestimates. Myers and Kent (2001) observe that many environmental externalities (including what could prove to be as big as the rest put together, namely global warming) are either underestimated or omitted from the final results through sheer lack of documentation of economic costs entailed. Thus, the total for perverse subsidies, approaching $1.5 trillion per year, should be considered an underestimate. van Beers and Moor (2001) estimate world subsidies for a few identified sectors. Estimates presented in Table 5.1 reveal the alarming levels of subsidy in OECD countries.

It can be seen from Table 5.1 that as a percentage of world GDP, global subsidies account for a staggering 4 percent. However, in terms of the magnitude in US dollars, OECD countries account of over two-thirds of the total subsidies. The environmental implications of the subsidies in these sectors are potentially substantial.

Table 5.1
Estimates of world subsidies: 1994–98 (US$ billion)

Sector	*OECD*	*Non-OECD*	*World*	*OECD as % of World*
Agriculture	335	65	400	84
Water	15	45	60	25
Forestry	5	30	35	4
Fisheries	10	10	20	50
Mining	25	5	30	83
Energy	80	160	240	33
Road transport	200	25	225	89
Manufacturing	55	Negligible	55	100
Total	725	340	1065	68
Total as % of GDP	3.4	6.3	4.0	

Source: van Beers and de Moor (2001).

Table 5.2
Some environmental effects of subsidies or subsidy removal

Study/Country	*Nature of Scenario*	*Environmental Impacts*
Cristofaro et al. (1995), USA	Removal of US$8.5 billion Energy subsidies Removal of US$15.4 billion Energy subsidies	10 mtC by 2010 37 mtC by 2035 64 mtC by 2010
Gurich et al. (1995), Russia	Removal of energy Subsidy effects in 2010	76% reduction in TSP 39% reduction in CO_2 43% reduction in NO_x 66% reduction in SO_x
IEA (1999)	Removal of consumer subsidies in Russia, China and six other countries	16% reduction in CO_2
Larsen and Shah (1992)	Removal of world energy subsidies of US$230 billion	21% reduction in CO_2
DRI in Michaelis (1996)	Removal of coal subsidies in Europe and Japan	10–50 mt. CO_2

Source: Compiled by the authors.

Results of studies presented in Table 5.2 cannot be strictly compared as different definitions and methodologies have been used in these studies. Yet, estimates of environmental impacts of subsidies are significant enough to say that the debate should move away from trying to build consensus on definition and analytical issues to another level to help governments develop a strategy for reduction in environmentally harmful subsidies.

Subsidies and natural capital: Many subsidies directly or indirectly contribute to the depletion of natural capital. Examples abound: water logging and salinization from subsidized irrigation water; excessive air pollution and greenhouse gas (GHG) emission transport fuel and stationary energy subsidization; deforestation from subsidies to forest clearance and logging; overfishing due to subsidization of the fishing fleet. However, actual quantification of the loss is difficult. In Table 5.2, some estimates that focus on GHG emissions and air pollution are presented. These estimates, however, need to be treated with caution. The loss of human capital cannot be blamed solely on subsidies.

Subsidies and social capital: The social capital dimension of sustainable development is one of the unexplored areas of research. Social capital relates to sets of interpersonal and inter-institutional relationships in society. The better these relationships, the lower is the transaction costs of economic exchange and better the chances of sustained development. There may be many links between social capital, the implicit trust in human relationship and subsidies. For example, subsidies generate rents and encourage rent-seeking activities. Rent seeking involves lobbying and, ultimately leads to corruption and bribes. Thus, the trust in government institutions is reduced, thereby lowering the stock of social capital. The cost is multidimensional: overall, economic efficiency gets lowered (under directly unproductive profit-seeking activities) and the poor, who cannot pay bribes to secure the subsidy, are excluded from the benefit of it. Losing social capital also means losing the concern for fellow human beings. Societies that tend to be more selfish also tend to be less caring of the natural environment.

Subsidies and technology: A final component of the subsidy–sustainability link is via technology. Subsidies can induce environmentally friendly technology (e.g. subsidies in renewable energy sector). But many subsidies provide 'lock in' effects to prevailing technologies, inhibiting the advance of new, cleaner technologies. For example, subsidies are often specified by fuel source or technology, e.g. subsidies to coal sector in the UK and Germany. These subsidies block the transition to renewable and low-pollution sources of energy. Nor is there any incentive to develop technologies that lower the pollution content of the fuels.

5.2 CASE FOR ENVIRONMENT-PROMOTING SUBSIDIES

5.2.1 Introduction

For promoting environment, among the market-based instruments both taxation and subsidies for goods and services have significance and serve as complementary instruments. In fact, tax revenues from environmental taxes can be used to finance environment-promoting subsidies. However using environmental subsidies requires suitable design of subsidies, which can differ from context to context. The idea is to induce the households or firms to find the cheapest possible way to reduce pollution. Such reduction can come through the three Rs (reduce, reuse and recycle) as well as through greener technologies (newer machines, labour-intensive production, etc.) or inputs (bio-fuels). In all cases, the idea is to develop a set of Pigouvian intervention for social welfare maximization through correction of externalities.

5.2.2 Combining Environmental Taxation and Subsidy

In administering environmental taxation as well as subsidies, it is important to recognize that it applies to the polluting activity rather than any market transaction. But polluting activities (say, SO_x generation) are hard to monitor (the firm or the consumer have incentive to under-report). This makes both determination and enforcement of taxation as well as subsidies difficult. In order to overcome the problem, Fullerton and Wolverton (1995) have suggested a two-part subsidy. They suggest an instrument that mimics the Pigouvian intervention (generating efficiency) consisting of a tax on the output/consumption of the good, and combining it with a subsidy to other inputs except waste.

To see the logic of the argument, one needs to think the pollution or waste generation as an input to production process. Mathematically, one may express the output as $Q = F(K, L)$ and waste generation as $W = \phi(K, L)$. It is possible then to express Q as a function of W, such as $Q = \Phi(K, L, W)$. Here, K and L are capital/labour and other material inputs.

Pigouvian taxes correct for externality in two different ways: the 'output effect' discourages production and hence consumption of polluting goods. On the other hand, the substitution effect makes pollution (as an input to production) more expensive relative to other inputs. The implied 'substitution effect' reduces waste generation per unit of the remaining amount of the output that still gets produced. A two-part instrument, consisting of a tax as well as a subsidy, accomplishes the same effects separately. The tax on polluting output reduces production and consumption of the good. The second part that subsidizes all non-waste inputs makes waste relatively more expensive and reduces waste per unit of output. An example of a two-part instrument is a deposit–refund system: the consumer pays a deposit (when she buys a bottle of milk or a can of soft drinks) under the presumption that the waste will be discarded improperly and gets a refund only with proper performance. The deposit equals the refund.

It is possible to extend the model to production, where direct taxes on emission are not possible to levy. By proper choice of (sales) tax on the *consumption of* brown goods and a subsidy on usage of clean inputs in *production*, one can achieve the social optimum. Given this equivalence between Pigouvian taxation and a two-part instrument, one needs to take into account other considerations like feasibility, administrative costs, political perception and enforcement for deciding the appropriate instrument. A Pigouvian tax on brown inputs or emissions may not be feasible, either because emissions cannot be measured or the tax is not enforceable. If Pigouvian tax is not viable, the equivalent two-part instrument has an obvious advantage.

Even if the Pigouvian tax is viable, the two-part instrument may have lower cost of administration. The Pigouvian tax requires the government to collect data on emissions of the polluter. In contrast, the two-part instrument places the data requirements on the polluters. The individual consumer or firm is required to provide the proof proper disposal has taken place in order to obtain the subsidy. The cost of the 'proof' must be lower for the firm and the consumer than for a government official who has less knowledge of the production and disposal process. The government only needs to set the deposit and the refund, and to check for the authenticity of a returned item or clean input.

Politically, Pigouvian tax may be resisted if it raises taxes on consumers or firms. A deposit–refund system may be more popular with the voters. If those who properly dispose off an item can receive a refund on the tax originally paid, then these taxes increase for those who refuse to participate. A second reason for the political appeal, at least in the case of deposit–refund system, that it could be self-financing: the refund can be taken directly from the funds generated by deposits. Even if the two-part instrument is not strictly a deposit–refund casc (funds from tax not to be used for the subsidy), this would generate flexibility in the use of funds. The other advantages of a two-part instrument (or, more specifically, the deposit–refund system) include job creation due to an increased demand for truck drivers, sorters and recyclers; and energy savings from the use of recycled rather than virgin materials.

The evidence for a two-part tariff comes mainly from the USA, where bottle bills and other forms of deposit–refund system are practiced extensively. The actual evidence of the states with bottle bills include (a) higher return rate of bottles, (b) lower solid waste generation, (c) reduction in injuries to children due to less littering and (d) higher quality of inputs to be recycled.

The evidence of other benefits seems to be mixed. For example, it is true that some jobs have been created mainly in retailing, transportation and recycling, but there could be a job loss in non-refillable industries. Taking another case, reduction in virgin material in glass production implies reduction in air pollution, water pollution and mining waste generation. On the other hand, fuel bill for transportation of re-usable materials may go up because reusable bottles (and other consumer goods) are bulkier than regular, 'use-and-throw' bottles.

Typical deposit–refund systems are also present in most of the OECD countries (other than the USA), and these include aluminium cans, beverage containers and car hulks. In literature, one can find other examples of deposit–refund system. Fischer et al. (1995), for example, have proposed a deposit–refund system for carbon removal from atmosphere. Here, citizens of each country would pay the proposed tax when they purchase a product manufactured using a polluting process. The subsidy, in the form of a credit to the country's emission quota, is given when a country demonstrates certified carbon removal. In the same vein, a tax and a subsidy are coupled to remove the CFCs from refrigerators and air conditioners. Bohm (1981) has proposed a deposit–refund system for removal of SO_x. A deposit would be required on fuel, based on the sulphur content, and refund would be paid to firms when the sulphur is removed from the air.

5.3 ENVIRONMENTAL SUBSIDIES: SELECTED INTERNATIONAL EXPERIENCE

In this section, we review the experience of selected countries that have used environmental subsidies. We look specifically at the experience of Sweden, Germany and China.

5.3.1 Environmental Subsidies in Sweden

In Sweden, environmental subsidies have been extensively used. For this purpose, it is useful to widen the definition of subsidies as given by the European System of Accounts 1995, which is as follows '... current unrequited payments from government to producers with the objective of influencing their levels of production, their prices or the remuneration of the factors of production' (European Commission, 1996). This definition may be broadened to include to the following:

1. capital transfers, such as investment subsidies and
2. current transfers from the government to households in their role as consumers.

Environmental subsidies in Sweden may be considered, as per the OECD rules as covering. 'environmentally motivated subsidies'. Most of these are related to energy and transport.

In Sweden, there are two major sources of subsidies—the government and the European Union (EU). The total amount of subsidies from the government has decreased from SEK 59833 million in 1993 to SEK 33898 million in 2000. Subsidies from the EU have, on the other hand, increased from SEK 4859 million to SEK 8887 million between 1995 and 2000. The SNA-subsidies are given to different recipients in the economy. The largest amount of subsidies, SEK 32000 million, was given to private companies in 1996. Other major receivers were state corporations, state businesses, private companies, the public sector and non-profit-making household associations. Of the state subsidies to private companies, more than 75 percent were interest subsidies for housing construction and approximately 15 percent were subsidies for creating employment. Subsidies from the EU come from a range of different funds, with a large part going to the agricultural sector.

i. Environmental Subsidies in Swedish National Account

In Sweden, the resource-related subsidies are dominated by subsidies to the agricultural sector. Other resource-related subsidies in Sweden affect the fishing sector as well as research. The majority of the energy-related subsidies aim to increase energy efficiency and improve energy technology. Table 5.3 shows the volume of subsidies, per Swedish National Income Accounts (SNA) calculations.

Environmentally motivated SNA-subsidies have increased as a percentage of the total SNA-subsidies in Sweden between 1993 and 2000. Since 1998, environmentally motivated subsidies as a percentage of the total subsidies in Sweden have been constant at around 6–7 percent. One explanation for this development is the decrease of the *total subsidies* over these years, together with the fact that the environmentally motivated subsidies increased rapidly between 1996 and 1998. In 2000, the total environmentally motivated subsidies came to 0.10 percent of GDP, which is a slight decrease compared to 1999.

a. Resource subsidies: Resource-related subsidies are dominated by subsidies to the agricultural sector, including the following items: 'landscape

Table 5.3
Total environmentally motivated subsidies in Sweden (SEK million)

	1993	*1994*	*1995*	*1996*	*1997*	*1998*	*1999*	*2000*
Resource subsidies	248	296	1110	947	1638	2694	2432	2028
Energy subsidies	121	71	152	141	165	178	191	154
Transport subsidies	0	0	14	2	3	3	14	0
Total	369	367	1276	1090	1806	2875	2637	2182

Source: SCB (2003).

conservation measures', 'supplementary measures in the agricultural sector' and 'measures for improving the environment in the agricultural sector', which went directly to the sector. The subsidy 'nature conservation measures in the agricultural sector' (NOLA) also went directly to the sector when it existed (1993–95). The purpose of this subsidy was to conserve the farmed landscape and its valuable semi-natural pastureland and meadows, including forest grazing land. Supplementary measures in the agricultural sector include three different supports:

1. environmental programme;
2. different forest measures;
3. plantation of energy forest.

Except for the financing of environmental measures in agriculture, similar to the objective of the subsidy NOLA before 1995, the programme finances forestry measures and for the plantation of energy forest. The main purpose with the environmental support given in this budget line is to reduce the pressure on the environment caused by agriculture.

b. Other subsidies for agriculture: The 'landscape conservation measure' was introduced in 1990 and was managed by the Ministry of Environment. The grant was used to protect arable land that was of interest for natural and cultural heritage reasons. The subsidies were also paid to farmers for maintaining the open landscape. Measures for improving the environment in the agricultural sector have existed all years between 1993 and 2000 and its purpose is to steer the development in the agricultural and horticultural industry towards reduced nutrient and ammonia leaching, safer and reduced use of pesticides, conservation of biodiversity and increased ecological production. It is primarily used to conduct experiments and for development in the area. Subsidy for fish cultivation has existed in different forms during the period 1993–2000 but always with the same purpose, to work towards a vital and rich stock of fish in Swedish waters. In later years, the environmental purpose has become more distinct. In the long run, the purpose is to maintain the biodiversity by promoting a rich and varied stock and an optimal use of resources.

c. Research on the environment and eco-cycles: There are two budget lines supporting environmental and eco-cycle research in

Sweden. The purpose is to discover and prevent new environmental threats by interdisciplinary research on, for example, waste and material flows. The research mainly takes place in universities and university colleges. Only the amount given as subsidies from this budget line is documented here.

d. Subsidy for environmental work: This budget line includes means for environmental measures managed by other authorities than the Swedish Environmental Protection Agency and by other organizations in this area. It mainly concerns means to restore damage caused by air pollution and acidification, but also to support other work for the control of the environment.

ii. Energy Subsidies

Governments in both developing and developed countries intervene considerably in the energy sector. Heat and power production, in particular, have been exposed to extensive attempts for control in Sweden and the motives for this control have differed over time. During the 1970s and early 1980s, the key focus was identifying a substitution for oil and, shortly thereafter, the preparations for the future phasing out of nuclear power. Since the late 1980s, intervention has gradually come to focus on environmental concerns. The subsidies in Table 5.3 were paid out between 1993 and 2000 with an environmental purpose. Other subsidies related to energy, not included in the definition of a subsidy used in this report, are several different tax subsidies. Here, we discuss the main energy subsidies.

The purpose of 'energy efficiency measures' is to support technology purchase, information, training, testing, marking and certifying to stimulate the development and introduction of energy efficient technology. The subsidies paid from the grant are principally managed by the Swedish Energy Agency (STEM) and a company can be subsidized for up to 50 percent of the costs for specific allowed activities. 'Energy technology support' aims to encourage the development of new energy technology in companies and industries. The payment can be given either as a loan or a subsidy. It can amount up to 50 percent of the investment cost or research collaboration. 'Introduction of new energy technologies' was introduced in 1999 and is managed by the Swedish Energy Agency. Subsidies are given in order to promote the development of technology based on renewable energy as well as an efficient use of energy in industrial processes. This support is similar to the energy technology support, but the purpose is more specific for promoting technology based on renewable energy. The subsidy can constitute a maximum of 50 percent of the cost for industrial research and a maximum of 25 percent, if the purpose is developing a goods item before it is introduced on the market (up to 30 percent for small- or medium-sized companies).

'Energy research subsidies' are connected to energy research and bio-energy research. Energy research is by far the larger subsidy, with disbursed payments as large as SEK 165 million in 1998, which is 93 percent of the total energy-related subsidies in that year. In 2000, the amount paid had decreased to SEK 66 million, 43 percent of the total energy-related subsidies.

iii. Transport Subsidies

Since the definition of an environmentally motivated subsidy focuses on its motive and not its effects, the large amount of subsidies for the purchase of rail transport in Sweden, the investment in railways or public transportation is not included. The main motives for these subsidies are regional and not environmental *per se*, according to the budget proposals. However, there are environmental reasons that have been made clearer in recent years, so some of these subsidies should be counted as environmental subsidies. Based on the narrow definition, the 'research subsidy for electrical and hybrid vehicles' is paid out as part of a research, development and demonstration programme initiated in 1993, concerning the use of electric and hybrid vehicles. The amount paid out as a subsidy has differed from year to year, the maximum was SEK 14 million given in 1995 and in 1999.

iv. Investment Subsidies

In the system of national accounts investment subsidies or support given to households are not included. But such subsidies may be disbursed with an environmental motive. Table 5.4 shows the volume of environment-motivated investment subsidies during the 1990s. It indicates that these subsidies were substantially increased 1998 onwards.

Table 5.4
Environmentally motivated investment subsidies in Sweden

Year	*1993*	*1994*	*1995*	*1996*	*1997*	*1998*	*1999*	*2000*
Amount (SEK million)	326	444	550	545	369	2907	2140	1998

Source: SCB (2003).

As before, the main components are resource and energy related. The purpose of 'investment subsidy for an ecological restructuring' (1995–96) was to encourage an eco-cycle adaptation of buildings and technological infrastructure. Another purpose was to bring about improvements in the environment. Measures included in the programme were focused on the development of technology, for example in the waste, water and construction area. The support was to be given for investments that would otherwise not occur and subsidies were given of between 15 and 30 percent of the total investment cost. The LIFE (Financial Instrument for the Environment) programme is entirely financed by the EU and was introduced in 1992. This is the only subsidy that is directly related to development and implementation of EU environmental policy. 'The investment subsidy for reducing the use of energy' was given until 2000 for several measures, such as the installation of effect guards, complementary sources of energy and equipment for heat accumulation. 'The grant for the conversion of heating systems', which still exists, is given for the conversion of electrically heated residential buildings to district heating or to another form of heating. The purpose for both subsidies was to stimulate measures in areas where it is not economically rational to connect to district heating.

'Subsidy for solar heat establishments' in houses, apartments and premises was introduced in 2000, and the size of the subsidy is decided on the basis of the calculated yearly production of the solar collector, or as a maximum of 25 percent of the investment cost.

'Investment for extension of district heating' is given for investments for reconstruction and connection of buildings heated by electricity into district heating.

v. *Environmentally Harmful Subsidies in Sweden*

Some examples of potentially environmentally harmful subsidies in Sweden are those geared towards transport, agriculture, fishing, housing construction, reindeer husbandry and forest roads. The largest 'environmental harmful' subsidies are the acreage support[2] and livestock support.[3] It is also of importance that the volumes of such subsidies are far higher than the environmentally motivating subsidies. However, with implementation of the EU guideline to decouple subsidies from production volume may reduce such environmentally harmful subsidies.

5.3.2 Environmental Subsidies in Germany

According to Article 6 of EU treaty, 'Environmental protection requirements must be integrated into the definition and implementation of the Community policies [...] in particular with a view to promote sustainable development'. Such a paradigm shift emphasizes the fact that existing policies have been highly fragmented and created institutions and incentive structure that generated an adverse bearing towards environment. In Germany, during the pre-EU days, subsidies were granted in favour of intensive farming, construction of single occupancy houses in the countryside or CO_2-intensive coal mining. The public finance system that taxed labour rather than natural resources accentuated the distortions generated by subsidy.

i. Regional Economic Policy of Germany

Regional economic policy in Germany attempts to reduce the locational disadvantages of regions (e.g. low per capita income and/or problematic economic structure). Such policies have the potential of improving national welfare and the overall efficiency of resource and factor allocation by removing market failures (e.g. agglomeration externalities) and regional bottlenecks. Traditionally, the focus of the policy has been quite narrow. The 'Joint Task Improvement of Regional Economic Structure' (GRW) facilitated cooperation between federal and provincial (*Länder*) governments and allowed the federal government to play a coordinating role. The key instrument used to be a capital grant in the form of a subsidy to local governments for economic development as well as investment in economic infrastructure (such as industrial parks). The projects were subjected to a number of restrictions put forward by land use planning, building and environmental regulations. As such, environmental concerns are seen as a necessary evil, one among the restrictions on regional economic development, which nonetheless has to be obeyed.

The unification of Germany with Europe brought an overall change in policy space. The EU structural fund has somewhat weakened the traditional authority of GRW. In contrast to the GRW, the European Commission has put more emphasis on regional programmes that took a holistic approach to development. Apart from infrastructural development, the structural funding programme also covers R&D and environmental protection. The emphasis on planning, implementation and evaluation has increased the scope for 'greening' the subsidy structure of Germany. At the other end, increasing influence of EU has created the space for less restricted regional policy formulation. As a consequence, the *Länders* can exploit the greater flexibility of the structural funds and spending for environmental purposes becomes an important component of the regional programmes.

On the other hand, the EU has discouraged the use of subsidies (with some exceptions). For the Member States, this trend created pressure to develop further alternatives to traditional forms of subsidization. For example, the traditional capital-intensive investment grants are less likely to pass state aid control than less intrusive subsidies, for example, for education and training, and broader strategies and instruments aiming at the promotion of endogenous development potentials. Secondly, the scope of subsidies has been continuously restrained over the years. On the one hand, EU funding in eligible German regions will be further restricted and concentrated in 2007 as a result of the enlargement of the EU. On the other hand, under Stabilization and Growth Pact (advocating fiscal sustainability), a strong pressure exists to put less strain on public budgets and rely less on spending (like subsidies) as a public policy instrument.

ii. Energy Policy in Germany

By and large, the German energy policy relate to the Energy Industry Act of 1935, the substance of which remained unaltered until 1998. The industry structure was centralized way and big private energy supply companies and public authorities were in close cooperation. The law against restraints on competition justified the existence of regional monopolies as a 'special case'. Such a structure generated high profits for electricity and gas supply companies with little or ineffective control mechanisms. It was thought that primary energy consumption is closely connected with GDP growth, and possible 'side-effects' of energy consumption were ignored.

The use of subsidies has for a long time been associated with coal, a non-renewable resource in which Germany is richly endowed with. After World War II, the mining sector expanded rapidly (from 38.9 million tons in 1945 to 151 million tons in 1956). This substantial rise in coal production led to Germany's quick economic post-war recovery and subsequent growth and prosperity. To meet the rising energy demand and reduce social hardships after the war, coal prices were regulated and fixed below the market price, and several policies were put in place to boost coal production even further (e.g. by putting restriction on oil-fired power plants). In the end, coal had to be apportioned due to excess demand.

From the late 1950s, coal policy aimed at restoring competitiveness to the domestic mining industry and limiting social and regional hardships in the mining areas. Most of these policies were based on the assumption that (market induced) downward trends for German coal production (which happened after 1958) could be stopped or reversed. To ensure these objectives, coal policy has heavily relied on subsidies, in conjunction with regulations and command-and-control (CAC) instruments. From 1958 to 2002, measures totalling €157.7 billion can be distinguished as having influence on energy, most of which qualify as subsidies. Unfortunately, these programmes developed a dynamics of their own, and programmes adopted for boosting coal production (e.g. immediately after the oil crisis) were not always abandoned after a crisis.

Coal policy was so sacrosanct that they were untouched even when the environmental issues became more important in the 1970s. It must be borne in mind that mining, energy conversion and use of coal have serious environmental implications vis-à-vis its substitutes. For example, emissions of particulates, dust, sulphur dioxide, nitrogen oxides and GHG emissions per unit of usable energy are typically higher. Mining itself remained a resource-intensive sector and causes a large number of local and regional environmental burdens (unusable waste land, waste water, change of groundwater table, water pollution, impairment of landscape and ecosystems, change of relief). To counteract (or rather alleviate) these problems, subsidy programmes were at least devoted to environmental investment. North-Rhine Westphalia (NRW) granted structural aids to limit pollution, noise and agitation between 1969 and 1990 which amounted to €74.1 million.

A more substantial amount of aid fell under the category R&D. Typically, these aids were accompanied by the introduction of CAC policies like (stricter) emission standards in the power sector. However, from the point of view of environmental policy, these measures qualify as add-on or end-of-pipe: They do not change the production and consumption patterns and provide marginal incentives for environmental improvements.

During the 1990s, two major changes occurred in Germany. One, the emphasis of the EU on competitiveness reduced subsidies in many parts. Second, there was greater concern for climate change. While coal subsidies were allowed to go on, for good, there were at least substantial changes in subsidy design. Adaptation pressure to reduce coal subsidies has come from the strain they impose on the public budget. An important stimulus for the reform of coal subsidies occurred in 1994 when the German Federal Constitutional Court declared the largest of all coal support measures, the *coal penny*[4] unconstitutional. This triggered reductions in aid volumes. Instead of subsidizing pre-defined quantities of coal and compensating electricity companies (for usage of coal) target ceilings were introduced and a fixed amount of subsidies (deficiency payments) included under these ceilings were passed on to the mining companies. The amount of subsidies paid was no longer dependent on the difference between import prices and domestic prices but the ceilings agreed upon by the parties were fixed in the budget. Due to budgetary pressure, these ceilings have been reduced, tightened and unified over the years.

However, some blind spots do remain. While coal support has decreased in the last decade, no clear commitment to end coal support policies has been made. The introduction of the Ecological Tax Reform (which includes eco-taxes) has, by and large, exempted coal. Finally, the trend towards market liberalization in the electricity market is accompanied by mergers and acquisitions. Thus, the scope for competitiveness, research and development gets diminished.

5.3.3 Environmental Subsidies in China

In the context of industrial pollution control in China, several management measures have been concurrently implemented in order to enforce the environmental protection law. The measures include both the CAC approach, such as discharge standards, abatement facility instalment deadlines and discharge permits, which provide a maximum discharge ceiling for firms, and market-based practices such as emission charges and pollution abatement subsidies. The market-based instruments have gained in importance since the 1980s. In 1982, after three years experimentation, China's State Council began nationwide implementation of pollution charges. Since then billions of Yuan have been collected each year from hundreds of thousands of industrial polluters for air pollution, water pollution, solid waste and noise. In 1996, the system was implemented in almost all counties and cities. About 4 billion Yuan ($1 = 8 Yuan) were collected from about half a million industrial firms. Table 5.5 lists information about the total levy collected.

Table 5.5
Total pollution levy collected in China: 1986–93

Year	*Total Levy (Million Yuan)*	*Industrial Output (Billion Yuan)*
1986	1190.2	1119.4
1987	1427.8	1381.3
1988	1609.0	1822.4
1989	1674.0	2201.7
1990	1751.6	2392.4
1991	2006.0	2824.8
1992	2471.0	3706.6
1993	2680.1	5269.3

Source: Wang and Chen (1999).

These incentives can be viewed as a charge-subsidy double incentive system with discharge standards embedded. In Wang and Wheeler (1996), province-level data on water pollution was analysed. The results suggest that province-level pollution discharge intensities have been highly responsive to provincial levy variations.

There are some unique features associated with the charge system. For wastewater, fees are calculated for each pollutant in a discharge stream and the polluter only needs to pay whichever amount has the highest value among all the pollutants. The Chinese central government constructs a uniform fee schedule; however, the implementation across the regions is not uniform. The levy collected is earmarked for institutional development, administration, environmental projects and subsidy to firms' pollution control projects. If a firm decides to invest in pollution abatement, a maximum of 80 percent of the levy paid by the firm can be used to subsidize the investment project proposed by the firm. For defaulters, there is a penalty; however, penalties cannot be used to subsidize firm-level pollution control projects. Wang and Chen (1999) used an econometric analysis to study the impact of environmental subsidies in China. The regression results of their study are presented in Table 5.6. For the sake of brevity, only the significant variables are included.

Based on this econometric study, Wang and Chen (1999) observe that effective levy rate leads to higher efforts to curb pollution, both in terms

Table 5.6
Analysis of environmental subsidies in China

Ind variables	*Model 1 (Depvar: Fixed Cost)*	*Model 2 (Depvar: Operating Cost)*
Effective levy rate	0.058	0.062
Industry share	0.826	1.38
Educational level	–0.745	–0.974
Pollution/output	0.38	0.482
Per capita output	–0.652	0.548
Coal	–0.425	0.76
Beer	1.16	1.15
Dye	0.707	0.919
Coking	0.84	1.22
Pesticide	–	0.767
Refinery	1.75	2.47
Steel processing		–1.32
Dye material	1.3	1.53

Source: Wang and Chen (1999).

of higher investment and higher operating costs. The coefficients on the productivity of a firm are negative. Firms who are more productive need to spend less investment effort in pollution control. The reason might be that more productive firms are also cleaner. Beer, dye, coking and refinery industries were found to have invested more on wastewater treatment facilities, while the cement industry invested less. This could be related to the difference in the efficiency of pollution abatement among different sectors. They also find that education has a significant and negative impact on total abatement investment and operation cost, which implies a strong negative correlation between subsidy and education. Without subsidy, education would have been expected to have positive impact on pollution control effort because education has been found to be positively correlated with pollution control pressures.

Empirical research has found that higher education generates higher pressure on industry for pollution control. Pargal and Wheeler (1996) found that while formal regulation was not in place, informal regulation could put significant pressure on the firms. When education is higher, the informal pressure would be stronger. Wang and Wheeler (1996) found that education was positively correlated with effective levy rate in China. While formal regulation is in place and effective levy is included in the modelling, education was found to have a negative impact on subsidy and therefore on total pollution control investment efforts. Consistent evidence was also found with firms' own characteristics on pollution abatement investment. Higher pollution is linked with higher investment. More productive firms need to invest less in pollution abatement. Neither the ownership effect nor the vintage effect is significant.

5.4 ENVIRONMENTAL SUBSIDIES IN INDIA

Measurement of the volume of subsidy is often not enough. What is required is the measurement of excess subsidization, that is, the volume or the degree of subsidy provision in excess of what is desirable or optimal. Further, the same subsidy programme may play different roles at different times. As such, subsidization programmes should not be thought of as static exercises. Rather they should respond to their past history and the changes that take place in the sector. Viewing subsidies in terms of a life cycle where they may grow in importance initially or in an expansion phase, reach a maximum and then are rolled back in the contraction phase may be the best method of promoting relevant objectives in a sector. When appropriate changes do not take place in response to the history of the subsidy and the external environment, the expansion phase may be over stated and contraction may prove to be very difficult. Subsidy programmes that are not scrutinized with respect to their desired life cycle pattern may prove to be more harmful than beneficial. Recognizing a suitable life cycle is especially important in the context of environment.

There is evidence in the literature to show that many subsidies have been constructive at the time of their introduction, but have later become harmful. They have completed their original purpose but have not been phased out afterwards. For instance, certain agricultural subsidies generated substantial and much needed positive spill-overs into other sectors in India. Input supports during the 1980s totalled 17 percent of total value added (25 percent for wheat and 35 percent for rice) (Gulati, 1989). They not only achieved much for the country's Green Revolution but also generated many spin-off benefits as well. From the early 1970s through the early 1990s, agricultural subsidies fed into infrastructure of many sorts, with the result that the length of surfaced roads more than doubled and the villages with electricity quadrupled (Repetto, 1994; Vaidyanathan, 1999). Yet many of the agricultural subsidies remain in place, even though they are now harmful to both the environment and the economy at large.

5.4.1 Identifying Environmentally Harmful and Positive Subsidies

The issue of subsidies in general and agricultural subsidies (including subsidy on fertilizer, pesticides, water, electricity) in particular has been in debate in India since early 1990s. It is both because farm subsidies put enormous strain on government budgets and that the environmental impacts of these subsidies are potentially substantial. Some of the reasons that have been advanced in support of farm subsidies are: food security, income redistribution, stability in food prices and encouragement to use new farming methods. In addition to straining government budgets, subsidies distort prices of agricultural inputs and thereby affect levels of input use. This has an effect on the availability of inputs and resources used in agriculture. When supply of inputs is constrained by natural or other factors, the sustainability of agricultural development may be affected. Excessive and inefficient use of agricultural inputs such as fertilizers, water and pesticides is also reported to have detrimental consequences for the environment and human health and welfare.

Agriculture has a significant impact on environment, particularly on soil, water, biodiversity and air. The specific impact depends, among other factors, on the type and quantity of crops produced, the farming practices employed, the level and mix of inputs such as fertilizers and pesticides applied, irrigation methods, and site-specific environmental conditions. Farmers will be concerned about the environmental performance of the agricultural sector if they are faced with adequate incentives to include the environmental costs and benefits of their activities in their production decisions. Markets do not penalize farmers for harming the environment, nor offer rewards for avoiding or reducing harmful effects. Government pricing policies of both agricultural inputs and outputs have encouraged a commodity mix narrower than would be the case if these policies were not in place, and have promoted high levels of water, fertilizer and chemical use. This, in turn, has exacerbated environmental pollution, especially soil erosion, and surface and groundwater pollution. The mechanism is a form of derived demand for inputs (Harold and Runge, 1993).

There are three main challenges involved in identifying/evaluating the environmental impact of both environmentally perverse and environment supporting subsidies:

1. The impact is likely to differ from one environmental situation to another, because the sensitivity of an ecosystem will differ according to the specific situation, and most subsidy measures will extend beyond a single ecosystem. Often environmental degradation is visible after a long period of time, so these long-term impacts have to be taken into consideration while analysing the environmental impacts.
2. Human behaviour will be affected not only by the particular subsidy in question but also by all the other government programmes that affect a given individual. There may be multiple subsidy programmes, perhaps with conflicting objectives, that are relevant.
3. Some subsidy programmes may make payments that are inconsistent with the programme's own goals. For example, the programme may have outlived the life span envisaged by its designers, or it may apply to 'fringe' areas where circumstances do not match those which its designers foresaw (Barg, 1996).

In order to evaluate the impact of subsidies to agricultural inputs, it is important to identify their potential impacts on environmental resources, and human health and welfare. The chemical and/or physical changes in the environment associated with an activity or source—in this case agricultural inputs—are described as stressors, which is a term used to denote the types and levels of pollutant emissions or habitat alterations. Through the media of air, land and water, such environmental changes and pollutants ultimately affect resources, people, wildlife and plants (Table 5.7). The impacts may have far reaching effects or may affect the receptor on a smaller scale. They can be on-site (localized) or off-site (regional or even global) impacts, physical (e.g. loss of species diversity) and chemical effects (such as diseases), socio-economic impacts (e.g. loss of income, resettlement of people or land abandonment) or near-term and long-term impacts.

Table 5.7

Taxonomy for evaluating potential impacts of environmental stressors

	Effects Category						
	Environmental Resources						
Potential burdens to water							
Stressor	Groundwater contamination	Surface water contamination	Groundwater level	Coastal, marine and fresh water ecosystems	Terrestrial ecosystems	Biodiversity/ endangered species	Sedimentation
Fertilizer	x	x		x		x	
Pesticides	x	x		x	x	x	
Irrigation (surface)	x	x	x				x
Electricity			x				
Potential burdens to land							
Stressor	Contamination	Waterlogging	Salinity	Erosion	Terrestrial ecosystems	Biodiversity/ endangered species	Nutrient leaching
Fertilizers	x				x		
Pesticides	x				x	x	
Irrigation (surface)		x	x	x	x		x
Electricity				x	x		
Potential burdens to air							
Stressor					Terrestrial ecosystems		
Pesticides					x		

Table 5.7 continued

Table 5.7 continued

	Effects Category				
	Human Health		*Human Welfare*		
Potential burdens to water					
Stressor	Mortality	Morbidity	Material loss	Aesthetics	Resource use
Fertilizer		x			x
Pesticides	x	x			x
Irrigation (surface)			x	x	x
Electricity				x	x
Potential burdens to land					
Stressor	Mortality	Morbidity	Material loss	Aesthetics	Resource use
Fertilizers					x
Pesticides		x			x
Irrigation (surface)			x		x
Electricity					x
Potential burdens to air					
Stressor	Mortality	Morbidity	Material loss	Aesthetics	Resource use
Pesticides	x	x			x

Source: Pandey and Srivastava (2003).

Notes: Changes in the productivity or value of commercial, subsistence or recreational uses of such natural resources as forests (e.g. for timber), agricultural lands (e.g. for crops), fisheries (e.g. for subsistence diets) or wildlife (e.g. for ecotourism). 'Coastal and other marine ecosystems': Includes reef, fishery and other biological resources in saline water. 'Freshwater ecosystems: Includes wetlands, watersheds and other biological resources in fresh water (sweet water). 'Biodiversity/endangered species': Impacts on the diversity of flora and fauna, species that are endemic or unique, and species habitats and corridors (e.g. flyways for birds). 'Terrestrial ecosystems': Flora and fauna, minerals, soil, forest or grassland habitat.

There is evidence in the empirical literature to show that agricultural yield is sensitive to the quality of environmental resources. There are a number of studies (Mausolff and Farber, 1995; Byiringiro and Reardon, 1996; Pattanayak and Mercer, 1998) which have incorporated environmental information directly into production function to determine the effects of environmental factor on yield. The limitation of this approach has been that these do not provide the information to quantify the dynamic effects and environmental stressors on yields. Analytical model presented in Pandey and Srivastava (2003) attempts to identify environmentally optimal levels of input use and to derive the price changes needed in order to move the farmers towards the social optimum.

5.4.2 Environmental Impacts of Subsidies: Evidence from Literature

In practice, many subsidies are not only excessive but ill-targeted and also tend to become open ended and continued long after they have served their purpose. Recently, it has been increasingly recognized that many subsidies directed towards agriculture impose a high cost on society through their adverse impact on environmental resources. In this context, this section reviews the existing literature on the subject with an objective to examine the environmental impact of the subsidies to fertilizers, surface irrigation, pesticides and power and its implications for the sustainability of natural resources and agriculture.

a. Power Subsidy: Impact on Groundwater Depletion

It is generally perceived that reducing energy consumption implies reducing production. However, Singh (1999) reports that this is a misconception. His study cites Mitra (1992) who found that the linkage between energy consumption and economic growth has been broken decisively by the developed countries after the oil crises, which broke out in the early 1970s. Middle-income and lower middle-income countries too have shown that efficiency of energy use can significantly reduce the consumption of energy without impairing economic growth targets. However, the low-income countries, among them India most prominently, have remained stuck with high energy intensity in their economic development processes and profiles. The persistent neglect of the energy conservation in agriculture is a glaring example of this. The irrational pricing policy of electricity results in the inefficient use of electricity on the one hand and inefficient use of water on the other.

Myers and Kent (2001) note that irrigation subsidies encourage wasteful use of scarce water worldwide. Power subsidies too, encourage withdrawal of groundwater for agricultural use, leading to a decline in the water table. These have implications for both the availability of scarce water resource and the environmental problems entailed by its overuse and wastage, namely groundwater depletion, and soil depletion which have serious impact on agriculture.

Sidhu and Dhillon (1997), on the basis of a study conducted in Punjab, show that the low rates of electricity and the flat rate system of charging have induced farmers to shift to tube well irrigation, water-intensive crops and over irrigation which have resulted in a sharp decline in the groundwater level and consequently, the electricity requirement for drawing groundwater is increasing year after year. The groundwater level has declined in 86 percent of the area of the state. The decline was more than 5 metres in 29 percent of the area implying 7–10 percent increase in electricity demand. Further, there was a sharp shift from dry crops to water-intensive crops. For instance, the area under rice which is an irrigation-intensive crop increased from 292000 hectares in 1970–71 to 2276000 hectares in 1994–95. The marginal lands too were put under the water-intensive crops. The study also reveals that the zero marginal cost of irrigation due to the rate system of charges for electricity has induced the farmers to over irrigate. Only 54.7 percent of the farmers applied the required number of irrigations, while the remaining over irrigated the rice crop to various degree.

Subsidy on electricity has affected the efficiency of irrigation systems too. A study conducted by the Punjab Agricultural University (1997)[5] on the operational efficiency of electricity operated tube wells found that 33 percent tube wells were operating at 50 percent of efficiency, 21 percent were at 40–50 percent level of efficiency and the remaining were operating at less than 45 percent level of efficiency. Joshi (1997) reports that the water table in the good aquifer regions of Haryana has declined ranging between 1 and 83 cm during the last one decade posing serious threat to the agricultural economy of Haryana.

In the coastal regions, fresh groundwater supplies are vulnerable to contamination by salt water intrusion. Overdraft of these fresh water zones causes salt water intrusions. Singh (1999) shows that the groundwater table has gone down drastically in many areas of the country such as Mehsana district in north Gujarat, and Coimbatore district in west Tamil Nadu. It is estimated that in Mehsana district, water table has been falling at the rate of 5–8 metres annually and that some 2000 wells dry up every year. In the coastal areas of Gujarat, excessive extraction has depleted the groundwater aquifers and the vacuum so created has been filled in by intrusion of sea water—a phenomenon called salinity ingress. It is estimated that salinity ingress is increasing at an alarming rate of one-half to one kilometre a year, along 60 percent of the 1100 km long Saurashtra coast. The salinity ingress has rendered groundwater in those areas unfit for both domestic and agricultural uses and has adversely affected crop yields. Singh fears that 'sometimes, these effects are slow in coming, but by the time they are recognized it may be too late to correct the damage'.

b. Irrigation Subsidy: Impact on Waterlogging, Salinity and Soil Erosion

Increase in soil salinity is recognized worldwide as a major deprecating factor in agricultural growth. Myers and Kent (2001) note that worldwide, 454000 sq. km of the 2.8 million sq. km of land is salinized which is enough to reduce crop yields, with crop losses worth almost $11 billion per year. The study also notes that the problem derives primarily from subsidies that encourage careless and prodigal use of seemingly plentiful water supplies. Government subsidies encourage wasteful use of water, and eliminate any incentive to use it sparingly. Mexico loses a million metric tons of grain a year because of soil salinity, enough to feed five million people and Pakistan today spends more on pumping out salt-laden water than on irrigation.

Joshi and Jha (1992) show that in the long run, water logging and salinity lead to land abandonment, while in the short term and medium term, there are adverse productivity impacts. Presently, salinity affects productivity in about 86 million hectares of the world's irrigated land. At least 2–3 lakh hectares of irrigated land are lost every year due to salinization and waterlogging. In developed and developing countries, salinity and waterlogging together are responsible for the decline of about 1.1 million tons of grain output each year.

India, being predominantly agriculture-based economy and with much inefficiency in its irrigation subsidy policies, is no exception to this problem. Myers (1998) notes that in India 100000 sq. km out of 420000 sq. km of irrigated croplands has been lost to cultivation through water logging, and 70000 sq. km are affected by salinization. It is estimated that Indian farmers could cut back on irrigation water use by 15 percent without reducing crop yields simply by eliminating over-watering. Marothia (1997) shows that subsidized canal irrigation and subsidized electricity (in some cases free) for tube wells, remunerative output price support, availability of high-yielding variety (HYV) seeds and higher returns encouraged the farmers to opt for water-intensive crops. Nearly one-fourth of the cultivable command area under all-canal projects in India is suffering from water logging and soil salinity. This has adversely affected the crop productivity and restricted the choice of crops. As precise statistical data are not yet available as to the amount of irrigated lands that have fallen into disuse because of water logging and salinity, these concerns are inadequately addressed in most of the irrigation investment decisions.

The study by Joshi and Jha (1992) focuses primarily on the problem of soil alkalinity and water logging in the Sharda Canal Command area and attempts to measure its impact at the farm level in terms of resource use, productivity and profitability of crop production. Four villages in the Gauriganj block were chosen for the study covering the 1985–86 cropping year. The study finds that overuse of canal irrigation and underuse of groundwater have disturbed the water balance of the area causing water logging and increase in salinization in the command area. The reason for under-exploitation of rather good quality groundwater is low water rate on canal irrigation. It has been shown that the cost of tube well irrigation is much higher (₹825 per hectare for paddy) as compared to the rate of canal water tariff (₹143.26 per hectare for paddy). Such a wide difference in the cost of irrigation has led the farmers to discontinue the use of groundwater, resulting in an increase in water table and soil alkalinity.

The study further notes that crop choices are severely restricted under degraded soil conditions. Under salt affected and waterlogged soils, crops like pulses, sugarcane, potato and a number of other crops are not grown. In such situations, intensity of land use goes down and in the extreme such problems lead to abandonment of cultivation. Thus, land degradation aggravates land scarcity. Results of the study on productivity and profitability of crop production were far more revealing. Though in farmers' perceptions, yields of paddy and wheat halved in about eight years' time due to increasing soil degradation, estimates of the study indicated that paddy and wheat yields went down by more than 51 percent and 56 percent, respectively, on salt-affected soils. For wheat, the net income fell by 92 percent. The unit cost of production rose by 59–61 percent for paddy and by 85 percent for wheat when cultivation is extended on salt-affected soils. The study concludes that with the same level of resources as used on normal soils, gross output would decline by 63–64 percent on salt affected or waterlogged soils. The study concludes that under-pricing in favour of canal irrigation is, by and large, responsible for such a situation. Joshi (1997) based on primary data reports that the crop productivity in Western Yamuna and Bhakra Canal Command showed a declining trend in comparison to normal soils.

Sharma et al. (1997) find that in Haryana about 70 percent of the geographical area is facing the problem of rising water table due to the dominance of canal irrigation, lack of adequate drainage and low extraction of groundwater. Gangwar and Toorn (1987) put the economic loss due to rising and poor quality of water in Haryana at ₹26.8 crore and anticipate it to rise to a level of ₹71.9 crore in 2000. The state is also salt affected. Singh (1984) estimates that an area of 450000 hectares under salinity/alkalinity and water logging. More severely affected districts are Karnal, Kurukshetra, Jind, Hisar, Sonipat and Rohtak. In the Central-Southern districts of Jind, Hisar, Sirsa and Bhiwani, where most of the area is canal irrigated, the water table rose at a fast rate during 1974–91 (0.7 metre in Rohtak to 6.5 metre in Sirsa district) leading to water logging and secondary salinity. Moreover, these areas are underlain by brackish water. So water logging is assuming gigantic proportions in various canal command areas. The worst affected districts are Rohtak, Jind, Hisar and Sirsa.

c. Fertilizer Subsidy: Impact on Soil Productivity, and Groundwater and Surface Water Contamination

Three main fertilizers used in agriculture are urea (N), di-ammonium phosphate (DAP) and potash (K). Of these, the production of urea is under the retention price scheme. There is a flat rate subsidy on DAP. Potash, which is mainly imported, also has a flat rate subsidy. One of the main purposes of retention price scheme is to develop the urea industry in the country. Every individual plant is assured a fixed rate of return. Hence, the retention prices are fixed for each individual plant. The subsidy on urea is the difference between the retention price (adjusted for freight, etc.) and the price that the farmer pays. According to Gulati and Narayanan (2000), the fertilizer subsidy bill in 1988–89 amounted to ₹112 billion. In the 1980s, there was an unprecedented growth in the fertilizer subsidy in India. Parikh and Suryanarayana (1992) show that the rate of fertilizer subsidy on domestic production has increased from ₹565.72 per ton to ₹1383.33 per ton in 1987–88.

Application of fertilizers and pesticides is essential in order to increase food production and achieve the targeted agricultural production. However, studies reveal that indiscriminate use of fertilizers has proved detrimental. According to a study, in Gujarat region, nitrogen leaching for 90 cm soil depth under 564 mm rainfall was 14 kg/ha out of 180 kg/ha N applied. In a rice field near Delhi, loss of 14.3 kg/ha was reported from an application of 120 kg/ha (Mahalanobis, 1971). Handa (1986) found that the main cause of groundwater pollution is indiscriminate and higher dose of fertilizers and pesticides. The study also finds that the nitrate content in the soil sample of the states where lower doses of fertilizers are used is considerably low as compared to the states where per hectare use of fertilizer is higher. It must be noted that the soil health has direct impact on crop yield.

According to Sidhu and Byerlee (1992), in relatively more developed districts of Punjab, such as Ludhiana, fertilizer use has already exceeded the recommended dose at least for nitrogen. Hence, marginal contribution of fertilizer to yield increases is predicted to be substantially lower in future. The study computed the land, labour and fertilizer productivity for the years 1975 and 1985 for various states of India and expressed them as percentages of Punjab charts. The results show a decline in fertilizer productivity in Punjab, Haryana, Uttar Pradesh, Madhya Pradesh and Rajasthan due to application of increasing amounts of fertilizers to maintain current levels of yield.

Sah and Shah (1992) find that in irrigated areas of Gujarat where fertilizer use is widespread and has reached 1.5 times or more than the recommended amounts, the issue of fertilizer use efficiency has become increasingly important. The analysis, based on a sample of 330 farmers located in 42 villages of five important soil-crop zones in Gujarat, finds that excessive use of fertilizers is widespread; only one out of five farmers, who had received soil test recommendations, used fertilizers as recommended. Farmers' inability to visualize the effect of nutrient balance on crop output distorts their perceptions about yield response, resulting in overuse.

Singh et al. (1997) analyse the environmental consequences of the rice–wheat cropping system in Haryana. The study finds that increasing fertilizer use has led to diminishing marginal gains to nutrient ratio from 14.65 to 9.36 for rice and from 21.5 to 8.67 for wheat between 1970–75 and 1990–94.

Nagaraj et al. (1998) examine the resource use efficiency in cultivation of various crops under different cropping systems in Tungabhadra Command Area (Karnataka). The results of the study show that the regression coefficients for manure and fertilizers are negative and non-significant in production of paddy indicating a negative influence on the gross returns from paddy and that the input is used in excess of requirements.

According to Joshi (1997), adoption of nutrient responsive high-yielding varieties and application of inorganic fertilizers without soil test and widespread application with wrong nutrient balance have resulted in nutrient imbalance of the soil in many parts of the country. As a result, the actual productivity from using inorganic fertilizers was much lower than that of the potential. Nearly, 70 percent of the fertilizer was applied to rice and wheat in Haryana. Several studies report that the farmers in Haryana were applying overdoses of fertilizer, particularly of nitrogenous fertilizer in most of the crops. The recommended ratio of N, P, K (4:2:1) is not being maintained due to subsidies in favour of nitrogenous fertilizers. Some economists argue that soil nutrient-related problems were due to imbalance of subsidies for the major nutrients. Nutrient deficiency and loss of organic matter were among other important reasons for declining productivity of rice and wheat.

Ray (1998) observed that although use of fertilizers, pesticides and water are unavoidable for achieving the targeted agricultural growth, indiscriminate use of these inputs creates environmental problems. The study analyses fertilizer consumption data for Andhra Pradesh, Punjab, Haryana, Tamil Nadu, Bihar, Madhya Pradesh, Odisha and Rajasthan from 1981 to 1995 and concludes that the following:

1. due to use of more and more fertilizers, the return from per unit of fertilizer was decreasing in almost all states;
2. the return from per kilogram of fertilizer is highest in less developed states where the rate of use of fertilizers is substantially lower as compared to the states where a high dose of fertilizer has been used and
3. due to the use of higher dose of fertilizers and pesticides, the pollution of soil and groundwater is more and as a consequence, the marginal physical productivity of fertilizers declined significantly.

The study notes that increasing trends in bringing land under rice and wheat and other profitable crops and applying higher doses of fertilizers are not likely to change in the near future. Therefore, efforts should be made to ensure judicial use of fertilizers and pesticides so that only a small portion is left unutilized which reaches the soil and groundwater.

Huang and Rozelle (1995), in an analysis of the slower growth of grain yields in China in the late 1980s, observe that the intensification of China's agricultural practices and other rural activities appear to have caused an increase in environmental stress that created a drag yield growth.

d. Environmental Impact of Indiscriminate Use of Pesticides

Deep concern is expressed about the excessive use of pesticides in developing countries, which is reported to have led to environmental degradation. Farah (1994) shows that some pesticides persist longer than others or break down to even more toxic components, extending the time span in which they could contaminate agricultural crops, underground water and surface water bodies. Pesticides affect not only the location of their application but also the ecosystems far removed due to their mobility in air and water. Further, pesticides usually kill pests and their natural enemies alike. Pests are also very adept at developing resistance against the chemical pesticides intended to control them. Thus, pesticide use initiated to suppress pests may lead to greater pest outbreaks. The study notes that towards the late 1980s, with the growth of herbicide use, at least 48 weed species had gained resistance to chemicals. Another source estimates that from 1930 to 1960, the number of resistant anthropoid species (insects, mites, ticks) rose from just 6 to 137, an average increase of four resistant species per year. In the period of 1960–80, on an average 13 species per year are reported to have gained resistance to chemical pesticides. It was estimated that in 1990 approximately 504 insect and mite species had acquired resistance to pesticides in use.

The wiping out of essential predatory insects due to excessive and uncontrolled pesticide treatments has created new pests. For instance, in cotton production in the Canete Valley in Peru, spraying to control the tobacco budworm led to the rapid build-up of the cotton aphid. As chemical treatment intensified to counteract this resistance build-up, other pests developed because their natural predators were eliminated. In Mexico, the tobacco budworm developed resistance to all known pesticides and caused the cotton planted area to drop from more than 280000 ha to a mere 400 ha in the 1960s. Similarly, in Nicaragua, 15 years of heavy insecticide use on cotton were followed by four years in which yields fell by 30 percent.

Pesticide-related poisoning could occur in human beings as a result of excessive exposure to pesticides, through inhalation or on consuming heavily or untimely pesticide-treated crops. Karwasra et al. (1997) assess the impact of agricultural development on nature and extent of resource degradation in Haryana. They observe that in the central-southern districts, intensive canal irrigation has led to water logging and increase in salinity and this has encouraged profuse growth of weeds and insect pests. To control such infestation and to propel any further harvest, intensive chemical control measures will have to be employed. The study notes that the direct ill-effects of farm chemicals have started showing its presence in the form of nitrate concentration in water and pesticides residue in different food items. Bhatnagar and Thakur (1998) observe that in Haryana from 1966 to 1993 both consumption and coverage of area by pesticides have shown accelerating growth rates. Consumption of pesticides has grown at a higher rate than the growth in areas covered by the use of pesticides.

Farah (1994) notes that the pesticide users are hardly aware of the negative externalities on the environment. In the absence of government intervention through regulations and taxation, they tend to overuse pesticides and this tendency is further exacerbated due to international and national institutional economic policies which directly or indirectly lead to farmers applying more pesticides than they would otherwise. According to Joshi (1997), pesticide consumption in Indian agriculture has increased manifold during the last three decades. Five states, namely Andhra Pradesh, Gujarat, Maharashtra, Punjab and Tamil Nadu, accounted for more than 90 percent of the pesticide use in the country, although the average consumption of pesticide in India is low, 33 grams/hectare. Indiscriminate use of pesticide in some pockets is causing several environmental and health problems. Farah (1994) reports that, during the 1989/90 season, $27 million worth of pesticides were used in the district of Guntur in the state of Andhra Pradesh. With an average overuse of 20 percent, $5.4 million of pesticides were wasted, which could have been avoided through better pest management. The yield losses due to pest resistance were estimated at $39.7 million. In pesticide application, the red triangle label (extremely hazardous) chemicals have a share of 26 percent in Andhra Pradesh, 39.7 percent in Punjab and as high as 65 percent in Gujarat of the reported use. The yellow triangle label (highly hazardous) group constitutes 59 percent each in Andhra Pradesh and Punjab and 34 percent in Gujarat of the reported use. An analysis of the pesticide use behaviour found that pesticide use levels are determined significantly by the extent of irrigation. The intensity of use is higher on small farms. Joshi (1997) shows that with the increase in pesticide use in Punjab, 525 insects have already developed resistance to pesticides. Marothia (1997) reports that nearly 70 percent of all pesticides consumed by Indian farmers belong to banned or severely restricted categories in the developed countries. The Indian Council of Medical Research conducted an extensive study in 1993 covering all the states of India. Results of this study indicate that the samples far exceeded the tolerance limits of pesticide residuals in the case of milk, canned fruit products, poultry feeds and vegetables. The report emphasizes that the private benefits of pesticides use should be evaluated against their social costs. It has been estimated that only 10 percent of the total food grains production can be saved from increased pesticides use. Once the health hazards and other costs are imputed, these benefits appear too meagre.

Pesticides also find their way into the river through agricultural runoffs because the upstream catchment areas are intensely cultivated. Around 150 tons of pesticides and herbicides are used in the agricultural and plantation areas. The deadly impact of these chemicals has caused destruction of several types of fish and aquatic organisms in recent years.

e. Electricity Subsidies

Electricity subsidies in India (measured as under recovery of costs) are very large and give rise to economic, environmental and social costs—although hidden in these estimates are substantial costs due to procurer and other systemic inefficiencies. The primary effect of the electricity subsidies is to distort the overall energy market in favour of electricity which results in higher electricity intensity of GDP. Production of electricity, which is largely coal based in India, has implications for both local and global pollutants. Electricity subsidies may also indirectly hold back rural development by undermining the ability of the state electricity boards to invest in extending distribution networks to villages. Lack of electricity contributes to poverty, as it precludes most industrial activities and the jobs they create. Subsidies also create incentives for both suppliers and users for inefficiency—which only harms environment, economy

Table 5.8
Size and impact of electricity subsidies in India

Sector	*Avg. Price (₹/kWh)*	*Reference Price (₹/kWh)*	*Rate of Subsidy (%)*	*Potential Primary Energy Saving from Subsidy Removal*
Households	1.50	3.56	57.9	48
Industry	3.50	3.42	–	–
Agriculture	0.25	3.56	93.0	86
Average	–		38.0	34

Source: IEA (2001).

and society (UNEP, 2003). Table 5.8 shows the extent of electricity subsidy across various sectors in India.

5.4.3 Reform of Environmentally Harmful Subsidies in India

The importance of review and potential reform of environmentally harmful subsidies is well recognized. Increasing support for analytical research and policy dialogue in developed countries underline that decisive progress is needed (e.g. OECD, 2006b, 2007; TEEB, 2009; Valsecchi et al., 2009) towards the reform of environmentally harmful subsidies.

The barrier to the reform on the one hand has been the resistance by vested interests and associated difficulty of gaining public support, on the other hand it is hindered by the lack of preparedness in terms of an agreed method to define, identify and quantify them, and the lack of application of the available tools in assessing the wider implications of the impact of their removal including the economic, social and environmental dimensions. There can be various ways to address these. One is to formulate alternative policies that target the same subsidy objectives better, while also compensating losers. A related measure is to develop an economic and environmental-policy context that encourages subsidy removal through reducing government controls generally and freeing up markets. A subsidiary measure is to introduce provisions that require surviving subsidies to be re-justified periodically, thus avoiding the perpetual subsidy problem. All these measures can be strongly reinforced by promoting transparency about perverse subsidies, especially in the context of their impacts both economic and environmental, and their costs to both taxpayers and consumers.

However, policy makers considering removing subsidies or considering reforming subsidies will need to understand the linkages between the existing subsidies and the underlying economic and environmental reality. This lack of preparedness (in reducing economically and environmentally harmful subsidies) in terms of both the magnitudes of subsidy and their impact on the environment is seen as equally challenging, if not more, as political and institutional concerns.

In the literature, quantification efforts have mainly focused on budgetary subsidies given that the quantification of off-budget subsidies is complex. In this context, two recent initiatives for the identification and assessment of environmentally harmful subsidy offer great promise.

One, various studies of the OECD (1998, 2005, 2007) have developed tools for the analysis of the linkages between financial support to an activity and its environmental impacts. These tools constitute an attempt to unfold the linkages and the circumstances that cause, mitigate, or have rebound effects on the environmental harmfulness of a subsidy. Three different tools have been developed to provide: (a) a framework for the identification of environmentally harmful subsidies, (b) to assess whether the subsidy removal will benefit the environment and (c) help to understand the wider implications of subsidy removal including the economic and social dimensions. The main features of the tools and insights on the crucial elements behind the tools are illustrated in OECD (2009). These tools have been used to develop a methodology such that these tools can be tested on the selected case studies. The aim of the tests were to assess the strengths and weaknesses, the effectiveness, the user friendliness and the data requirements of the tools as well as gain an overall impression of their use and develop guidelines for removal of environmentally harmful subsidy.

Two, the System of Environmental-Economic Accounting (SEEA) is a satellite system to the system of national accounts that has been under development since the early 1990s. The system brings together economic and environmental information in a common framework to measure the contribution of the environment to the economy and the impact of the economy on the environment. It aims to provide policy makers with indicators and statistics to monitor these interactions and provide a database for strategic planning. This is an international system based on a UN initiative. In Europe, the information is harmonized and coordinated by Eurostat. The SEEA covers: flows of materials per industry (energy, material and emissions waste); economic variables (labour taxes, subsidies, costs, products and services) and natural resources (stocks, quality, value).

Under the Swedish system of SEEA, subsidies are classified as environmentally motivated subsidies, potentially damaging subsidies and other subsidies. Subsidies are classified through a detailed review of budget proposals to determine which budget lines have an environmental motive. The SEEA definition of subsidies covers on-budget subsidies to industry, transfers to international beneficiaries and households, as well as capital transfers. While some off-budget subsidies such as tax exemptions can be calculated from SEEA data where there is a direct link between emissions and taxes, other off-budget subsidies such as preferential market access and exemptions from government standards are not currently included given difficulties in obtaining such data (cited in Valsecchi et al., 2009).

Methodology developed in OECD (2009) not only helps to identify and prioritize those subsidies that have clear environmental implication and are more politically viable for reform but also helps to identify information and analytical gaps with regard to identifying environmental benefits and trade-offs with social and economic objectives, subsidy reform can potentially bring about. There is merit in using this methodology in future work on environmentally harmful subsidies in a developing country like India with a view to develop a strategy for reform of such subsidies.

5.5 ENVIRONMENTALLY PERVERSE SUBSIDIES IN INDIA: BUDGETARY COSTS

In this section, we estimate the budgetary cost of subsidies in India that have a bearing on environment. We identify both environment friendly budgetary subsidies and environmentally harmful subsidies. We focus on three agricultural inputs, namely power, irrigation and fertilizer where perverse subsidies are pervasive. We also look at the environmental-friendly subsidies in the budget heads like soil and water conservation, sewerage and sanitation, forest conservation, development and regeneration, afforestation and ecology development, ecology and environment, flood control, anti-sea erosion projects, drainage, non-conventional sources of energy, environmental research, prevention and control of pollution, mining in iron and steel industries, and mineral exploration in non-ferrous mining and metallurgical industries.

5.5.1 Identifying Environmental Subsidies

In this section, we identify the heads that have a bearing on environment, both in the central and state budgets. Subsequently, these identified environmental-related subsidies are categorized into two groups. The first group where the subsidies are designed to have a positive impact on the environment and second group where environment may get adversely affected. It is important to note that it is not the *activity*, but the *subsidy* that may be classified as perverse.

There are some subsidies which *prima facie* may have a positive impact on environment. Subsidies that are likely to have a beneficial effect on environment are sewerage and sanitation, and non-conventional sources of energy. Also, subsidies like forestry and wildlife, soil and water conservation and fisheries can be considered necessary for environmental protection. However, there are several budgetary heads, where subsidization may have a mixed or adverse effect as in the case of 'irrigation'. Here, subsidization may lead to both positive and negative effects. Irrigation as an activity is extremely beneficial to agriculture, but excess use of water due to excess subsidization of irrigation may damage the fertility of soil, leading to an adverse impact. When subsidy is given in excess, it leads to problems that may sometimes be unanticipated. Environment may be adversely affected by the overuse and/or inefficient use of resources due to improper pricing engendered by the subsidies. It is therefore important that, while framing a subsidy policy and determining agricultural prices, the shadow price of environmental resources be properly taken into account.

In the case of some other items also, the impact of subsidy may be mixed, such as command area development programmes and agricultural research in forestry. Many subsidy-induced research programmes may contribute to commercial forestry rather than environmental forestry and may ultimately induce a negative consequence for the environment. Similarly, large irrigation projects may not be the best way of providing irrigation for agriculture. How these areas should be dealt with is an important question.

The budgetary heads that have an environmental impact both in the social and economic services need to be first identified. With this in view, the services are classified into two groups, Group A and Group B. Those that have a 'direct positive' effect on environment are included in Group A. The remaining services, those that have an adverse or mixed effect on environment, are placed in Group B. Most Group B items will be judged by the fact that the primary objective of the service is not related directly to environment and the adverse or mixed effects are likely to be generated indirectly or incidentally. The grouping categorization is similar to the study by Pandey and Srivastava (2003). The grouping is detailed below.

Group A

1. Sewerage and sanitation
2. Soil and water conservation
3. Fisheries
4. Forestry and wildlife
   - Forest conservation, development and regeneration
   - Environmental forestry and wildlife
   - Afforestation and ecology development
5. Agricultural research and education
   - Soil and water conservation
   - Fisheries
   - Forestry
6. Special areas development programme
   - Drought prone areas
   - Desert development programme
   - Wasteland development programme
7. Flood control and drainage
   - Flood control
   - Anti-sea erosion
8. Non-conventional sources of energy
9. Ecology and environment
   - Prevention and control of pollution

Group B

1. Major and medium irrigation
2. Minor irrigation

3. Command area development programme
4. Fertilizer
5. Pesticide and chemicals
6. Mining in iron and steel industries
7. Cement and non-metallic industries
8. Non-ferrous mining and metallurgical industries
   - Mineral exploration in geological survey of India
   - Mineral exploration in regulation and development of mines

The volume of subsidies has been estimated for these budgetary heads for the central government and for four states, namely Maharashtra, Gujarat, West Bengal and Rajasthan for the year 2008–09. The basic data are drawn from the finance accounts of the central and the state governments.

5.5.2 Methodology of Measuring Subsidies

In this study, subsidies are measured as unrecovered costs of governmental provision of goods and services that are not classified as public goods. The unrecovered costs are measured as the excess of aggregate costs over receipts from the concerned budgetary head. The methodology, described in detail in Mundle and Rao (1991), and with modification in Srivastava et al. (1997), Srivastava and Amar Nath (2001), Srivastava and Rao (2001) and Srivastava et al. (2003), has been followed.

In the calculation of capital costs, accumulated capital stock pertaining to a service head is divided into three parts: (a) investment in physical assets in departmental activities including departmental enterprises, (b) investment in equities and (c) loans. In all cases, an accumulated investment as outstanding at the beginning of the financial year is taken. In the case of physical capital, a depreciation rate is applied.

Since estimates are made with respect to a financial year, annualized cost of capital needs to be estimated. In this context, two rates are important, namely the depreciation rate and the effective interest rate. The methodology enunciated in Srivastava and Amar Nath (2001) and Srivastava et al. (2003) has been followed. The average life of a capital asset is taken to be 50 years. The depreciation rate is worked out as a function of the parameters, namely the rate of growth of nominal investment (z) and the long-term rate of inflation (p). Investment data given in finance accounts are accumulated stock in the terms of the nominal values prevalent in the year of acquisition of the asset. The depreciation rate is given by d^* as indicated below.

$$d^* = \left(\frac{1}{50}\right)\left[\frac{\{1+w+w^2+\ldots+w^{49}\}(1+p)}{\{1+x+x^2+\ldots+x^{49}\}}\right],$$

with $w = (1 + p)/(1 + z)$ and $x = 1/(1 + z)$.

Here, p is the long-term rate of inflation and z is the growth rate of investment. 'p' has been taken to be 7.89 percent and 'z' has been calculated to be 13.04 percent. d^*, the depreciation rate, was calculated to be 0.05308, that is, 5.31 percent, by the above method (Appendix A5.1). Apart from depreciation, the effective interest rate is calculated to indicate the opportunity cost of funds. This is to be used in the case of all categories of capital expenditure, that is, loans and advances, equity investment and own capital expenditure on the functional head. The effective interest rates are calculated as interest payments as percentage of total borrowing by the concerned government (centre/state). The effective interest rates used for the centre and the four states, namely Maharashtra, Gujarat, Rajasthan and West Bengal for the year 2008–09 are shown in Table 5.9. Rajasthan seems to have a higher effective rate as compared to the other states and centre.

The estimation methodology has certain important assumptions and limitations arising from those. In particular, the life of an asset is assumed to be 50 years. Estimated subsidies include inefficiency costs. These are integral to the public provision of private goods. Subsidies due to tax expenditures are not captured. Subsidies are calculated with respect to actual prices,

Table 5.9
Effective interest rate in India: 2008–09 (percent)

States	*Interest Rate*
Maharashtra	9.200
Gujarat	9.291
West Bengal	9.200
Rajasthan	10.592
Centre	9.293

Source (Basic Data): Centre and respective State Finance Accounts.

even if these are administered, and not on the basis of market prices which would prevail if there were no regulated prices.

5.5.4 Estimation of Environment-related Subsidies

Subsidies having a bearing on environment in respect of the budgetary heads that have been identified by Pandey and Srivastava (2003) amounted to ₹5320 crore in 1994–95 and ₹6471 crore in 1996–97. These as percentage to GDP[6] in the respective years, translate to 0.53 and 0.47 percent, respectively. In this paper, the estimates for 2008–09 environmental subsidies amounted to ₹26322 crore and as percentage of GDP remained at 0.47 percent (Table 5.10). Out of these, subsidies on the following items, namely irrigation (major, medium and minor), fertilizers, pesticides and chemicals and command area development, mining in iron and steel industries, cement and non-metallic industries, non-ferrous mining and metallurgical industries (mineral exploration) are separated as pertaining to Group B.[7] The subsidies which remain may be identified as unambiguously having a positive impact on environment. These have been referred to as Group A

Table 5.10
Environment-related subsidies of centre: India (₹ crore)

Groups/Heads	*1994–95**	*1996–97**	*2008–09*
Group A	333.89	624.18	5231.67
Group B	4986.85	5847.11	21090.60
Irrigation (including CAD)	129.88	166.62	486.91
Fertilizers	4793.2	5586.94	20782.62
Pesticides and chemicals	63.77	93.54	89.86
Mining in iron and steel industries			10.28
Cement and non-metallic industries			–203.69
Non-ferrous mining and metallurgical industries			–75.39
Total	5320.74	6471.29	26322.28
As % of GDP	0.53	0.47	0.47

Source *(Basic Data):* GoI, Union Finance Accounts; GDP at market prices are taken from National Accounts Statistics, CSO. 2001, 2010.

Note: *Pandey and Srivastava (2003); CAD: command area development; GDP at market prices (at 2004–05 base) for the year 2008–09 is ₹5,574,449 crore; (–) sign indicates that the sector generated surplus in the given year.

Table 5.11
Environment-promoting subsidies (Group A) of centre: India (₹ crore)

Group A	*1994–95**	*1996–97**	*2008–09*
Sewerage and sanitation	42.00	17.10	1236.06
Soil and water conservation	20.45	23.14	26.04
Fisheries	61.16	57.70	221.52
Forestry and wildlife	–22.83	36.55	696.36
Agricultural research and education	52.20	56.96	365.11
Special areas development programmes	0.62	224.66	1560.29
Flood control and drainage	32.90	65.83	175.28
Non-conventional sources of energy	147.34	142.24	477.21
Ecology and environment			473.80
Total	333.84	624.18	5231.67

Source *(Basic Data):* GoI, Union Finance Accounts.
Note: *Pandey and Srivastava (2003); (–) sign indicates that the sector generated surplus in the given year.

subsidies. It will be seen that Group A subsidies are a very small portion of the total subsidies having an environmental impact.

The magnitudes of Group A subsidies, identified as having direct positive effect on environment, are shown in Table 5.11. Detailed estimates for 2008–09 is given in Appendix A5.2 while the detailed estimates for the years 1994–95 and 1996–97 given in Pandey and Srivastava (2003). These include estimated costs comprising actual and imputed components and receipts. The annualized cost of capital is obtained by applying the effective interest and depreciation rates to the relevant capital stock.

5.6 FINANCING AND RESTRUCTURING ENVIRONMENTAL SUBSIDIES IN INDIA

In this section, we look at issues in regard to financing environmental subsidies. In particular, we examine possible sources of such finance in the Indian context, the allocation of such financing, the targets or objectives and delivery of such financing. Alongside, we also look at the scope of restructuring subsidies to increase their positive environmental impact.

5.6.1 Sources of Finance

The financing of environment-promoting subsidies can come from the following sources: government (central and state governments), private sources, and international sources. Government financing can be drawn from general tax revenues as also earmarked cesses. Some funds can be released by expenditure restructuring, particularly by reforming environmentally perverse subsidies.

Government Budget

a. Taxation: Considering that promotion of environment can be considered a public good with associated high positive externalities, common property features, non-excludability and non-rivalry in consumption, the ideal method of financing is through taxation. Suitable allocation from the general budgetary resources should be made to finance environment-promoting activities, directly or through subsidies.

b. Cess or earmarked revenues: However, given competing claims on budgetary resources, it is often the case that adequate priority to environment promotion is not accorded. Often the committed expenditure in the budget becomes very large and the discretionary space becomes limited and promotion of environment gets relegated in terms of importance. Therefore, a more practical strategy may be to earmark amounts through cess or excise duties that must be used only for purposes of promoting environment. Examples are coal cess and petroleum cess, which are earmarked for expenditure on the concerned sector or industry. The coal cess is meant to be spent for cleaning of coal. In the context of GST, this question has to be rethought. In the current discussions on GST, the idea is to abolish all cess and surcharges. However, in the scheme proposed here, in the case of the taxation of petroleum and other major polluting goods and services, a non-rebatable excise or cess over and above the core GST rate has been proposed. The revenue from this additional non-rebatable rate can be earmarked for use for environmental purposes only. Here also, an excise may be preferable over a cess since the cess will be sector specific but the overall revenue from the non-rebatable excise can be earmarked for reducing pollution and promoting environment considering all sectors together. These revenues can be used for environment-promoting subsidies.

c. Restructuring subsidies: A third source for financing environment-promoting subsidies can be restructuring of subsides. In particular, resources can be released from environmentally perverse subsidies and these resources can then be allocated towards correcting the environmental damage. In this chapter, we have estimated that the share of environmentally perverse subsidies in India is quite large and that considerable resources can be released by discontinuing these subsidies and using these resources for environment-promoting subsidies.

d. Private resources: The idea of a subsidy is to induce the private sector also to commit to expenditure that may promote environment. Government subsidies can then leverage private resources.

e. International resources: Individual countries can also access international resources. Many of these resources are asking for matching contributions. The government's resources can be leveraged to get international resources also. In international funding for environmental objectives, 'mitigation specific' and 'mitigation relevant' support are being distinguished. 'Mitigation-specific support' aims to achieve GHG mitigation in developing countries as its main objective. Mitigation-specific financial support may include public and/or private support pertaining to investment flows under the clean development mechanism under the Kyoto Protocol.

'Mitigation relevant support' covers funding for development in key sectors that affect emissions in developing countries and thus mitigation potential. Such support includes bilateral as well as multilateral official development assistance in emission-intensive sectors, such as energy, transport and/or water infrastructure, waste management, agricultural or forestry sector development. These also include collaborative research and development initiatives that may not target climate change *per se* (e.g. in the energy and agricultural sectors). 'Mitigation relevant' flows of support may have either a positive or a negative effect on GHG emissions.

Under the global environment facility (GEF), public funding in the GEF has shown a leveraging ratio of about 7 (i.e. the GEF investment leads to a total investment that is roughly 7 times greater due to co-financing largely from the private sector). Both the estimates of large private financial flows under the CDM and the GEF co-financing from the private sector indicate the potential of public–private partnerships.

The UNFCCC monitoring system requires Annex I (developed country) Parties to periodically report information on bilateral financial support for mitigation in developing countries. These countries reported annual flows of financial support of between US$2 and 5 billion, for the period between 1999 and 2003 although this may give only a partial picture. Available data indicate that industry, energy and transport sectors have received the largest share of total bilateral mitigation relevant assistance (50 percent, 12 percent and 29 percent, respectively) and that mitigation far surpasses adaptation spending (the latter represents only 0.2 percent of total).

5.6.2 Financing Subsidies: Fiscal Federalism Implications

Oates (2001) distinguishes between three cases in the context of environment issues in a federal context: with environmental quality being (a) a pure public good, (b) a local public good and (c) local public good with spill-over effects. In the first case, there is a reason to argue that for setting environmental standards, the central government may be best placed to set the standards. Oates (2001) observes:

> There is consequently a need for the central government to set standards. On efficiency grounds, the central environmental authority should set a standard for environmental quality that satisfies the basic Samuelson condition: one for which the marginal benefits (i.e. benefits from a unit of improvement in environmental quality summed over everyone in the nation) equal marginal abatement cost. Efficiency would further require some kind of program (such as a national uniform effluent charge or a nationwide system of tradable emissions permits) that results in an equating nationwide of marginal abatement costs across sources.

In the second case, with local level variation in the environmental quality and impact of pollution, local level financing or setting of standards can be argued for. However, if the standards are set nationally, local level instruments should be available to meet the cost of extra pollution for reasons beyond its control. In a coal-rich state, there may be extra pollution for meeting national-level demands for energy. If the country goes for destination-based tax system like the GST, there are issues regarding meeting the cost of mitigation and adaptation for local pollution. If no suitable tax instrument is available for the sub-national governments, the cost may have to be subsidized by the national government.

In the case of environmental quality being a local public good with inter-state spill-over, the ideal method would be either differentiated tax structure to internalize the cost of pollution externalities or subsidies emanating from national resources but designed to take account of regional effects. In this context, Oates (2001) observes:

> The economist's usual response to such externalities is to prescribe a set of emissions taxes that internalize the social damages. But in an intergovernmental setting, this solution is less practical. The central government must either specify some set of differentiated taxes directly on polluting sources across the nation, or offer an appropriate and differentiated subsidy to local governments to induce them to internalize the inter-jurisdictional benefits from pollution control.

5.6.3 Design of Environmental Subsidies

Environmental subsidies aimed at pollution mitigation may be designed with four primary objectives: (a) to encourage the use of environmental-friendly inputs; (b) to encourage the use of outputs that intensively use environmental-friendly inputs; (c) to encourage technological innovation that will reduce the use of polluting inputs and (d) to facilitate adoption of environment-promoting technologies.

a. Allocation and Delivery of Environmental Subsidies

Fortunately, the major sources of pollution including carbon generation are limited in number. In terms of industries, attention has to be focused on coal, iron and steel and power sectors. A major impact on carbon emissions and other local pollutants can be generated through incentivizing technological innovation that promotes environment.

b. Environment-promoting Innovation and Subsidies

Market forces will generally not lead to development of new green technologies. Subsidies can significantly support environment-promoting innovation. These can be financed by suitable environmental subsidies, which in turn can be financed by environmental taxation.

A combination of taxes levied on environmentally harmful activities and subsidies that promote environment-promoting technologies and innovations can lead to acceptable environmental outcomes without sacrificing growth. Innovation can play a key role in promoting long-term economic growth. New products and more efficient processes can lead to new business opportunities and greater profitability for innovating firms. In respect of innovation, inventors would not generally have the foresight about the opportunities ahead and have access to the necessary financial support. Innovation is also characterized by risk of failure and need for lumpy initial investments. Individual innovators cannot take into account the positive benefits of knowledge spill-over effects.

Popp (2004) developed a model where innovation is brought about because of the new environmental policies. The effect of this innovation is an increase in welfare of 10 percent under an optimal carbon tax scenario, driven primarily by cost savings rather than additional environmental improvement. Gerlagh and Lise (2005) find that including technological change into a climate change model with a constant carbon tax brings about three times more emissions reductions than scenario without innovation being present. Kemfert and Troung (2007) find that accounting for induced technological change significantly reduces the negative GDP impacts of climate change policies.

In modelling exercises undertaken by the OECD, potential innovation was found to have a large impact on the costs and the climate change mitigation policies. Since innovation tends to be capital intensive, innovation adoption is likely to occur as older technology is replaced and new technology is needed. Further, the diffusion of innovation is not just limited to firms within the same country. The transfer of innovation across countries can accelerate the reach of innovation and increase abatement options for foreign polluters.

5.6.4 Targeting Specific Industries in India for Subsidy Support

Although a large volume of resources can be released by converting the environmentally harmful subsidies into environment-promoting subsidies supplemented by revenues from earmarked eco-taxes, their impact can be maximized by suitably targeting the most polluting industries. In the Indian context, the main industries that can be supported for encouraging innovations and substitution of cleaner inputs can be listed as energy, particularly thermal energy, iron and steel, motor vehicles, paper, textiles and plastics. Brief observations on the kind of support are given below.

1. Energy and Coal

Given the dependence of growth on supply of energy and the dependence of energy on coal, subsidies need to be stepped for cleaner coal technologies and cleaner energy production through solar and wind energy as well as run of the river mini-hydro power plants. In all these cases, the costs of technological innovation, high unit costs of energy and high initial set-up costs have so far proved to be prohibitive. This has resulted in slow growth of these cleaner energy supply sources.

It is well known that the combustion power plants manufactured by Bharat Heavy Electricals Limited (BHEL) constitute the core of the coal-power sector in India. Although the unit size and efficiency of these BHEL-manufactured power plants have gradually increased, the basic technology remains highly polluting. As observed by Chikkatur and Sagar (2007), there is now a range of advanced, more efficient, and cleaner technologies for producing electricity using coal. Combustion, based on supercritical steam, offers higher efficiencies than sub-critical PC. These are commercially viable and internationally available. Ultra-supercritical PC, which offers even higher efficiency, is also being deployed. Among other initiatives, Chikkatur and Sagar also suggest investment in a focused plan for geological carbon storage options, with detailed assessment of CO_2 storage locations, capacity and storage mechanisms in order to collect valuable information for India's carbon mitigation options and inform future technology selection as well as siting decisions for coal-power plants. Similarly, washing of coal at the mine heads will reduce the weight to be transported to the power plants and reduce pollution from transport vehicles apart from that in the power production.

2. Iron and Steel

In the case of iron and steel, cleaner technologies must start from the mining of iron ore itself. Recycling of iron is another area where cleaner technologies can be encouraged. Iron and steel industry also uses a lot of coal, and clean coal technologies would help reduce pollution through the iron and steel industry also.

Innovative technology of micro addition of more earth to liquid steel is being advocated for production of cleaner and quality steel. Another clean technology being advocated is the use of energy optimizing furnace (EOF), which is the basic unit proposed in place of basic oxygen furnace used for conventional steel making process. The process is being commercially exploited since 1982 but has been introduced in India, only recently. The EOF process is essentially an oxygen steel making process using combined submerged (bottom) and atmospheric (top) blowing. Oxygen is injected horizontally into the molten bath, and also into the furnace atmosphere through water-cooled injectors. These technologies need support for their fast and wide-spread adoption.

3. Textiles

Throughout the value chain in the production of textiles as also for cleaning of garments, cleaner technologies have become available. In textile production, five main segments are fibre production, spinning, weaving and knitting, dyeing-printing and finishing, and garment production. In the conversion of yarn from fibre, solid waste, fibre waste, yarn waste, dust, etc. are created. In the conversion of grey fabric from yarn, waste water containing cellulose derivatives comes out. From grey fabric to finished textile, at different stages, high BOD, high TS, neutral pH, high alkalinity, wasted dyes and solids become by-products. These processes also use up considerable amount of energy. A large number of washing steps involved in the production process also consume substantial amount of water. Due to the use of a variety of dyestuffs and auxiliary chemicals, lots of colour and metals appear in the wastewater and also give rise to Volatile organic compounds (VOC) emissions. Good housekeeping, reducing excessive use of water, recovery and recycling of waste, reuse of dye solutions from dye-bath, recovery of caustic in mercerising (by effective evaporation, using membrane technology) and recovery of size in cotton, processing (using technologies like ultra-filtration), recovery of grease in wool processing by acid cracking, centrifuging or by solvent extraction are steps that need to be encouraged not just by regulatory norms but by training, demonstration, etc. New technologies in textile manufacturing take advantages of size by using bigger scale like Jigger-Jumbo jigger-super jumbo equipment sizes, process control like micro-processor controlled pad-batches and single stage design scour-bleach processes. Eco-labelling is being used in many developed countries to distinguish between products produced by dirtier vis-à-vis cleaner technologies. Again, most of these initiatives need support.

4. Plastics

While the production and usage of plastics is slated to grow, its production and disposal are major environmental hazards. New ways to use plastics like in road construction, new technologies for plastic recycling show considerable possibilities for reducing the environmental costs, and thus provide scope for intervention and encouragement.

5. Clean Materials Initiative

More generally, across the spectrum of industries, usage of cleaner materials needs to be encouraged. Based on the 'best available techniques reference documents' (BREFs) drafted at the European Integrated Pollution Prevention and Control Bureau in Seville (see Ecofys, 2002 for details), other sources of information and expert opinion, an inventory has been established technologies with the potential to become important for reducing future environmental impact related to material demand. The potentials of reducing the environmental impacts have been quantified for the following categories of technologies:

1. material production technologies;
2. material application technologies;
3. material recycling and product recycling technologies;
4. end-of-pipe technologies.

It has been argued that there is strong potential for cleaner production technologies and recycling technologies to reduce environmental effects for all environmental impact categories. For a number of impact categories, such as 'carcinogenic', 'summer smog' and 'ozone depletion', end-of-pipe technologies have a substantial potential to reduce environmental impacts. One important area where technologies for limiting environmental impacts are missing is the recycling of cement/concrete and ceramics. Another issue is the use of oil as feedstock in the production of plastics, leading to a growth in fossil fuel depletion. Only few technologies are emerging in this area, for example, the development of bio-plastics. Support for innovations in such technologies can go long way in enhancing the environmental quality.

NOTES

1. For instance, the total volume of the budgetary subsidy will be of particular interest to those wanting to assess the drain on the public money; the resource use perspective will consider subsidies looking at whether the price reflects the true resource price (shadow price) of the good; implicit subsidies relating to not paying for environmental impacts may concern not only the local people and the local governments but also the neighbouring jurisdictions/countries and the society at large depending upon the nature of environmental impact.
2. Price support designed to compensate farmers for falls in the prices of crops.
3. To compensate meat producers for fall in the prices of meat.
4. The programme levied a special tax on the price of electricity that was used to subsidize generator's consumption of domestic coal.
5. Cited in Shergill (2005).
6. At current market prices, 1993–94 base series.
7. In Pandey and Srivastava study, mining in iron and steel industries, cement and non-metallic industries, non-ferrous mining and metallurgical industries (mineral exploration) are not included.

6

Conclusion and Prospects

D.K. Srivastava and K.S. Kavi Kumar

6.1 INTRODUCTION

The quality of environment and the quality of life are nearly synonymous. Maintaining the environment at an acceptable level of quality is the duty of central, state and local governments and also the duty of all citizens as per the provisions of the Constitution of India read with the relevant Supreme Court judgements. The process of economic growth, however, entails myriad activities that generate pollution affecting the quality of air, water and land. If the level of pollution increases beyond acceptable thresholds, it can potentially cause major health hazards, entailing both economic and welfare costs.

Some of this pollution is cleared up by natural processes. Others like carbon dioxide and other greenhouse gases (GHGs) remain in the atmosphere for a long time due to high life time. Accumulated pollution over a long period of time as a result of economic activities is a stock; current pollution is a flow that adds to that stock. This flow of pollution can be mitigated to a certain extent by policy intervention. Pollution has serious implications for economic growth and welfare because of its impact on health, resource depletion and natural calamities linked to climate change. Though it is well established that market based and fiscal instruments for pollution control (such as taxes, subsidies and trading instruments) have many desirable properties compared to the command-and-control (CAC) mode of environmental regulation, many countries including India still use the latter. Carefully designed use of fiscal instruments such as eco-taxes (tax the polluting inputs and outputs rather than pollution directly) provides a framework in which the central and the state governments can develop a coordinated intergovernmental approach to tackle issues of pollution in the light of India's growth requirements while keeping pollution within acceptable limits. Eco-taxes are not meant to be a revenue-augmenting device. Instead, the idea is to change the structure of taxation without putting additional burden on the tax payers. They reduce the use of resources and pollution by making them more expensive. At the same time, they facilitate reduction of distortionary taxes on labour and capital, making them cheaper, leading to increased output, employment and resource productivity. Many European countries have now started extensively using a number of eco-taxes for controlling pollution and meeting environmental targets including those relating to climate change. Consideration of the fiscal instruments for environmental management is particularly important at the present juncture as India is in the process of bringing in comprehensive reforms in the system of taxation of goods and services.

This chapter summarizes the arguments made so far for integrating eco-taxes and eco-subsidies in the goods and services tax (GST) regime in India. The chapter is structured as follows: the next section highlights the constitutional provisions in regard to environment in India and argues in favour of managing environment through economic instruments (EIs). The third section looks at the implications of integrating eco-taxes in the GST framework in terms of revenue potential and impact on pollution besides providing a comprehensive discussion on basic features of the proposed GST and some of its variants, complementary role of environment-promoting subsidies and industry perspectives. The final section provides concluding remarks.

6.2 MANAGING ENVIRONMENT: NEED AND SCOPE

Article 21 of the Constitution, relating to the fundamental rights, states that 'No person shall be deprived of his life or personal liberty except according to procedure established by law'. This article has been repeatedly interpreted by the Supreme Court as ensuring 'right for clean environment'—arguing that right for life is not feasible without protection and preservation of natures' gift. Any disturbance to the basic environment elements, namely, air, water and soil necessary for life, could thus be interpreted as hazardous to life within the meaning of Article 21 of the Constitution.

Article 47 of the Constitution requires the state to improve the standard of living and public health. To fulfil this constitutional goal, it is necessary that the state should provide among other things a pollution-free environment. The United Nations Conference on Environment held at Stockholm in 1972 placed the protection of biosphere at the centre of international policy and law. India through its participation in the Stockholm convention and explicit statement has committed itself to the protection of the environment. Relevant constitutional changes were brought about through the 42nd Amendment Act in 1976 relating to Articles 48 and 51.

1. *Directive Principles of State Policy:* Article 48 A—'The State shall endeavour to protect and improve the environment and to safeguard the forest and wildlife of the country'.
2. *Fundamental Duty:* Article 51-A (g)—'It shall be the duty of every citizen of India to protect and improve the natural environment including forests, lakes, rivers and wildlife and to have compassion for living creatures'.

Amendments to the Constitution were also made to accelerate the pace for environmental protection through changes in the Seventh, Eleventh and Twelfth Schedules of the Constitution. Under the Constitution, three important subjects concerning environment, namely, water, land, and gas and gas-works are placed in the State List of the Seventh Schedule of the Constitution as items 17, 18 and 25. Forests are placed in the Concurrent List.

From the economic viewpoint also, reduction in pollution is of considerable importance. The Thirteenth Finance Commission (THFC) observed (GoI, 2009, para 10.179), 'During field visits in the states we witnessed significant environmental degradation affecting the lives of people in the mining regions.' The economic costs associated with pollution can be significant although there are very limited number of studies that systematically assess such costs. For example, Brandon and Hommann (1996) for the first time provided an aggregate economy-wide estimate of cost due to various environmental pollution in India. The study estimated the health impact of water pollution to be $5710 million and the agricultural output loss due to soil degradation as $1942 million. The health impacts of air pollution were assessed as $1310 million and the loss of live-stock carrying capacity due to rangeland degradation was found to be $328 million. The cost of deforestation came to $214 million and the loss of international tourism was found to be $213 million. Overall, the results show that the total environmental damage was $9.7 billion per year, or 4.5 percent of gross domestic product (GDP) in 1992 values.

In a subsequent estimate, World Bank (2005) assessed that the annual economic cost of damage to public health from increased air pollution alone based on respirable suspended particulate matter (RSPM) measurements for 50 cities with the total population of 110 million was close to US$3 billion in 2004.

Smith and Mehta (2002) have analysed the years of life lost (YLL) and disability adjusted life years (DALY) among the rural and urban children below the age of five years and estimated the YLL and DALY attributable to the use of solid fuels in the household. It is estimated that annually about 20 million YLL and DALY in India can be attributed to not using the clean fuels.

Recently, Green Indian States Trust (GIST, 2008) has made an attempt to estimate the aggregate impact of natural resource degradation on Indian economy. The resources covered included depletion of forest resources, biodiversity loss, agricultural and pasture land degradation, and loss in ecological services. The gain/loss due to change of these resources is estimated across major states of India and expressed with reference to the Net State Domestic Product (NSDP) in 2002–03:

1. In terms of loss due to depletion of timber, fuel wood and non-timber forest products, Bihar is estimated to have incurred significant burden—about 5 percent of its NSDP, followed by Himachal Pradesh (2 percent of its NSDP) and Odisha (1 percent of its NSDP). At the all-India level, the losses are estimated at about 0.5 percent of national domestic product (NDP).
2. With regard to loss due to depletion and degradation of agricultural and pasture land, Rajasthan, Madhya Pradesh and Odisha registered high losses (4 percent, 3.5 percent and 3 percent, respectively of NSDP).
3. Himachal Pradesh, Uttar Pradesh and Kerala registered significant loss due to biodiversity loss from the forest degradation.

Thus, maintaining good quality environment is mandated both under the fundamental rights of the constitution and the directive principles. There is also a strong economic rationale to justify this. Under the constitutional provisions, the central, state and local governments must make the necessary effort to promote activities that maintain the acceptable quality of the environment.

Regulatory and EIs for Environmental Management

Environmental legislations in India come under criminal laws.[1] In implementation of the laws as well as in judicial decisions, the issue is on compliance or non-compliance, and not on the extent of compliance. The penalties for non-compliance are unrelated to the compliance costs. This type of pollution control regime creates an opportunity for corruption and rent seeking. The present standards and control regime—particularly the ones based on technology standards and input usage norms—provides no incentive for polluters to search for and adopt environmentally sound cost minimizing technologies/practices. EIs like taxation and subsidies, on the other hand, use incentives and disincentives to affect the decisions of producers and consumers. These are self-administered and allow the possibility of affecting the extent of pollution.

The main criticism against the CAC instruments is the high cost of emission reduction and government implementation failures. Given that all industries do not have the same abatement cost, it is cost efficient for some industries to abate more and others to abate less than required. However, regulations require all industries to adhere to similar standards irrespective of their cost of abatement which increases the overall cost of abatement. Regulation is also more difficult to implement as they require considerable information and involve significant administrative costs for implementation and monitoring. Further, the penalty for non-compliance does not depend on the extent of non-compliance. In case of non-compliance, everyone pays the same fine irrespective of the difference in their level compliance.

Market-based EIs, on the other hand, are intended to internalize environmental costs and externalities and hence influence decisions of agents by sending signals through price and other variables. These provide financial incentives to make environment-friendly decisions. It is in the economic interest of the polluter or the consumer to reduce pollution voluntarily by using better inputs and techniques or consume less polluting goods by conservation or substitution.

The main strength of EIs is the flexibility they allow leading to a reduction in the overall cost of abatement in comparison to other regulatory approaches. EIs call for an overall level of environmental performance in the economy. The private players, depending on their relative costs, can decide their respective levels of abatement. This ensures that industries with lower abatement cost abate more than those with higher abatement costs. Market-based instruments are of three broad types: price-based, quantity-based and informational-policy instruments.

Eco-tax is a broad term used to denote a variety of negative price incentives including not just taxes that directly tax pollution but also other indirect taxes which discourage the consumption of polluting outputs and the use of polluting inputs in production. For example, a tax on automobiles would lead to a reduction in pollution indirectly through lesser usage of automobiles. A tax on coal, which is regarded to be highly polluting, will discourage its use as raw material in production process and encourage its substitution with other environment-friendly materials. From the perspective of implementation, taxing an output or input rather than pollution is preferred due to availability of information on outputs and inputs and familiarity of tax authorities with input/output data.

Hence, eco-taxes (the way they are referred here) can be levied directly on pollution or on pollution-causing inputs and outputs signalling the price for the unpaid factor of production, thereby internalizing the externality. However, taxing pollution directly is often difficult due to measurement problems. Further, in some countries like India pollution taxes necessitate significant legal and institutional reforms. In such circumstances, taxing polluting inputs and outputs is considered a second-best solution. Eco-taxes, levied on output, are aimed at raising the price of the output, inducing consumers to reduce consumption levels or shift to non-polluting substitutes. Reduction in consumption will subsequently lead to a reduction in production and hence in pollution load. Impact of eco-tax in this case depends on the price elasticity of the polluting good and the availability of close substitutes. If levied on inputs, the burden of the tax is borne partly by the producers and is partly passed on to the consumers in the form of increased prices. This will encourage producers to invest in technological innovations and to use non-polluting inputs if substitutes are available.

Since the primary objective of environmental taxes is to bring about a reduction in environmental damages from different polluting sources, existing eco-taxes have targeted three main areas that are major contributors to pollution: (a) transport, in the form of differential taxation on vehicles based on fuel efficiency and congestion charges such as the one in London; (b) energy, where fuels which feed into energy generation are taxed and (c) waste and use of natural resources, where pollution, waste disposed and exploitation of natural resources is taxed so that an industry that is more polluting or is more natural resource intensive ends up paying a higher amount in taxes. Available evidence indicates that nearly 8–10 percent of total tax revenues are being raised by eco-taxes in countries that have implemented such taxes (Ekins, 2009).

6.3 INTEGRATING ECO-TAXES IN THE GST FRAMEWORK

6.3.1 GST and Eco-taxes—Alternative Versions

The variants of GST currently under consideration emanate, respectively, from (a) the Empowered Committee of State Finance Ministers (see, Empowered Committee, 2010), (b) the THFC (Task Force on Goods and Services Tax, 2009) and (c) the model implicit in central government's proposed constitutional amendment (GoI, 2011, revised in 2013). A major achievement is that the basic features of GST, namely, that it will be a concurrent GST, consistent with India's federal structure has been agreed upon. In all the three versions, the GST consists of central and state GST components (CGST and SGST) with the following main features:

1. The basic features of law such as chargeability, definition of taxable event and taxable person, measure of levy including valuation provisions, basis of classification, etc. would be uniform across central and state statutes as far as practicable.
2. The CGST and SGST would be applicable to all transactions of goods and services made for a consideration except for the exempted goods and services, goods which are outside the purview of GST and the transactions which are below the prescribed threshold limits.
3. The CGST and SGST are to be paid to the accounts of the centre and the states separately. Taxes paid against the CGST and SGST will get input tax credit (ITC) within the CGST and SGST chains,

respectively, but cross utilization of ITC between CGST and SGST would not be allowed.

4. The administration of the CGST will be with the centre and that of SGST with the states. The GST will be based on the destination principle. This requires that inter-state sales of goods and services and exports are zero-rated.

As discussed above, there are also issues concerning whether the proposed GST will have adverse environmental implications and what can be done to bring environmental considerations in the GST framework. Treatment of polluting inputs and outputs for effective environmental management is of critical importance in the context of GST as these inputs and output create negative externalities. Thus, a select number of polluting goods should bc subjected to either a non-rebatable excise over and above the GST or a cess. When a cess is levied, the revenue should be earmarked for the same industry for environmental promoting activities. It may be noted that in the GST, effective tax rate of some of the polluting goods are bound to come down compared to present tax rates, central and state rates taken together. This is bound to encourage pollution. This needs to be corrected in moving to GST by a non-rebatable excise or cess. In Indian context, a key component of the environmental taxes will have to relate to taxation of coal. In the Union Budget of 2010–11, for the first time the central government has taken the initiative of levying a cess of ₹50 (now increased to ₹100) per ton on domestically produced and imported coal. The revenue of this cess will form the resource pool for a 'clean coal fund'.

There are three routes for the environmental taxes to be part of the overall scheme of indirect taxes in India the core of which can be the GST. These are: (a) non-rebatable excise duties on identified polluting goods and services by the centre and the states, (b) environmental cesses where a link can be established between the revenue from the cess and the environmental promoting activities and (c) user charges. In addition, at the local government level, environmental taxes like the congestion charges can be levied. The most important of these will be the non-rebatable excises and the selection of goods that can be placed under these. This has been recognized in all the three variants of GST.

1. In its Draft Discussion paper, the Empowered Committee has discussed about the demerit goods including petroleum products

(which, as already discussed above, are one of the main polluting goods in India). The Empowered Committee has argued in favour of keeping the demerit goods including petroleum products, tobacco and alcohol out of the GST purview. These goods in turn will be subjected to separate non-rebatable excise duty/sales tax.

2. The Task Force set-up for the Thirteenth Finance Commission clubbed the petroleum products, tobacco and alcohol under the category 'sin goods'. The Task Force recognized the issue of negative externalities in a clearer way and collectively referred to these as sin goods and services and makes a distinction between sin goods and non-sin goods. The Task Force defines sin goods as goods whose consumption create negative externalities and for the purposes of their Report these, collectively or severally, refer to emission fuels, tobacco goods and alcohol. The Task Force notes that generally, goods with negative externalities should be subjected to excise duties in respect of which ITC is not to be allowed.
3. No other specific polluting input or output is mentioned although the environmental objective is clearly recognized by the Thirteenth Finance Commission. The Commission observes (GoI, 2009, para 5.28):

> The taxation of petroleum products and natural gas would be rationalised by including them in the tax base. HSD, MS, and ATF could be charged GST and an additional levy by both the Central and State Governments. No input credit would be available against either CGST or SGST on the additional levy. A similar treatment would be provided to alcohol and tobacco. Such an arrangement would ensure protection of existing revenues while taking care of environmental concerns.

In addition to these variants of GST under discussion, other Constitutional Bodies have recognized the need for integrating the eco-taxes in the GST framework. For instance, the Commission on Centre-State Relations has endorsed the idea (Commission on Centre-State Relations, 2010, para 9.5.02):

> In view of the dire need to arrest environmental degradation it is necessary to integrate environmental considerations within the framework of GST. Environmental taxes act as an indirect mechanism to control pollution and are likely to induce appropriate environmental decisions. We therefore recommend that polluting inputs and outputs may be subjected to a special non-rebatable levy by both the Centre and the States. In addition petroleum products alcoholic beverages and tobacco products may also be subjected to a non-rebatable levy.

6.3.2 GST and Eco-taxes—Implications for Revenue Potential and Pollution

Central to the acceptance of GST in India is to form an idea of the short- and long-run revenue potential of the GST. States fear that the movement to GST and abolition of CST would erode their revenues. Some of the producing states would particularly suffer as the basis of taxation moves to the destination principle. The revenue potential depends very largely on the GST rate structure and the efficiency effects that the GST can create thereby increasing the tax base.

In India, the debate on revenue implications has focused on determining a 'revenue neutral rate (RNR)' or a 'structure of RNRs', which would generate the same amount of revenues as presently under the taxes that are to be replaced by the GST. With such a RNR, two additional questions are: a division of the overall rate between the centre and states; and if for the states taken together, the rate is revenue neutral, then some states are bound to lose while others will gain. If so, how to compensate the losing states for their losses and for how long can such compensation continue.

Here, an attempt has been made to assess the revenue impact of GST in the Indian economy not in the narrow sense of working out a GST rate or rate structure that will produce the same amount of revenue as currently generated by the taxes that the GST will replace. Instead, GST is placed in the overall context of the size of the government that will be consistent with the changing needs of the Indian economy to provide the required size of government. In that context, the contribution of the indirect taxes levied by the central and state governments is worked out to see how the GST, in combination with the extra taxes on petroleum products and the demerit/polluting goods, taken together can generate the required increase in the tax–GDP ratio. This is done using a macro-econometric model of the Indian economy with a longer-term perspective going up to 2029–30. The model is extended for the generation of indirect taxes using a disaggregated sectoral detail. In the macro-model, output at factor cost is generated for eight sectors. These are further disaggregated into six additional sectors. The input–output table (IOT) is used for the generation of intermediate demand for output.

The empirical exercises start with the GST model and examine the possibilities of revenue neutrality arguing that the core GST rate can start with 14 percent divided into two parts for the centre and states. It argues that if provision is made for a non-rebatable excise/cess on polluting goods, then it is possible to reduce the core GST rate within a few years, if revenue neutrality is considered in a broader context where the overall contribution of taxation of goods and services (excluding local taxes) is taken into consideration. Three important features are: with the international crude oil prices continuing to rise in the future, the tax on petroleum products will continue to contribute progressively higher amounts; with the Indian economy progressively opening out, import duties will continue to have significant revenue importance; and with the provision of non-rebatable excise on polluting goods, these will lead to additional tax revenues permitting reduction in the core GST rate and more environment-friendly output structure. The following are some of the notable features:

1. The core GST rate is kept at 14 percent.
2. Without changing the core rate, and compliance rate, the desired buoyancy comes from the petroleum taxes.
3. The core rate can be further reduced if higher rate is charged on polluting goods/petroleum products or if the compliance rate improves.
4. Overtime, the GST share in total tax revenues goes down as the share of exports in GDP increases, but this is compensated by the higher share of import duties.

In this framework, the future pollution load is generated by: (a) estimating growth of output at 14 sector disaggregation (GDP at factor cost) up to 2029–30; (b) converting output in to gross output (sum of GDP at factor cost/gross value added, net indirect taxes and input requirements) using technology assumptions from the 2006–07 IOT and (c) using pollution load matrix giving pollution per unit of gross output. Pollution levels into the future can then be analysed and modified either by changing the growth and/or structure of output, or by changing the input-use coefficients (substitution of inputs/changed technology) or by changing the pollution load coefficients (more environment-friendly technology).

In the base growth scenario, sectoral growth is projected as per potential growth. These growth rates can be considered potential growth since they assume a supporting policy scenario and are based on supply side considerations. Pollution load, both of local and global pollutants, is generated using the projected output at 1999–2000 prices and the pollution coefficients.

In the base scenario, the structure of output keeps changing in favour of the services sector. As a result, even while the input-coefficients and the pollution load coefficients are held constant, the CO_2-intensity of output falls. The policy options used in scenario simulations may be summarized as follows:

1. Allow growth at less than potential rate as deliberate policy;
2. Modify the input-use coefficients of major sources of pollution and
3. Restructure output in favour of less polluting sectors while maintaining growth at about potential rate.

The environmental impacts of policy simulations are assessed through the emission trajectory of carbon dioxide. The effect of two simulations on the global pollution load (CO_2) is summarized in Table 6.1. In simulation 1, the sectoral growth rates across the board are reduced by one percentage point except for agriculture and allied services, which is retained at the base level. In simulation 2, the pollution load of selected sectors is changed by 5 percent and in the case of 'other polluting goods' and 'electricity, gas and water supply' by 10 percent and combine it with reduction in growth of one percentage point in coal and lignite, crude petroleum and petroleum products, polluting goods, alcoholic beverages, and electricity, gas, and water supply. In this scenario, growth across the board is not reduced. It is reduced only in sectors more directly responsible for pollution combined with improvement in technology that causes less pollution. Table 6.1 summarizes

Table 6.1

Progressive reduction in carbon intensity (Progressive percent reduction relative to 2006–07 level)

	Base	*Sim1*	*Sim2*
2007–08	1.78	1.78	1.70
2010–11	3.47	3.47	3.29
2014–15	8.29	8.78	9.91
2019–20	15.33	16.24	18.62
2024–25	23.25	24.36	27.46
2029–30	33.05	34.30	37.23

Source: Based on model projections.

the reduction in carbon intensity in select years in the base and two policy simulation scenarios.

It may be noted that the difference in percentage reduction in the carbon intensity in the three scenarios is not much. As such, there is no need to consider sacrificing the growth rate as a desirable option, if the target is only reduction in carbon intensity.

6.3.3 Complementary Role of Eco-subsidies

Fiscal intervention for promoting environment will be most effective if environmental taxation is complemented by environmental subsidies. In India, the design of fiscal instruments for environmental management has additional considerations arising because of the federal arrangements. Combinations of taxation and national subsidies can suit handling different types of environmental quality considerations in a federal context.

Subsidies in India require considerable restructuring to play an effective positive role in promoting environment. Quite a number of subsidies in the present regime can be considered environmentally perverse. These will have to be modified and replaced by environment-promoting subsidies. Restructuring of subsidies can provide source for financing environment-promoting subsidies. In particular, resources can be released from environmentally perverse subsidies and these resources can then be allocated towards correcting the environmental damage. It has been estimated that the share of environmentally perverse subsidies in India is quite large and that considerable resources can be released by discontinuing these subsidies and using these resources for environment-promoting subsidies.

Given competing claims on budgetary resources, it is often that adequate priority to environment promotion is not accorded. The revenue from the additional non-rebatable eco-taxes discussed above can be earmarked for use for environmental purposes only. Here also, an excise may be preferable over a cess since the cess will be sector specific but the overall revenue from the non-rebatable excise can be earmarked for reducing pollution and promoting environment considering all sectors together. Alongside, these revenues can also be used for financing environment-promoting subsidies.

Although a large volume of resources can be released by converting the environmentally harmful subsidies into environment-promoting subsidies supplemented by revenues from earmarked eco-taxes, their impact can be maximized by suitably targeting the most polluting industries. In the Indian context, the main industries that can be supported for encouraging innovations and substitution of cleaner inputs can be listed as energy, particularly thermal energy, iron and steel, motor vehicles, paper, textiles, and plastics.

6.3.4 Complementary Environmental Tax Reforms at State and Local Level

In most states, a compounded system of motor vehicle tax exists where a one-time levy is paid for the life of the vehicle. Such a system cannot distinguish between the pollution impacts of old vehicles vis-à-vis new vehicles who may also meet more up to date emission norms. In many states, motor vehicles are taxed at 12.5 percent of the purchase value. This covers two and three wheelers as well as cars, trucks and buses. Only in the case of tractors and trailers a concessional rate is applied, which may be of 4 percent.

The motor vehicle tax should be levied every five years and the older cars should be subjected to an increasing level of eco-cess every five years. After 15 years, the vehicles should be compulsorily taken out of the road.

Many cities in the world impose a congestion tax on certain specified segments of the city area, where there is a heavy density of vehicular traffic. This is implemented through suitable software and monitoring mechanisms so that taxes may be collected without any disruption to the traffic. In London, for example, in the central area, an entering vehicle is charged a congestion tax of £8, and in case of evasion, a fine of £50 is levied. This is applicable from 7 am to 6 pm, every day except Sundays and excepting certain types of vehicles like hospital ambulances. The enforcement system includes database of registered vehicles, a number of cameras guarding the entrance and exits of congestion zones, apart from the inner roads in the zone and Automatic Number Plate Recognition (ANPR) Software. The use of ANPR software is needed for this purpose.

The construction of 'Green' buildings may be encouraged by property tax concession. A rating mechanism called 'Griha' (Green Rating and Integrated Habitat Assessment) has been developed by the Tata Energy and Resources Institute (TERI) and the Ministry of New and Renewable Energy Sources based on inputs from the Power Ministry's Energy Conservation Building Code.

6.3.5 Industry Perspectives

The industry looks for a system of taxation of goods and services that would have among others, the following features:

1. The tax system should be based on self-assessment as far as possible.
2. The tax structure including the rates, exemptions and laws should be uniform across the country.
3. There should be no tax-barriers on state borders creating a genuine integrated all-India market.
4. Goods and services should be treated on par.
5. There should be no cascading, that is tax on tax and all goods and services within the purview so that no input tax remains un-rebated.
6. The tax rates should be low; ideally, a low single rate would be desirable.
7. There should be minimum compliance costs.
8. The tax regime should promote environment and conservation of resources so that growth can be sustained for a long period.

The GST can satisfy all of these requirements, if properly designed and implemented.

6.4 CONCLUSIONS

The present discussions around GST are characterized by a number of concerns.

1. First, the states fear loss of autonomy. Sales taxes and 'State VAT' are their main revenue sources. With these merged in GST, states fear that they will completely lose autonomy in determining tax rates and raising more or less revenues according to their needs.
2. Second, many states fear that with the central sales tax abolished, they will lose revenue in the long run. While the central government may compensate them for a few years, eventually this compensation will dry up. This concern is particularly true of the so-called 'producing' states.
3. Third, in a destination-based system, the tax revenue will accrue to the consuming states, while considerable amount of pollution will remain in the producing states.

4. Fourth, states are talking about dual rates for goods: one lower rate for goods of mass consumption and the other, the core rate for all other goods. This would necessitate having two rates for goods and possibly a third rate for services. This will bring back classification disputes amongst goods and between goods and service.
5. Fifth, the GST as presently envisaged is environmentally perverse, since it will tax polluting and non-polluting goods and services at the same rate.
6. Sixth, in spite of the reforms, taxation of petroleum products is still being kept out of the purview of GST where cascading is allowed to continue.

As argued here, if environmental taxes are integrated in the GST, almost all of these concerns can be effectively addressed. The environmental taxes can be introduced in the form of non-rebatable excises or cesses on polluting goods and services. With respect to these non-rebatable excises, the states can be given autonomy to select the goods from within a list approved by the GST Council. The rates may also be fixed by them subject to bands approved by the GST Council. Second, the revenue from environmental taxes can be used to bring the overall GST rate down to say 14 percent, divided between centre and states, at 7 percent each. Third, the producing states will get a long-term source of additional revenue enabling them to cope with the problems of localized pollution. Fourth, the 7 percent rate is low enough obviating the need to have dual rates for goods. We can then have a single rate for goods and services. Fifth, we will then have an environmental-friendly taxation regime. Sixth, the provision of non-rebatable excise will allow petroleum products also to be brought under GST. On the whole, a Green GST (GGST) will be far more welfare improving and acceptable than the narrowly formulated GST.

NOTE

1. National Environmental Policy (2006) notes that, 'Civil law offers flexibility and its sanctions can be more effectively tailored to particular situations. The evidentiary burdens of civil proceedings are less daunting than those of criminal laws. It also allows for preventive policing through orders and injunctions' (GoI, 2006; p. 17).

Appendix A1.1

Polluting Inputs and Outputs in India: Identification and Effective Tax Rates

A1.1.1 INTRODUCTION

A uniform rate of GST does not discriminate between polluting/non-polluting inputs or outputs. This may not be adequate for environmental protection. The policy makers have so far viewed the proposed tax regime as a tool of maximizing government revenues through simplified tax structures and (hopefully) through higher rate of compliance than before. The role of taxes in correcting (mainly environmental) externalities is ignored.[1] Allowing for this second scope of a tax system must compromise the uniform nature of the GST regime. The objective of this annexure is to identify, based on some current research, the most polluting industrial inputs and outputs within Indian states. Since the effects of such pollutants are mostly local (i.e. they are 'public bad' within the state), corrective actions must be taken by states themselves.[2] Moreover, different states are characterized by different industrial composition and hence different pollution patterns. The corrective policy, if any, should differ from one state to the other. This provides a rational for modifying the uniform GST regime across states.

A1.1.2 METHODOLOGY

The first step is, then, to calculate industrial pollution loads for different sectors across the states. We follow the pioneering effort of Gupta (2002) in this regard. In India, state-wise or nation-wise measurements of annual pollution loads are not available. However, industrial pollution intensities, defined by the ratio of pollutant output to total manufacturing activity,[3] are available in the World Bank Industrial Pollution Projection System (IPPS) database. However, there are some debates regarding the suitable choices of denominator as well as the numerator.

For example, denominator choices can be (a) suitable volume of output,[4] (b) shipment value, (c) value added and (d) employment. In practice, pollution loads are estimated separately by multiplying the pollution intensities (available by industrial sector) by the value of output and number of persons employed in each industry. Hettige et al. (1995) have shown that in the case of the USA, the ranking of industrial sectors by their pollution load is almost identical, irrespective of whether the value of output or employment is used as the unit of measurement. The total value of output is judged superior to value added because the energy and materials inputs are critical in the determination of industrial pollution. On the other hand, lack of physical data on volume of output in several countries limit the application of this system and for cross-country analysis.

The second major problem is to choose a suitable estimate of numerator. There is a difference between emission and pollution, and the effects of different pollutants on environment and human health are different (e.g. some pollute the soil more than water). The IPSS measurement uses different toxicity ratings for each industry.[5] The IPSS pollution intensities are based on US technology. One justification of working with them in Indian scenario is the fact that technologies do converge across countries. On a different level, the industrial classification system in vogue for the USA and India may not match. One must employ due caution in applying those indicators to other countries.

Gupta (2002) has also identified the CPCB notified 17 categories of polluting industries[6] and measured pollution load for them. However, only 16 categories are considered since Thermal Power Plants are not treated under IPSS as a separate category. Using the same methodology, Pandey (2005) has extended and updated Gupta's (2002) initial findings of state-level pollutants. As an indicator of output, she has used data on value of output and number of persons employed. These have been obtained from Annual Survey of Industries (ASI), which uses National Industrial Classification (NIC).

A1.1.3 OVERVIEW OF THE INDUSTRIES

The CPCB notified 16 industries are mostly concentrated in seven states namely, Maharashtra, Gujarat, Uttar Pradesh, Tamil Nadu, Bihar, Andhra Pradesh and Madhya Pradesh. Together, these account for more than 70 percent of the total value of production of these industries in India. Among these states, while iron and steel industry dominates Bihar (now Jharkhand) and Madhya Pradesh; oil refinery is largely concentrated in Maharashtra and Tamil Nadu; fertilizer in Gujarat, Maharashtra and Uttar Pradesh; sugar in Uttar Pradesh and Maharashtra; and the cement industry dominates in Madhya Pradesh and Andhra Pradesh. In 1994, among the 16 most polluting industries in terms of both values of production and employment, the largest industry was iron and steel. The five largest industries contributing 74 percent of the total value of industrial production and nearly 67 percent of total employment in these industries were iron and steel, oil refinery, fertilizer, sugar and cement. The estimates of industrial pollution load have been obtained using the industrial value of production and employment as a measure of industrial activity. Pollution loads are estimated according to the nature of pollutants (water, air, toxic and metal) and also by medium (air, water and land) for the toxic and metal pollutants.

The relative contribution of each industry to total pollution load at the all-India level shows that the iron and steel industry is the highest polluting industry in terms of all four pollutants except air where it ranks second to cement. Iron and steel is the largest water polluting industry in India with 87.4 percent of the total pollution load. The pulp and paper and aluminium industries rank second and third, respectively, with their contribution to total water pollution load at 4.6 and 2.5 percent. Sugar and distillery industries rank fourth and fifth, respectively (Table A1.1.1).

Table A1.1.1
Ranking of industrial sectors by estimated pollution load (Tons)

S. No.	*ISIC Code*	*Industry*	*Water*	*Air*	*Toxic*	*Metal*
A: By Output Volume						
1	3720	Aluminium	3	6	5	1
2	3720	Copper	6	8	9	2
3	3720	Zinc	8	10	11	3

Table A1.1.1 continued

Table A1.1.1 continued

S. No.	*ISIC Code*	*Industry*	*Water*	*Air*	*Toxic*	*Metal*
4	3710	Iron and steel	1	1	1	4
5	3692	Cement	11	2	14	5
6	3530	Oil refinery	12	3	4	6
7	3522	Drugs	10	15	12	7
8	3513	Petrochemicals	13	7	2	8
9	3512	Fertilizer	4	9	3	9
10	3512	Pesticide	9	12	8	10
11	3511	Caustic soda	15	13	10	11
12	3411	Pulp and paper	2	4	6	12
13	3231	Leather	14	14	7	13
14	3211	Dyes and dye intermediate	16	16	16	14
15	3131	Distillery	7	11	15	15
16	3118	Sugar	5	5	13	16
B: By Employment						
1	3720	Aluminium	16	7	8	2
2	3720	Copper	9	10	11	4
3	3720	Zinc	12	13	13	5
4	3710	Iron and steel	1	2	2	1
5	3692	Cement	11	1	15	11
6	3530	Oil refinery	13	5	5	10
7	3522	Drugs	8	16	12	14
8	3513	Petrochemicals	14	9	7	9
9	3512	Fertilizer	7	11	4	6
10	3512	Pesticide	10	15	9	8
11	3511	Caustic soda	5	6	1	3
12	3411	Pulp and paper	3	3	3	12
13	3231	Leather	2	14	6	7
14	3211	Dyes and dye intermediate	15	12	14	13
15	3131	Distillery	6	8	16	16
16	3118	Sugar	4	4	10	15

Source: Pandey (2005).

The cement industry is the biggest air polluter emitting nearly 34 percent of the total air pollution load. Iron and steel stands second, emitting 32 percent, while oil refinery ranks third contributing 7.4 percent to the total industrial air pollution load.

The iron and steel industry is also the largest metal polluter accounting for more than 71 percent of the total metal pollution load. Aluminium industry is the second highest contributor (nearly 16 percent) to metal pollution. In the toxic pollution category also, iron and steel industry is the highest polluter contributing 39 percent of the total pollution load. The second most polluting industry in this category is leather with about 14 percent share in total toxic load. Iron and steel, leather, petrochemical and oil refinery industries together account for 70 percent of total toxic pollution load. The main implication of these results is that substantial reduction in total pollution loads can be achieved by focusing pollution control efforts in a limited number of industrial sectors.

Except water pollution, the ranks of different industries either by output volume or by employment are highly correlated. Pandey (2005) posits that Indian industries are overstaffed vis-à-vis the US ones. Hence, it is better to work with output-based measurements of pollution load.

A1.1.4 MAJOR POLLUTING STATES

In toxic pollution, there are seven states that account for about 70 percent of the total toxic industrial pollution. Maharashtra, the largest contributor, accounts for about 15.9 percent of the total toxic pollution in the country followed by Gujarat at 15.5 percent and Tamil Nadu at 8.5 percent. Bihar (undivided) is at the fourth place with a share of 8.4 percent followed by Uttar Pradesh with 7.3 percent of the total toxic pollution load. Madhya Pradesh and Odisha contribute 7.0 and 6.2 percent, respectively, to this category of pollution.

Sixty-eight percent of the total industrial metal pollution load in the country is contributed by six states. Bihar ranks first with a share at 15.1 percent followed by Maharashtra at 14.2 percent. 12.1 percent of the total metal pollution load is generated by Odisha. Madhya Pradesh's contribution to this category of pollution is 12.1 percent followed by West Bengal at 7.4 percent. Uttar Pradesh with a metal pollution load of 6.6 percent of the total load ranks sixth.

The ranking of states in water pollution is somewhat similar to that of metal pollution. The four largest water polluting states are the same as in the case of metal pollution. Bihar with 17.1 percent of the load leads the group and is followed by Madhya Pradesh with 12.9 percent, Maharashtra with 12.5 percent and Odisha with 10.9 percent of the total water pollution load. Andhra Pradesh and West Bengal, respectively, have a share of 6.7 and 6.9 percent of the total water pollution load. Uttar Pradesh with a share of 5.5 percent of the total pollution load puts the cumulative share of these seven states at about 73 percent.

As in the case of toxic pollution, Maharashtra is the largest polluter of air with a share of 15 percent of the total industrial air pollution followed by Madhya Pradesh at 11.2 percent. Gujarat ranks third with a share of 9.3 and is followed by Andhra Pradesh and Bihar at 8.9 and 8.6 percent share, respectively. Tamil Nadu and Uttar Pradesh contribute 7.9 and 7.5 percent of air pollution load, respectively. Odisha with a share of 6.6 percent takes the cumulative contribution of these eight states to 74.8 percent of total industrial air pollution load. In Table A1.1.2, following top five states in each category are mentioned:

1. Water: Bihar, Maharashtra, Madhya Pradesh, Odisha, West Bengal.
2. Air: Maharashtra, Madhya Pradesh, Gujarat, Andhra Pradesh, Bihar
3. Toxic: Maharashtra, Gujarat, Tamil Nadu, Bihar, Uttar Pradesh
4. Metal: Bihar, Maharashtra, Odisha, West Bengal, Uttar Pradesh

Table A1.1.2

Contribution of select states to industrial pollution load (Percent)

State	*Water*	*Air*	*Toxic*	*Metal*
Andhra Pradesh	7.0	8.9	5.8	5.8
Bihar	17.1	8.6	8.4	15.1
Gujarat	4.2	9.3	15.2	4.2
Karnataka	3.1	4.3	2.0	2.9
Madhya Pradesh	12.9	11.2	7.0	12.1
Maharashtra	12.5	15.0	15.9	14.2
Odisha	10.9	6.6	6.2	12.1
Punjab	5.1	2.7	2.8	4.0
Rajasthan	1.3	3.8	1.9	1.7
Tamil Nadu	4.5	7.9	8.5	4.1
Uttar Pradesh	5.5	7.5	7.3	6.6
West Bengal	6.9	7.3	5.4	7.4

Source: Pandey (2005).

Since we are concerned about the local effects of pollution, one should also take the population density of the states into consideration. A high density state (like West Bengal or Kerala) will face higher per capita burden of pollution and the policy should be stricter there.

A1.1.5 MAJOR POLLUTING INDUSTRIES AND THEIR POLLUTION LOAD: ACROSS STATES

Table A1.1.3 provides the distribution of polluting industries, as a whole, across some selected states. We take the output (in 1994–95 prices) as the indicator of scale. It is clear that polluting industries are most heavily concentrated in five states, namely, Maharashtra, Gujarat, Uttar Pradesh, Andhra Pradesh and Bihar (together, they account for almost 55 percent of production).

Table A1.1.3
Percent distribution of CPCB notified polluting industries

State	*Percent of Polluting Output*
Andhra Pradesh	7.0
Assam	1.2
Bihar (Jharkhand)	7.0
Delhi	0.4
Goa	0.02
Gujarat	12.6
Haryana	1.6
Karnataka	3.0
Kerala	0.7
Maharashtra	18.3
Odisha	4.8
Tamil Nadu	8.4
Uttar Pradesh	10.4
West Bengal	4.2

Source: Pandey (2005).

A comparison between Tables A1.1.2 and A1.1.3 quickly reveals why one should be careful with the pollution control exercise based on distribution of polluting industries. For example, Bihar does not figure into the top five industry concentration, yet figures in the top five pollution load in all categories. Combining the elements of Tables A1.1.1 and A1.1.2, we try to predict major pollutants for different states.

In all the states except Goa, iron and steel is the major water polluting industry in terms of contribution to the total water pollution load in the state (Table A1.1.4). In fact, in all the states except Goa and Kerala, iron and steel industry contributes more than 50 percent to the states' total water pollution load. However, in Goa, distillery industry which ranks fifth at the all-India level in terms of its contribution to total pollution load, is the only water polluting industry. The pulp and paper industry is the second largest contributor (5–20 percent) to states' water pollution load in Andhra Pradesh, Haryana, Karnataka, Tamil Nadu, Gujarat and Uttar Pradesh. Aluminium, fertilizer and drugs and pharmaceuticals are the other major water polluting industries besides iron and steel in the state of Kerala.

Table A1.1.4

Major sources of water pollution: By states

States	*Industries (Except Iron and Steel)*
Andhra Pradesh	Pulp and paper
Assam	NA
Bihar	NA
Goa*	Distilleries
Gujarat	Pulp and paper
Haryana	Pulp and paper
Karnataka	Pulp and paper
Kerala*	Aluminium, fertilizer, drugs and pharmaceuticals
Maharashtra	NA
Odisha	NA
Rajasthan	NA
Tamil Nadu	Pulp and paper
Uttar Pradesh	Pulp and paper
West Bengal	NA

Note: *Major pollutants, not iron and steel; NA: not available.

Table A1.1.5
Major sources of toxic elements: By states

States	*Industries (Except Iron and Steel)*
Andhra Pradesh	NA
Assam*	Oil refinery
Bihar	NA
Goa*	Distilleries
Gujarat*	Petrochemical and fertilizer
Haryana	NA
Karnataka	NA
Kerala*	Aluminium, fertilizer
Maharashtra	NA
Odisha	NA
Rajasthan*	Fertilizer
Tamil Nadu*	Leather
Uttar Pradesh	NA
West Bengal	NA

Note: *Major pollutants, not iron and steel; NA: not available.

In terms of discharge of toxic pollutants, the iron and steel industry is the largest contributor to states' total toxic pollution load in all states except Assam, Gujarat, Goa, Kerala, Rajasthan and Tamil Nadu. In this category, the petrochemical and fertilizer industries are major contributors in Gujarat, distilleries in Goa, the fertilizer and aluminium industries in Kerala, oil refinery in Assam, leather in Tamil Nadu and the fertilizer industry in Rajasthan (Table A1.1.5).

For metal pollutants, iron and steel is the largest polluting industry in all the states except Goa. The oil refinery industry contributes substantially to states' total toxic pollution load in Assam, the copper industry in Delhi, Maharashtra and Rajasthan, petro-chemicals in Gujarat, the aluminium industry in Karnataka, Kerala, Madhya Pradesh, Maharashtra, Odisha, Rajasthan, Uttar Pradesh and West Bengal and the leather industry in Tamil Nadu (Table A1.1.6).

For air pollutants, the iron and steel industry is again the major polluting industry in all states except Assam, Goa and Kerala. Oil refinery, paper and cement are the major air polluting industries in Assam. While distillery is the

Table A1.1.6
Major sources of metal pollutants: By states

States	*Industries (Except Iron and Steel)*
Andhra Pradesh	NA
Assam*	Oil refinery
Bihar	NA
Delhi	Copper
Goa*	Distilleries
Gujarat	Petrochemical
Haryana	NA
Karnataka	Aluminium
Kerala	Aluminium
Madhya Pradesh	Aluminium
Maharashtra	Copper, aluminium
Odisha	Aluminium
Rajasthan	Aluminium
Tamil Nadu	Leather
Uttar Pradesh	Aluminium
West Bengal	Aluminium

Note: *Major pollutants, not including iron and steel; NA: not available.

single most polluting industry in Goa, cement and aluminium are the major air polluting industries in Kerala. Cement is the major air polluting industry for the states of Andhra Pradesh, Assam, Gujarat, Haryana, Himachal Pradesh, Karnataka, Kerala, Madhya Pradesh, Rajasthan and Tamil Nadu. Among other industries, the paper industry in Assam, Haryana and Karnataka; the oil refinery industry in Assam, Gujarat, Maharashtra, Tamil Nadu, Uttar Pradesh and West Bengal; the aluminium industry in Kerala, Odisha, Uttar Pradesh and West Bengal; the copper industry in Delhi; petrochemicals in Gujarat; distillery in Jammu and Kashmir; and the sugar industry in Uttar Pradesh.

A1.1.6 DESIGNING AN EFFLUENT CHARGE

An important aspect of designing an effluent charge is to determine the *right* rate of charge. Theoretical literature prescribes that the rate of charge should be set such that the marginal gains from the pollution reduced

Table A1.1.7
Major sources of air pollutants: By states

States	*Industries (Except Iron and Steel)*
Andhra Pradesh	Cement
Assam*	Oil refinery, paper, cement
Bihar	NA
Delhi	Copper
Goa*	Distilleries
Gujarat	Petrochemicals ,cement, oil refinery
Haryana	Cement, paper
Karnataka	Cement, paper
Kerala*	Aluminium, cement
Madhya Pradesh	Cement
Maharashtra	Aluminium, oil refinery
Odisha	Aluminium
Rajasthan	Cement
Tamil Nadu	Oil refinery
Uttar Pradesh	Oil refinery, aluminium, sugar
West Bengal	Oil refinery, aluminium

Note: *Major pollutants, not including iron and steel; NA: not available.

equals the marginal cost of reducing it (MBA = MCA). In other words, a rate of charge equal to the marginal pollution abatement cost at the socially optimum level of pollution will induce the polluter to reduce his/her pollution to the socially efficient level. However, given the practical difficulties in measuring the damage due to pollution and also gains from reduction in pollution at the margin, the above approach is difficult to put in practice. Economists have suggested an alternative approach which is popularly known as 'standards and taxes' approach. This approach involves a pre-specified emission/discharge standard for each pollutant, together with a charge that is levied on the polluter if he/she exceeds the prescribed norms (Table A1.1.8).

We want to stress the following points. First, it has been shown that market-based instruments are superior to CAC principles. To discourage usage of polluting inputs and outputs, the states may levy a (quasi-Pigouvian) tax on the sectoral output. Whether such a tax will reduce pollution depends

Table A1.1.8

Abatement cost coefficients (US$, 1994) per ton of pollutant abated

S. No.	*Industry*	*ISIC*	*PT*	*SO_2*	*NO_2*	*VOC*	*PB*
1.	Sugar	3118	57.50	234.92	330.51	195.35	236.93
2.	Distillery	3131	176.39	622.54	2963.14	195.35	236.93
3.	Dye	3211	243.80	270.85	2670.28	819.34	1362.29
4.	Leather	3231	329.64	300.13	300.13	366.79	300.13
5.	Pulp and paper	3411	40.74	106.22	136.26	157.42	236.93
6.	Caustic soda	3511	2.42	222.48	146.34	133.38	444.34
7.	Fertilizer and pesticide	3512	69.01	183.94	510.55	295.79	79.32
8.	Petrochemical	3513	71.23	222.48	120.66	81.70	1413.43
9.	Drugs	3522	260.47	1311.88	706.55	141.26	354.34
10.	Oil refinery	3530	23.50	187.83	65.71	188.38	3.84
11.	Cement	3692	13.00	14.08	330.51	327.03	236.93
12.	Iron and steel	3710	167.8	40.69	106.03	2420.94	2176.47
13.	Aluminium, copper and zinc	3720	199.42	151.14	116.75	1326.9	874.22

		TXAIR	*AOTH*	*WCON*	*WNON*	*WTXMT*	*WTXOG*
1.	Sugar	1277.21	387.36	5.92	71.68	671.93	286.71
2.	Distillery	1277.21	387.36	183.49	319.26	671.93	286.71
3.	Dye	544.18	387.36	83.58	319.26	785.63	167.83
4.	Leather	300.13	300.13	148.50	442.17	2753.81	167.83
5.	Pulp and paper	544.18	62.94	84.17	185.36	671.93	286.71
6.	Caustic soda	22.46	39.87	175.72	281.69	671.93	205.95
7.	Fertilizer and pesticide	1352.11	159.73	954.46	487.03	671.93	448.19
8.	Petrochemical	70.04	51.05	592.01	369.16	671.93	532.80
9.	Drugs	81.94	387.36	452.89	397.00	671.93	1793.01
10.	Oil refinery	3.84	3.84	269.27	724.01	671.93	1016.51
11.	Cement	544.18	387.36	11.73	2741.22	671.93	286.71
12.	Iron and steel	667.97	387.36	91.25	279.01	486.93	87.32
13.	Aluminium, copper and zinc	2021.18	387.36	85.09	78.46	671.93	100.74

Source: Pandey (2005).

Note: PT, particulate; AOTH, others air pollutants; TXAIR, toxic air pollutants; SO_2, sulphur di-oxide; WCON, conventional water pollutants; NO_2, nitrogen dioxide; WNON, non-conventional water pollutants; WTXOG, toxic organic water pollutants; PB, lead; VOC, volatile organic compounds; WTXMT, toxic metal water pollutants.

on the elasticity (which, in turn, depends on the availability of a greener substitute) of the sectors (from the demand side) as well as the cost of abatement (from the supply side). If the tax rate is higher than cost of abatement, the industry will abate and not pay any tax. On the other hand, if abatement cost is higher, the industry will continue to pollute and pay taxes. An estimate of the cost of abatement is given in Table A1.1.7.

A1.1.7 TOWARDS A TAX PRESCRIPTION

It is imperative to know that some of the most polluting inputs are also taxed heavily. This is shown in Table A1.1.9.

Table A1.1.9
Effective tax rate as percent of value added

	2003–04		*2006–07*	
Industries	*Effective Tax Rate (Percent)*	*Rank Out of 107 Industries*	*Effective Tax Rate (Percent)*	*Rank Out of 103 Industries*
Cement	9.89	61	12.54	50
Drugs and medicines	24.97	30	23.30	32
Fertilizers	28.08	26	24.67	28
Iron and steel, casting and forging	34.95	13	35.48	14
Iron and steel, foundries	56.68	6	52.04	7
Iron, steel and Ferro alloys	17.09	42	9.11	55
Leather and leather products	17.05	43	8.21	59
Motor vehicles	34.07	17	36.98	11
Non-ferrous basic metals	24.08	31	31.97	16
Paper, paper prods. and newsprint	31.45	22	35.30	15
Pesticides	23.35	34	20.15	38
Petroleum products	56.94	5	31.86	17
Sugar	6.69	68	24.07	31
Average of all industries	(total = 107) 17.41		(total = 103) 18.15	

Source (Basic Data): CSO, 2003–04 and 2006–07 Input–Output Tables. Authors' calculation.

One can argue that the most polluting inputs are already heavily taxed (except energy inputs like coal and lignite, natural gas and crude petroleum), such that there is a disincentive for intensive use of these inputs. If we allow for uniform tax rates across the board, such impediments vanish, and environmental problems will accentuate.

A1.1.8 SUMMARY

The above discussion presents a case against uniform treatment of various polluting and non-polluting inputs under the forthcoming GST regime. Also, different states have different polluting industries, and the nature of pollution is not same across states. This calls for differential treatment by the states over and above what the uniform rate suggests. Some of the polluting inputs are already very heavily taxed; any attempt to remove these taxes will remove market incentive to move towards greener substitutes.

A1.1.9 END NOTE: MEASURING THE BENEFIT

One faces serious informational problem in order to estimate the (health) benefits of reduced pollution (or costs of higher pollution). There are two dimensions of the problem. First, the health implications of different types of pollutants are not well understood. Even if they are, direct data, at least in case of India, are not forthcoming. One should therefore measure such benefits with extreme caution.

Brandon and Hommann (1996) have estimated the excess morbidity due to air and water pollution using data on 36 Indian cities. Thus, one can estimate, however crudely, the benefit from reducing, say total suspended particulates (TSP). The reason behind focusing TSP is as follows. At least in this respect, the health issues are more or less clear. Some researchers (Kandlikar and Ramachandra, 2000) have argued that 'particulate matter is the major cause of human mortality and morbidity from air pollution'. If the ambient particulate concentrations are reduced to the WHO annual-average-standard, then 40,300 premature deaths together could have been avoided. This translates into, by a rough estimate, a benefit of the order \$170–\$1675 million.[7]

However, in India where discharge standards are in force for more than two decades and firms have adjusted their abatement activities to the discharge standards, a full charge system may not be acceptable to industries. There may also be resistance because of factors such as non-availability of technology for meeting more stringent targets and economic viability of meeting such targets. Since efficiency is by no means the only factor in designing a pollution control instrument, we may take an approach in which efficiency may have to be sacrificed marginally for the gain in its acceptability hence, implementation and enforcement ease.

NOTES

1. Baumol and Oates (1988).
2. In India, environmental management is a state subject. This is true for natural resources as well as for ambient air and water quality and solid waste pollution.
3. Analogous to, say, the input–output coefficients.
4. Output volume, although attractive at the first look, runs into problem since the measurement of units may be different in different industries.
5. Hettige et al. (1995).
6. These sectors get more attention from the CPCB than the rest. These are (a) aluminium, (b) basic drugs and pharmaceuticals, (c) caustic soda, (d) cement, (e) copper smelting, (f) distillery, (g) dyes and dye intermediates, (h) fertilizer, (i) iron and steel, (j) leather, (k) oil refineries, (l) pesticides, (m) petrochemicals, (n) paper and pulp, (o) sugar, (p) thermal power plants and (q) zinc smelting. They are also important in terms of employment and output. (See http://cpcb.nic.in/17cat/17cat.html)
7. This is the value statistical life: discounted value of a 10-year wage stream. The numbers are the lower and upper bounds of wage stream. The marginal benefit of reducing particulate concentration is thus (money saved)/Δ(TSP). Given the large concentration of TSP in Indian cities, even a 50 percent reduction may not be enough to achieve the WHO par.

Appendix A1.2

Recommendations of Earlier Eco-tax Studies

Earlier studies have closely looked into some of the highly polluting inputs and outputs and recommended the use of appropriate market instruments—eco-tax rates and subsidies—to limit or at least reduce the rate of pollution. The following paragraphs provide a brief review of earlier recommendations.

A1.2.1 COAL

Chelliah et al. (2007) recommended the levy of an eco-cess to provide suitable incentives for reducing the ash-content. The additional burden of the cess measured in terms of percent of base price of different grades of both coking and non-coking coal was also estimated. Srivastava and Rao (2008) recommended a similar but somewhat simplified structure of the eco-cess as given in Table A1.2.1

It was proposed that the existing provision of collecting a uniform cess of ₹10 per ton of coal be applied to levying an environmentally rational cess which will be passed on to the consumers. This will reduce pollution as well as improve efficiency of production without causing loss either to consumers (who need less of a better quality of coal) or producers of coal since they do not bear the cess. The receipt from the cess was proposed to be allocated for setting up facilities for washing and treating coal and related research and development.

Table A1.2.1
Rates of eco-tax on coal

Type of Coal	*Rate (₹ Per Ton)*
All varieties of coking coal where ash content is 18 percent or less	Nil
All varieties of coking coal where ash content is between 19 percent and 28 percent	20
All varieties of coking coal where ash content is higher than 28 percent	40
All varieties of non-coking coal where ash content is 28 percent or less	Nil
All varieties of coking coal where ash content is higher than 28 percent	50

A1.2.2 PETROLEUM PRODUCTS

As part of the overall tax reforms, it was suggested that in the case of petroleum products, states may levy differential special rates but agree on floor and ceiling rates. The existing floor rate may be increased from 20 percent to 25 percent:

1. Considering the revenue-importance of this tax, in order not to have detrimental effects either on growth on prices, the core (floor) State VAT rate on all other goods may be reduced from 12.5 percent to 10 percent.

This would also facilitate introducing a comprehensive GST regime where both the core rates of CENVAT and State VAT will need to be reduced from the present levels of 14 and 12.5 percent, respectively.

A1.2.3 CHEMICAL FERTILIZERS

Given the large volume of subsidies given by the central government, it does not seem feasible for the central government to impose an eco-tax for reducing the consumption of chemical fertilizers. As far as the state governments are concerned, they have also put fertilizer rates that vary between total exemption and 12.5 percent. In some cases, naphtha is rated at 20 percent.

At the present juncture, the following are recommended:

1. Overall volume of subsidy for chemical fertilizers should be reduced in stages and eventually eliminated.
2. Encourage a more balanced use of fertilizers by following a nutrient-based subsidy regime.
3. Reduce the overall cost by shifting away from naphtha as feedstock.
4. States should keep chemical fertilizers in the 12.5 percent category and bio-fertilizers in the exempted category.

A1.2.4 CHEMICAL PESTICIDES

In order to discourage the use of chemical pesticides, an effective pricing policy would be to levy an eco-tax on chemical pesticides based on toxicity levels. It was recommended that the tax should be a separate eco-cess which could be levied on the pesticide manufacturers. The yield from the cess could be used to promote the use of bio-pesticides and integrated pest management.

An additional cess based on toxicity of chemical pesticides could be collected as an eco-tax. The Central Insecticides Board has designated a colour coding based on toxicity. This code could be used as a basis for levying the eco-cess (Table A1.2.2).

Keeping in view findings of Chelliah et al. (2007), Srivastava and Rao (2008) recommended that:

1. Chemical fertilizers be placed at 14 percent under CENVAT and at 12.5 percent under State VAT.

Table A1.2.2
Rates of eco-cess on chemical pesticides

Toxicity	*Colour*	*Cess (Percent)*
Extremely toxic	Bright red	8
Highly toxic	Bright yellow	6
Moderately toxic	Bright blue	4
Slightly toxic	Bright green	2
	Average	5

Source: Central Insecticides Board and Regulation Committee.

2. CENVAT on bio-pesticides be decreased from 16 percent to 8 percent and it should be put under the exempted category in State VAT.

A1.2.5 PLASTICS

Plastic products like carry bags, beverage containers and thin sheets cause significant solid waste problems. There is a concern that recycling may not be environmentally safe. The studies recommended the following:

1. *Biodegradable plastics:* The 16 percent CENVAT on biodegradable plastics be removed. In State VAT also, these should invariably be placed under the exempted category.
2. *Deposit refused on polyethylene terephthalate (PET) bottles:* A deposit of ₹1 per bottle should be levied on PET bottles at the time of sale which can be refunded when the bottle is returned. Manufacturers would have to set up a network of collection centres which will collect the bottles and send them for recycling.
3. *Incentive to rag pickers:* Households can be encouraged by their respective municipal authorities to segregate their plastic wastes and hand over the low value wastes to the rag pickers. The plastic industry can provide a matching incentive amount (say ₹10 per kg of plastic bags) to the rag pickers in addition to the amount that the recycler would pay.
4. *Recycling:* Municipalities can also set up a central facility/complex with assistance from the industry to recycle low value plastic wastes in an environmentally sound manner.
5. *Incentive to recyclers:* Fifty percent reduction in customs duty be given to recyclers who wish to import equipment and machinery for upgradation of recycling technology for a limited period of 10 years.

A1.2.6 AUTOMOBILES

As the proposed eco-tax directly targets the fuel consumption of vehicles, it may be more appropriate to call it a resource tax. In addition to conservation of the exhaustible resource, the resource tax will reduce the emissions of local pollutants and global pollutant (CO_2). The proposed

Table A1.2.3
Rates of resource tax

Vehicle	*Fuel Economy*	*Resource Tax Factor*	*Rate of Resource Tax (Percent)*
Two-wheelers	0–40	1.50	3.0
	41–50	1.33	2.5
	51–60	1.09	2.0
	>61	1.00	–
Passenger cars/jeeps	<10	1.67	5.0
	10–14	1.25	3.0
	12–18	1.11	2.0
	>18	1.00	–

resource tax rates for two-wheelers, passenger cars and jeeps are given in Table A1.2.3. The bases of resource tax would be the prices of various categories of vehicles before CENVAT.

Chelliah et al. (2007) recommended an annual emission tax of ₹750 on diesel cars based on estimates of income loss and medical costs attributable to particulate matter.

A1.2.7 PULP AND PAPER

Pulp and paper mills as well as viscose rayon mills could be encouraged to move towards chlorine substitutes like hydrogen peroxide. It was recommended that:

1. The rebate on the basic excise duty (BED) of 16 percent on chlorine in the VAT system be withdrawn. The additional excise revenue would be of the order of ₹5.3 crore for pulp and paper plants and about ₹0.65 crore for viscose rayon plants or a total of about ₹6 crore per year.
2. Provide incentives to switch over to chlorine substitutes by continuing to provide rebates on such substitutes (even if they contain chlorine) like chlorine dioxide or hypochlorite.
3. An accelerated depreciation (at the rate of 50 percent) be provided to promote investment in new machinery.

A1.2.8 PHOSPHATE-BASED DETERGENTS

In line with the precautionary principle, it is desirable to limit the use of phosphates in detergents, even though there is not much information on the impact of phosphate-based detergents in India. The major input in detergents which contributes to the phosphate content is sodium tri-poly phosphate (STPP). In order to limit the use of phosphates in detergents, it is recommended that:

1. The rebate of the CENVAT levied on the phosphate compounds used as inputs (such as STPP) can be denied. At a 16 percent excise duty, this would imply an additional revenue of ₹32 crore to the government.
2. Non-phosphate detergents could be promoted by decreasing the excise duty from 16 percent to 8 percent which would be revenue negative. It was estimated that such reduction in excise duty would result in a revenue loss of about ₹28 crore.

A1.2.9 LEAD ACID BATTERIES

In order to check the proliferation of battery re-building and smelting activity in the unorganized sector and to improve the competitiveness of licensed recyclers vis-à-vis informal sector smelters, the following recommendations were proposed:

1. Reduction in excise duty on production of secondary lead by the organized smelters.
2. Levy of an environment cess on the sale of scrap batteries in auctions by the bulk consumers. The environment cess should be allowed to be set off against the levies on production of secondary lead. This could be expected to check the participation of the unorganized smelters/traders in auctions.

Appendix A2.1

Environmental Public Goods and Eco-tax Revenue

Nature serves as natural sink for the pollution generated by the anthropogenic activities. If the pollution is within the carrying capacity of the natural sink, then local pollutants such as SPM, sulphur dioxide, etc. are absorbed by the nature.[1] However, this extremely useful function of nature fails if the pollution flow rate exceeds the absorption capacity of the nature. Thus, nature serves as environmental public good neutralizing the adverse effects of the pollution. Nature's public good contribution can be enhanced through anthropogenic interventions such as cleaning-up of rivers, restoring the nutrient balance of soils, afforestation and other similar programmes.

In this context, eco-taxes can serve two purposes: one, stem the flow of additional pollution by discouraging the use of polluting inputs and outputs (disincentive effect), and two, generate additional revenue which can be used partly or fully for providing environmental public goods (revenue effect). An important issue is whether eco-tax revenue should be fully earmarked for environmental public goods.

In taxation, there is no quid pro and one-to-one relationships between tax payments and services provided are generally avoided. This is because public goods are characterized by properties of non-excludability and non-rivalry. Demand for public goods is likely to remain understated as people know that they cannot be excluded from its consumption, and they need not reveal how much tax price they are willing to pay for the public good. This problem remains for environmental public goods also. People are not likely to reveal what is the value of environment to them if they have to pay for it. The link between tax price and provision of environment public good would therefore lead to an understatement of demand for such goods or resistance to tax payments for the provision for such goods. They would argue for shifting the burden of taxation to future generations for financing remedial treatment of the environment and go on adding to the stock of pollution.

A suitable analytical framework for examining this issue is the concept of 'SMCPF'. The supply of all public goods/projects including the environmental public good can be determined by reference to the principle of 'SMCPF'. The SMCPF is defined as the ratio between the shadow price of tax revenues and the population average of the social marginal utility of income.

Given social utility and cost functions, the SMCPF analysis leads to the following result for determining the size of public goods:

$$B' = \eta C' \tag{A2.1}$$

Here, B' is the social marginal benefit of the provision of public goods and C' is the social cost of the provision of such goods and η is the SMCPF. Marginal social benefit may be derived from a social utility function defined over private (x) and public goods (y):

$$U = U(x, y) \tag{A2.2}$$

For an optimal tax system, η should be equal to 1 (Lundholm, 2005). This implies that if the provision of public goods is financed with an optimal tax system, then the social marginal benefit of public goods should be equal to social marginal cost of provision of such goods. However, if the system is using distortionary taxes, the value of η may be higher than 1, which implies that in the presence of taxation inefficiencies, public goods should be provided to the extent such that the social marginal benefit of the public goods is higher than the social marginal cost of providing the public goods financed by taxation to account for welfare loss due to distortionary taxation. It may be noted that there are various measurement issues concerning the SMCPF and different authors have often used the term with different meanings.[2]

Starting from Equation A2.1, any substitution of distortionary taxation by environmental taxes will reduce the value of η, say by a fraction λ (<1) and therefore would be welfare improving even without provision of environmental public goods. Ignoring the disincentive effects of environmental taxation, if resources are fully employed and there is no change in the quantities of private and public goods, this would imply improvement in welfare because the deadweight and inefficiency costs of taxation will go down. If resources are not fully employed, then existing supply of public goods can be increased (even that of non-environmental public goods) leading to increase in total social benefit. The process can be pursued up to the point where environmental taxes force the economy to lower production possibility frontiers when substitution possibilities between polluting goods are exhausted given the state of technology. At the same time, an additional source of social benefit is the reduction in the use of polluting goods leading to better environment yielding direct benefits to the society.

In this framework, we may now introduce the provision of environmental public goods, say by dividing the public goods into two components: non-environmental public goods and environmental public goods. Then the social utility function is as follows:

$$U = U(x, y(y1, y2)) \tag{A2.3}$$

The marginal social benefit of public goods will then depend on both non-environmental and environmental public goods. There will now be interaction terms between non-environmental and environmental public goods. First, as the quality of environment improves, there will be reduction for the need for both private and public sector provision for health services, for example. The released resources from the general pool of taxes can then be used for environmental public goods. Similarly, higher provision of better and wider roads or better traffic management, which is a non-environmental public good will reduce carbon emissions and reduce say, the need for providing additional forestation.

Thus, the provision for environmental public goods will require the expansion of the public sector but because of interactions between private goods, non-environmental and environmental public goods, environmental tax revenues can be used to enhance welfare by adjusting the supply of non-environmental as well as environmental goods and/or reducing the MSCPF. A one-to-one relationship between environmental taxes and environmental public goods is not necessarily warranted.

Earmarking of specific tax revenues for specific purposes can be done only in a limited way by making the environmental tax as a cess. For all other environmental taxes, the decision for allocation across different budget heads under our constitutional arrangements is the prerogative of the Parliament and state legislatures according to the priorities reflecting preference of the voters.

Some other relevant considerations may be listed as follows:

1. For a society, given the law of entropy, it may often be impossible to restore the environment to its original position after having been polluted. It may be physically not possible or technologies may not exist for the purpose or it may be prohibitively costly to clean up the environment. The key to maintaining acceptable quality of environment is therefore to keep in check the current flow of pollution that adds to the stock of pollution. The distinctive effect of eco-taxes may be far more important than the revenue effect.
2. There are important intergenerational issues in the need to correct for the stock of environmental pollution. This stock is the outcome of the cumulated contributions of all previous generations. How much of this needs to be corrected by the current generation can be decided by the current generation in conjunction with how much tax-price they would be willing to pay for it if the tax-price is entirely additional.
3. Some part of pollution, particularly in the context of climate change has global dimensions. Any single country may not be willing to pay the tax-price for the provision of mitigation. A one-to-one link between tax revenue and environmental public goods and subsidies is difficult to establish in a country-specific context because of global externalities.
4. There is a difference between the tax–GDP ratios of developed and developing countries, the former being much higher than the latter. In developed countries, the environmental tax reform entails using a significant part of the revenue for reducing other distortionary taxes as the political acceptability of a higher tax burden is very limited. In developing countries where the tax–GDP ratio is still low, environmental taxes may provide a route for increasing the tax revenue and increasing the size of government, which may use the additional revenues for both environmental and non-environmental public goods.

In deriving practical results, there are measurement difficulties both in relation to SMCPF and the social utility function. In one of the earliest papers on the concept and measurement of marginal cost of public funds, Browning (1976) observes:

> It is important to recognize that it is literally impossible to determine the exact source of finance when governments use general fund financing (enacting tax and expenditure bills separately). In this type of situation, what is clearly needed is a convention or rule of thumb … this convention should represent a judgment of the type of change that a government typically makes when more or less revenue is required.

Such conventions need to be different between developed and developing countries. In the former, where the tax–GDP ratios are high, it will be difficult to use environmental tax revenue aimed at increasing the tax–GDP ratio. In this case, environmental taxes will mostly be used to replace conventional distortionary taxes, and most of the revenue will be used for general public goods. Discussions with experts suggest on an anecdotal basis that 85 percent of environmental tax revenue can be used for general public goods and 15 percent for environmental public goods. In developing countries, environmental taxes can be used to some extent in increasing the tax–GDP ratio and a higher percentage can be allocated for environmental public goods.

NOTES

1. This does not apply to the global pollutants like carbon dioxide, whose life-time is typically in excess of several decades.
2. There are two traditions in the literature in this context (see, e.g. Ballard and Fullerton, 1992). In the Harberger-Pigou-Browning tradition, the marginal cost of public funds is always larger than unity and the Dasgupta-Stiglitz-Atkinson-Stern tradition where it may be larger or lower than one. In the first tradition, the marginal project is a lump sum transfer to a representative consumer financed by a distortionary tax.

Appendix A4.1

Description of Variables, Units and Data Sources

Table A4.1.1
Variable list

S. No.	*Variable Name*	*Description*	*Unit*	*Source of Basic Data*
1	AINF	Annual rate of inflation with respect to deflator of GDP at market prices	Percent per annum	NAS
2	BM	Government borrowing from the market	₹ crore	IPFS, RBI
	BPR	Policy interest rate (bank rate/rep rate)	Percent	RBI
3	CAS	Current account surplus	₹ crore	NAS
4	CBDEBT	Combined debt	₹ crore	IPFS
5	CBDTR	Combined direct tax revenues	₹ crore	IPFS
6	CBFDD	Combined fiscal deficit derived (annual increase in outstanding liabilities from central and state governments)	₹ crore	IPFS
7	CBITR	Combined indirect revenues	₹ crore	IPFS
8	CBKE	Combined capital expenditure	₹ crore	IPFS
9	CBPRE	Combined primary revenue expenditure	₹ crore	IPFS
10	CDEBT	Central debt (outstanding liabilities)	₹ crore	IPFS
11	CEIR	Combined effective interest rate	₹ crore	IPFS
12	CFC	Consumption of fixed capital	₹ crore	IPFS
13	CFDD	Central fiscal deficit derived (annual increase in outstanding liabilities of central government)	₹ crore	IPFS
14	CG	Government consumption expenditure at current prices	₹ crore	NAS

Table A4.1.1 continued

Table A4.1.1 continued

S. No.	*Variable Name*	*Description*	*Unit*	*Source of Basic Data*
15	CGTR	Gross central tax revenues	₹ crore	IPFS
16	CIP	Central interest payment	₹ crore	IPFS
17	CKE	Central capital expenditure	₹ crore	IPFS
18	CKR	Central capital receipts	₹ crore	IPFS
19	CNTR	Central non-tax revenue	₹ crore	IPFS
20	COTR	Central other tax revenues	₹ crore	IPFS
21	CPR	Private consumption expenditure at 1999–2000 prices	₹ crore	NAS
22	CPRE	Central primary revenue expenditure	₹ crore	IPFS
23	CPTR	Corporation tax revenue	₹ crore	IPFS
24	CRD	Central revenue deficit	₹ crore	IPFS
25	CRE	Central revenue expenditure	₹ crore	IPFS
26	CRR	Central revenue receipts	₹ crore	IPFS
27	CRRATIO	Cash reserve ratio	₹ crore	RBI - HBMS
	CSTR	CIS at 1999–2000 prices	₹ crore	NAS
28	CTR	Central net tax revenues (net of states' share in central taxes)	₹ crore	IPFS
29	DADJ	Residual for adjustment in GDP at factor cost in the context of changing the series from 1950–51 to 1999–2000 prices (sectoral sums do not add to totals as given in NAS)	₹ crore	NAS
30	DLM3	Change in money stock (log M3-log M3-1)	₹ crore	RBI
31	DNBCB	Change in net current RBI credit to government	₹ crore	RBI
32	DR	Dependency ratio	Percent	World Bank
33	DRAIN10	Dummy for deficiency in rainfall of more than 10 percent of average rainfall		

Table A4.1.1 continued

Table A4.1.1 continued

S. No.	*Variable Name*	*Description*	*Unit*	*Source of Basic Data*
34	DSER-VICE	Dummy for service sector (one for the years 2000–01 to 2002–03 and zero for other years)		
35	DUMYIR	Dummy for industrial output (one for selected peak growth years, zero for other years)		
36	EMPA	Work force in agriculture	Crore	Census, NSS
37	EMPI	Work force in industry	Crore	Census, NSS
38	EMPS	Work force in services	Crore	Census, NSS
39	EXPN	Exports at current prices	₹ crore	NAS
40	EXPR	Exports at constant prices (1999–2000)	₹ crore	NAS
	FINV	Foreign investments	₹ crore	NAS
	GIR	Gross investment at 1999–2000 prices	₹ crore	NAS
41	GRANTS	Total grants from centre to states	₹ crore	IPFS
42	IAR	Investment in agriculture	₹ crore	NAS
43	IDLS	Indirect taxes net of subsidies	₹ crore	NAS
44	IDR	Import duty revenues	₹ crore	NAS
45	IG	Government investment expenditure at current prices	₹ crore	NAS
46	IIR	Investment in industry	₹ crore	NAS
47	IMPN	Imports at current prices	₹ crore	NAS
48	IMPR	Imports at 1999–2000 prices	₹ crore	NAS
49	IPPDEBT	Interest payment on public debt	₹ crore	NAS
50	IPR	Private investment expenditure at constant prices	₹ crore	NAS
51	IPUB	Excess of government investment as given in National Income Account over combined capital expenditure of central and state governments	₹ crore	NAS & IPFS

Table A4.1.1 continued

Table A4.1.1 continued

S. No.	*Variable Name*	*Description*	*Unit*	*Source of Basic Data*
52	ISR	Investment in services at constant prices	₹ crore	NAS
53	ITR	Income tax revenue	₹ crore	NAS
54	KAR	Net fixed capital stock in agriculture	₹ crore	NAS
55	KIR	Net fixed capital stock in industry	₹ crore	NAS
56	KR	Total capital stock	₹ crore	NAS
57	KSR	Capital stock in services	₹ crore	NAS
58	M0	Reserve money	₹ crore	RBI-HBMS
59	M3	Broad money	₹ crore	RBI-HBMS
60	NAIRU	Non-accelerating inflation rate of unemployment	Percent	Estimated
61	NBCB	Net RBI credit to government	₹ crore	RBI-BMS
	NIB	Net invisibles	₹ crore	NAS
62	PCRUDE	International price for crude petroleum	US$ per barrel	IMF, Financial Statistics
63	PDYR	Personal disposable income at 1999–2000 prices	₹ crore	NAS
64	PEXP	Unit value of exports	Index (1999–2000 = 100)	NAS
65	PI	Implicit price deflator of investment	Index (1999–2000 = 100)	NAS
66	PIMP	Unit value of imports	Index (1999–2000 = 100)	NAS
67	PVDYR	Private income at 1999–2000 prices	₹ crore	NAS
70	PWR	Private wealth in real terms	₹ crore	NAS
	PYAR	Implicit deflator of agriculture	Index (1999–2000 = 100)	NAS

Table A4.1.1 continued

Table A4.1.1 continued

S. No.	*Variable Name*	*Description*	*Unit*	*Source of Basic Data*
	PYNAR	Implicit deflator of non-agriculture	Index (1999–2000 = 100)	NAS
68	PYN	Implicit price deflator of GDP at market prices	Index (1999–2000 = 100)	NAS
69	PYR	Implicit price deflator of GDP at factor cost	Index (1999–2000 = 100)	NAS
71	RESCAS	Excess of current account balance over trade account balance	₹ crore	NAS & IPFS
72	RESCBIP	Excess of interest payment on public debt over combined interest payment of central and state governments	₹ crore	NAS
73	RESIDLS	Excess of indirect taxes net of subsidies over combined indirect tax revenues	₹ crore	NAS
74	RESIN	Residual reflecting excess of some of sectoral investments in agriculture, industry and services over sum of private and public investment in nominal terms	₹ crore	NAS
75	RESITR	Excess of combined indirect taxes over sum of union excise duties, import duty revenues, state sales taxes and states other indirect taxes	₹ crore	IPFS
76	RESM0	Sum of components of monetary base other than net RBI credit to government	₹ crore	RBI - HBMS
77	RESPDY	Excess of private disposable income over the sum of personal disposable income and combined direct taxes	₹ crore	NAS
78	RESPVY	Other transfers derived as (GDP at factor cost net of consumption of fixed capital + interest on public debt - private income)	₹ crore	NAS

Table A4.1.1 continued

Table A4.1.1 continued

S. No.	*Variable Name*	*Description*	*Unit*	*Source of Basic Data*
79	RESYN	Excess of GDP at market prices over the sum of private consumption and investment expenditure, public consumption and investment expenditure, exports net of imports in nominal terms	₹ crore	NAS
80	RLN	Long-term interest rate defined as interest rates on deposits above 3–5 years maturity	₹ crore	RBI-HBMS
81	RLNR	Real long-term interest rate	Percent per annum	RBI-NAS
82	RSN	Short-term interest rate on deposits of 1–3 years maturity	₹ crore	RBI-HBMS
83	SBITEMS	Central revenue receipts	₹ crore	IPFS
84	SCIP	Interest paid by states to centre	₹ crore	IPFS
85	SCLAD	Net lending by centre to states	₹ crore	IPFS
86	SCTR	State shares in gross central taxes	₹ crore	IPFS
87	SDEBT	State debt (outstanding liabilities)	₹ crore	IPFS
88	SEIR	State effective interest rate	₹ crore	IPFS
89	SFDD	State fiscal deficit derived	₹ crore	IPFS
90	SIP	State interest payment	₹ crore	IPFS
91	SKE	State capital expenditure	₹ crore	IPFS
92	SKR	State capital receipts	₹ crore	IPFS
93	SOITR	States own indirect taxes	₹ crore	IPFS
94	SONTR	States own non-tax revenues	₹ crore	IPFS
95	SOTR	State tax revenues other than sales tax and other own indirect taxes	₹ crore	IPFS
96	SPRE	State primary revenue expenditure	₹ crore	IPFS
97	SRD	State revenue deficit	₹ crore	IPFS
98	SRE	State revenue expenditure	₹ crore	IPFS
99	SRR	State revenue receipts	₹ crore	IPFS
100	SS	Share of states in central gross tax revenues	₹ crore	IPFS

Table A4.1.1 continued

Table A4.1.1 continued

S. No.	*Variable Name*	*Description*	*Unit*	*Source of Basic Data*
101	SSR	States sales tax revenue	₹ crore	IPFS
102	STRF	Transfer to funds from state revenue receipts	₹ crore	IPFS
103	UDR	Union excise duties	₹ crore	IPFS
104	WF	Aggregate work force	Crore	Census, NSS
105	XECPTR	Expected effective rate of corporative tax	Percent	IPFS
106	XGYR	Expected growth rate of GDP at factor cost	Percent per annum	NAS
107	XINF	Expected inflation rate	Percent per annum	NAS
108	YAR	Agricultural output at 1999–2000 prices	₹ crore	NAS
109	YIR	Industrial output	₹ crore	NAS
110	YN	GDP at market prices	₹ crore	NAS
111	YR	GDP at factor cost at 1999–2000 prices	₹ crore	NAS
112	YSR	Service sector output at 1999–2000 prices	₹ crore	NAS
113	ZCBDTR	Excess of combined direct tax revenues over sum of income tax and corporate tax revenues	₹ crore	IPFS
114	ZCBKE	Excess of combined capital expenditure over sum of central capital expenditure and state capital expenditure net of central loans to states	₹ crore	IPFS
115	ZCBPRE	Excess of combined primary revenue expenditure over sum of central primary revenue expenditure and state primary revenue expenditure net of grants from centre to states	₹ crore	IPFS
116	ZCKE	Excess of central capital receipts net of central revenue deficit over central capital expenditure	₹ crore	IPFS

Table A4.1.1 continued

Table A4.1.1 continued

S. No.	*Variable Name*	*Description*	*Unit*	*Source of Basic Data*
117	ZSKE	Excess of state capital receipts minus state revenue deficit over state capital expenditure	₹ crore	IPFS
118	ZYMR	Residual in GDP at market prices at 1999–2000 prices	₹ crore	NAS

Appendix A4.2

Mapping Polluting Industries with ISIC Codes

Table A4.2.1
Mapping of major polluting industries with ISIC codes

CPCB Category	*Group Name*	*ISIC Description*	*ISIC Code*
Cement	Cement	CEMENT, LIME AND PLASTER	3692
Oil refinery	Crude oil	PETROLEUM REFINERIES	3530
Drugs and Pharma	Drugs and medicines	DRUGS AND MEDICINES	3522
Fertilizer, pesticide	Fertilizers and pesticides	FERTILIZERS AND PESTICIDES	3512
Caustic soda	Industrial chemical except fertilizer and other chemicals	INDUSTRIAL CHEMICALS EXCEPT FERTILIZER	3511
Iron and steel	Integrated iron and steel	IRON AND STEEL	3710
Leather	Leather and leather products	TANNERIES AND LEATHER FINISHING	3231
Aluminium, copper, zinc	Non-ferrous basic metals	NON-FERROUS METALS	3720
Distilleries	Other chemicals	DISTILLED SPIRITS	3131
Pulp and paper	Paper, paper prods. and newsprint	PULP, PAPER AND PAPERBOARD	3411
Sugar	Sugar	SUGAR FACTORIES AND REFINERIES	3118
Petrochemical	Synthetic fibres, resin	SYNTHETIC RESINS, PLASTICS MATERIALS AND MANMADE FIBRES	3513

Table A4.2.1 continued

Table A4.2.1 continued

CPCB Category	*Group Name*	*ISIC Description*	*ISIC Code*
Dyes and dye intermediaries	Textiles and apparel	SPINNING, WEAVING AND FINISHING TEXTILES	3211
	Coal and lignite	MISC. PETROLEUM AND COAL PRODUCTS	3540
	Coal tar products	MISC. PETROLEUM AND COAL PRODUCTS	3540

Table A4.2.2
Mapping of other industries with ISIC codes

Group Name	*ISIC Description*	*ISIC Code*
Animal husbandry	MEAT PRODUCTS	3111
Beverages	WINE INDUSTRIES	3132
Ceramic	STRUCTURAL CLAY PRODUCTS	3691
Edible oil	OILS AND FATS	3115
Electrical machinery and equipment	ELECTRICAL INDUSTRIAL MACHINERY	3831
Electronic and non-electrical machinery	MACHINERY AND EQUIPMENT, N.E.C.	3829
Fishing	FISH PRODUCTS	3114
Machinery, tools and implements	SPECIAL INDUSTRIAL MACHINERY AND EQUIPMENT	3824
Miscellaneous food products	FOOD PRODUCTS, N.E.C.	3121
Miscellaneous manufacturing	MANUFACTURING INDUSTRIES, N.E.C.	3909
Miscellaneous metal products	STRUCTURAL METAL PRODUCTS	3813
Other non-metallic mineral prods.	NONMETALLIC MINERAL PRODUCTS, N.E.C.	3699
Petroleum products	MISC. PETROLEUM AND COAL PRODUCTS	3540
Plastic products	PLASTICS PRODUCTS, N.E.C.	3560

Table A4.2.2 continued

Table A4.2.2 continued

Group Name	*ISIC Description*	*ISIC Code*
Rail and other transport equipment	RAILROAD EQUIPMENT	3842
Rubber products	RUBBER PRODUCTS, N.E.C.	3559
Tobacco products	TOBACCO MANUFACTURES	3140
Wood and wood products	WOOD AND CORK PRODUCTS, N.E.C.	3319

Table A4.2.3
Sectors with no corresponding IPPS coefficients

*Electricity**	*Mineral Products*
Banking and insurance	Natural gas
Cash crop	Other crops
Communication	Otherservices1
Construction	Otherservices2
Food crops	Plantation crop
Forestry and logging	Railway and other transport service
Fruits and vegetables	Tea and coffee processing
Gas and water supply	Trade

Note: *The maximum of all the coefficients are assumed; the remaining sectors are assumed to have the minimum of all the coefficients.

Appendix A5.1

Estimating Depreciation Rate—A Note

Table A5.1.1
Estimation of depreciation rate (₹ crore)

Year	GDCF Public Sector	Gross Domestic Capital Formation (GDCF)			GDCF-Public Sector after Adjustment
	Current Prices Nominal Investment	Current Prices	Constant Prices at 1999–2000 Prices	Deflator (Long-term Rate of Inflation)	
1955–56	563	1395	39798	0.04	16061.85
1956–57	738	192	48223	0.00	185357.16
1957–58	908	1829	44927	0.04	22303.84
1958–59	989	1755	44633	0.04	25152.16
1959–60	1000	1951	44355	0.04	22734.50
1960–61	1259	2433	52500	0.05	27167.08
1961–62	1272	2419	51617	0.05	27142.13
1962–63	1590	2880	58725	0.05	32421.09
1963–64	1852	3143	63651	0.05	37506.09
1964–65	2146	3677	69412	0.05	40510.78
1965–66	2438	4432	77792	0.06	42792.62
1966–67	2366	5251	84686	0.06	38157.89
1967–68	2570	5130	79229	0.06	39691.72
1968–69	2422	5073	77235	0.07	36874.27
1969–70	2530	6285	87852	0.07	35364.45
1970–71	3104	6965	89870	0.08	40051.18
1971–72	3631	7759	94318	0.08	44138.25
1972–73	4152	8085	93933	0.09	48238.69
1973–74	5212	11304	111567	0.10	51440.84

Table A5.1.1 continued

Table A5.1.1 continued

Year	GDCF Public Sector Current Prices Nominal Investment	Gross Domestic Capital Formation (GDCF) Current Prices	Constant Prices at 1999–2000 Prices	Deflator (Long-term Rate of Inflation)	GDCF-Public Sector after Adjustment
1974–75	6083	12951	100075	0.13	47004.57
1975–76	8236	14079	103685	0.14	60654.14
1976–77	9360	16011	117640	0.14	68772.12
1977–78	8689	18530	129808	0.14	60868.95
1978–79	10805	23729	156955	0.15	71469.46
1979–80	12898	24793	141769	0.17	73752.13
1980–81	12994	28975	149728	0.19	67146.35
1981–82	18092	33507	144196	0.23	77858.18
1982–83	21543	36353	143958	0.25	85310.35
1983–84	22810	40608	151247	0.27	84957.25
1984–85	27366	48745	163269	0.30	91661.08
1985–86	32063	59623	178991	0.33	96254.61
1986–87	37275	64391	179971	0.36	104182.56
1987–88	26361	79089	205216	0.39	68400.14
1988–89	43137	99470	233728	0.43	101360.46
1989–90	49707	118371	249711	0.47	104860.01
1990–91	56874	148206	291611	0.51	111905.62
1991–92	62052	144466	246099	0.59	105706.08
1992–93	68533	173498	269647	0.64	106512.57
1993–94	75923	194724	286305	0.68	111630.48
1994–95	94775	259355	349266	0.74	127630.80
1995–96	97749	311782	375888	0.83	117847.33
1996–97	103159	330806	374006	0.88	116630.55
1997–98	107830	385808	419378	0.92	117212.52
1998–99	122849	408109	419885	0.97	126393.81
1999–2000	144610	506244	506244	1.00	144610.00
2000–01	144638	488658	511788	0.95	151484.25
2001–02	156537	474448	520655	0.91	171782.31

Table A5.1.1 continued

Table A5.1.1 continued

	GDCF Public Sector	Gross Domestic Capital Formation (GDCF)			GDCF-Public Sector after Adjustment
Year	*Current Prices Nominal Investment*	*Current Prices*	*Constant Prices at 1999–2000 Prices*	*Deflator (Long-term Rate of Inflation)*	
2002–03	149399	555287	619485	0.90	166671.36
2003–04	174579	665625	775647	0.86	203435.38
2004–05	216962	795642	1013761	0.78	276440.43
2005–06	272002	950102	1271953	0.75	364143.81
2006–07	321753	1053323	1487786	0.71	454466.11
CGR	0.1304			0.0789	4.77
	(z)			(ρ)	

Source (Basic Data): GoI (2007; 2009; 2010).

Appendix A5.2

Environment-related Subsidies in India: 2008–09

Table A5.2.1

Estimating environment-related budgetary subsidies for centre: 2008–09 (units in ₹ lakh)

INDIA (Centre)					*Effect. Int. Rate 0.09293*				
Parameters:									
Description	*Rev Rec.*	*Rev Exp.*	*Div.*	*Int. on Loans*	*Annualised Cost of Cap.**	*Total Costs*	*Total Rec.*	*Subsidy*	*Recvy. Rate (%)*
Sewerage and Sanitation	3.64	123379.39			230.21	123609.60	3.64	123605.96	
Soil and Water Conservation		2312.67		19.24	310.87	2623.54	19.24	2604.30	0.73
Fisheries	610.53	18875.07		1.42	3889.01	22764.08	611.95	22152.13	2.69
Forestry and Wildlife	**2151.52**	**68185.10**	**0.51**		**3603.23**	**71788.33**	**2152.03**	**69636.30**	**3.00**
Forest Cons., Dev., and Regen.	953.53	23352.96			3338.98	26691.94	953.53	25738.41	3.57
Environ. Forestry and Wildlife	1197.99	8816.11	0.51		264.24	9080.35	1198.50	7881.85	13.20
Afforestation and Ecology Development		36016.03				36016.03		36016.03	
Agri. Research and Education	0.11	36511.00				36511.00	0.11	36510.89	
Special Areas DevProg.		156028.71				156028.71		156028.71	
Flood Control and Drainage		17527.81				17527.81		17527.81	

Non-Conv. Sources of Energy	51.62	37699.35		180.63	10254.20	47953.55	232.25	47721.30	0.48
Ecology and Environment		47379.87				47379.87		47379.87	
Total A	**2817.42**	**507898.97**	**0.51**	**201.29**	**18287.51**	**526186.48**	**3019.22**	**523167.26**	**0.57**
Industry									
Mining	27.03			112.55	1167.88	1167.88	139.58	1028.30	11.95
Cement and Non-metallic Industries	40437.66	201.84		1886.04	21753.33	21955.17	42323.70	-20368.53	192.77
Fertilizer	140.82	1945573.10	8285.79	568.70	141684.34	2087257.44	8995.31	2078262.13	0.43
Pesticide and Chemicals	908.02	1738.50			8155.78	9894.28	908.02	8986.26	9.18
Non-Ferrous Mining and Metallurgical Industries		2691.05	54089.17		43859.30	46550.35	54089.17	-7538.82	116.19
Irrigation									
Major and Medium Irrigation	663.89	29809.87			4065.46	33875.33	663.89	33211.44	1.96
Minor Irrigation	39.41	14638.81			759.88	15398.69	39.41	15359.28	0.26
Command Area DevProg.					120.40	120.40	0.00	120.40	
Total B	**42216.83**	**1994653.17**	**62374.96**	**2567.29**	**221566.38**	**2216219.55**	**107159.08**	**2109060.47**	**4.84**
Total (A+B)	**45034.25**	**2502552.14**	**62375.47**	**2768.58**	**239853.89**	**2742406.03**	**110178.30**	**2632227.73**	**4.02**

Basic Source: GoI, Union Finance Accounts 2007–08 and 2008–09.

Notes: * including imputed interest on investment, dividends and return on capital stock.

Agricultural Research and Education comprises of Soil and Water Conservation (02), Fisheries and Forestry (05). Special Areas Development Programme comprises Drought Prone Areas (02), Devlp./Desert Devlp. Progs. (03) and Wasteland Devlp. Progs. (05). Flood Control and Drainage comprises Flood Control (01) and Anti-Sea Erosion (02). Non-Ferrous Mining and Metallurgical Industries includes Geological Survey of India's Mineral Exploration [2853 (01/102)] and Regulation and Development of Prevention [2853 2/102)] and Control of Pollution under Ecology and Environment [3435 (04)]. Mining under Iron and Steel Industries [2852 (01/101)]. Pesticide and Chemicals under Chemicals and Pharmaceutical Industries [2852 (05/205)].

Table A5.2.2

Estimating environment-related budgetary subsidies for Maharashtra: 2008–09 (units in ₹ lakh)

Maharashtra					*Effect. Int. Rate 0.09200*				
Parameters:				*Int. on*	*Annualized*				*Recvy.*
Description	*Rev Rec.*	*Rev Exp.*	*Div.*	*Loans*	*Cost of Cap.**	*Total Costs*	*Total Rec.*	*Subsidy*	*Rate (%)*
Sewerage and Sanitation	229.24	5697.50			96.49	5793.99	229.24	5564.75	3.96
Soil and Water Conservation		3086.87			48415.21	51502.08		51502.08	
Fisheries	675.93	14780.78			4053.44	18834.22	675.93	18158.29	3.59
Forestry and Wildlife									
Forest Cons., Dev., and Regen.	24728.41	54752.21			7207.79	61960.00	24728.41	37231.59	39.91
Environ. Forestry and Wildlife	1247.47	7031.25			–66.81	6964.44	1247.47	5716.97	17.91
Agri. Research and Education		1007.75			188.38	1196.13		1196.13	
Special Areas DevProg.		14328.79				14328.79		14328.79	
Flood Control and Drainage					2442.06	2442.06		2442.06	
Non-Conv. Sources of Energy	12.99	2339.43				2339.43	12.99	2326.44	0.56
Ecology and Environment		3915.02				3915.02		3915.02	
Total A	**918.16**	**45156.14**			**55195.58**	**100351.72**	**918.16**	**99433.56**	**0.91**
Industry									
Mining					19.01	19.01		19.01	
Cement and Non-metallic Industries									

Fertilizer				60.68	60.68		60.68	
Pesticide and Chemicals				2.52	2.52		2.52	
Non-Ferrous Mining and Metallurgical Industries	121566.56	9747.40		40.31	9787.71	121566.56	–111778.85	1242.03
Irrigation								
Major and Medium Irrigation	63176.40	143202.32		719657.55	862859.87	63176.40	799683.47	7.32
Minor Irrigation	4755.03	48543.26		167612.22	216155.48	4755.03	211400.45	2.20
Command Area DevProg.		1371.15		41.04	1412.19		1412.19	
Total B	**189497.99**	**202864.13**		**887433.33**	**1090297.46**	**189497.99**	**900799.47**	**17.38**
Total (A+B)	**190416.15**	**248020.27**		**942628.91**	**1190649.18**	**190416.15**	**1000233.03**	**15.99**

Basic Source: GoI, State Finance Accounts 2007–08 and 2008–09.

Notes: *Including imputed interest on investment, dividends and return on capital stock.

Agricultural research and education comprises of soil and water conservation (02), Fisheries and forestry (05).

Special areas development programme comprises drought prone areas (02), Devlp./desert Devlp. Progs. (03) and Wasteland Devlp. Progs. (05). Flood control and drainage comprises flood control (01) and Anti-sea erosion (02). Non-ferrous mining and metallurgical industries includes Geological Survey of India's mineral exploration [2853 (01/102)] and Regulation and development of prevention [2853 2/102)] and Control of pollution under ecology and environment [3435 (04)]. Mining under iron and steel industries [2852 (01/101)]. Pesticide and chemicals under chemicals and pharmaceutical industries [2852 (05/205)].

Table A5.2.3

Estimating environment-related budgetary subsidies for Gujarat: 2008–09 (units in ₹ lakh)

Gujarat					*Effect. Int. Rate 0.09291*				
Parameters:									
Description	*Rev Rec.*	*Rev Exp.*	*Div.*	*Int. on Loans*	*Annualized Cost of Cap.**	*Total Costs*	*Total Rec.*	*Subsidy*	*Recvy. Rate (%)*
Sewerage and Sanitation		2634.62			0.81	2635.43		2635.43	
Soil and Water Conservation		31934.57			1543.37	33477.94		33477.94	
Fisheries	510.17	13371.36			465.97	13837.33	510.17	13327.16	3.69
Forestry and Wildlife									
Forest Cons., Dev., and Regen.	4050.69	15370.79			34446.01	49816.80	4050.69	45766.11	8.13
Environ. Forestry and Wildlife		4967.06			1.98	4969.04		4969.04	
Agri. Research and Education		118.95				118.95		118.95	
Special Areas DevProg.		3760.15				3760.15		3760.15	
Flood Control and Drainage		2922.36			1709.80	4632.16		4632.16	
Non-Conv. Sources of Energy		200.00				200.00		200.00	
Ecology and Environment									
Total A	**510.17**	**54942.01**			**3719.95**	**58661.96**	**510.17**	**58151.79**	**0.87**
Industry									
Cement and Non-metallic Industries					0.61	0.61		0.61	
Fertilizer					112.88	112.88		112.88	
Pesticide and Chemicals					0.09	0.09		0.09	

Non-Ferrous Mining and Metallurgical Industries	154956.08	129.61	2353.20		81.97	211.58	157309.28	-157097.70	74348.80
Irrigation									
Major and Medium Irrigation	45577.18	34313.46			317822.65	352136.11	45577.18	306558.93	12.94
Minor Irrigation	1456.60	36627.34			48692.37	85319.71	1456.60	83863.11	1.71
Command Area DevProg.		964.01			0.74	964.75		964.75	
Total B	**201989.86**	**72034.42**	**2353.20**		**366711.32**	**438745.74**	**204343.06**	**234402.68**	**46.57**
Total (A+B)	**202500.03**	**126976.43**	**2353.20**		**370431.26**	**497407.69**	**204853.23**	**292554.46**	**41.18**

Basic Source: GoI, State Finance Accounts 2007–08 and 2008–09.

Notes: *Including imputed interest on investment, dividends and return on capital stock.

Agricultural research and education comprises of soil and water conservation (02), Fisheries and forestry (05).

Special areas development programme comprises drought prone areas (02), Devlp./desert Devlp. Progs. (03) and Wasteland Devlp. Progs. (05).

Flood control and drainage comprises flood control (01) and Anti-sea erosion (02).

Non-ferrous mining and metallurgical industries includes Geological Survey of India's mineral exploration [2853 (01/102)] and Regulation and development of prevention [2853 2/102)] and Control of pollution under ecology and environment [3435 (04)].

Mining under iron and steel industries [2852 (01/101)].

Pesticide and chemicals under chemicals and pharmaceutical industries [2852 (05/205)].

Table A5.2.4

Estimating environment-related budgetary subsidies for Rajasthan: 2008–09 (units in ₹ lakh)

Rajasthan					*Effect. Int. Rate 0.10592*				
Parameters:				*Int. on*	*Annualised*				*Recvy.*
Description	*Rev Rec.*	*Rev Exp.*	*Div.*	*Loans*	*Cost of Cap.**	*Total Costs*	*Total Rec.*	*Subsidy*	*Rate (%)*
Sewerage and Sanitation	3013.50	18082.81			1033.64	19116.45	3013.50	16102.95	15.76
Soil and Water Conservation		4280.42			4136.46	8416.88		8416.88	
Fisheries	740.48	1122.09			106.26	1228.35	740.48	487.87	60.28
Forestry and Wildlife									
Forest Cons., Dev., and Regen.	5131.42	25953.51			9269.05	35222.56	5131.42	30091.14	14.57
Environ. Forestry and Wildlife	642.21	31182.25			288.33	31470.58	642.21	30828.37	2.04
Agri. Research and Education		13.86			2.84	16.70		16.70	
Special Areas DevProg.		6673.70			0.00	6673.70		6673.70	
Flood Control and Drainage					2732.97	2732.97		2732.97	
Non-Conv. Sources of Energy		30.17			18.28	48.45		48.45	
Ecology and Environment									
Total A	**3753.98**	**30203.05**			**8030.46**	**38233.51**	**3753.98**	**34479.53**	**9.82**
Industry									
Mining					0.26	0.26		0.26	

Cement and Non-metallic Industries									
Pesticide and Chemicals					18.38	18.38		18.38	
Non-Ferrous Mining and Metallurgical Industries	122181.24	634.53	1550.83		3312.77	3947.30	123732.07	–119784.77	3134.60
Irrigation									
Major and Medium Irrigation	5415.78	101680.87			147124.81	248805.68	5415.78	243389.90	2.18
Minor Irrigation	1735.91	10477.04			25660.27	36137.31	1735.91	34401.40	4.80
Command Area DevProg.		3511.31			22233.86	25745.17	0.00	25745.17	
Total B	**129332.93**	**116303.75**	**1550.83**		**198350.36**	**314654.11**	**130883.76**	**183770.35**	**41.60**
Total (A+B)	**133086.91**	**146506.80**	**1550.83**		**206380.81**	**352887.61**	**134637.74**	**218249.87**	**38.15**

Basic Source: GoI, State Finance Accounts 2007–08 and 2008–09.

Notes: *Including imputed interest on investment, dividends and return on capital stock. Agricultural research and education comprises of soil and water conservation (02), Fisheries and forestry (05). Special areas development programme comprises drought prone areas (02), Devlp./desert Devlp. Progs. (03) and Wasteland Devlp. Progs. (05). Flood control and drainage comprises flood control (01) and Anti-sea erosion (02). Non-ferrous mining and metallurgical industries includes Geological Survey of India's mineral exploration [2853 (01/102)] and Regulation and development of prevention [2853 2/102)] and Control of pollution under ecology and environment [3435 (04)]. Mining under iron and steel industries [2852 (01/101)]. Pesticide and chemicals under chemicals and pharmaceutical industries [2852 (05/205)].

Table A5.2.5

Estimating environment-related budgetary subsidies for West Bengal: 2008–09 (units in ₹ lakh)

West Bengal					*Effect. Int. Rate 0.09200*				
Parameters:				*Int. On*	*Annualized*				*Recvy.*
Description	*Rev Rec.*	*Rev Exp.*	*Div.*	*Loans*	*Cost of Cap.**	*Total Costs*	*Total Rec.*	*Subsidy*	*Rate (%)*
Sewerage and sanitation	1.41	1358.81			25.44	1384.25	1.41	1382.84	0.10
Soil and water conservation		2409.52			9.99	2419.51		2419.51	
Fisheries	411.11	7520.47			2958.07	10478.54	411.11	10067.43	3.92
Forestry and wildlife									
Forest Cons., dev. and Regen.	4418.76	14698.43			550.28	15248.71	4418.76	10829.95	28.98
Environ. forestry and wildlife	114.70	4684.94				4684.94	114.70	4570.24	2.45
Afforestation and ecology development									
Agri. research and education									
Special areas DevProg.									
Flood control and drainage									
Non-conv. sources of energy		1100.59				1100.59		1100.59	
Ecology and Environment									
Total A	412.52	12389.39			2993.49	15382.88	412.52	14970.36	2.68
Industry									
Mining									
Cement and Non-metallic Industries									

Fertilizer				9.39	9.39		9.39	
Pesticide and Chemicals				6000.88	6000.88		6000.88	
Non-ferrous mining and metallurgical industries								
Irrigation								
Major and medium irrigation	693.22	24736.18		29414.65	54150.83	693.22	53457.61	1.28
Minor irrigation	2033.38	28028.21		10157.49	38185.70	2033.38	36152.32	5.32
Command area DevProg.		452.81	0.15	1155.94	1608.75	0.15	1608.60	0.01
Total B	2726.60	53217.20	0.15	46738.35	99955.55	2726.75	97228.80	2.73
Total (A+B)	3139.12	65606.59	0.15	49731.85	115338.44	3139.27	112199.17	2.72

Basic Source: GoI, State Finance Accounts 2007–08 and 2008–09.

Notes: *Including imputed interest on investment, dividends and return on capital stock.

Agricultural research and education comprises of soil and water conservation (02), Fisheries and Forestry (05).

Special areas development programme comprises drought prone areas (02), Devlp./desert Devlp. Progs. (03) and Wasteland Devlp. Progs. (05). Flood control and drainage comprises flood control (01) and Anti-sea erosion (02). Non-ferrous mining and metallurgical industries includes Geological Survey of India's mineral exploration [2853 (01/102)] and Regulation and development of prevention [2853 2/102)] and Control of pollution under ecology and environment [3435 (04)].

Mining under iron and steel industries [2852 (01/101)].

Pesticide and chemicals under chemicals and pharmaceutical industries [2852 (05/205)].

Bibliography

Ballard, C. L. and D. Fullerton (1992), 'Distortionary Taxes and the Provision of Public Goods', *Journal of Economic Perspectives*, 6(3): 117–31.

Barg, S. (1996), 'Eliminating Perverse Subsidies: What's the Problem?' *Subsidies and Environment: Exploring the Linkages* (23–41). Paris: Organisation for Economic Cooperation and Development.

Baumol, W. J. and Oates, W. E. (1988), *The Theory of Environmental Policy*. Cambridge: Cambridge University Press.

Bhatnagar, V. B. and D. S. Thakur (1998), 'Effect of Nitrogen and Phosphorus Levels on Growth, Yield and Quality of Toria (Brassica compestrisL.) Under Irrigated Condition', *Crop Research* 15(1): 26–30.

Blow, Laura, Andrew Leicester, and Zoe Smith (2003), 'London's Congestion Charge', Briefing Note No. 31, The Institute for Fiscal Studies, available at www.ifs.org.uk/bns/bn31.pdf.

Bohm, P. (1981), *Deposit Refund Systems*. Washington, DC: Resources for the Future Press.

Borup, Mads (2007), 'Environmental Vehicle Excise Duty in Sweden', *Proceedings: Cases in Sustainable Consumption and Production: Workshop of the Sustainable Consumption Research Exchange (SCORE!) Network*, supported by the EU's 6th Framework Program, Paris, 4–5 June 2007, available at http://www.risoe.dk/rispubl/art/2007_161_paper.pdf.

Brandon, C. and K. Hommann (1996), 'Cost of Inaction: Valuing the Economy-wide Cost of Environmental Degradation in India', *UNU/IAS Working Paper No. 9*, Institute of Advanced Studies, UNU, Tokyo.

Branlund, Runar and Bengt Kristrom (1999), 'Energy and Environmental Taxation in Sweden: Some Experience from the Swedish Green Tax Commission, in T. Sterner (ed.), *The Market and the Environment* (233–54). Cheltenham: Edward Elgar Publishing.

Brécard, D., F. Fougeyrollas, P. Le Mouël, L. Lemiale, and P. Zagamé (2006), 'Macroeconomic Consequences of European Research Policy: Prospects of the Nemesis Model in the year 2030', *Research Policy*, 35(7): 910–24.

British Columbia Government (2008), 'Revenue Neutral Carbon Tax', available at http://www.bcbudget.gov.bc.ca/2008/backgrounders/2008_Backgrounder_Carbon_Tax.pdf.

Browning, Edgar K. (1976), 'The Marginal Cost of Public Funds', *Journal of Political Economy*, 84(2): 283–98.

Butcher, L. (2009), 'Parliament Briefing Paper on Vehicle Excise Duty', Library of House of Common, Business and Transport Sector. Available at www.parliament.uk/briefing-papers.

Byiringiro, F. and T. Reardon (1996), 'Farm Productivity in Rwanda: Effects of Farm Size, Erosion, and Soil Conservation Investments', *Agricultural Economics*, 15(2): 127–36.

Cambridge Econometrics (2005), 'Modelling the Initial Effects of the Climate Change Levy', available at www.hmrc.gov.uk.

Canadian Union of Public Employees (CUPE) (2008), 'Impact of Carbon Tax on Different Household Income Groups', CUPE Economic Brief, June.

Cao, J. and J. Zeng (2010), 'The Incidence of Carbon Tax in China', paper presented at Lincoln Institute China Program Annual May Conference, Cambridge, 17 May.

Center for International Earth Science Information Network (CIESIN) (1995), *Thematic Guide to Integrated Assessment Modeling of Climate Change*. Palisades, NY: CIESIN.

Chelliah, R. J., P. P. Appaswamy, U. Sankar, and R. Pandey (2007), *Ecotaxes on Polluting Inputs and Outputs*. New Delhi: Academic Foundation.

Chikkatur, A. P. and A. D. Sagar (2007), 'Cleaner Power in India: Towards a Clean-Coal-Technology Roadmap', Discussion Paper 2007–06, Energy Technology Innovation Policy Research Group, Belfer Center for Science and International Affairs, Harvard Kennedy School, December.

Commission on Centre-State Relations (2010), 'Centre-State Financial Relations and Planning: Volume 3', March, Government of India.

Cristofaro, A. B., R. Schillo, R., Shackleton, and M. Shelby (1995), 'The Climate Change Implications of Eliminating US Energy Subsidies', USEPA Report to OECD, OECD: Paris.

Datta, Ashokankur (2008), 'The Incidence of Fuel Taxation in India', Discussion Paper 08-05, ISI, Planning Unit, Delhi.

de Jaeger (2007), Presentation at the Brussels Tax Forum 2007, State Secretary for Finance, The Netherlands.

de Mello, L. (2008), 'Avoiding the Value Added Tax: Theory and Cross-Country Evidence', *OECD Economics Department Working Papers, No. 604*, OECD Publishing.

Driesen, David (2006), 'Economic Instruments for Sustainable Development' in B. J. Richardson and S. Wood (eds), *Environmental Law for Sustainability* (277–308). Oxford: Hart Publishing.

Ecofys (2002), 'Assessing the Environmental Potential of Clean Material Technologies', *Report EUR 20515 EN*, European Commission Joint Research Centre, October, available at http://ftp.jrc.es/EURdoc/eur20515en.pdf.

Edmonds, J., H. Pitcher, and R. Sands (2004), *Second Generation Model 2004: An Overview*. College Park, MA: JGCRI.

Ekins, Paul (2009), 'Resource Productivity, Environmental Tax Reform and Sustainable Growth in Europe', Anglo-German Foundation for the Study of Industrial Society, available at http://www.petre.org.uk/pdf/FinRepFin.pdf.

Empowered Committee of State Finance Ministers (2010), 'First Discussion Paper on Goods and Services Tax in India', Empowered Committee of State Finance Ministers, Government of India.

EPA (1990), *Policy Options for Stabilizing Global Climate: Report to Congress*, Technical Appendices, EPA Doc: EPA-600/8-90-079, EPA, Washington, DC.

Eschborn/Bonn (2004), *Environmental Fiscal Reform for Sustainable Development and Poverty Reduction: Workshop Proceedings and Country Case Studies*. Bonn: GTZ.

European Commission (1995), The PRIMES Energy Model, Report number EUR 16713, DG-XII, Brussels.

European Commission (1996), *European System of Accounts—ESA 1995*. Luxembourg: Office for Official Publications of the European Communities.

European Environmental Agency (EEA) (1996), *Environmental Taxes: Implementation and Environmental Effectiveness*, Environmental Issues Series, No. 1, Luxembourg.

European Environmental Agency (EEA) (2000), *Environmental Taxes: Recent Development in Tools for Integration*. Copenhagen: European Environmental Agency.

European Environmental Agency (EEA) (2007), 'Greenhouse Gas Emissions: Trends and Projections in Europe 2007', *EEA Report No 5/2007*, available at http://reports.eea.europa.eu/eea_report_2007_5/en.

Farah, Jumanah (1994), 'Pesticide Policies in Developing Countries: Do They Encourage Excessive Use?', *World Bank Discussion Paper 238*. Washington, DC: World Bank.

Fischer et al. (1995), 'An Economic Assessment of Policy Instruments to Combat Climate Change', in James P. Bruce, Hoesung Lee, and Erik F. Haites (eds), *Climate Change 1995: Economic and Social Dimensions of Climate Change*, Intergovernmental Panel on Climate Change. Cambridge: Cambridge University Press.

Fullerton, D. and A. Wolverton (1995), 'The Case for a Two Part Instrument: Presumptive Tax and Environmental Subsidy', *Working Paper 5993*. New York: National Bureau of Economic Research.

Gangwar, A. C. and W. H. van den Toorn (1987), 'The Economics of Adverse Groundwater Conditions in Haryana State', *Indian Journal of Agricultural Economics*, 42(2): 160–72.

Gerlagh, R. and W. Lise (2005), 'Carbon Taxes: A Drop in the Ocean, or a Drop that Erodes the Stone? The Effect of Carbon Taxes on Technological Change', *Ecological Economics*, 54(2–3): 241–60.

Ghoshal, T. and R. Bhattacharyya (2007), 'State Level Carbon Dioxide Emissions of India: 1980–2000', available at SSRN: http://ssrn.com/abstract=999353.

GIST (2008), *Green Accounting for Indian States Project*, Various Monographs, available at http://www.gistindia.org/publications.asp

GoI (2006), *National Environmental Policy 2006*, Ministry of Environment and Forests, GoI.

GoI (2007), *National Accounts Statistics*, Ministry of Statistics and Programme Implementation, New Delhi.

GoI (2009), *National Accounts Statistics*, Ministry of Statistics and Programme Implementation, New Delhi.

GoI (2010), *National Accounts Statistics*, Ministry of Statistics and Programme Implementation, New Delhi.

GoI (2011), 'The Constitution (One Hundred and Fifteenth Amendment) Bill 2011', Bill No. 22, Lok Sabha.

Goulder, L. H. (1995), 'Environmental Taxation and the Double Dividend: A Reader's Guide', *International Tax and Public Finance*, 2(2): 157–83.

Green Fiscal Commission (2009), 'How Effective are Green Taxes?', Briefing Paper 2, April, available at www.greenfiscalcommission.org.uk.

Gulati, A. (1989), 'Input Subsidies in Indian Agriculture—A Statewise Analysis', *Economic and Political Weekly*, June 24.

Gulati, A. and S. Narayanan (2000), 'Demystifying Fertiliser and Power Subsidies in India', *Economic and Political Weekly*, March 4.

Gupta, Sreekant (2002), 'Environmental Benefits and Cost Savings through Market Based Instruments: An Application using State level Data from India', paper presented at the National Law School of India, Bangalore, India.

Gurich, E., A. Golub, M. Vzyakov, A. Mukhin, N. Koroborva, G. Hughes, K. Lvovsky, and A. Gorman (1995), 'Impact of Russian Energy Subsidies on Greenhouse Gas Emissions', *Report to OECD*, OECD: Paris.

GTZ (2007), 'Environmental Fiscal Reform in Developing, Emerging and Transition Economies: Progress & Prospects', Documentation of the 2007 Special Workshop hosted by the Federal Ministry for Economic Cooperation and Development (BMZ) and the Deutsche Gesellschaft für Technische Zusammenarbeit (GTZ) GmbH, Bonn: GTZ.

GTZ (2009), 'International Fuel Prices', available at http://www.gtz.de/de/dokumente/en-int-fuel-prices-6th-edition-gtz2009-corrected.pdf.

Handa, B. K. (1986), 'Pollution of Ground Water by Nitrate in India', *BHU-JAL News: Quarterly Journal of Central Ground Water Board*, 1(3): 16–9.

Harold, C. and C. F. Runge (1993), 'GATT and the Environment: Policy Research Needs', *American Journal of Agricultural Economics*, 75 (August): 789–93.

Heady, C. J., A. Markandya, W. Blyth, J. Collingwood, and P. G. Taylor (2000), 'Study on the Relationship Between Environmental/Energy Taxation and Employment Creation', report prepared for the European Commission Directorate General XI, University of Bath, available at http://ec.europa.eu/environment/enveco/taxation/pdf/entaxemp.pdf.

Hettige, M., P. Martin, M. Singh, and D. Wheeler (1995), 'The Industrial Pollution Projection System', *World Bank Policy Research Working Paper 1431*, March, World Bank.

HMT (2006), 'The Climate Change Levy Package', HM Treasury, London, March, available at http://www.hmtreasury.gov.uk/media/8/B/bud06_climate169.pdf.

Huang, Jikun and Scott Rozelle (1995), 'Environmental Stress and Grain Yields in China', *American Journal of Agricultural Economics*, 77(4): 853–64.

IEA (1999), 'Looking at Energy Subsidies, Getting Energy Prices Right', *World Energy Outlook*. Paris: OECD/IEA.

IEA (2001), 'Energy Subsidies in India', *Economic Analysis Division Working Paper*, International Energy Agency, Paris.

IEA (2009a), 'CO_2 Emissions from Fuel Combustion: Highlights', International Energy Agency Statistics, 2009 Edition, France.

IEA (2009b), 'Energy Prices and Taxes Quarterly Statistics: Fourth Quarter', International Energy Agency Statistics, 2009 Edition, France.

IIASA (2005), 'Model for Energy Supply Strategy Alternatives and their General Environmental Impact (MESSAGE): Model Description', available at http://webarchive.iiasa.ac.at/Research/ECS/docs/models.html#MESSAGE.

Joshi, P. K. (1997), 'Rapporteur's Report on Technology and Environmental Management in Agriculture', *Indian Journal of Agricultural Economics*, 52(3): 673–87, July–September.

Joshi, P. K. and D. Jha (1992), 'An Economic Enquiry into the Impact of Soil Alkalinity and Waterlogging', *Indian Journal of Agricultural Economics*, 47(2): 195–204, April–June.

Kainuma, M., Y. Matsuoka, and T. Morita (2003), *Climate Policy Assessment: Asia-Pacific Integrated Modeling.* Tokyo: Springer-Verlag, 402 pp.

Kandlikar, M. and G. Ramachandran (2000), 'The Causes and Consequences of Particulate Air Pollution in Urban India: A Synthesis of Science', *Annual Review of Energy and Environment*, 25: 629–84.

Kolhaas, Michael (2000), 'Ecological Tax Reform in Germany: From Theory to Policy', *Economic Studies Program Series*, Vol. 6, American Institute for Contemporary German Studies, The Johns Hopkins University.

Karwasra, J. C., S. P. Singh, and S. N. Singh (1997), 'Impact of Agricultural Development on Nature and Extent of Resource Degradation in Haryana', *Indian Journal of Agricultural Economics*, 52(3): 541–42, July–September.

Kavita, Rao (2010), 'GST Design Needs a Rethink', *The Business Standard*, September 9.

Kemfert, C. and T. Truong (2007), 'Impact Assessment of Emissions Stabilization Scenarios with and without Induced Technological Change', *Energy Policy*, 35(11): 5337–45.

Larsen, B. and A. Shah (1992), 'World Fossil Fuel Subsidies and Global Carbon Emission', *World Bank Policy Research Working Paper 1002.* Washington, DC: World Bank.

LEAP (2005), *Long-range Energy Alternatives Planning System: User Guide for LEAP 2005*, Stockholm Environment Institute, Boston Centre, Tellus Institute.

Leicester, A. (2006), *The UK Tax System and the Environment.* London: Institute for Fiscal Studies.

LGEEPA (1988), Ley General de Equilibrio Ecologico y Proteccion al Ambiente, SEMARNAT, Mexico.

Lundholm, M. (2005), 'Cost Benefit Analysis and the Marginal Cost of Public Funds', *Research Papers in Economics 2005:3*, Department of Economics, Stockholm University.

Mahalanobis, J. K. (1971), Emerging Soil Pollution Problems in Rice and their Amelioration', M.Sc. Thesis, IARI, New Delhi.

Marothia, D. K. (1997), 'Agricultural Technology and Environmental Quality: An Institutional Perspective', *Indian Journal of Agricultural Economics*, 52(3): 473–87, July–September.

Mausolff, C. and S. Faber (1995), 'An Economic Analysis of Ecological Agricultural Technologies among Peasant Farmers in Honduras', *Ecological Economics*, 12(3): 237–48.

Metcalf, Gilbert and David Weisbach (2009), 'The Design of a Carbon Tax', *Harvard Environmental Law Review*, 33(2): 499–556.

Michaelis, L. (1996), *OECD Project on the Environmental Implications of Energy and Transport Subsidies: Summary Report*. Paris: OECD.

Ministry of Environment, New Zealand, available at http://www.mfe.govt.nz/issues/waste/actimplementation.html.

Mitra, N. (1992), 'Energy Policy Planning in India—Case of Petroleum and Natural Gas', *Economic and Political Weekly*, 27(35): M109–15.

MoEF (2009), 'India's GHG Emissions Profile: Results of Five Climate Modelling Studies', *Climate Modeling Forum*, India and Ministry of Environment and Forests, Government of India, September, available at http://moef.nic.in/downloads/home/GHG-report.pdf.

MoEF (2010), *India: Greenhouse Gas Emissions 2007*, Indian Network for Climate Change Assessment, Ministry of Environment and Forests, Government of India, New Delhi.

Mundle, S. and M. Govinda Rao (1991), 'The Volume and Composition of Government Subsidies in India: 1987–88', Current Policy Issues No. 13, December, National Institute of Public Finance and Police, New Delhi and in Economic and Political Weekly, 4 May 1992.

Myers, N. (1998), 'Threatened biotas: 'hotspots' in tropical forests', *Environmentalist* 8, 1–20.

Myers, N. and J. Kent (2001), *Perverse Subsidies: How Tax Dollars can Undercut the Environment and the Economy*, International Institute for Sustainable Development and Island Press.

Nagaraj, T., H. S. S. Khan, and N. N. Karnool (1998), 'Resource use Efficiency in Various Crops Under Different Cropping Systems in Tungabhadra Command Area (Karnataka)', *Agricultural Situation in India*, 55(3): 135–39.

Nakicenovic, N. and K. Riahi (2003), *Model Runs with MESSAGE in the Context of the Further Developments of the Kyoto-Protocol*, WBGU Special Assessment Report, WBGU II/2003, Laxenburg.

National Treasury (2006), A *Framework for Considering Market-based Instruments to Support Environmental Fiscal Reform in South Africa*, Tax Policy Chief Directorate, April.

NCAER (2009), *Moving to Goods and Services Tax in India: Impact on India's Growth and International Trade*, report prepared for the Thirteenth Finance Commission, Government of India.

NEERI (2010), *Air Quality Assessment, Emissions Inventory and Source Apportionment Studies: Mumbai*. Nagpur: National Environmental Engineering Research Institute.

Nordic Council (1999), *The Use of Economic Instruments in Nordic Environmental Policy 1997–1998*. Copenhagen.

Nordic Council (2006), *The Use of Economic Instruments in Environmental Policy in the Nordic and Baltic Countries 2001–2005*. Copenhagen, Denmark, available at http://www.norden.org/pub/miljo/ekonomi/sk/TN2006525.pdf.

Oates, W. E. (2001), 'A Reconsideration of Environmental Federalism', discussion paper 01-54, Resources for the Future, Washington, DC.

OECD (1998), *Improving the Environment Through Reducing Subsidies*. Paris: OECD.

OECD (2001), *Environmentally Related Taxes in OECD Countries*. Paris: OECD Publishing.

OECD (2003), 'Environmental Performance Reviews: Mexico', available at http://www.oecd.org/env/country-reviews/18385233.pdf.

OECD (2005), *Environmental Fiscal Reform for Poverty Reduction*, DAC Guidelines and Reference Series, Paris: OECD.

OECD (2006a), *The Political Economy of Environmentally Related Taxes*. Paris: OECD.

OECD (2006b), *Subsidy Reform and Sustainable Development: Economic, Environmental and Social Aspects*. Paris: OECD.

OECD (2007), *Instrument Mixes for Environmental Policy*. Paris: OECD, available at http://dx.doi.org/10.1787/9789264018419-en.

OECD (2009), *Environmentally Harmful Subsidies: Identification and Assessment*, Final Report for the European Commission's DG Environment, November.

Panayotou, T. (1992), 'The Economics of Environmental Degradation: Problems, Causes and Responses', in A. Markandya and J. Richardson (eds), *The Earthscan Reader in Environmental Economics* (pp. 319–23). London: Earthscan.

Pandey, R. and D. K. Srivastava (2003), *Subsidies and the Environment: With Special Reference to Agriculture in India*, National Institute of Public Finance and Policy, New Delhi.

Pandey, Rita (2005), 'Estimating Sectoral and Geographical Industrial Pollution Inventories in India: Implications for Using Effluent Charge Versus Regulation', *Journal of Development Studies*, 41(1): 33–61.

Pargal, S. and D. Wheeler (1996), 'Informal Regulation of Industrial Pollution in Developing Countries: Evidence from Indonesia', *Journal of Political Economy*, 104(6): 1314–27.

Parikh, K. S. and M. H. Suryanarayana (1992), 'Food and Agricultural Subsidies: Incidence and Welfare under Alternative Schemes', *Journal of Quantitative Economics*, 8(1): 1–28.

Pattanayak, S. K. and E. Mercer (1998), 'Valuing Soil Conservation Benefits of Agroforestry Practices: Contour Hedgerows in the Eastern Visayas, Philippines', *Agricultural Economics*, 18(1): 31–46.

Patuelli, R., E. Pels, and P. Nijkamp (2002), 'Environmental Tax Reform and Double Dividend', Tinbergen Institute Discussion Paper 02-095/3, Tinbergen Institute.

Poddar, S. and A. Bagchi (2007), 'Revenue-neutral Rate for GST', *The Economic Times*, November 15.

Popp, D. (2004), 'ENTICE: Endogenous Technological Change in the DICE Model of Global Warming', *Journal of Environmental Economics and Management*, 48(1): 742–68.

Raina, V. K. (2009), 'Himalayan Glaciers: A State-of-Art Review of Glacial Studies, Glacial Retreat and Climate Change', Discussion Paper, Ministry of Environment and Forests, Government of India, available at http://moef.nic.in/sites/default/files/MoEF%20Discussion%20Paper%20_him.pdf.

Ray, A. K. (1998), 'The Present Status of Soil and Ground Water Pollution and Its Impact', *Agricultural Situation in India*, 55(7): 417–20.

Repetto, R. (1994), *The "Second India" Revisited: Population, Poverty and Environmental Stress over Two Decades*. Washington, DC: World Resources Institute.

Sah, D. C. and A. Shah (1992), 'Incentives for Adopting Soil Test Based Fertiliser Use: Evidences from ABC Trials', *Indian Journal of Agricultural Economics*, 47(4): 631–43, October–December.

SCB (2003), *Environmental Subsidies—A Review of Subsidies in Sweden between 1993 and 2000*, Report No. 2003:4, Statistiska Centralbyran, Sweden.

Seely, Antony (2009), 'Landfill Tax: Recent Developments', available at www.parliament.uk/briefing-papers/SNO1963.pdf.

Sharma, V. P., R. Parshad, and B. L. Gajja (1997), 'Land Degradation: Dimensions, Causes and Consequences—A Case of Haryana', *Agricultural Situation in India*, 54(6): 357–60.

Shergill, H. S. (2005), 'Wheat and Paddy Cultivation and the Question of Optimal Cropping Pattern for Punjab', *Journal of Punjab Studies*, 12(2): 239–50.

Sidhu, D. S. and D. Byerlee (1992), 'Technical Change and Wheat Productivity in the Indian Punjab in the Post Green Revolution Period', *CIMMYT Economics Working Paper 92-02*, CIMMYT, Mexico.

Sidhu, R. S. and M. S. Dillon (1997), 'Land and Water Resources in Punjab: Their Degradation and Technologies for Sustainable Use', *Indian Journal of Agricultural Economics*, 52(3): 508–18.

Silvani, C. and S. Wakefield (2002), 'Relación entre la Tasa y la Productividad de un Impuesto', Paper presented at the XXXVI Meeting of the Inter-American Centre of Tax Administration (CIAT), Quebec, Canada.

Singh, A. (1984), 'Economic and Policy Dimensions of Irrational Use of Electricity in Agriculture in India', *Indian Journal of Economics*, 79(313): 187–93.

Singh, J., V. K. Singh, and K. K. Kundu (1997), 'Modern Technology vis-à-vis Environmental Degradation—A Case of Rice-Wheat Cropping System', *Indian Journal of Agricultural Economics*, 52(3), July–September.

Singh, K. (1999), 'Sustainable Development: Some Reflections', *Indian Journal of Agricultural Economics*, 54(1): 6–41.

Smith, K. R. and S. Mehta (2002), 'The Burden of Disease from Indoor Air Pollution in Developing Countries: Comparison of Estimates', *International Journal of Hygiene and Environmental Health*, 206(4&5): 279–89.

Speck, Stefan (2008), 'Possibilities of Environmental Fiscal Reform in Developing Countries', paper presented at Bank Indonesia Annual International Seminar,

Macroeconomic Impact of Climate Change: Opportunities and Challenges, Nusa Dua, Bali, August 1–2.

Srivastava, D. K. (2011), *A Long-term Model of the Indian Economy*. Chennai: mimeo, Madras School of Economics.

Srivastava, D. K. and C. B. Rao (2001), 'Government Subsidies in India: Issues and Approach', in E. Favaro and A. Lahiri (eds), *Fiscal Policies and Sustainable Growth in India* (pp. 148–65). New Delhi: Oxford University Press, 2004.

Srivastava, D. K. and K. S. Kavi Kumar (2011), 'Impact of Fiscal Instruments in Environmental Management through a Simulation Model: Case Study of India', Technical Paper 2 of the project Integrating Pollution-Abating Economic Instruments in Goods and Services Tax Regime, Monograph 14/2011, Madras School of Economics, December.

Srivastava, D. K. and H. K. Amar Nath (2001), *Central Budgetary Subsidies in India*. New Delhi: National Institute of Public Finance and Policy.

Srivastava, D. K., C. B. Rao, P. Chakraborty, and T. S. Rangamannar (2003), *Budgetary Subsidies in India Subsidising Social and Economic Services*. New Delhi: mimeo, National Institute of Public Finance and Policy, March.

Srivastava, D. K., K. R. Shanmugam, and C. Bhujanga Rao (2010), *Structural Breaks in the Indian Economy: A Study of Major Aggregates*. Chennai: mimeo, Madras School of Economics.

Srivastava, D. K., T. K. Sen, H. Mukhopadhyay, C. B. Rao, and H. K. Amar Nath (1997), *Government Subsidies in India*. New Delhi: National Institute of Public Finance and Policy, August.

Srivastava, D. K. and Bhujanga C. Rao (2008), 'Feasibility of Incentive Based Environmental Instruments and State and Central Taxation Regimes', Chennai: Madras School of Economics.

Sterner, T. (2007), 'Fuel Taxes: An Important Instrument for Climate Policy', *Energy Policy*, 35(6): 3194–202.

Task Force on Goods and Services Tax (2009), *Report of the Task Force on Goods and Services Tax*, Thirteenth Finance Commission, Government of India.

Tax Policy Chief Directorate (2006), 'A Framework for Considering Market-Based Instruments to Support Environmental Fiscal Reform in South Africa', Draft Policy Paper, Tax Policy Chief Directorate, National Treasury.

TEEB (2009), *The Economics of Ecosystems and Biodiversity for National and International Policy Makers*, November, available at http://www.teebweb.org/ForPolicymakers/tabid/1019/Default.

UNEP (2003), *Energy Subsidies: Lessons Learned in Assessing their Impact and Designing Policy Reforms*, United Nations Environment Programme, Geneva.

Vaidyanathan, A. (1999), *Irrigation Management in India: Role of Institutions*. New Delhi: Oxford University Press.

Valsecchi, C., P. ten Brink, S. Bassi, S. Withana, M. Lewis, A. Best, F. Oosterhuis, C. Dias Soares, H. Rogers-Ganter, and T. Kaphengst (2009), *Environmentally Harmful Subsidies: Identification and Assessment*, Final report for the European Commission's DG Environment, November.

van Beers and S. de Moor (2001), *Public Subsidies and Policy Failures: How Subsidies Distort the Natural Environment, Equity and Trade and How to Reform Them*. Cheltenham: Edward Elgar.

Wang, Hua and D. Wheeler (1996), 'Pricing Industrial Pollution in China', *Policy Research Working Paper 1644*, World Bank, Washington, DC.

Wang, Hua and M. Chen (1999), 'How the Chinese System of Charges and Subsidies Affects Pollution Control Efforts by China's Top Industrial Polluters', *Policy Research Working Paper 2198*, World Bank, Washington, October.

Weizsacker, E. U. Von. (1992), *Ecological Tax Reform*. London: Zed Books.

World Bank (2005), *For a Breath of Fresh Air: Ten Years of Progress with Urban Air Quality Management in India*, Environment and Social Development Unit, South Asia Region, New Delhi: World Bank.

World Bank (2007), 'India: Strengthening Institutions for Sustainable Growth—Country Environmental Analysis', South Asia Environment and Social Development Unit, World Bank, Washington.

Yusuf, A. A. (2008), 'The Distributional Impact of Environmental Policy: The Case of Carbon Tax and Energy Pricing Reform in Indonesia', *Research Report No. 2008-RR1*, Environment and Economy Program for Southeast Asia, Singapore.

Ziramba, E., W. L. Kumo, and O. A. Akinbiade (2009), 'Economic Instruments for Environmental Regulation in Africa: An Analysis of the Efficacy of Fuel Taxation for Pollution Control in South Africa', *CEEPA Discussion Paper No. 44*, available at http://www.ceepa.co.za/Discussion paper no 44.pdf.

About the Editors and Contributors

THE EDITORS

D.K. Srivastava is Chief Policy Advisor, Ernst and Young, and Honorary Professor Madras School of Economics (MSE). He was earlier member of the Twelfth Finance Commission, and served as Director, MSE. He was also Professor, National Institute for Public Finance and Policy (NIPFP). His latest books include *Development and Public Finance: Essays in Honour of Raja J. Chelliah* (with Professor U. Sankar), published by SAGE India and *Federalism and Fiscal Transfers in India* (with Dr C. Rangarajan) published by Oxford University Press India.

K.S. Kavi Kumar is Professor, Madras School of Economics. He has been coordinating activities of the Centre of Excellence in environmental economics, supported by the Ministry of Environment and Forests, at MSE for the past six years. He is also Member, Expert Committee of Climate Change, Government of India; Member, State Environment Appraisal Committee, Tamil Nadu; and Member National Initiative on Climate Resilient Agriculture (NICRA) Expert Committee—working at MSE since 1999.

THE CONTRIBUTORS

Rita Pandey is Professor, National Institute of Public Finance and Policy (NIPFP), New Delhi. She has a PhD in economics and did her postdoctoral research at the School of Forestry and Environmental Studies, University of Yale. She has undertaken a broad range of studies examining the different links between environment and resources and the economy, and has worked extensively on economic instruments and environmental fiscal reforms for environmental management, resource conservation, and climate change. She has published widely in national and international journals and has four books to her credit.

C. Bhujanga Rao is Senior Economist, NIPFP, New Delhi. He held faculty positions at Ramakrishna Mission Vivekananda College, Chennai; Institute of Economic Growth (IEG); National Council of Applied Economic Research (NCAER); Delhi School of Economics (DSE); Madras School of Economics (MSE); and served as Joint Director in the Eleventh Finance Commission. His research interests cover wide areas of public finance, applied econometrics, developmental issues, agricultural economics, macro-economics and banking.

Index